ROUTLEDGE LIBRARY EDITIONS:
ENVIRONMENTAL AND NATURAL RESOURCE ECONOMICS

Volume 3

GREEN PAGES

GREEN PAGES
The Business of Saving the World

JOHN ELKINGTON, TOM BURKE AND JULIA HAILES

LONDON AND NEW YORK

First published in 1988 by Routledge

This edition first published in 2018
by Routledge
2 Park Square, Milton Park, Abingdon, Oxon OX14 4RN

and by Routledge
711 Third Avenue, New York, NY 10017

Routledge is an imprint of the Taylor & Francis Group, an informa business

© 1988 John Elkington, Tom Burke and Julia Hailes

All rights reserved. No part of this book may be reprinted or reproduced or utilised in any form or by any electronic, mechanical, or other means, now known or hereafter invented, including photocopying and recording, or in any information storage or retrieval system, without permission in writing from the publishers.

Trademark notice: Product or corporate names may be trademarks or registered trademarks, and are used only for identification and explanation without intent to infringe.

British Library Cataloguing in Publication Data
A catalogue record for this book is available from the British Library

ISBN: 978-1-138-08283-0 (Set)
ISBN: 978-1-315-14775-8 (Set) (ebk)
ISBN: 978-1-138-50323-6 (Volume 3) (hbk)
ISBN: 978-1-138-50325-0 (Volume 3) (pbk)
ISBN: 978-1-315-14532-7 (Volume 3) (ebk)

Publisher's Note
The publisher has gone to great lengths to ensure the quality of this reprint but points out that some imperfections in the original copies may be apparent.

Disclaimer
The publisher has made every effort to trace copyright holders and would welcome correspondence from those they have been unable to trace.

Preface to the 2017 edition of *Green Pages*

Time machines come in many forms, including the DeLorean car featured in the *Back to the Future* films. When Tom Burke, Julia Hailes and I were working on *Green Pages* back in 1987, Stephen Spielberg's film had been out for a couple of years, but it was no part of our plan to create another time machine. Looking back, though, that is exactly what we did.

When the book's publishers, Routledge, approached us thirty years later to ask if we would support the book's republication in 2017, we were skeptical, given that so much had changed in the intervening decades. But then we went back to the book and read it again.

Sustainable development is back in the spotlight with the UN's 2015 launch of the "Sustainable Development Goals", so it struck us that there could be real value in winding back the clock to the late 1980s—particularly to the Brundtland Commission's 1987 report, *Our Common Future*.

Quoted in *Green Pages* (page 46), two-time Norwegian Prime Minister Gro Harlem Brundtland argued that: "What is needed now is a new era of economic growth—growth that is forceful and at the same time socially and environmentally desirable."

Such thinking had spurred the *Green Pages* team to set up a new company in 1987, SustainAbility, billed as "The Green Growth Company". Later, in 1994, I would coin the terms "Triple Bottom Line" and "People, Planet, Profit" to spotlight the fact that the sustainability agenda extends well beyond the natural environment.

This approach shaped key organisations in the field, among them the Dow Jones Sustainability Indices (DJSI) and the Global Reporting Initiative (GRI). More recently, the Triple Bottom Line has also become central to the B Corporation movement, which promotes businesses acting as a force for good. At the time of writing, over 2,000 businesses worldwide had become B Corps.

Back in the day, the sub-title of *Green Pages* spelled out our intent: "The Business of Saving the World." At the time, industry was generally viewed as the cause of a series of major disasters, such as Bhopal and Chernobyl. And, the scale of the negative impacts was just beginning to dawn as the world became aware of the destruction of the stratospheric ozone layer, tropical deforestation and climate change.

Whilst we were writing *Green Pages*, the world's human population hit the 5 billion mark. Today we've already passed 7 billion, with forecasters anticipating our reaching 9 or even 10 billion later in the century. The nature and scale of the likely consequences will be huge, as highlighted by the work of the Stockholm Resilience Centre, in such areas as the "Global Acceleration" and "Planetary Boundaries".

On the plus side, we have seen rapid growth in the number of organisations seeking to address such issues. The pro-better-business stance of *Green Pages* was unusual back then, but is now pretty much taken for granted.

A story that underscores the immensity of the changes that have happened since 1988 involves one of our contributors, the German Green politician Petra Kelly. *Green Pages* was published before the extraordinary events of 1989, which saw the Communist world rocked by the fall of the Berlin Wall and the Tiananmen Square Massacre.

One of our contributors would die in a glider crash while another committed suicide, but Kelly's story was the most tragic. She was shot in 1992 by her lover, Gert Bastian, who then turned the gun on himself. A former general, he apparently feared that unsettling aspects of his past could be revealed with the publication of secret police records in the old East Germany.

In her *Green Pages* contribution, Kelly warned about tokenism—something we have seen much evidence of since, both in business and in politics. But the general trajectories identified in the book have stood the test of time. For example, when we produced the book:

Corporate sustainability reporting did not exist, so we reviewed the limited coverage of relevant issues in corporate annual financial reports (pages 40–44).

The potential contributions of computers and IT were already clear (pages 94–107), but the dawn of the Internet was still 6–7 years in the future.

The falling price of oil was seen as a threat to the nascent renewable energy industry (pages 136–137), whereas today low oil prices are no deterrent to the Moore's Law-driven success of renewable energy technologies.

Our concluding remarks are as true today as they were then. "We emerge from *Green Pages* as optimists," we said (page 239). We were acutely aware of the problems facing the world, but concluded that the best way of promoting difficult changes was to show people what was in it for them, whether they were operating as voters, investors, managers, employees, consumers or, perhaps most important of all, businesses.

Tomorrow's market opportunities are immense. The Business & Sustainable Development Commission forecasts that just four markets of the many they surveyed could be worth $12 trillion a year by 2030. So, despite ongoing fallout from globalization and populism, we expect the business of saving the world to achieve a degree of traction and impact by 2030 that is almost unimaginable today.

John Elkington, on behalf of the *Green Pages* team

NOTE: The original *Green Pages* included a number of advertisements, in the spirit of *Yellow Pages*. With two exceptions, we have left these in, as illustrations of the environmental and sustainability sectors' commercial priorities at the time. In terms of the exceptions, we have dropped ads from two energy companies, Shell and BNFL, which appeared on the front and back inside covers. At the time we felt that the messages these two companies featured in their ads aligned with the spirit of *Green Pages*, though subsequent events have continued to raise major concerns over the fossil fuel and nuclear industries.

What the authors did next

Green Pages helped catalyse a period of rapid social change. John Elkington and Julia Hailes followed up with *The Green Consumer Guide* in 1988, which went on to sell a million copies worldwide.

John remains Honorary Chairman of SustainAbility, but co-founded Volans in 2008, where he is Chairman and Chief Pollinator. His nineteenth book, *The Breakthrough Challenge*, was co-authored with PUMA Chairman and CEO Jochen Zeitz. See www.volans.com, www.johnelkington.com and www.projectbreakthrough.io.

Julia set up her own consultancy in 1995. In 2004, she co-founded the Haller Foundation (www.haller.org.uk), promoting sustainable living in Kenya. In 2007, she published *The New Green Consumer Guide*. See http://juliahailesblog.blogspot.co.uk and www.juliahailes.com.

Tom co-founded E3G www.e3g.org/people/tom-burke), where he is now Chairman—focusing on "Third Generation Environmentalism". He had previously developed the Rio Tinto-led Global Mining Initiative on sustainable development and served as a senior advisor to the British Government.

GREEN PAGES

THE BUSINESS OF SAVING THE WORLD

JOHN ELKINGTON / TOM BURKE / JULIA HAILES

First published in 1988 by Routledge,
11 New Fetter Lane, London EC4P 4EE
Design by Tim Moore Associates
Typeset in Times Roman by Eager Typesetting and
printed by The Guernsey Press Co. Ltd., Guernsey, Channel Islands

© Ecological Studies Institute

All rights reserved. No part of this book may be reprinted or utilised in any
form or by any electronic, mechanical, or other means, now known or
hereafter invented, including photocopy and recording, or in any information
storage or retrieval system, without permission in writing from the publishers.

British Library Cataloguing in Publication Data
Elkington, John, 1949 –
Green pages: the business of saving the world
1. European Economic Community. Environment.
Conservation role of industries. Directories.
i. Title ii. Burke, Tom, 1947 – iii. Hailes, Julia, 1961 –
333.7'2'0254

ISBN 0 415 00232 X

PREFACE

Looking Beyond EYE

EEC Environment Commissioner Stanley *Clinton Davis* introduces *Green Pages,* a venture which was part-funded by the European Year of the Environment (EYE) Task Force. The aim has been to look beyond EYE – beyond the 1980s – to the new market opportunities of the 1990s.

'I should like to begin by welcoming *Green Pages*. This is a timely and useful initiative which fits in well not only with the objectives of European Year of the Environment (EYE) but also with the European Community's longer-term goals of environmental policy.

Ultimately, environmental policy will only be successful if it has the support of all relevant sectors of the Community. It is critically important that business and professional people understand the nature of the challenge we face and that we win their backing. This is every bit as important as winning the active participation of the man or woman in the street, or in the countryside, who are the final 'consumers' of efforts in this field.

EYE was launched in March of 1987 to achieve a number of closely interrelated objectives. The European Community aimed to:
- make all Community citizens aware of the importance of environmental protection;
- promote the better integration of environmental policy into the different policies of the Community and its Member States, particularly their economic, industrial, agricultural and social policies;
- emphasise the European dimension of environmental policy; and
- demonstrate the progress and achievements realized by the Community's environment policies.

It was always understood that the EYE agenda could not simply be limited to the year from March 1987 to March 1988. Indeed, the goals which were defined for EYE will, in essence, constitute not merely the environmental agenda for the remaining years of this decade, but also the environmental agenda for the 1990s.

Most important, perhaps, is the question of job-creation. This was certainly a major concern of the European Council when it first proclaimed the European Year of the Environment at its Summit in March 1985 and of the Environment Ministers when, a year later, they adopted the detailed action programme for EYE.

Recent estimates suggest that between 1.5 and 2 million people are employed in the growing environmental industry which supplies pollution control equipment, cleaner products and related services in the European Community. Demand for these goods and services is rising rapidly and we can expect to see a doubling of these jobs by the end of the century.

In 1985, 9,000 companies exported air pollution control and waste-water treatment equipment to 130 countries, earning in excess of 10 billion million ECU (approximately £5 billion). In relation to air and water purification equipment alone the EEC exported 730 million ECU compared with only 177 million ECU of imports – a substantial, favourable trade balance.

Green Pages provides many useful pointers to the market opportunities in environmental technology and services. This sector of the economy can only become more important in the future and it is essential that Europe stakes its claim both in domestic and overseas markets. Later sections of this publication show how far we have come – and how far we still have to go.'

STANLEY CLINTON DAVIS, *the EEC Commissioner for the Environment, became a Member of the Commission of the European Communities in 1985. Originally a solicitor, he was Member of Parliament for Hackney Central from 1970 to 1983. From 1974 to 1979, he was Parliamentary Under-Secretary of State for Trade. Subsequently, he was Opposition spokesman for Trade and then Foreign Affairs. He is a Member or Chairman of a number of national and international associations and committees, and, in the environmental field, currently chairs the Advisory Committee on Pollution of the Sea (ACOPS).*

Contents

Preface: Stanley Clinton-Davis	3
Perspectives: List of contributors	4
List of advertisers	7

INTRODUCTION

Working for SustainAbility	8
Green Pages team	9
Europe's green economy	10
The front line	12
Questions and answers	14
Boxes	
Greener Pages	10
Why not recycled paper?	11
Issues for the 1990s	16
Which is the greenest company?	18
Gaining purchase	19

THE BUSINESS ENVIRONMENT

The Business environment	20
All the colours of the rainbow, but what about green?	40
Boxes	
Environmental guidelines for business	30

Perspectives
Robert Worcester and Michelle Corado, Nigel Haigh, Richard Macrory, Petra Kelly and Jaqueline Aloisi de Larderel

GREENER GROWTH

Greener growth	46
Boxes	
A new era of growth	46

Perspectives
Sir David Nickson, Lloyd Timberlake and Sheila Moorcroft

1. MARKETS

Targeting the Green Consumer	56
Boxes	
The Green Consumer Guide	71

Perspectives
Keith Brunt, Richard Adams, Charles Secrett, Paul Harrison and Anita Roddick

2. DESIGN

Designs with a future	72
Boxes	
Solutions on a stick	74
Worlds within worlds	76
Polmark: key to a £20 billion clean-up market	79
10 questions for the green designer	83

Perspectives
Adrian Judd and Keith Grant

3. RESEARCH

More questions than answers	84
Boxes	
Green framework for research	87
A disruptive technology	92

Perspectives
Dr John Bowman and Florence Fisher

4. COMPUTERS

Wheels for the brain	94
The green computer survey	98
Information at the touch of a button	101
Boxes	
Keying in to disaster	96
The environment on-line	105

Perspectives
Dr Jeremy Cherfas

5. POLLUTION AND WASTE

Cleaning up	108
Boxes	
Feeling guilty, but will they recycle?	115
Roads to cleaner motoring	116

Perspectives
Tim Clark, Dr Mike Flood, Dr Ernst von Weizsacker and Mike Flux

6. ENERGY

Finding the energy	128
Boxes	
From mileage marathon to formula one	133

Perspectives
Christopher Harding and Andrew Warren

7. FARMING AND FORESTRY

Growing pains	138

Boxes
Going organic	143
Farm foresters	146

Perspectives
David Baldock and Robin Grove-White

8. URBAN RENEWAL

Urban revolutions	152

Boxes
Who's who in the liveable city	159

Perspectives
John and Joan Davidson, Max Nicholson and Dr David Goode

9. TOURISM

Boon or bane?	166
The green tourist	174

Boxes
Don't go near the water	171

Perspectives
Brian Jackman	172

10. HEALTH

A picture of health	178
Goodbye to pesticides?	183

Boxes
Irradiated food	180
Healthy growth in alternative medicine	182

11. MONEY

Money matters	184

Boxes
Raising money	194

Perspectives
Giles Chitty, Robert Lowman and Dr Norman Myers

12. MEDIA AND PUBLISHING

News and the world	196
The Green Bookshelf	208

Boxes
Where to find the green media	198
Green publishers	198
The green magazine	199
Books reviewed	216

Perspectives
Charles Clover, Robert Lamb, Jon Tinker, Harford Thomas and Julia Hailes.

13. ADVERTISING & PUBLIC RELATIONS

Acceptable faces	218
10 steps to environmental excellence	226

Boxes
British Nuclear Fuels request the pleasure	22
ARC: responsible communications	223

Perspectives
Jackie Dickens and Robin Sadler

14. CAREERS AND EDUCATION

A Job to find	228

Boxes
Getting started	233

Perspectives
Debbie Bruce, Roger Hammond and Niall Marriott

INTO THE 90s

Into the 90s	238

Perspectives
Lester Brown, Janet Barber and Geoffrey Lean

Boxes
British Coal – A Mine of the Times	239

FOLLOW UP	246-250
INDEX	251-256

List of Contributors

Richard **Adams**,
Traidcraft.
Markets, pages 62
'The Alternative Traders'

Jacqueline **Aloisi de Larderel**,
United Nations Environment
Programme (UNEP).
Business Environment, pages 39
'Countdown to the Year 2000'

Janet **Barber**,
World Wildlife Fund (WWF).
Into the 90s, pages 242–243
'How Long a Spoon?'

David **Baldock**,
International Institute for
Environment and Development (IIED).
Farming, pages 148–149
'Can the CAP be Made to Fit?'

John **Bowman**, Dr,
Natural Environment Research
Council (NERC).
Research, pages 88–89
'Asking Difficult Questions'

Lester **Brown**,
Worldwatch Institute.
Business Environment, pages 240–241
'The State of the World'

Debbie **Bruce**,
Central Electricity Generating
Board (CEGB).
Careers & Education, pages 234–235
'An Electrifying Start'

Keith **Brunt**,
Boots Biocides.
Markets, pages 60–61
'The Commercial Environmentalist'

Jeremy **Cherfas**, Dr,
New Scientist.
Computers, pages 106–107
'Nature on a Silver Platter'

Giles **Chitty**,
The Financial Initiative Ltd.,
Money, pages 186–187
'The Green Investor'

Tim **Clarke**,
Farm Gas.
Pollution & Waste, pages 110–111
'Stepping on the Gas'

Stanley **Clinton-Davis**,
Commission of the European
Communities.
Introduction, page 3
'Looking Beyond EYE'.

Charles **Clover**,
Daily Telegraph.
Media & Publishing, pages 200–201
'Interesting, but is it News?'

John **Davidson** & Joan **Davidson**,
Groundwork Foundation.
Urban Renewal, pages 158–160
'Livable Cities'

Jackie **Dickens**,
Leo Burnett Advertising Ltd.
PR & Advertising, pages 224
'The Growth of Issues Advertising'

Florence **Fisher**,
Environmental Resources Ltd.
Research, pages 90–91
'Trends in Environmental Consulting'

Mike **Flood**, Dr,
Natural Resources Research.
Pollution, pages 120–122
'Fuels from Waste'

Mike **Flux**,
ICI.
Pollution & Waste, pages 126–127
'Don't Expect Instant Fixes'

David **Goode**, Dr,
London Ecology Unit.
Urban Renewal, pages 164–165
'Wild about the City'

Keith **Grant**,
Design Council.
Design, pages 80–81
'Designed for Sustainability'

Robin **Grove-White**,
Imperial College, Centre for
Environmental Technology.
Farming, pages 150–151
'The Changing Countryside'

Nigel **Haigh**,
Institute for European
Environmental Policy (IEEP).
Business Environment, pages 26–27
'Emerging Trends in EEC Environmental Policy'

Julia **Hailes**,
SustainAbility Ltd
Media & Publishing, pages 214–215
'Ecovisions'

Roger **Hammond** & Niall **Marriott**,
Marriott Hammond Resource
Consultants.
Careers & Education, pages 236–237
'Seeds of Understanding'

Christopher **Harding**,
British Nuclear Fuels Ltd.
Energy, pages 134–135
'The Nuclear Balance Sheet'

Paul **Harrison**,
Author: The Greening of Africa.
Markets, pages 68–69
'Coming to the Boil'

Brian **Jackman**,
Sunday Times.
Tourism, pages 172–173
'The Millionaire Lions'

Adrian **Judd**,
Friends of the Earth (FOE).
Design, pages 78–79
'Conspicuous Consumption'

Petra **Kelly**,
Bundestag.
Business Environment, pages 36–37
'Do the Impossible'

Robert **Lamb**,
Television Trust for the
Environment (TVE).
Media & Publishing, pages 202–203
'Behind the News'

Geoffrey **Lean**,
The Observer.
Into the 90s, pages 244–245
'My Five Billionth Baby'

Bob **Lowman**,
Ecology Building Society.
Money, pages 188–189
'Mortgaging the Future?'

Richard **Macrory**,
Imperial College, Centre for
Environmental Technology.
Business Environment, page 28
'The Green Arm of the Law'

Sheila **Moorcroft**,
Taylor Nelson Applied Futures.
Greener Growth, pages 52–55
'The Emergence of Inner-Directed Europe'

Norman **Myers**, Dr.,
Norman Myers Consulting Ltd.
Money, pages 190–192
'Writing off the Environment'

Max **Nicholson**,
Trust for Urban Ecology.
Urban Renewal, pages 162–163
'The Cinderella Science'

David **Nickson**, Sir,
Confederation of British
Industry (CBI).
Greener Growth, pages 48–49
'Exporting Environmental Excellence'

Anita **Roddick**,
The Body Shop.
Markets, pages 70–71
'The Beauty of Green'

Robin **Sadler**,
McCann Erickson Advertising Ltd.
PR & Advertising, pages 225
'Green Accounts'

Charles **Secrett**,
Friends of the Earth (FOE).
Markets, pages 64–66
'The Good Wood Guide'

Harford **Thomas**,
The Guardian.
Media & Publishing, pages 206–208
'In the Beginning was the Word'

Lloyd **Timberlake**,
Earthscan.
Business Environment, pages 50–51
'What is Sustainability?'

Jon **Tinker**,
Panos Institute.
Media & Publishing, pages 204–205
'How Panos Makes the Headlines'

Ernst **von Weizacker**, Dr,
Institute for European
Environmental Policy (IIEP).
Pollution, pages 124–125
'Clean Technologies?'

Andrew **Warren**,
Association for the Conservation
of Energy.
Energy, pages 136–137
'A Rush to Profligacy?'

Robert **Worcester**, Michelle **Corado**,
Market and Opinion Research
International (MORI).
Business Environment, pages 22–24
'No Meltdown yet in Public Opinion'

Advertisers

Biotreatment (BTL)	page 114
British Nuclear Fuels (BNFL)	Inside Back Cover
Central Electricity Generating Board (CEGB)	page 45
Common Ground	page 47
Commonwork Land Trust	page 168
Conder (Clearwater)	page 112
DOCTER	page 195
Ecology Building Society	page 141
English Estates	page 154
Environmental Data Services (ENDS)	page 34
Esso	page 38
Farm Gas	page 142
Friends of the Earth (FoE)	page 82
Groundwork	page 161
International Biochemicals	page 125
John Elkington Associates	page 18
Landscape Institute	page 140
Mercury Provident	page 193
Michael Boddington Associates	page 156
Natural Environment Research Council (NERC)	page 93
NIREX	page 135
Peak District National Park	page 170
Rechem	page 123
School of Combined Honours, University of Liverpool	page 238
Shell	Inside Front Cover
Tim Moore & Associates	page 81
Traidcraft	page 66

Working for Sustainability

What *is* sustainability? First and foremost, it is an idea. Indeed, as Lloyd Timberlake argues on page 50, it is potentially one of the most powerful ideas to have emerged in the 20th century.

The World Commission on Environment and Development concluded that an industry or an activity is sustainable if it 'meets the needs of the present without compromising the ability of future generations to meet their own needs.' Inevitably, many of those who have contributed to *Green Pages* may have their own definitions of sustainability, but there is a great deal more common ground than there was even a few years ago.

Green Pages is the first of a series of publications initiated and compiled by a new enterprise, SustainAbility. Designed as a first-stop information source on the rapidly growing environment business, *Green Pages* encapsulates our basic philosophy and approach. Like most of our projects, it aims to help build bridges between business, public sector and environmental interests.

Formed in 1987, SustainAbility draws on an expanding web of talent. The company's founder-Directors are John Elkington and Tom Burke. The *Green Pages* project, however, was very much a team effort. Assistant Editor Julia Hailes co-ordinated one of the most complex tasks we have yet undertaken. Elaine Elkington and Debbie Bruce helped edit the contributions and running text. Jonathan Shopley, Nick Rowcliffe, Lisa Silcock, Laura Kelly, Julie Seppings and Toby Adamson helped with the research. Ian McKinnell produced the cartoons and Tim Moore was responsible for design and layout. Others who have made major contributions include Georgina McAughtry of Environmental Data Services and Wendy Morris of Routledge.

We have enjoyed generous support from a number of sponsors during the life of the project. The **Network Foundation** gave an initial start-up grant, while the **Earthlife Foundation** provided office space and computer services until the launch of **SustainAbility** early in 1987. **The Department of the Environment,** the **EYE Task Force** at the **Community of the European Communities, ICI plc** and the **British Coal Corporation** all grant-aided the project. We are particularly grateful to Philip Dale of the DoE and Joanna Tachmintzis of the Commission. But the project would never have come through to completion without a major grant from the **Central Electricity Generating Board** (CEGB), where we should like to thank both Dr. Peter Chester (Director, Environment) and Debbie Bruce for their support. We are also grateful to the **Green Alliance** for its help in bringing this project through to completion.

Our ability to attract such a wide range of contributors, from Petra Kelly, the internationally known Green member of West Germany's Bundestag, to Christopher Harding, Chairman of British Nuclear Fuels, reflects one of SustainAbility's key strengths: our ability to communicate with all those involved in the environmental debate. While we do not subscribe to all the views put forward in our series of *Perspectives,* we believe that, in one way or another, they are all worth airing.

Clearly, sustainable development links together many different constituencies. We have had to be selective in choosing material to include in this first edition of *Green Pages,* but we are always interested to hear of new initiatives in the areas reviewed within these covers.

Let us know what you are doing. Write to us at: SustainAbility Ltd., 1 Cambridge Road, Barnes, London SW13 0PE. Or call us on 01 876 1125 (International: +44 1 876 1125).

INTRODUCTION

The Green Pages Team

1. Tim Moore
2. Tom Burke
3. Jonathan Shopley
4. John Elkington
5. Julia Hailes
6. Nick Rowcliffe

John Elkington

The founder-Editor of the *ENDS Report*, and subsequently Managing Director of Environmental Data Services Ltd., John Elkington has worked in the environmental field for over 15 years. Before being recruited to ENDS by Max Nicholson (page 162), he carried out postgraduate research at the School of Environmental Studies, University College London, and then worked for four years as a town planner at TEST, one of the early environmental consultancies. During that period, he was a frequent contributor to *New Scientist* on environment and development issues.

In the five years since he left ENDS, he has built up a reputation as one of Europe's leading authorities on the role of industry in sustainable development. He runs an independent environmental consultancy whose clients have included BP, Glaxo, Groundwork, ICI, the International Institute for Environment and Development (both IIED UK and IIED USA), Monsanto, the Nature Conservancy Council (NCC), the Natural Environment Research Council (NERC) and the World Resources Institute (WRI).

He wrote the industrial component of the UK response to the *World Conservation Strategy (1980)*, launched by Prince Charles in 1983, and has since worked on a wide range of innovative projects at the interface between business and environment. A Fellow of the Royal Society of Arts, he has been an Assessor of the Pollution Abatement Technology Awards since 1983, and of the Better Environment Awards since 1987. He served on the Industry Year Environment Panel and played a key role in organising the Design Council's 'Green Designer' exhibition in 1986. He is a member of the Nature Conservancy Council's Advisory Committee, England, and of the Central Electricity Generating Board's Environmental Development Advisory Panel.

A widely published writer and journalist, he has been Editor of *Biotechnology Bulletin* since 1982. His previous books include *The Ecology of Tomorrow's World* (Associated Business Press, 1980), *Sun Traps* (Pelican, 1984), *The Gene Factory* (Century, 1985), *The Poisoned Womb* (Viking 1985/Pelican, 1986) and – with Tom Burke – *The Green Capitalists* (Victor Gollancz, 1987). He was also a member of the editorial team which produced *The Gaia Atlas of Planet Management* (Pan, 1985).

Tom Burke

One of the most forceful voices in environmental politics, Tom Burke is Director of the Green Alliance and Policy Adviser of the European Environment Bureau. A vigorous environmental campaigner through the 1970s, he has devoted much of his time in the 1980s to developing an effective environmental lobby in Westminster and Brussels.

A member of the Board of Directors of Earth Resources Research (1981–), he has served as a member of the Waste Management Advisory Council (1976–81) and the Packaging Council (1978–82) and of the Executive Committee of the National Council for Voluntary Organisations (1984–), and as Executive Director of Friends of the Earth (1975–79). He served as a member of the UK National Committee for European Year of the Environment and of the Industry Year Environment Panel.

His publications include: *Europe: Environment* (1981); *Pressure Groups in the Global System* (1982); *Ecology 2000* (1984); and *The Green Capitalists: Industry's Search for Environmental Excellence*. He was a contributor to *The Gaia Atlas of Planet Management* (Pan, 1985).

Julia Hailes

SustainAbility's Company Secretary and Assistant Editor on the *Green Pages* project, Julia Hailes previously worked in television production and in advertising (Leo Burnett, see page 224). Following extensive travel in Latin America, she joined the Earthlife Foundation, working for Earthlife Publications.

Subsequently she helped to found SustainAbility, where she has worked on a number of projects, including *Green Pages* and *The Green Consumer Guide*, which she is co-authoring with John Elkington. She is interested in the potential for developing sustainable forms of tourism.

Jonathan Shopley

With considerable experience in civil engineering and environmental science, Jonathan Shopley has been an Associate with John Elkington Associates since 1985. Previously he had carried out environmental assessment, pollution research and land rehabilitation projects for a number of major mining and energy companies, including Shell, Anglo American and De Beers.

Since joining JEA, his work has taken him to France, Spain, Kenya and the United States. He played a leading role in a major project for the Nature Conservancy Council and British Petroleum, which involved the preparation of nature conservation guidelines for onshore oil and gas development.

He has also worked on two projects for the World Resources Institute, one focusing on the potential role of information and remote sensing technologies in sustainable development in the Third World, the other on waste management technologies.

Nick Rowcliffe

With a BSc in Environmental Sciences from the University of Southampton, Nick Rowcliffe worked briefly at the Institute of Terrestrial Ecology. He then spent a year doing practical conservation work with the British Trust for Conservation Volunteers (BTCV).

Working part-time for two years with the Green Alliance, he focused on such issues as acid rain, the Chernobyl disaster and the electoral implications of environmental issues. He was instrumental in bringing activist Jeremy Rifkin to Britain in 1987 to discuss the implications of biotechnology. He now works with Environmental Data Services Ltd., publishers of the *ENDS Report*.

Tim Moore

When he left the London School of Printing in 1979, Tim Moore decided to concentrate on work with creative and progressive clients in the theatre, music and environmental businesses. After a Master's course at Rhode Island School of Design, he formed Tim Moore Associates in 1982 and has since worked for such clients as CBS, Channel 4, TV AM, *Vogue, Business, New Scientist* and the Ballet Rambert. With John Elkington he has worked on projects for Earthlife, Groundwork and the Nature Conservancy Council.

Europe's Green Economy

Pollution has turned the Rhine successively red, blue and green. The public reaction to such disasters is forcing European industry to green its own operations.

In 1986, dubbed Industry Year in Britain, we helped the Design Council put together *The Green Designer* exhibition, which ran for six weeks at the Design Centre before transferring to Glasgow. The exhibition, highlighting new products and technologies which were cleaner, quieter and more energy-efficient, was described by *New Scientist* as possibly 'the most significant exhibition that the Design Council has mounted in 10 years.'

The scores of companies whose technologies and products were featured were delighted with the exposure they received, but many asked why there was no yearbook or directory covering this area? Their interest spurred us on to think of ways in which we could produce a more lasting record of progress in Europe's emerging 'green economy'. *Green Pages* is the end-result.

Overdrawn

The central message which we are aiming to communicate in *Green Pages* is that business and industry can play – and increasingly are playing – a crucial role in the transition to more environmentally sustainable forms of economic development. But, even in straightforward economic terms, the challenge facing world industry is formidable.

It is worth recalling that the world manufactures seven times more goods today than it did as recently as 1950. 'Given population growth rates,' the World Commission on Environment and Development concluded in its report, *Our Common Future*, 'a five- to tenfold increase in manufacturing output will be needed just to raise developing-world consumption of manufactured goods to industrialized world levels by the time population growth rates level off next century.'

While many of the environmental organisations covered in the *Green Pages* survey (page 14) would not see this either as a desirable or feasible goal, most would accept the Commission's assertion that 'a world in which poverty is endemic will always be prone to ecological and other catastrophes.'

Nor would they dispute its claim that current styles of economic development 'draw too heavily, too quickly, on already overdrawn environmental resource accounts to be affordable far into the future without bankrupting those accounts. They may show profits on the balance sheets of our generation, but our children will inherit the losses.'

Our environmental problems are more serious today than they have ever been, as later sections of *Green Pages* confirm, but some leading environmentalists are convinced that new styles of development, new styles of growth, could help us meet both our economic and our ecological goals.

Don't expect harmony

Today, environmentalists increasingly talk in terms of 'sustainable development'. In so doing, they recognise that, as the Commission put it, 'sustainable development is not a fixed state of harmony, but rather a process of change in which the exploitation of resources, the direction of investments, and institutional change are made consistent with future as well as present needs.'

Green Pages provides progress reports on a number of the most important green business sectors which are beginning to effect a similar transformation of Europe's economy. It is worth stressing that we are not simply talking about manufacturing, but also about a wide range of service, investment and educational activities.

Green Pages also contains contributions from a number of those who are playing a leading role in developing those sectors. These contributions, which appear under the heading 'Perspectives', add up to

---

Greener Pages

While compiling this edition of SustainAbility's *Green Pages,* we heard of two other initiatives which had adopted the same name. Both are very much more 'alternative' publications, but complement our work rather than competing with it. *Green Pages South-West* (84 Colston Street, Bristol BS1 5BB), with whose originators we have worked almost from the outset, aims to provide local information on the green economy in the West Country.

Macdonald & Co. are also planning a *Green Pages,* written by John Button, which will apparently be rather more like a UK version of the pathfinding Whole Earth Catalog (first published in the States in 1968). Button's opus will cover 'everything and anything available in Britain today which is truly life-enhancing'. He can be reached at Myrtle Cottage, Slogarie, Laurieston, Castle Douglas, Kirkudbrightshire DG7 2NL.

fascinating overview of the green economy. We would stress, however, that the fact that we have chosen to publish a particular contribution does not necessarily imply that we subscribe to all the views expressed therein.

We start off by looking at some of the trends in European politics and the ways in which they are creating new pressures on business. Different industries and different companies within given industries are responding to these pressures in very different ways. As later sections show, there have been both striking failures and striking successes.

Overall, however, the *Green Pages* survey of environmental organisations (page 14) confirmed that, while many were prepared to admit that various sectors of industry have dramatically cleaned up their act, there is unlikely to be any let-up in the pressure on environmentally problematic industries and companies.

The Technicolor Rhine

Meanwhile, how green *is* European business? Our survey shows that leading environmentalists accept that the image of some industries and many companies has improved, but they note that they find it very difficult to assess whether their environmental performance has improved to the same extent. This will remain a problem until there is free exchange of information between environmental and industrial organisations.

Meanwhile, however, there are a number of barometers you can use to check European industry's awareness of – and responsiveness to – environmental issues. We chose to look at the annual reports produced by a sample of leading companies (page 40). Many will not have worked through each of the '10 Steps to Environmental Excellence' (page 226), although the extent to which such companies now feel they need to discuss their stance on environmental issues – and, in IBM's case, on sustainable development itself – is a real indication of the way that business is beginning to take some of these issues on board.

As the Sandoz example shows, companies may prettily describe their environmental sensitivity in successive annual reports while teetering on the verge of a major disaster. The smouldering sacks of prussian blue dye which caused the massive pollution of the Rhine in 1986 were destined for a use with which few environmentalists would sympathise: the dye is used to colour agrochemicals to make them attractive to users! Because of the mixture of chemicals sluiced into the Rhine by the fire hoses used to fight the resulting inferno, the river turned red. The following year, Sandoz contrived – through two more accidental spills – to turn the Rhine first blue, then green.

Companies that get the equation wrong risk going out of business. While *Green Pages* was in the final stages of preparation, for example, it was reported that Land Rover had lost an £85 million, 4,100 vehicle Swiss Army contract because it could not fit anti-pollution equipment in time. Although the company later retorted that it had yet to hear anything formally from the Swiss Government, there is growing pressure on such manufacturers to consider the environmental performance of their products. Austin Rover, in fact, were able at the time to sell only one model in Switzerland, the new Rover 800.

For this reason, while there will always be many recalcitrants and even renegades, growing numbers of companies are moving ahead of the legislation to ensure that their environmental performance is going to be acceptable for the foreseeable future. Often, as CBI President Sir David Nickson points out on page 48, they are winning real commercial prizes as a result.

Why Not Recycled Paper?

Green Pages should have been printed on recycled paper. Unfortunately, we couldn't afford it.

Recycled paper offers a number of environmental advantages. It saves trees, energy and water. Ultimately, when economies of scale begin to feed in, it should also become cost-competitive – and in some applications it already is.

When Routledge sought quotes from the main suppliers of recycled paper, however, their product turned out to be around 40% more expensive than non-recycled paper. More problematically still, they could not guarantee the thickness of the paper, which would have introduced difficulties at the book binding stage. On a tight budget, we had no option but to go the non-green route. Next time, perhaps.

Leading UK suppliers of recycled paper include Paperback Ltd and Conservation Books. One of the achievements of firms like Paperback has been to dispel the idea that recycled products are necessarily inferior. Indeed, the range of quality products is constantly expanding.

Paperback Ltd, *8–16 Coronet Street, Hoxton, London N1 6HD. Tel: 01 729 1382.*

Conservation Books, *228 London Road, Reading RG6 1AH. Tel: 0734 668611.*

The Front Line

Love them or loathe them, environmental campaigners have helped force many issues onto the political agenda. And the results of the *Green Pages* survey suggests that their influence is likely to grow.

If any one image sums up the collision between market values and radical environmentalism, it is a newswire picture of a Greenpeace inflatable slicing in towards an 'enemy' ship.

Whether the ship is dumping or incinerating wastes, or transporting nuclear materials, the impact is the same. The David versus Goliath angle ensures that an industrial practice which might otherwise have remained comfortably out of sight and out of mind, is brought into sharp focus as headline news.

But this piratical approach is only one of many campaigning styles adopted by Europe's environmental organisations. Other groups, including Friends of the Earth (FoE), have gone for other types of publicity 'stunts' and for rallies. Organisations like the World Wildlife Fund (WWF), may come across as much more sedate – but are often involved in vigorous behind-the-scenes lobbying (page 242).

Groups like the WWF also provide a vehicle for establishment figures, including royalty, to become involved in conservation. Increasingly, too, they are helping to pull in corporate sponsorship for conservation and sustainable development programmes. But the importance of individual fundraising initiatives remains as considerable as ever.

Ultimately, however, the success of environmental organisations in saving the world will depend on the extent to which they can parlay the funds they raise, whether in the high street or the board room, into greener forms of enterprise, investment and employment.

Green Pages provides a progress report on key sectors of the emerging green economy. In many respects it is a rather more positive picture than one might expect from reading the newspapers or watching the TV. But with the world's human population likely to double before it stabilises (page 244), the green economy will need to gear itself up for a period of super-rapid growth. The risks are great, but the opportunities are also probably greater than at any previous time in human history.

Greenpeace is prepared to put lives on the line . . .

. . . and its inflatables help blow up complex issues into headline news.

INTRODUCTION

1 *The lion may have been left in the dark as Friends of the Earth rally support for their campaign against acid rain, but one benefit of cleaner air would be longer lives for monumental cats.*

2, 3 *It's one thing to organise a stunt against the trade in endangered species, quite another to hunt down well-organised poachers and traders. Inset: one of 141 rhino horns from Kenya confiscated by Customs in Bremen, West Germany. Friends of the Earth are settling in for the long haul with tropical hardwoods (page 64).*

4 *A race against time. Sponsored by Armstrong World Industries, British Airways and British Eagle, rhino peddlers Charlie Hewat and Julie Edwards cycled from the UK to Zimbabwe to raise money for rhino conservation.*

5 *Increasingly, environmentalists recognise that campaigns must be complemented by green enterprise. Anti-pesticide stunts may give the Government food for thought, but organic farmers are likely to be much more important in the transition to sustainable agriculture (page 143).*

Questions and Answers

Which company has the best environmental reputation – and which has the worst?
What are the priority targets for European environmentalists in the 1990s?
Which single environmental organisation has had the greatest impact in the 1980s?

To take the last question first, no prizes for guessing the answer: Greenpeace.

Asked to name the most effective environmental organisation – other than their own – the 69 organisations responding to the *Green Pages* questionnaire had a huge range to choose from. But they put Greenpeace in first place (28% of mentions), Friends of the Earth in second place (18%), and the Royal Society for the Protection of Birds and World Wildlife Fund in joint third place (13%). Dozens of other organisations received lower rankings.

Carried out by SustainAbility in European Year of the Environment (EYE), the *Green Pages* survey achieved an unusually high (67%) response rate – and uncovered some important facts and trends.

CAP shadows EYE

EYE, for example, was an EEC initiative and was launched by the Commission of the European Communities. So what do environmentalists think of the EEC?

On balance, just over half (54%) thought that the EEC had been a 'good thing' for the environment. But most of those who supported the EEC and its fourth Environmental Action Programme (page 26) felt that any benefits from a continent-wide approach to environmental problems were almost outweighed by the environmental damage caused by the Common Agricultural Policy (page 148). And fully 20% felt that, on balance, the EEC had been a bad thing, bringing food mountains, wine lakes and heavier lorries in its wake.

But where, one might ask, does Britain rank among European Community member states in terms of environmental sensitivity? The answers here very much depended on whom you talked to.

Many of those who felt that the EEC has had a positive impact noted that EEC Regulations and Directives have helped push forward UK legislation. There was a tendency, too, to agree with European greens such as Petra Kelly (page 36), who see Britain as the 'dirty man of Europe'. The British government, noted Holland's Stichting Natuur en Milieu, 'has unfortunately slowed down a lot of decision-making on environmental issues. However, Britain is not the only country here!' In some areas, too, particularly in bird conservation, the consensus was that Britain is still ahead of the field.

Given the wide range of organisations who replied, such differences in perspective are to be expected. But there were very marked differences between organisations of different ages. The most radical, Greenpeace and Friends of the Earth among them, were founded during the 1970s. The age of the organisation was also strongly reflected in the resources available to it.

Green budgets

Those with the biggest turnovers and staffs were almost exclusively founded over 30 years ago. Among the big employers were the Royal Society for the Prevention of Cruelty to Animals (founded 1824; 700 employees), the Royal Society for the Protection of Birds (1889; 469 employees); the National Trust for Scotland (1931; 300 employees), the Nature Conservancy Council (1950; 800 employees); and the World Wildlife Fund (1961; 103 employees).

The average staff size for organisations founded in the 1960s was 18 (and their average turnover was £1.3 million). The Nature Conservancy Council's £36.5 million turnover was the largest in the sample, but the Royal Society for the Protection of Birds is perhaps the model which most green organisations would love to emulate, with its 500,000-plus membership and £18.3 million turnover.

Other well-endowed organisations included the RSPCA (which reported a £16.8 million turnover), the National Trust for Scotland (£7.2 million), the World Wildlife Fund (£5.9 million), the British Trust for Conservation Volunteers (£2.6 million) and the Jersey Wildlife Preservation Trust (£1 million).

Groups founded in the 1970s reported an average 7 employees and £288,000 in turnover, while organisations launched in the 1980s had an average of 6 employees and an average turnover of around £160,000 – roughly a tenth of that reported by their counterparts launched in the 1960s.

Because of widespread interest in environmental conservation, many organisations are able to make considerable use of volunteers. The British Trust for Conservation Volunteers (BTCV) and the Sussex Trust for Nature Conservation both reported using 500 volunteers; the National Trust for Scotland and the Hertfordshire and Middlesex Trust for Nature Conservation were using 300 apiece; and the Marine Conservation Society reported 100.

Some organisations which did not send their questionnaires in time, like Groundwork (page 158), make even greater use of voluntary help.

But, however many volunteers they may have at

INTRODUCTION

their disposal, these organisations still need to raise money. And they do so in many different ways. Some have developed a considerable number of branch organisations, for example. In our sample, Friends of the Earth led with 220 branches, followed by the RSPCA with 211, the Royal Society for Nature Conservation with 128 and the British Trust for Conservation Volunteers with 56.

Industrious search for money

Seven main sources of income were mentioned. 38% of the organisations said they were grant-aided, with the Countryside Commission for Scotland, the Urban Spaces Scheme, the Institute for European Environmental Policy and the Nature Conservancy Council all getting 97% or more of their funding in this form.

A green royal. Prince Charles launches the Conservation and Development for the UK *in 1983.*

Membership fees are the second most important source of funds, mentioned by 21% of respondents. Many of the biggest organisations have diversified their income sources. The RSPB, for example, gets 47% of its income from fund-raising activities and 38% from membership subscriptions, but others – among them the Christian Ecology Group and the Association for the Protection of Rural Scotland – depend on their members for more than 80% of their income.

Corporate sponsorship, mentioned by just 6% of respondents, is a growing source of income. 69% of those receiving such sponsorship said that it was on a rising curve. The organisation depending most heavily on this source (59%) is the UK Centre for Economic and Environmental Development (CEED), set up to implement the *Conservation and Development Programme for the UK*. This, the UK response to the 1980 *World Conservation Strategy,* was prepared by a consortium of environmental organisations, including the Nature Conservancy Council, the Countryside Commission and the World Wildlife Fund.

Other organisations were much less dependent on corporate sponsorship. The RSPB, for example, reports that only 1% of its funds comes from industry. This does not mean that such organisations would not accept funds, if suitable terms could be arranged. Even Friends of the Earth has accepted corporate sponsorship, albeit from one of the greenest businesses in the country, the Body Shop (page 70). 'We accept very little such funding,' noted FoE Director Jonathon Porritt, 'and have very tight guidelines. It must also be said,' he wryly noted, 'that we are hardly industry's dream organisation!'

The four other sources of income most frequently mentioned were fees from conferences and training programmes; merchandising (page 19); the sale of publications; and 'investments', although it was not always clear what the respondents meant by this term.

In good company?

The fact that particular organisations received corporate sponsorship was no guarantee that they supported current business practices. Indeed, in several cases they named major sponsors as among the worst environmental offenders. Not surprisingly, the 1970s organisations were much more likely to agree with the proposition that economic growth inevitably damages the environment (54% did so) than were those formed in the 1950s (33%), 1960s (8%) or 1980s (33%).

Most respondents (93%) said that industry's environmental performance had improved significantly, although many distinguished between the image projected by industry (Jonathon Porritt mentioned industry's growing fluency in 'greenspeak') and the actual facts of the matter.

Asked to rank the environmental performance of specific industrial sectors on a scale running from 1 (excellent) to 5 (appalling), respondents ranked the oil industry top (albeit awarding it a distinctly cool average score of 2.6) and the financial sector bottom (a chilly 4.0). In between came, in deteriorating order, the food and drink sector (2.9), the water and sewage industry (3.2), the motor industry (3.3), the waste management industry (3.4), five sectors clustering at 3.5 (chemicals, construction, electricity supply, forestry and general manufacturing), agriculture (3.8) and packaging (3.9).

About half of our respondents, however, felt that economic growth could be squared, to some considerable extent, with the pursuit of environmental quality. The concept of 'sustainable development' was mentioned time and again, although it was far from clear that everyone was using the term in the same way.

A fair number of respondents accepted that further economic growth in the industrialised countries could be achieved with cleaner, less energy-intensive technologies, but wondered whether the same would be true of the Third World. And the Nature Conservation Bureau noted that even if improved technologies were adopted in the North, our economies would continue to trigger enormous environmental damage in the South.

Green growth?

We also asked whether 'green growth' was possible or desirable? By this we meant growth directed at switching European economies away from environment-intensive sectors and activities into cleaner, more resource-efficient alternatives. Only Friends of the Earth argued that green growth was logically impossible.

'As it is presently understood and pursued as the sole determinant of economic success,' Jonathon Porritt noted, 'economic growth *per se* must damage the environment.' But even he recognised that greener growth is not only desirable but already taking place – he mentioned energy efficiency and renewable energy technologies, organic agriculture and mass-transit transport systems.

Indeed everyone generally supported the concept of greener growth and encouraging examples were given from many of the economic sectors covered later in *Green Pages*. The extent to which such improvements are sustained and built upon, however, will depend on the vitality and impact of the world-wide environmental movement. So what about the prospects for environmentalism in the closing years of the 20th century?

Overall, our respondents were surprisingly optimistic. The environmental movement has already had a considerable impact on public opinion (page 22) and 92% felt that they would have an even greater impact in the 1990s. In Britain, the pessimists were all involved in nature conservation and presumably felt that any gains would no more than slow the erosion of vulnerable habitat and the loss of endangered species.

Issues for the 1990s

Atmospheric pollution is the number one concern.

Asked to list the issues which most concern them, half (54%) of the survey respondents mentioned *atmospheric pollution* problems. Of particular concern are acid rain, the depletion of the ozone layer and the build-up of atmospheric carbon dioxide (page 86). The last two are direct contributors to the 'greenhouse effect', a general planetary warming trend which could lead to untold knock-on effects.

The second cluster of issues which emerged, gaining 41% of mentions, focused on *rural land use and ownership*. Among the issues highlighted were changes in the farming and forestry industries, the pressure on green belts and the demand for increased public access to the countryside. 17% of the sample also mentioned agricultural pollution, particularly that caused by agrochemicals.

The third set of concerns revolved around *nuclear energy*. 37% of respondents mentioned the nuclear industry and 27% specified nuclear waste disposal. Some organisations, however, felt that this was the number one priority. In Spain, for example, AEDENAT (Asociacion Ecologista de Defensa de la Naturaleza) reported that its main campaign for the 1990s would aim to achieve the closure of all the country's nuclear power stations.

Linked to the concern about the greenhouse effect, and to many other issues, the loss of the planet's *tropical forests* was mentioned by 30% of the sample. This has proved a particularly difficult problem for conservation organisations to address, because most tropical forests are in countries where population pressures are greatest and environmental controls weakest.

Population growth, in fact, was mentioned by 21% of respondents. (Geoffrey Lean focuses on population pressures on page 244.) *Third world poverty* and *foreign debt* problems were mentioned by 10% of respondents, as were *urban dereliction*, the management of *hazardous waste* and the introduction of *advanced biotechnologies*.

INTRODUCTION

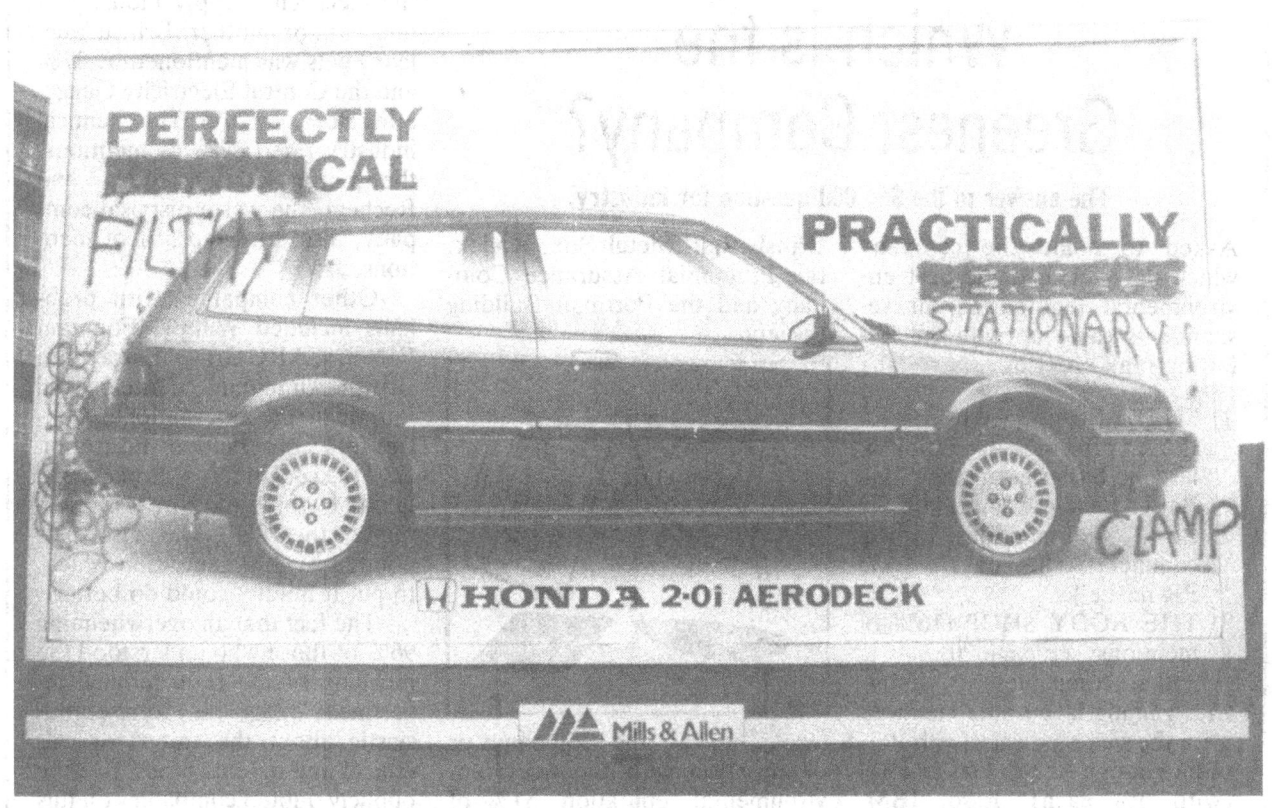

Green graffiti, above, may be the cheapest way of getting the message across, but a growing number of environmental groups are commissioning their own advertising campaigns (page 224). Below: a still from 'Meltdown', a Greenpeace film. The next step: to sell the concept of sustainability.

Which is the Greenest Company?

The answer to the $64,000 question for industry.

Asked to name the company which they felt had the best environmental reputation, our respondents came up with the following rank ordering:

1. SHELL (mentioned by 31% of those offering an opinion, largely because of the Shell Better Britain Campaign).
2. BP (22% of mentions. Typical comment: 'They have a good PR image').
3. THE BODY SHOP (16% of mentions: see page 70).

Other companies and industries gaining favourable mentions were the water industry (with 10% of mentions), British Gas and 3M (with 6% each), Esso, IBM, Traidcraft (page 62), Sainsbury, British Rail, Metal Box, Kodak, the Prudential Assurance Company and the Portman Building Society.

As far as the company or organisation with the *worst* environmental reputation, 51% of those offering an opinion picked the electricity supply industry in one form or another. British Nuclear Fuels was mentioned by 37% and the Central Electricity Generating Board by 20%. The chemical industry rated 12% of mentions, the motor industry 5% – and Rechem, the waste disposal company, also attracted 5% of mentions.

Other companies with problems included Wimpy, Fountain Forestry, ARC Gravel Extraction, British Aluminium, British Coal (although the International Centre for Conservation Education gave the coal industry its backing), Union Carbide and Nirex. Interestingly, the TUC was also pinpointed as an organisation which, to put it mildly, could do better.

The fact that an overwhelming 96% of those who understood the meaning of the term 'ethical investment' (page 186) were enthusiastic about the trend towards ethical investment should give the publicly quoted companies on this 'black list' pause for thought.

JOHN ELKINGTON ASSOCIATES

Helping business and industry, national and international government agencies, and non-governmental organisations to achieve environmental excellence.

Our client list includes:

The Design Council · Glaxo · Groundwork · ICI · the Institute of Petroleum
the International Institute for Environment and Development (both in the UK and USA)
Monsanto · the Nature Conservancy Council · the Natural Environment Research Council
the United Nations Environment Programme and the World Resources Institute.

1 Cambridge Road, Barnes, London SW13 0PE or on 01-876 1125 (Int'l: +44 1 876 1125)

Gaining Purchase

Who will benefit from the Green Consumer?

When SustainAbility and The Other Economic Summit (TOES) hosted a workshop on the 'Conscious Consumer', early in EYE, it attracted a wide range of organisations, from the Consumers' Association to ethical investment consultants. And some interesting facts emerged.

When *Which?* magazine surveyed its readers in 1986, for example, 9 out of 10 said that pollution was important to them. And Kirk McNulty of Taylor Nelson Applied Futures (page 52) pointed out that about a third of Britons now subscribe to attitudes which make them potential Conscious Consumers.

The main question addressed by the workshop was: How can consumers who want to be part of the solution, rather than part of the problem, influence the environmental performance of the European economy through their purchasing power? This theme was then picked up by a second all-day meeting organised by Turning Point.

Interestingly, three-quarters (74%) of the respondents in the *Green Pages* survey of environmental organisations felt that the Green Consumer has an important potential role to play in saving the world. 14% of the organisations had boycotted products and 13% had endorsed products.

Holland's Stichting Natuur en Milieu was the most specific in terms of brand names: it had boycotted Duracell batteries (until the company stopped the manufacture of cadmium batteries), Heineken beer (until Heineken agreed not to use cadmium-containing plastics in its crates) and Shell (which 'spent a great deal of money on a campaign to tell the public that they didn't make all that much acid rain').

The UK boycotts range from Friends of the Earth's campaigns against most tropical hardwoods (page 64) and aerosols to the British Hedgehog Society's opposition to the use of hedgehogs for food. Such boycotts have rarely been completely successful: the Soil Association's campaign for 'Real Milk' foundered, for example, while the victories (e.g. endangered species or furs) were often partial at best. The endorsements reported were mainly of recycled paper, organically grown produce and free-range eggs, although Friends of the Earth endorses the Body Shop's produce range and the World Wildlife Fund, for example, backs certain holiday packages.

A small number of environmentalists expressed concern that Green Consumers would always be in the minority, but supporters of greener consumption patterns could point to many examples where there have been major shifts in buying behaviour:

- 69% mentioned health foods, for example, and 29% the cut-back in food additives.
- 18% pointed to the desire to see more recycling.
- 14% highlighted the increasing concern for animals welfare, leading to growing pressures on intensive livestock farming and on the use of animals in toxicity testing.
- 8% mentioned the consumer boycotts against the fur trade.

Some organisations were distinctly bullish. 'The sky's the limit' was the TOES reaction to the question about the potential for the Green Consumer. Among the other targets mentioned by respondents were unleaded petrol, energy conservation, non-meat or low-meat diets, clean cars, conservation holidays and ethical investment.

Interestingly, half (52%) of the organisations responding to the *Green Pages* survey are now involved in some form of merchandising. Over a quarter (28%) produce catalogues and two-thirds (67%) of those responding to this question felt that merchandising would become increasingly important as a source of income. Some of the products on offer, though, are slightly dubious: one of the County Nature Conservation Trusts thought it slightly ironic, for example, that the World Wildlife Fund's catalogue offered an electric carving knife!

The range of products given the green catalogue treatment is considerable and growing, from the obvious T-shirts and calendars through posters and car-stickers to books and videos. 68% produce newsletters, 35% magazines and 74% have published at least one book. In addition to the educational products, there is also a growing emphasis on gifts, including cuddly toys, animal models, tea towels, cards and wildflower seeds.

Among recent books which have looked at the links between consumption and the environment are *The Friends of the Earth Handbook* and *Blueprint for a Green Planet*, both of which are reviewed in our Green Bookshelf section.

More specific advice on what to buy – and what not to buy – will be given in *The Green Consumer Guide*, compiled by John Elkington and Julia Hailes of SustainAbility, and published in the summer of 1988 by Victor Gollancz.

The Business Environment

Industry and investors normally think of the 'business environment' in terms of interest and tax rates, industrial relations or international competition. Now, says *Tom Burke*, they must add other priorities to the list. Among them, environmental protection and sustainable development.

Green is the new political colour of Europe. Greens sit in the Bundestag and both houses of the Belgian Parliament. They are credited with having ended Bruno Kreisky's decade long domination of Austrian politics and have now entered the Italian Parliament for the first time. There is a multinational Green group in the European Parliament. Green parties now put forward candidates in 16 out of the 17 European countries which hold free elections. In Eastern Europe, ecological groups are to be found at the cutting edge of the political renewal movements in Poland, Czechoslovakia, Hungary and even the Soviet Union itself.

This greening of politics is one of the most striking social phenomena of the decade. The electoral successes of the Greens, limited though these may have been, have had a transforming effect on the whole of European politics as the orthodox parties responded by hastily sewing a green stripe into the red or blue flag. The environment has been legitimised as a political issue. It is now a respectable subject for serious politicians.

The elevation of environmental issues to the mainstream political agenda also lifts their prominence as a feature in the business environment. Public support for tougher action on environmental protection has been consistently apparent in opinion polls since the late sixties. But it has, for the most part, been very general in character. As long as all the political parties were equally indifferent to the environment such a generalised aspiration had little real political effect. Only massive accidents or the rare successful campaign from a pressure group focused public attention sufficiently to achieve political action.

This cosy conspiracy of indifference has now been broken. There is real competition between all the political parties to seize the environmental high ground. From a political perspective, the environment is uncolonised territory. No political party is automatically associated with good environmental performance in the way that they are with, say, strong defence, proportional representation or preservation of the health service. Yet, in Britain, a poll conducted by Friends of the Earth before the 1987 election found that for more than 30% of voters the environment was very important in determining their choice of party.

Golden circle

The emergence of the German Greens to political prominence has triggered an iterative process throughout Europe whereby an already high level of public concern, long ignored by the politicians, has now been endorsed and legitimised by them. Because it is now an area for inter-party struggle it is in the interest of opposition parties to stress the urgency of the problems and the failures of the governing parties to act strongly or effectively enough. This, in its turn,

---

Business operates in a context set by the activities of many other interests, individuals and institutions. This context both establishes the external constraints on business activity and identifies opportunities for new goods and services. Accurate assessment of the 'business environment', as it is known, is a key element in business success.

Environmental issues and pressures now represent an important component of the business environment, both in Europe and elsewhere. This section of Green Pages *examines the politics of the environment, the policy and legislative pressures which are driven by those politics, and the state of the environment itself. It also pinpoints 'sustainability' as a central concept for reconciling economic and ecological goals, highlighting emerging areas for partnership between business and the environment.*

---

stimulates further public concern and raises the electoral stakes for which the politicians are competing, so prompting another round of environmental bidding by the political parties.

Thus did democracy ever work. The real significance of the greening of politics is that the environment has now entered the golden circle of problems on which governments must act and be seen to act. It is not a step that will be readily reversed, thus it is worthwhile examining further the forces which have driven this political transformation.

The now universal image of a painfully beautiful blue and white planet, photographed against the deep black loneliness of space, has become a symbol of our era. Yet whilst planetary consciousness has been

BUSINESS ENVIRONMENT

expanding, European horizons have been shrinking. Europeans have come to doubt their place in the world. After centuries of expansionary self-confidence, a deep anxiety about the future has become Europe's dominant mood. Poised between the grumbling giants of East and West, frozen into the brittle and unnatural posture imposed at Yalta, an insidious weariness with the world has permeated, and frequently paralysed, European policy making. Only in the sparsely populated Scandanavian countries has there been any real vigour of response to the fate of the earth.

But the reflexes missing from official Europe have not been lost to the European people, especially among those born since 1945. This generation, now on the verge of power, and its successors, form an emergent majority. Three experiences, wholly new to humankind, mark their lives: the threat of nuclear war, the magnitude of global poverty and the destruction of the planetary environment.

The vigour of the political impulse to which these experiences have given birth cannot be denied. The staggering response to the Band-Aid concerts is only the latest and most spectacular event to give testimony to its force. Massive popular movements, intensely international both in spirit and practice, led, for the most part, by the emerging generation, have swept across Europe in the past three decades. Their abrasive attempts to break the stifling grasp of the post-war orthodoxy on Europe's political agenda have been the principal source of originality and vitality in European policy making.

A new generation

It is as mistaken to think of these movements merely as spasms of reaction against the side-effects of progress as it is to think of them as simply movements of the left against the right. Rather, they represent far deeper shifts in the emotional ground of European politics. A new generation is giving voice to new concerns pressed upon it by the new, and intolerable, conditions under which it lives. The sheer scale of the problems posed by the remorseless spread of nuclear weapons or the ecologically destructive capability of five billion human beings armed with modern technology has created a new realm of politics.

The environment occupies a pivotal place in these emerging politics. Environmentalism is the leading edge of the post-war generation's assault on the orthodox agenda. As a political force it spans the great European divides. It is as deeply felt in the communist East as in the capitalist West, albeit in different forms, and as strong in the Catholic South as the Protestant North. It evokes responses equally on the authoritarian right or democratic left; among working class poor and middle class affluent. It contains within its compass the traditional European tensions between idealist and pragmatist; between romantic and rationalist; between revolutionary and reformer.

These tensions are the driving force of change in European politics. They are clearly seen in the contrast between the greening of politics in Britain and Germany. These countries are at the poles of a European spectrum of environmental politics, the one pragmatic, rationalist and reformist, the other idealist, romantic and revolutionary.

On March 22nd, 1983, 27 newly elected members took their seats in the Bundestag. Deliberately choosing to sit between Social Democrats on the left and the Christian Democrats to the right in obedience to their campaign slogan, 'Neither right nor left but out in front' and disdaining obeisance to the dress conventions of their temperamentally formal fellow members, the casually dressed Greens, potted plants, beards, badges and all had arrived. Five years and a further election later, they were still there and had increased in number to 44.

The social and political pressures underpinning the rise of the Greens had been long building. In part, they were a product of the extraordinary strength of the post-war political consensus in Germany. There was little disagreement between right and left on the central economic and security issues throughout the three decades of the German 'economic miracle'. The division of the country into two blocs, each just unable to dominate on their own, balanced by a small centre party willing to swing between the two, created a remarkably stable political climate. The Social Democrats, alone or in coalition, had ruled since 1966. The result was a stifling orthodoxy with no room for either dissent or innovation.

Not surprisingly, it had no room either for an emerging generation born since the war. The 'generation gap', common to most affluent societies, was deepened and hardened in Germany by the sterile unresponsiveness of this orthodoxy. The German student activists of the 1960s ran head on into an authoritarian and inflexible Government, unwilling and unable to make any concessions to new ideas. The Greens' systematic rejection of the goals and values of the German consensus is rooted in the alienation experienced during this period.

Unstable compound

This immunity of German politics to criticism from either within or outside the political parties drove increasing numbers of those engaged in change into the extra-parliamentary opposition. The urban terrorists of the Baader-Meinhoff gang were the most extreme manifestation of this process. But its strongest expression lay in the growth of the wholly legal, and often very effective, citizen's initiative movements (Burgerinitiativen) throughout the 1970s. These groups focused their efforts on tackling discrete local problems directly. Inevitably, many of the issues around which they organised were environmental:

24→

PERSPECTIVES

No Meltdown Yet in Public Opinion

What measures are Europeans prepared to take to protect their environment?
How concerned are we about the environmental prospect?
Robert Worcester and *Michele Corrado* of MORI report

'The word 'meltdown' got into the Longman's English Dictionary for the first time in 1987, in the wake of the Chernobyl disaster. Among other words which are increasingly known to members of the public are 'acid rain' and 'tropical rainforests'. But how is public opinion in Britain and the rest of Europe reacting to the increased coverage of such issues in the media?

A MORI opinion poll commissioned by Friends of the Earth (FoE) and the World Wildlife Fund (WWF) in May 1987, immediately prior to the British General Election, revealed that 81% believed that the 'Government should give a much higher priority to protecting the environment.' Even among Conservative supporters the figure ran as high as 77%.

The same poll showed that 69% of the public felt that the environmental policies of political parties were at least 'fairly important' in determining which political party, if any, they would vote for at the impending General Election. In the event, it is far from clear that such considerations had much influence on voting patterns, but the results were a general indicator of the level of concern about environmental issues.

Europe's mood

And it looks as though the mood in Europe is similar. Eurobarometer, which polls opinion in the twelve member States and is co-ordinated by 'Faits et Opinions' in Paris, asked EEC citizens in March and April of 1986 whether they saw pollution as an 'urgent and immediate problem', 'more a problem for the future' or 'not really a problem'. Nearly three-quarters (72%) said it was 'urgent and immediate'. Only a very small minority (3%) considered pollution no problem at all.

Concern was greatest in Italy, Greece, Luxembourg and Germany, where at least four in five respondents described pollution as an urgent, immediate problem. But in France and Ireland, only around half of those interviewed thought it so pressing.

A Chernobyl in Britain?

Pulling back to British public opinion for a moment, the MORI poll for FoE and WWF revealed that there are a number of areas of particular concern. Over 80% of the public felt that the Government should: set maximum levels of pesticides and residues in food and drinking water; provide funds to help finance local authority waste recycling schemes; and withdraw proposals for the shallow burial of nuclear waste,

ROBERT M. WORCESTER *is Chairman and Managing Director of Market & Opinion Research International (MORI). Prior to founding MORI in 1969, he was an officer of Opinion Research Corporation, Princeton, New Jersey. He is a past-President of the World Association for Public Opinion Research (WAPOR), and is a council member of the UNESCO International Social Science Council and of the World Wildlife Fund (UK). He is a consultant to the* Times, Sunday Times *and* Economist *newspapers and co-editor of the* Consumer Market Research Handbook. *The author of many papers, he has also co-authored a number of major publications, including* Private Opinion Public Polls *(1986).*

BUSINESS ENVIRONMENT

pending further research into other storage options. The public's concerns about the last issue may have been allayed since the NIREX proposals *have* been withdrawn.

Another concern was revealed by a MORI poll for the *Reader's Digest* in 1987. On the basis of these results, half of the British public believe that a Chernobyl-like accident could happen here. The same poll suggested that the public is much more inclined to trust environmental pressure groups than Government ministers (50% to 25%) when it comes to the environmental impact of nuclear power.

And the British public's general level of concern is further reflected by a number of measures they are prepared to take. At least a quarter are willing to pay more for petrol to combat acid rain and other forms of air pollution, to pay more tax for measures to protect the environment, to pay more for their food bill in return for pesticide-free food, and to stop buying wood products unless they could be guaranteed to come from countries that are protecting their forests.

When it comes to measures which Europeans are prepared to take to protect the environment, there are wide variations by country. Overall, two-thirds are prepared to take some form of minor action when presented with a list (such as taking care not to drop litter or waste water), and a quarter are willing to take a minor *and* a major action (such as converting their car exhaust system or demonstrating against projects that might damage the environment).

Those living in Luxembourg and the Netherlands are most inclined to take action, while those in Ireland, Greece or Portugal are least willing. Indeed, willingness to take action seems to increase significantly with national prosperity.

Read all about it

In Britain, the public is not only concerned about various environmental issues, but another MORI poll, conducted for WWF in 1986, revealed that they also want to read more about the environment in their newspapers, a demand which the new breed of environmental correspondents (page 200) is seeking to satisfy. Nearly one in five of the British public want to read more about conservation. It ranked fourth after news about Britain, social issues and overseas news, and took the lead over women's articles, sport and letters to the editor, among others.

Readers of the *Financial Times, Guardian* and *Daily Mail* were particularly inclined to want more coverage of conservation. Among the Sunday papers, *Observer* and *Sunday Times* readers headed the list, but even 10% of *News of the World* readers said they wanted more coverage of conservation.

Some of MORI's privately commissioned surveys have shown growing concern about a number of environmental issues. This is also generally true in Europe, as shown by the results reported by the European Omnibus. The fastest growth in concern was in Italy, with a particular focus on drinking water quality, damage to the landscape and air pollution (page 171).

When it comes to the national and world environment, concern has risen in Europe since 1982, though again there are wide differences by country. The biggest changes recorded were for water pollution, air pollution and the extinction of plants and animals. Concern in Denmark and Italy was higher than the Community average on six of the seven measures than in 1982, while in other member States, such as Germany, Belgium, Ireland, Greece and Luxembourg, the level of concern (which has been high for some time) has changed relatively little.

Overall, Europeans are much more aware of environmental issues than they were. Most are concerned about some form of pollution, a fair proportion want more information on environmental issues and many are prepared to do something concrete. Whilst few are likely at this stage of the game to join Greenpeace in their daredevil pursuits, they may well be open to more mainstream suggestions.

MICHELE CORRADO *joined MORI in 1981, where she is now a Senior Research Executive. A graduate in psychology from the University of Reading, she worked for MMI, an agency specialising in medical work, before joining MORI. She now concentrates on social and health-related work and has done extensive research for a wide range of charities, including a number of environmental organisations.*

Market & Opinion Research International (MORI), *32 Old Queen Street, London SW1H 9HP. Tel: 01 222 0232.*

motorways, airports and, in particular, nuclear power.

This unstable compound of restless young and obdurate old was ignited by two events: the decision to deploy Cruise and Pershing missiles and the discovery that half of Germany's forests were dying. The former event brought back to life a unilateral disarmament movement that had lain dormant for twenty years. In a country with a long tradition of romantic naturalism, news of the tree deaths triggered a massive wave of public concern. The network of citizens initiatives provided a ready-made focus for protest coordinated nationally by the BBU, a national federation of environmental initiatives, many of whose leaders went on to lead the Green Party. The fusion of these two waves of protest created the broadly based political impulse that projected the Greens into the Bundestag.

Under Green pressure, Helmut Kohl's Christian Democrat Government has taken an aggressive lead within the EEC on issues such as acid rain and vehicle emission standards, forcing other governments to respond. The opposition Social Democrats have countered by taking a tough stance against nuclear power in order not to be outflanked by the Greens. Furthermore, both Peter Glosz, secretary-general of the Social Democrats, and Oskar Lafontaine, a future candidate for the leadership of the SPD, have urged their party to adopt an eco-socialist approach aimed at reconciling economic and ecological imperatives.

The Greens did not set out to educate or change the other political parties. Their own ambition is the wider transformation of society as a whole. But in placing the environment high on the political agenda in Germany they have had a significant impact on political perceptions throughout Europe. Germany is the most powerful economy in Europe and its unchallenged political leader. As the principal contributor to the funds of the EEC its bargaining power is considerable. Under the domestic pressures stimulated by the Greens, Germany has become a much more powerful advocate of higher environmental standards internationally. The example has not been lost on environmentalists elsewhere and even in Britain, where the opportunities for direct political participation by new parties is considerably restricted, the success of the German Greens has helped to precipitate significant shifts in political perceptions.

Green first

It is rarely remembered that Europe's first Green Party was founded in Britain in 1973. Indeed, the first 'green' anywhere to win public office was also British – a Cornish County Councillor elected in May 1977. The then People Party had been founded to give political effect to *A Blueprint for Survival,* a seminal document published in 1972 by the *Ecologist* magazine. Two subsequent name changes, first to the Ecology Party

and then, in 1985, to the Green Party, have brought it into line with the broader European movement.

Despite this early start, the Green Party remains firmly on the margins of British politics, rarely achieving more than the 1-2% of the vote typically granted to any fringe party in general elections. In recent local elections it has, for the first time, made a much stronger showing in some localities. It is not that the British people, and its post-war generation in particular, are immune from the tides of popular feeling sweeping Europe. Rather, the political and cultural geography into which these tides are flowing is different.

It is not only Britain's archaic electoral system which has counted against the Greens. The post-war political orthodoxy has never been as stifling in Britain as in Germany. Some concerns of the emerging generation have occasionally struck a chord of response from both Left and Right. A resurgent CND, for instance, was able to capture the Labour Party for unilateralism with relative ease. Thus frustration with the existing political parties has been lower and was reduced even further with the break-up of the Labour Party and the formation of the Alliance. Nor has there been an emotional trigger comparable to the destruction of the German forests by acid rain to catalyse public protest into political impulse.

But perhaps the most significant difference is the presence in Britain of a long-standing tradition of extra-parliamentary opposition dating back to Wilberforce and the campaign against slavery. This tradition is much less developed in Germany. Thus much of the political energy that in Germany could only find expression through the creation of a new political party was in Britain channelled into the pragmatic pursuit of change through the pressure groups.

Three pillars

The past decade has been marked by an explosive growth in the membership of Britain's environmental organisations. Total membership of the thousand or so national bodies involved in some way in environmental protection is over 3 million – far more than the combined membership of all the British political parties. There is no accurate estimate of their total expenditure, but it is unlikely to be less than £100 million a year. This level of manpower and resources represents a considerable capability to influence public policy.

There are three pillars to the environment movement in Britain. The oldest and least organised is that preoccupied with the search for alternative lifestyles. It is in the line of a distinguished British tradition of radical dissent beginning with John Ball, running through the Levellers and the Diggers of the 17th century and drawing new inspiration from the anarchist and cooperative movements of the 19th century. In temperament it is the closest part of the British environment movement to the German Greens. Today it manifests itself in the myriad small groups that make up the self-sufficiency, community arts, alternative health, organic farming and similar movements. More personal than institutional in strength and concerned to act rather than argue about change, it nevertheless adds considerable moral momentum to Britain's environment movement.

The respectable centre of gravity derives its inspiration from, and laid its institutional foundations in, the second half of the 19th century. Its central preoccupation is the preservation of natural features or cultural artefacts cherished for their aesthetic, intrinsic or amenity value. Represented by such bodies as the Royal Society for the Protection of Birds, the National and Civic Trusts and the Council for the Protection of Rural England, these are well resourced, frequently influential bodies.

They have been joined since the late 1960s by a new set of organisations concerned more with the future than the past and more with the planet than the nation. More aggressive in their campaigning style and appealing to a younger generation, bodies such as Friends of the Earth, Greenpeace and Transport 2000 were set up specifically to achieve changes in national policy and legislation. Although much weaker than the older bodies institutionally, they have rapidly acquired influence as a result of their ability to project the environment into public awareness by the skilful and sustained use of the mass media.

By dint of vigorous campaigning on single issues at both local and national level the British environmentalists not only succeeded in winning a large number of battles, but also built an impressive body of public support. Since the early 1970s, polling evidence has consistently shown a high, and growing, level of public concern about the state of the environment. One recent poll found that 60% of Britons thought it more important to protect the environment than to keep prices down. A similar proportion thought that the environment should be given more priority even at the risk of slowing economic growth.

No Green Paper

Yet for all this, Britain's politicians paid relatively little attention to the environment. There has never been a Green or White Paper on the full range of environmental issues from any Government. There is no environmental equivalent of the Beveridge Report. There is no environmental budget. Until 1983, no leader of a British political party had made a major speech on the environment and when one did so he was able to point out that the Control of Pollution Act, given the Royal Assent in 1974, was then, nine years and two Governments later, still not fully implemented. Until recently there was no debate on environmental policy inside any of the political parties, with the exception of the Liberals, and no publication of significance from any of them.

Recently, this sorry state of affairs has been transformed. In late 1985, the Prime Minister invited six environmentalists to lunch at Downing Street. Though not a particularly successful occasion, it did signal a marked shift in the politics of the environment. Since that date, all of Britain's political parties have published comprehensive statements of environmental policy. The politicians have finally caught up with public opinion. In the run up to the 1987 election, there was frequent public discussion of the greening of British politics which was reflected by the inclusion, for the first time, of clear commitments on the environment in all the manifestos. The most lasting effect of this political activity is that on the many of thousands of political party members who also belong to environmental bodies. The current circumstances when the parties are competing with each other to capture the environment as an issue, has brought them closer to the centre of their parties and legitimised and encouraged their efforts to influence party policy. Within the political parties, the environment is no longer simply an issue for the fringe ghettos, but now belongs firmly in the mainstream.

Thus, by very different routes, the greening of politics in both Britain and Germany has arrived at a similar point. In both countries, there are now well established environmental interests within the orthodox political parties that have obtained some hold on the policy making process. Their grip will not easily be loosened. Indeed, if the Greens sustain the pressure in Germany through the electoral system, as current polls suggest they will, and the British environmental bodies maintain the momentum they have established

PERSPECTIVES

Emerging Trends in EEC Environmental Policy

Enacting European legislation is one thing, ensuring that it is implemented in all Member States quite another. *Nigel Haigh* looks at some recent trends in the light of the fourth Environmental Action Programme.

'The provision of large sums of money for agriculture by the European Community (EC) distracts attention from the EC's other main activity, which is to legislate. Although there is a tiny sum of EC money available for environmental protection – and this will surely grow – the EC's main impact in the environmental field to date has been to produce a number of important items of detailed legislation which the Member States then have to implement. This has had some impact in all countries, and some have founded their own environmental policies on EC Directives. The amendment of the Treaty of Rome by the 'Single European Act' now allows some environmental legislation to be adopted by majority vote in the Council of Ministers instead of unanimously as before. The consequences of this will not be clear for some time, but it could result in more legislation and more stringent standards.

Although Commission officials tend to boast about the EC having adopted over 100 items of legislation since its environmental policy began in 1973, its reputation really rests on a limited number of these. To mention a few, there are the Directives on: preventing major accidents at industrial plants; testing new chemicals before marketing; vehicle emissions and lead in petrol; drinking water; discharges of dangerous substances to water; bird protection; and, finally environmental impact assessment, which is to be implemented in 1988. Combating acid rain is not yet an area of success, although some things have been achieved in setting standards for ground level concentrations of certain air pollutants that effect human health.

Official blueprint

There is no reason to suppose that the introduction of new legislation will not continue to be the EC's main contribution in the coming years. For example, proposals are already being prepared in the field of biotechnology, to prevent nitrate pollution of water, and for the recycling of batteries. But all this output only means anything if it is effectively translated into national legislation by the Member States and is then put into practice. Otherwise the output simply remains an impressive amount of paper. The recognition of this danger is one of the principal features of the EC's fourth Action Programme on the Environment, which sets out the Commission's plans for the next six years. This document was drafted in 1986 and approved by the Council of Ministers in 1987. It is the official blueprint for the future.

Unlike national governments, the EC has no adminstration able by itself to implement the legislation it produces. This is something that has to be done by the appropriate authorities within the Member States. Until recently, many Commission officials accordingly took the view that their job finished when an item of EC legislation had been produced. The fourth Action Programme now changes that. It recognises that the Commission must follow the legislation through to see what actually happens in practice.

According to the Programme, the dialogue with implementing authorities will be intensified, EC environmental policy will be given greater publicity, private persons and organisations will be encouraged to bring instances of non-compliance to the attention of the Commission, and further studies of implementation will be initiated. The implications of this new found emphasis have probably not yet been thought through, but if it is really taken seriously Commission officials are bound to spend much more of their time trying to understand the problems of particular countries and will have less time to develop new proposals for legislation. Already the Commission has started to call meetings of national officials to discuss how they are going to implement a Directive even before the due date for doing so. Commission officials will inevitably come to understand what national officials learn very quickly, which is that there are often big gaps between intention and reality.

Integrate

The second key idea in the fourth Action Programme is that environmental policy is not just a self-contained activity that can be carried out by the Directorate-General responsible for the environment. Environmental policy has to be 'integrated' with other policies, for example policies for agriculture, regional development, transport, energy and so on. It is becoming clear, for example, that the EC policies in the Mediterranean area – the agricultural policy and the special 'Integrated Mediterranean Programme' in particular – are having severe environmental effects.

The Commission proposes to tackle this broad subject initially at the level of the EC's own policies and actions; and secondly at the level of the policies implemented by Member States. It intends to develop internal procedures to ensure that environmental requirements are built into the processes for assessing and approving proposals for all developments to be financed from EC funds. In other words, officials in the Directorate-General responsible for the environment will somehow have to vet the environmental consequences of finance being distributed by other Directorates-General pursuing other policies. In this they will be enormously helped by the Single Act which requires that 'environmental protection requirements shall be a component of the Community's other policies'.

Other ideas in the Action Programme include developing the use of economic instruments as tools for pollution control and a proposal to subsidise the implementation of environmental Directives in disadvantaged areas. The Commission believes it should be possible to devise ways of improving public access to information held by environmental authorities and will make proposals on freedom of information. It will also publish a State of the Environment report every three years.

Rethinking

In the field of pollution control there is some rethinking of the traditional approach to dealing with problems as they arise in the different media (air, water, soil). The Commission proposes a reassessment of the 'source oriented' approach (e.g. all emissions from a plant to whatever medium) and proposes to extend the 'substance oriented' approach by attempting to develop control strategies for individual substances, whatever medium they are

released into. The whole subject of different kinds of standards that can be set to control pollution (e.g. emission standards, environmental quality standards, and product standards) will also be reviewed.

In all, the Action Programme is an ambitious document and not everything that is proposed will necessarily be realised. But it certainly suggests no shortage of real problems to be solved and plenty of ideas intended to deal with them.

NIGEL HAIGH *has been Director of the London office of the Institute for European Environmental Policy since 1980. Trained as an engineer, he practised as a Chartered Patent Agent for ten years before moving to the environmental field. While working at the Civic Trust on town planning matters he was a Vice-President of the European Environmental Bureau from 1975 to 1979. He is the author of* EEC Environmental Policy and Britain – *the standard work on the subject.*

The Institute for European Environmental Policy, *3 Endsleigh Street, London WC1H 0DD. Tel: 01 388 2117.*

---

during the last Parliament, then there is every likelihood that this process will go further. At the moment, Britain and Germany are often at odds over the pace of, and priorities for, the development of environmental policy in Europe. As both respond to strong domestic pressures, however, it seems likely that their interests will begin to converge more closely. Should this occur, a very powerful axis for a more progressive and powerful EEC environment policy will exist. This would make the environment an even more significant feature of the business environment than it is already.

Policies and legislation

The chief determinant of the policy and legislative context for Europe is the Fourth Action Programme on the Environment of the European Community adopted by the member states early in 1987. Since the declaration by Heads of State and Government in 1972 that first established a basis for a common environment policy, Brussels has come to dominate policy making on the environment within the twelve countries of the Community. Furthermore, since the EEC countries almost always act together on international environmental issues, Brussels is now a key arbiter of global environmental policy.

The EEC's environment policy has been elaborated in a series of action programmes. These action programmes are themselves very general in character, establishing a set of objectives and principles and setting out an agenda for future legislative action. The first two, which ran from 1973 until 1982, were primarily concerned with tackling the most urgent pollution problems, mainly by setting standards for the quality of drinking and bathing waters, controlling the emission of particularly dangerous substances and beginning to tackle the problem of hazardous wastes. They were essentially remedial in character.

29→

PERSPECTIVES

The Green Arm of the Law

Environmental law is a rapidly developing area of legal practice and teaching across Europe. *Richard Macrory* of the UK Environmental Law Association reviews the trends.

‘An American lawyer told me in 1987 that the number of lawyers who work full-time in the environmental field in the States had just overtaken those working in employment law. I am not predicting – nor would I wish to – that the same will happen in Europe, but the rapid growth in EEC environmental policies and legislation during the past decade has considerably heightened the public profile of lawyers active in this area.

1986, of course, saw the agreement by EEC Member States to the Single European Act. One result of that has been the addition of the new Article 130 to the Treaty of Rome, which for the first time provides an explicit remit for environmental policy at the EEC level. Indeed, it lays down the broad principles on which such policy should be based.

Environmental lawyers may not have all the answers, but we members of the profession and of the new Environmental Law Association have an important role to play in addressing such key questions as: What is the most appropriate role for the law in the field of environmental management? How far do new policy proposals make sense from a purely legal perspective? How well are existing environmental laws understood and effectively applied in practice?

All words, no action?

Launched in 1986, the Environmental Law Association is not without pedigree or precedent. Thirteen years earlier, for instance, the Solicitors' Ecology Group, as it then was, held its first conference.

Reviewing the conference, however, *New Scientist* noted sourly that, knowing lawyers, it would all end up in words and no action. Such a comment undervalues the importance of words. The environmental field bristles with ambiguities, imprecise language and consequent misunderstandings. At the very least, lawyers can play an important role in helping to clarify and elucidate the terminology and concepts currently used.

In any event, the years following that first conference saw intense activities by members of what subsequently became the Lawyers' Ecology Group. But the unfavourable financial climate of the time largely thwarted the Group's ambitious plan to set up a national environmental law centre.

Coming of age

But the tide has been moving in our direction. Many lawyers have long practised – and still do – in areas of law relating to the environment without calling themselves environmental lawyers. The subject has an identifiable core, but no precise boundaries. At this stage, though, we have concluded that it is an unrealistic exercise to construct such boundaries, however intellectually enjoyable the challenge might have been.

Perhaps the Lawyers' Ecology Group was ahead of its time, but I believe that there are now clear signals that we have recently reached a significant turning point. Indeed, in retrospect, European Year of the Environment may coincidentally be seen as the year that environmental law came of age in Britain.

The Environmental Law Association provides a professional forum for members involved in private practice, industry, the public sector, academia and environmental and amenity associations. Since the practice of environmental law involves many disciplines, the Association welcomes the fullest participation of non-lawyers, who can apply for Associate Membership, in all its activities. A bulletin, *Environmental Law*, is circulated to members and the Association also organises seminars, working groups, field trips and an annual conference.’

RICHARD MACRORY is *Chairman of the Environmental Law Association, a Barrister and a University Lecturer at the Imperial College Centre for Environmental Technology (ICCET).*

The United Kingdom Environmental Law Association, *Centre for Energy and Natural Resources Law, Faculty of Law, Southampton University, Southampton SO9 5NH. (Contact: Andrew Waite, Honorary Secretary).*

The Third Action Programme, dating from 1983, reflected a key change in perception that had occurred. Under the stimulus of the Environment Committee of the Organisation for Economic Cooperation and Development (OECD), attention began to shift from remedial to anticipatory policies. As the most urgent of the accumulated problems had been brought within the bounds of the policy framework so the need to prevent new problems emerging became apparent.

Within the EEC, this placed a high priority on the development of European legislation requiring the preparation of environmental impact assessments for all major developments. The force of an EEC Directive is to insist that member states adapt national legislation to conform with the requirements of the Directive. There is normally a period between the agreement of a Directive and its coming into force. The E.I.A. Directive, as it is known, was agreed in July 1985. Compliance with its provisions must take place by 1988. In those EEC countries where development control procedures are not already well established the Directive will have a very significant role in preventing avoidable environmental damage.

The Third Action Programme also gave formal expression for the first time to a powerful new principle of environment policy. It specifically recognised the need to integrate the environment with other areas of policy in order adequately to prevent environmental degradation. Harmful impacts on the environment cannot be eliminated simply by trying to constrain other areas of policy within a corset of ever more detailed and restrictive regulation. Rather, policies which generate damaging environmental impacts should be adapted so as to reduce or remove those impacts. The Third Action Programme itself contains few clues about the precise nature of integrative policies or the appropriate mechanisms for developing and implementing them.

The principle was strongly reinforced, however, by the Seven Nations Summit held in Bonn in 1985. This meeting of the leaders of the seven major industrial nations issued a declaration on the environment stressing the 'interdependence' of economic and environmental policy and calling for the better integration of the environment with other areas of policy.

Unstoppable momentum

The EEC's Fourth Action Programme restates a commitment to this principle and sets itself the task of making the environment an essential element of all the Community's own policies. Its first priority is to see that environmental requirements are built into the assessment procedures for all developments financed from the Community's Funds. It then sets out a large shopping list of possible initiatives for integration in areas ranging from agriculture, industry and energy, through the internal market, social policy and consumer protection to development assistance. Neither the scale of the task ahead, nor the absence of any clearly wrought instruments, seem likely to halt the momentum for integrative policies.

The second major policy shift in the Fourth Action Programme is a new emphasis on the enforcement, or in the EEC's lower key phrase, implementation of existing policy. Until the passage of the Single European Act, the legal basis for the EEC's environmental policy was weak. The Treaty of Rome contained no provisions for a European Environment Policy and such measures as had been adopted were justified under catchall powers or those relating to the prevention of barriers to trade. This did not provide the best foundation for a vigorous enforcement policy. The Single Act formalises the creation of an environment policy as a goal of the Community and makes tough enforcement that much easier (page 26). Furthermore, the pressure to achieve a single European market on target is leading those Government's with high compliance standards to seek a more even level of environmental performance across the Community so as not to disadvantage their own industries.

As well as a series of measures to give effect to this new policy emphasis, the Commission has outlined a substantial programme of new legislation. This will include new measures to control chemicals, a programme of legislation on air pollution in the light of the EEC's recently published long term strategy, much tougher controls on agricultural pollution and the first EEC legislation covering biotechnology. One of the most crucial areas of Community action, however, was not specifically foreshadowed in the Fourth Action Programme. Nevertheless, in the wake of the Sandoz incident on the Rhine and the questions raised by Chernobyl, there will certainly be new legislation on environmental liability and transfrontier pollution.

No one could accuse the British Government of over-reacting to an impressively dynamic Brussels by seeking to compete in the legislative stakes. Indeed, it often seems as if the Government is working hard to avoid further embarrassment of the kind associated with the notorious Control of Pollution Act (still not fully implemented after 13 years on the statute book) by the simple device of not introducing any new legislation at all. Although consultative papers have finally been issued on prospective legislation for both wastes and air pollution, there is little prospect of Parliament seeing a Bill on either during the course of 1988.

Privatisation of water and electricity will have significant environmental implications, however. The underlying problem facing the Government is that of designing a regulatory framework for the newly private industries that is, at one and the same time, attractive to both investors and environmentalists. The Government's first effort to square this circle with the water industry fell foul of the EEC, which made it pretty clear that it was not prepared to have private companies recognised as 'competent authorities' for the purposes of EC legislation. The subsequent proposal to establish a new National Rivers Authority was unwelcome to the water industry and mistrusted by environmentalists. It also ran the risk of effectively breaking up the newly created unified pollution inspectorate, which was the most substantial environmental gain of the previous Parliament. The principle questions raised by electricity privatisation concern the willingness of a privately owned utility to face up squarely to the problems of acid rain and carbon dioxide build-up. There are also considerable questions about the wisdom of transferring the management of nuclear power stations and their associated wastes to the private sector.

States of the environment

The large uncertainties about the real state of the environment compound the difficulties of arriving at national or international consensus about the most effective environmental policies and of generating the political will to adopt them. Is the fluctuation in the thickness of the ozone layer a man-induced or a natural phenomenon? Are car emissions or those from power stations more important as a cause of tree death in Europe? What is the real rate of loss of the tropical rainforests? How serious is the state of the North Sea? What climatic effects will be produced by what levels of carbon dioxide pollution? These, and

Environmental Guidelines for Business

Ever since Moses came down the mountain with the Ten Commandments, there has been considerable interest in laying down guidelines on what constitutes acceptable behaviour. The approach has been increasingly used in the environmental field, too.

It was the late Buckminster Fuller who said that the main problem with Spaceship Earth was that no-one had issued us with an operating manual. A growing range of environmental guidelines for industry – prepared by or with industry – are being published to fill the gap. Some recent examples are reviewed below.

The only environmental guidelines which apply to all forms of industry, worldwide, are those first produced by the **International Chamber of Commerce** (ICC) in 1974, and subsequently updated a number of times. The *ICC Guidelines* have been translated into a number of languages, including French, German and Spanish.

Among the factors that the *ICC Guidelines* suggest should be considered in industrial planning and operations are the following:
- the importance of protecting human health;
- the need to maintain species diversity and the balance of ecological systems;
- the need to develop alternatives to non-renewable resources;
- the cumulative effects on the environment of harmful wastes and other industrial activities;
- the potential effects of products on the environment;
- the existence and impact of transfrontier pollution;
- the law of diminishing returns, with the point inevitably reached where the incremental benefit from environmental investment is less than the value of the resources expended; and
- the need to minimise risks to the environment arising from industrial activities, bearing in mind that we are always exposed to some degree of risk, whatever we happen to be doing.

Openness is essential

In Britain, the **Confederation of British Industry** (CBI: see page 48) has issued guidelines on the disclosure of safety, health and environmental information to the public. While recognising that some information need to be kept confidential, for reasons of commercial or national security, the CBI stresses that 'firms should establish policies to secure openness in safety, health and environmental information, and should make adequate arrangements for their application in practice.' A popularly written CBI publication on the theme is *Clean Up: It's Good Business*, sub-titled 'How companies can profit from good environmental practice'.

Ideally, each sector of industry would have its own comprehensive guidelines explaining how companies should define and pursue 'environmental excellence' (page 226). To show how it might work, consider the chemical sector.

The **European Council of Chemical Manufacturers' Federations** (CEFIC) has prepared a set of guidelines for the European chemical industry, which stem directly from the ICC initiative. Other CEFIC guidelines cover the safe transfer of technology between countries, safe warehousing and the provision of information on hazardous substances in the workplace.

In Britain, the **Chemical Industries Association** (CIA), in turn, has listed a dozen environmental objectives for its members – with

BUSINESS ENVIRONMENT

there are many more, are questions for which there are not yet uncontested answers. Yet without answers, the development of appropriate responses is barely practicable.

For many of these issues firm answers may not come in time to take remedial action. No one knows how, or if, the ozone layer might be restored should it disappear. For others, delayed response simply increases the eventual cost of dealing with the problem. If accumulations of carbon dioxide and other greenhouse gases does change climatic conditions significantly, the costs will be literally incalculable. The absence of a clear policy response also slows technical development. There is, for instance, no clear signal being given to the motor industry on vehicle emissions, thus creating indecision about whether to pursue lean-burn engines aggressively or stick with catalytic converters (page 116). Where such signals can be clearly given, as they were for example with aircraft noise (page 73), they act as a stimulus to technical development.

As the pressures for effective action on environmental problems grow, so does the requirement for a clearer picture of the real state of the planet. There is currently no one series of environmental data that is complete and authoritative. The United Nations Environment Programme published the first really useful review of changes in the global environment in 1982, to mark the tenth anniversary of the Stockholm Conference. Sadly, it has not repeated the exercise. Both the EEC and the OECD have published

32 →

the key objective focusing on the preparation (and subsequent review) of corporate environmental policies. Copies of the *Environmental Objectives* are available from the CIA. The CIA also offers guidelines covering, for example, the use by member companies of waste disposal contractors and the responsible use of landfill.

Guidelines can also then play a role at the level of the individual company. **Essochem Europe,** now part of Exxon Chemical International, has for some time handed to new employees, on their first day at work, a booklet describing the company's policies on health, safety and environment. More companies should adopt this approach.

Oil, gas and turtles

One initiative which demonstrates the way that industrial and conservation interests can work together dates from 1982. Worried by their poor environmental reputation, Greek shipowners decided to develop an environmental code of conduct.

As a result, the **Hellenic Marine Environmental Protection Association** (HELMEPA) was formed. However, recognising that it needed to get internationally known environmental organisations involved if the code was to be remotely credible, HELMEPA turned to five – the Club of Rome, the International Institute for Environment and Development, (IIED), the International Union for the Conservation of Natural Resources (IUCN), the International Oceans Institute and the World Wildlife Fund. Considerable progress was achieved and the approach could well be adopted with other national fleets – and, indeed, other industries.

One of the most ambitious guideline projects in Britain was the joint venture between the **Nature Conservancy Council,** BP and John Elkington Associates,

which resulted in the *Nature Conservation Guidelines for the Onshore Oil and Gas Development*. Copies are available from the NCC.

It is one thing dealing with large and environmentally responsible companies, however, but quite another to deal with individual tourists – the target of guidelines designed to protect the loggerhead turtles of Laganas Bay, on the Greek island of Zakynthos (page 169). Prepared by the Greek **Sea Turtle Protection Society** and the World Wildlife Fund UK, the guidelines leaflet was printed with financial assistance from Grecian Holidays and distributed to visitors to Zakynthos by Grecian Holidays, Horizon, Sun Med Holidays and Thomson Holidays. Given the rapid worldwide growth of tourism, such initiatives are likely to be increasingly important.

Product and process

However, even at their best, such efforts are only a partial answer to the problem of ensuring that more industries and more industrial companies pursue environmental excellence. All these guidelines are *voluntary* and largely unenforceable by the issuing organisations. Legislation and the tough enforcement of the relevant standards by the regulatory authorities are also likely to be essential if the more unscrupulous operators are to be prevented from taking advantage of their competitors' sense of responsibility.

Clearly, the more specific and practical the guidelines can be, the more likely they are to help change industrial attitudes and behaviour. But, at whatever level such guidelines are prepared, if conservation interests work closely with industry while preparing the guidelines, that very process may bring important longer-term benefits, making it more likely that there will be close co-operation in future.

intermittent State of the Environment reports, but inevitably, their data series have been confined to those from member countries. The longest running series of regular updates is the Worldwatch Institute's annual *State of the World* report, published since 1984 (page 240). Though providing a valuable survey of global developments on a selection of key issues, the data series are very limited in scope.

The most successful attempt yet to provide an annual survey of comparable data covering both a wide range of issues and the complete list of countries is the *World Resources* report, published annually since 1986 by the World Resources Institute and the International Institute for the Environment and Development. *World Resources* is intended to provide 'an objective, current, global assessment of the natural resource base that supports the world economy.' It may not quite have got all the way there yet, but it comes closer than any other document.

Continuing decline

The decade and a half since the Stockholm Conference has seen an explosion in environmental legislation at every level in society – local, national, regional and international. Not all this legislation has been well designed, however, and less of it is well observed or enforced. Nevertheless, much of it, sometimes perhaps as an excuse to defer immediate action, has contained provisions for monitoring and research. It is only now that the fruits of this effort to acquire information are beginning to appear. Thus the capability for creating the scientific consensus without which political consensus is impossible has been much enhanced.

But, despite the successes that can be pointed to, the overall state of the world environment has declined during that same period. New problems have emerged faster than old ones have been remedied. Whilst some of the grossest environmental abuses have been reduced in some regions, most notably North America and Western Europe, in much of the rest of the world new problems have simply been piled on top of the old.

In these circumstances it is not surprising that, in those countries for which data is available, there is constant public pressure for a better environment (page 22). In one twelve country survey between 55%-90% of people described themselves as concerned about national or global environmental issues. In 1986, only 6-38% of people in 11 countries thought their government was doing a good job at protecting the environment. On air and water pollution in particular, public concern has increased steeply in recent years. Within the OECD countries, only Japanese public opinion seems relatively little troubled by the state of the environment.

Sustainability

Gro Harlem Brundtland, the Prime Minister of Norway, has long had a rare reputation as a politician with a passionate commitment to the environment. When, as chairman of the World Commission on Environment and Development, she introduced her Commission's report by calling for 'a new era of economic growth – growth that is forceful and at the same time socially and environmentally sustainable', she caused something of a stir. Few people are accustomed to hearing avowed environmentalists call for *more* economic growth.

Since the fifties and sixties, economic growth has been seen as the principal enemy of the environment. It was thought by many that the economy and environmental quality were at either end of a see-saw: the one could only grow at the expense of the other. Eco-fundamentalists faced a stark choice between abandoning economic growth or abandoning a livable environment. Industry was seen as the motor of growth. If growth destroyed the environment and industry was the motor of growth and the only way to protect the environment was to halt growth, then industry was the enemy and must be defeated. The logic of this position was as powerful as it was simple.

Industry reciprocated vigorously. Environmentalists were simply sentimental members of the affluent society hankering after a wholly illusory past. Fears about new technologies were simply spasms of latter-day Luddism by those too lazy or too timid to understand their potential and too selfish to care about the plight of those who were not yet affluent. Environmental pressure was a crippling constraint on the economic growth essential to improving human well-being. If environmentalists were anti-industry and thus anti-growth they were the enemy and must be defeated.

Fortunately for us all, the nature of the environmental debate has begun to change. As crisis turned to catastrophe in the African drylands, it soon became apparent that economic and ecological failure were intimately engaged. In the industrial North it was equally apparent that every call for economic regeneration began with pleas to invest in environmental improvements – energy conservation programmes, housing rehabilitation schemes, derelict land reclamation projects or better public transport systems. Economic growth was an unavoidable consequence of investing in environmental improvement.

The publication of the *World Conservation Strategy* by the International Union for the Conservation of Nature (IUCN) first gave global currency to the idea of sustainable development. It argued that environmental conservation and sustainable development were mutually dependent. Without development, over a billion of the world's rural poor had no choice but to destroy the fragile environments in which they lived in pursuit of the food and fuel essential for their survival. This key document served as the stimulus for many countries to draw up national

BUSINESS ENVIRONMENT

conservation strategies which attempted to reconcile conservation and development.

Double trouble

The Brundtland Report takes this process a stage further. Set up by a resolution of the General Assembly of the United Nations, the World Commission on Environment and Development was given the specific task of proposing long term strategies for achieving sustainable development. The Commission systematically examined the ways in which national and international policies on industrial and economic development, peace and security, trade and aid and population and agriculture must adapt if we are to succeed in managing the global environment.

The world's population has already tripled since the beginning of the century. It will double again within fifty years. The economic, social and political forces released by adding another whole world on top of the one we already have are barely comprehensible. As are the environmental impacts they will generate. The collision between the awesome momentum of these forces and the uncertain elasticities of the biosphere will shape the prospects for every individual and enterprise over the next half century.

Sustainable development is nothing more than the means of managing the biological and mineral resource base of the economy in such a way that it retains its capacity to meet the demands of this explosive growth. The choice is no longer between growth and no growth, but the much more difficult task of identifying and promoting that growth which is sustainable in the ecological as well as the economic sense. The sustainable growth for which Mrs Brundtland has called – we might call it 'green growth' to distinguish it from the orthodox economist's use of 'sustainable' to mean 'endless' – reconciles economic and ecological imperatives.

In the industrial economies at least, the principal elements of a determined drive for green growth are already emerging. We can already begin to see the kinds of investments, in both public and private sectors, that will generate *both* economic and environmental benefits.

In the public sector there is a growing need for greater investment in the water and sewage system. A decaying sewage system will destroy decades of effort to clean up our rivers. Unrepaired water supply pipes lead to the loss of up to a third of all the water collected, increasing the need for new water storage capacity. The environmental benefits of making these investments are obvious. So, too, are the economic benefits of stimulating an under-used construction industry with high job creation potential. Investment in domestic insulation not only brings rapid social benefits, particularly to the poor and elderly, but it reduces the costs of social service and health provision and creates employment in precisely those localities and labour market sectors where they are most needed. By reducing energy demand it helps solve the problems of acid rain, carbon dioxide and radioactive waste.

Similar stories can be told for public sector investment in rail electrification, road maintenance, improved bus services, housing rehabilitation, derelict land reclamation and waste recycling. In all these areas, economic growth accompanies environmental improvements and thus contributes to the sustainability of the resource base. Nowhere would this be more beneficial than in a shift of agricultural investment away from the surplus producing high input, high-output approach currently causing substantial environmental degradation to a lower input, lower output style of farming (page 150). Farm incomes could be sustained and the costs of producing, storing and disposing of surpluses reduced – at the same time as pollution loads are reduced, soil quality restored and wildlife habitats preserved.

In the private sector there is a large and growing range of green growth investments. Many of these have been described in *The Green Capitalists* (page 214). Developments in ceramics and carbon-based composites allow the replacement for structural uses of scarce metals with lighter materials made from abundant raw materials. Fibre optics similarly replace metals of inferior performance in dozens of communications applications. As the transformation to a carbon and silicon economy proceeds, the environmental impacts of the extractive industries are reduced at the same time as high value added goods, with all their economic advantages, are produced. Johnson-Matthey and Davey are among the leading British companies that have already profited from their share of the burgeoning pollution abatement industry.

These are all concrete examples of how sustainable development is already beginning to happen. There are growing signs that as mass consumer markets mature they, too, begin to create patterns of demand that place a high value on sustainability and the environment – with an emphasis on natural materials for clothing, additive-free foods (page 178), alternative therapies (page 182), wilderness vacations, natural cosmetics (page 70) and many more. The recent growth in ethical investment funds (page 186), many of them setting a premium on good environmental performance, suggest that even the financial institutions, the last bastions of unsustainable development, are beginning to respond to the rapidly changing realities of life on an overcrowded planet.

Partnerships

The search for sustainable growth is an enterprise in which ecologist and economist, industrialist and environmentalist, can join together wholeheartedly. This will not eliminate all the conflicts between industry and the environment, especially on a small

Report 149: June 1987

PERHAPS IT'S TIME TO TAKE A CLOSER LOOK AT ENVIRONMENTAL INTELLIGENCE

Every month the ENDS Report offers a unique digest of news, features and policy analysis which includes:

Practical information *on how named companies organise for environmental protection – and why they do it*
Regular news *of improved technical solutions to pollution problems*
Early warning *of changes in policy and legislation (UK and EEC)*
Market opportunities *created by cleaner products and processes and environmental services*
Concise background briefing *on environmental topics as diverse as acid rain and wind energy, landfill management and sewage sludge*

If you're ready for a new perspective on the problems and opportunities created by pressures for a cleaner environment – you should be reading the ENDS Report.

ENVIRONMENTAL DATA SERVICES LTD., FINSBURY BUSINESS CENTRE, 40 BOWLING GREEN LANE, LONDON EC1R 0NE (01 278 7624)

and overcrowded island such as Britain, where land use is the dominant environmental issue. But it does provide an opportunity to balance conflict with cooperation. On some issues the conflict of interest between industry and the environment simply cannot be avoided and they will have to be fought out in the arena of public policy. But on many more there are an increasing number of occasions when industrialist and environmentalist would both benefit from forming partnerships.

What is required is mutual respect for, and tolerance of, the other viewpoint. There are those among the environmentalists who, in their heart of hearts, believe industry to be an irredeemable victim of its own dynamics, doomed, however hard it tries, to be an environmental destroyer. They would rather not have any industry at all. Among industrialists, there are those who have an equally powerful wish to remove all environmentalists from the face of the earth, seeing them as unwanted and unwarranted interferers with the free play of market forces. They see no point in talking to environmentalists. Fortunately, both sets of extremists are an increasingly endangered species. The majority of both industrialists and environmentalists have come to accept that the other is not going away and that therefore a less mutually suspicious manner of living together must develop.

It would be foolish to pretend that this will be an easy task. The basis for the antagonism that existed throughout most of the past two decades may no longer be there, but the legacy remains. Positions once adopted are not lightly dropped, nor attitudes once established easily changed. Nevertheless, a common agenda is now beginning to emerge on which environmentalist and industrialist can work together.

Common agenda

The Government's original proposals for privatising the water industry were a clear example of such a common interest. For different, but entirely complementary reasons, industrialists and environmentalists were both unimpressed by the idea of selling off the water authorities' regulatory functions as well as its assets – a proposal likened to selling the police force to the mafia. Having both lobbied for the creation of a unified pollution inspectorate, both sides had an interest in ensuring that the proposed creation of a National Rivers Authority does not abort the inspectorate.

As we move closer to a single European market, both industry and environmental opinion share a common goal in seeing existing legislation equally and adequately enforced. Revision of the patent laws to extend patent times on certain classes of product would serve environmentalists by allowing more time for pre-market testing for any environmental impacts while at the same time allowing manufacturers more time to recoup their investment. If more of the investment can be recouped, more of it can be devoted to reducing or removing environmental impacts.

But the common agenda extends beyond the most immediate interests into more general issues of public policy. Cuts in the scientific research or education budgets are damaging to both industrialist and environmentalist. Our failure to understand the basic science of acid rain, for example, has slowed economic development as much as environmental improvement. A constant supply of highly motivated and scientifically trained graduates is as necessary for our environmental survival as it is for our economic survival. Too low a level of public capital expenditure hits the environment as hard as it hits the membership of the CBI.

Environmentalists may set different priorities for capital expenditure from industrialists, favouring, say, the water system rather than the road system or housing rehabilitation rather than new building, but both would benefit from some relaxation of fiscal policy. So the list could continue – high interest rates, short-termism in the City, hazardous waste disposal, the business school curriculum – the items of the common agenda are as diverse as they are many.

In all these areas, the possibility of developing partnerships between industry and the environment is growing. In other areas it is already well established. A great many companies support environmental enterprise in the form of grants and awards to organisations such as the Groundwork Foundation, the British Trust for Conservation Volunteers, U.K. 2000 or the N.C.V.O.'s Waste Watch programme that are mobilising volunteers to tackle local environmental problems directly. Others join in promotions to raise funds for organisations such as the World Wildlife Fund who have benefited from products ranging from breakfast cereals to butter. As more people want to do more to protect their own immediate environment, particularly in the inner cities, the opportunities for these practical partnerships are also growing.

But it is the overarching logic that is most compelling. In order to protect and maintain the environment and to pursue sustainable development for an extra five billion people on top of the existing five billion, we will have to invest. In order to invest, we must earn. In order to earn, industry must succeed.

In Britain, we live in an anti-industrial culture. Hostile attitudes to industry are deeply ingrained in our national character. For industry to succeed, we must first roll back those anti-industrial attitudes. In recent years this has become a key strategic goal for those concerned with Britain's economic survival. But poor environmental performance legitimises and reinforces anti-industrial attitudes. Improving industry's environmental performance is thus a necessary condition for achieving economic success and, in its turn, economic success is essential if Britain is to make any worthwhile contribution to the daunting task of sustaining the global environment. ☐

PERSPECTIVES
Do the Impossible!

Green politics will flourish in the 1990s, says *Petra Kelly*, even if some of today's Green Parties do not survive. But Green politicians, she argues, must beware of being co-opted into the system.

'The proliferation of mass destructive weapons has given us the ability to obliterate civilisations in a flash, while the growing environmental crisis threatens to choke the planet's life support systems. All over the world, Green Parties have emerged in response to such problems, using the colour green as a symbol of new hope and new thinking.

'The splitting of the atom has changed everything,' said Albert Einstein, 'except the way people think.' Now, all over the world, the Green movement is hoping to change the way people think. The Green perspective tries to integrate non-violence, decentralism, ecological principles and a feministic philosophy into all areas of our society and economy. Perhaps surprisingly with such an ambitious agenda, some European Green Parties have scored notable political successes. These include the Green Party in the Federal Republic of Germany and its counterparts in Austria, the Netherlands and Belgium.

But what are the likely trends for the 1990s? Personally, I believe that the Green Parties should not make any major compromises in their political programmes. In the end this would make them simply the 'lesser of the political evils'. They would be increasingly co-opted into the existing political and economic systems. These are based on economic growth as an end in itself, a concept we reject!

New age politics

We should not compromise when it comes to life and death questions. Just as there cannot be a 'bit of cancer' or a 'little bit of death', so we should beware of thinking in terms of a 'little bit of destruction'. It will not help, for example, if we begin looking for lower, safer levels of radioactivity or for lower, safer levels of dioxin. We all know that radioactivity and chemicals such as dioxin are dangerous right down the scale of exposure. So we must resist *any* activities likely to expose us to such threats.

I believe that the Green perspective is here to stay, even if some of the Green Parties may not survive into the 1990s. I also believe that 'New Age' politics are here to stay, with the New Age philosophy suggesting that the basic problems we face reflect the sheer scale of our society. Nearly everything we do is too big, too powerful and too speedy.

A third path

By contrast, a sustainable future will depend on small-scale, labour-intensive, soft, ecological and appropriate technologies. The Green Parties reject both capitalism and state socialism, seeking a third path. Fundamentally, however, many Greens believe that our environmental problems are a product of the patriarchal system of power, in which men determine what role women shall or shall not play. Patriarchal attitudes are found throughout the world, underpinning such rival systems as capitalism and state socialism. Getting rid of such attitudes is one of our most important goals for the 1990s and beyond.

We also have to move away from the monolithic mode of production. Ivan Illich noted that each institution eventually comes to frustrate the end it was originally designed to serve. In transportation, for example, the creation of faster and faster vehicles led to the creation of longer and longer distances between cities, so in the end it takes us even longer to get to work.

A nuclear monoculture?

Just as monocultures have come to dominate world agriculture, so monlithic technologies have come to dominate our society in ways which most of us hardly suspect.

Nuclear power is one of those technologies. As Amory Lovins put it: 'Discouraging nuclear violence and coercion requires some abrogation of civil liberties; guarding long-lived wastes against geological or social contingencies implies some form of hierarchical social rigidity or homogeneity to insulate the technocrats from social turbulence; and making political decisions about nuclear hazards which are compulsory, disputed, unknown, or unknowable, may tempt governments to bypass democratic decision in favour of elitist technocracy.' What Robert Jungk has dubbed the 'Atomic State' curtails human and civil rights and makes us all nuclear hostages.

Our defence and security systems are also totally dependent on monolithic institutions. The Greens are struggling against a governing elite which monopolises key decisions. The 500 largest industrial corporations in the United States, for example, control nearly one trillion dollars in corporate assets. And the 600 largest multi-national corporations will control over 40% of planetary production by the end of the 1990s.

Alternatives to 'jobs'

In contrast to such organisations, which foster wastefulness and over-dependence, Green politics and the emerging New Age economy emphasise life-oriented behaviour. In developing alternatives to the 'job economy', the Greens aim to promote local and regional self-sufficiency. Among the possibilities are a guaranteed subsistence income or guaranteed access to basic products and services.

There are also some marked green trends in the service economy, including growing employment in such areas as reforestation, alternative forms of production, work with the mentally ill and alcoholics, child-care, and the provision of sanitary services for the Third World.

Another trend will be continuing growth of interest in the craft-based economy. Human beings, as E. F. Schumacher pointed out, enjoy nothing more than to use their hands and brains creatively and skillfully. Most of this work can take place in workshops, rather than in factories.

Another fundamental trend will be a growing move towards genuine participation and genuine decentralisation. Already there is an alternative Green economy growing up within our capitalist system. I think here of the many self-help centres and networks, the self-governing work-teams in ecological jobs areas, all small islands in an almost hopeless economy.

Consumer power

And there is a definite trend towards people becoming more aware of the implications of their consumer choices. It may not instantly change the world if we stop buying products from South Africa, or products made by multinationals, but we must not underrate the impact that such boycotts can have. At the same time, too, more people are becoming critical about the type of food they eat and are beginning to look for more organic forms of food production.

The new interest in health creation, instead of the old reliance on drugs and high technology medicine, is an important trend. It runs hand-in-hand with the increasingly successful 'stop-smoking' campaign. A person who smokes half a pack a day surrenders an average five-and-a-half years of life. Directly and indirectly, these trends provide part of the momentum now building for community-based initiatives, such as community credit unions or ecological banks.

When peace breaks out

But Greens will also have to think at the national and international scale. What happens, for example, if peace does break out? What shall we do with the 6–7% of the workforce now employed in the arms industry in Europe? The Green Bans in Australia during the 1970s, the Lucas Aerospace initiatives (and Mike Cooley's subsequent work), and the studies being done by the European Confederation of Trade Unions in the area of alternative production – all these offer useful pointers. And there is a continuing, urgent need for practical, small-scale experiments and demonstration projects, showing how human-scale technologies can be put to work.

But even if the focus is often on local or regional initiatives, planetary co-operation will need to be a pronounced feature of the New Age economy. The hope – the demand – for a truly free society is shared not only with our friends in Europe, but also with the many *independent* ecological groups in Eastern Europe, with grass-roots Church initiatives in Latin America, with the 'other' America, and with the many other groups now active around the world.

Only an ecological society is a truly free society, as Murray Bookchin put it. He also recalled, in *The Ecology of Freedom,* that: 'Years ago, the French students in the May/June uprising of 1968 expressed their sharp contrast of alternatives magnificently in their slogan, *Be practical! Do the impossible!* To this demand,' Bookchin noted, 'the generation that faces the next century can add the more solemn injunction, *If we don't do the impossible, we shall be faced with the unthinkable.*'

I believe that the paths now being sketched out by the Greens offer the only way of surviving in dignity and freedom on this Planet Earth. But one or two Green ministers in a 'non-Green' government will not bring about the changes we desire. Instead, we need to create a new form of power, not a power over people but a power that will encourage them to take responsibility not only for their own lives but for the world in which we all live.

PETRA K. KELLY *is currently serving a second term (1987–1991) in the West German Parliament, the Bundestag, where she is a member of the Foreign Relations Committee. Educated in Washington, D.C., and Amsterdam, she was co-founder of Die Grünen, the West German Green Party. She was Speaker of the Parliamentary Greens in the Bundestag from 1983 to 1984. From 1972 to 1983, she was a European administrator of social and environmental affairs for the Economic and Social Committee of the European Community.*

Die Grünen, *Bundeshaus, 5300 Bonn 1, Federal Republic of West Germany. Tel: +49 228 16 92 06.*

 In the recent Budget, the duty on unleaded petrol was reduced – so now it's no more expensive than leaded petrol.

"What's it to do with me?" you may ask. "My car can't run on it."

Well, it may interest you to know that already many cars can run on unleaded petrol, and the number is increasing daily. In fact, very soon all new cars will be designed to run on unleaded.

Along with our EEC partners, the UK has agreed that unleaded petrol should be made widely available by October 1989.

And in this 1987 European Year of the Environment, Esso is taking firm steps to help achieve this goal.

In fact, since mid-1986 we have already introduced a national network of over 100 strategically chosen sites selling Esso Unleaded.

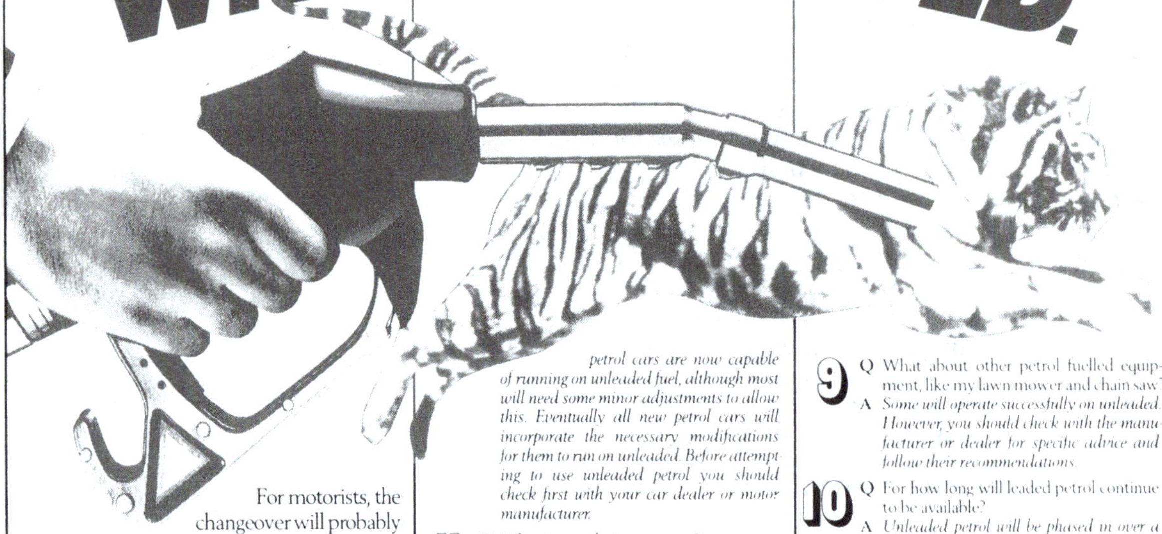

LEAPING FORWARD WITH UNLEADED.

For motorists, the changeover will probably raise more questions than answers, which is why we've produced this page.

Alternatively, pick up the Esso Unleaded leaflets, including our Service Station Site Directory, at your nearest Esso Station.

We hope you will find them helpful.

1 Q What is unleaded petrol?
A It is petrol to which no lead has been deliberately added.

2 Q Why is lead added to petrol?
A Small quantities of lead compounds can be added to petrol to increase its octane number. This allows the use of higher compression ratio engines with more ignition spark advance, which means improved engine efficiency and fuel economy. To replace lead we have to introduce more high octane compounds to compensate.

3 Q What is 'low lead' petrol compared to unleaded?
A Low lead refers to the normal leaded petrol which is currently available. This is because the lead content was reduced in all petrol to 0.15g per litre on 1st January 1986 from its previous level of 0.40g per litre, in line with British Standard 4040. Unleaded petrol is allowed to contain up to 0.013g per litre which is why it cannot be called 'lead free', although on the Continent this term may be used where unleaded cannot be translated.

4 Q Can I use unleaded petrol in my car?
A The majority of cars in the United Kingdom have been designed to run on leaded petrol. However, nearly 40% of post 1985 petrol cars are now capable of running on unleaded fuel, although most will need some minor adjustments to allow this. Eventually all new petrol cars will incorporate the necessary modifications for them to run on unleaded. Before attempting to use unleaded petrol you should check first with your car dealer or motor manufacturer.

5 Q What is a catalytic converter?
A Although not legally required in the UK at present, a catalytic converter is a device that can be fitted to the exhaust system. When the exhaust fumes pass through the converter, emissions such as nitrogen oxide and carbon monoxide are burnt up or oxidised. Unfortunately, lead damages the catalysts, so they are only effective on cars already using unleaded petrol.

6 Q Where can I buy unleaded petrol?
A Esso were the first company in the UK to put unleaded on sale. And since then we have been increasing the number of our service stations that sell unleaded petrol. We now have more stations selling unleaded than all our competitors put together. For details of where you can buy Esso Unleaded please pick up a FREE copy of our latest site directory from any Esso station.

7 Q How will I know which pump dispenses unleaded petrol?
A Esso Unleaded pumps are clearly marked UNLEADED and will usually have a small pump nozzle and identification cover marked UNLEADED on the nozzle.

8 Q What happens if I inadvertently put the wrong fuel in my car?
A Given the safeguards mentioned above it would be very difficult for you to do so. However, an isolated incident may not be too serious. Unleaded petrol used in an engine designed to take leaded, or leaded petrol used in an unleaded engine, could eventually cause damage to the engine.

9 Q What about other petrol fuelled equipment, like my lawn mower and chain saw?
A Some will operate successfully on unleaded. However, you should check with the manufacturer or dealer for specific advice and follow their recommendations.

10 Q For how long will leaded petrol continue to be available?
A Unleaded petrol will be phased in over a number of years. Therefore both leaded and unleaded will be available for a transition period which will be as long as the present product is required to supply today's cars.

11 Q What happens if I take my car to the Continent?
A Both leaded and unleaded petrol are available in Europe. There may be slight differences in unleaded to take account of local conditions, but this is unlikely to affect a car that can run on unleaded petrol.

(Esso) Quality at work for Britain.
A MEMBER OF THE EXXON GROUP

BUSINESS ENVIRONMENT

Countdown to the Year 2000

Once cast as the environmental villain, industry is increasingly seen as a vital ally in sustainable development. Jacqueline Aloisi de Larderel, the new director of the UNEP Industry & Environment Office in Paris, foresees a much closer working relationship between environmental interests and the business community.

Astonishingly, it is now sixteen years since the Stockholm Conference on the Human Environment. The immediate outcome of the event was the setting up of the United Nations Environment Programme (UNEP), but it also helped trigger the flood-tide of environmental legislation which swept through the 1970s and into the 1980s.

At the time, industry was cast as the villain of the piece. Now, as we move towards the 1990s and the dawn of the 21st century, industry is increasingly seen in a very different light. 'UNEP must work much more closely with industry, which has much to contribute in the environmental field,' says Jacqueline Aloisi de Larderel, the recently appointed director of UNEP's Industry and Environment Office (IEO) in Paris. And the feedback she is getting from industry suggests that she will get much of the help she needs.

Large to small

Set up in 1975, IEO aims to bring economic and environmental interests together into productive partnerships. Initially, IEO concentrated on the major industrial sectors, including the agro-industry, aluminium, chemicals, iron and steel, motor vehicle, non-ferrous metals, petroleum, and pulp and paper industries. Increasingly, however, it is focusing on some of the smaller industries found in the Third World, such as tanneries, textiles, cement, tourism and agricultural industries.

At the same, too, IEO is becoming more cross-sectoral in its work, developing projects which cut across the interests of many of these industries. Examples include hazardous waste management, the promotion of low- and non-waste technologies, risk assessment, cost-benefit analysis and environmental impact assessment.

High on Ms Aloisi's list of priorities is the implementation of the recommendations of the World Industry Conference on Environmental Management (WICEM), held in Versailles in 1984. 'WICEM,' says Ms Aloisi, 'was a great step forward.' In fact, one of her first visits on taking up her new post in early 1987 was to visit the International Environmental Bureau (IEB) in Geneva, set up by the International Chamber of Commerce to ensure industry plays an active role in the follow-up to WICEM.

Formerly deputy director of the Pollution Prevention Directorate of the French Ministry of Environment, Ms Aloisi is particularly keen to promote the development and use of 'clean technologies', which cause no (or less) pollution. 'And,' she promptly adds, 'of clean products.'

No quick solutions

She is realistic about what can be achieved. 'We recognise that it is best to aim for goals we can reach, rather than aiming too high and missing,' she says, but is determined to carry the debate deep into the heart of industry. 'We are involved in many training programmes,' she notes, 'and are working with the International Labour Organization to get environmental issues onto the agenda of business schools around the world.'

Having herself earned an MBA from INSEAD, the European Institute of Business Administration in 1969, she knows that this will be no easy task. But she is settling down for the long haul. 'Often we are dealing in time-scales of decades, rather than years,' she explains.

IEO has been in existence for thirteen years and a good deal has been achieved. But, industry cannot afford to relax, Ms Aloisi stresses. Perhaps even more than the environmental lobbying organisations covered in the *Green Pages* survey (page 14), she recognises that industry has already made some fairly extraordinary advances.

But, she argues, the next twelve years – which will take us to the threshold of the new century and to the Industry and Environment Office's 20th birthday – will need to see a further quantum leap in industry's environmental capabilities.

Industry and Environment

IEO publishes a quarterly technical newsletter, *Industry and Environment,* which is available on subscription (*details:* United Nations Publications, CH-1211 Geneva 10, Switzerland). Details of the various IEO programmes can be requested from the Industry and Environment Office, United Nations Environment Programme, Tour Mirabeau, 39–43 quai Andre Citroen, 75739 Paris Cedex, France or on (1) 45 78 33 33.

ANNUAL REPORT

All the Colours of the Rainbow – But What About Green?

Some people collect birds' eggs for the colours, others to find out something about birds. SustainAbility collects annual reports not for the colours but as a litmus test of industry's sensitivity on environmental issues.

Lay them out in front of you and the colours dazzle. Once a dull collection of facts and figures on a company's financial performance, annual reports have become an art-form in their own right. Top-flight designers are hired to produce the sort of look likely to appeal to a mass audience in this new age of 'people's capitalism'. Every colour of the rainbow is harnessed to sell the corporate image, but where does green fit in?

On the surface, it all looks rather reassuring. 'Changes were made to the structure of Ecology, Safety and Quality Assurance, the department responsible for these matters at Group level,' reported one company in its annual report, 'in order to enable it to continue to take account of the growing demands worldwide for better environmental protection and accident prevention measures.' This was the 1985 annual report from **Sandoz,** published six months before the Rhine pollution disaster on 11 November 1986 projected the company into the world's headlines.

'Painful'

In 1987, the company's annual report spoke of the 'painful and distressing' experience which followed the Schweizerhalle warehouse fire. It noted that Sandoz would go to 'even greater lengths to reduce the risks inherent in the production, storage and transport of chemical substances, and we shall intensify our efforts to develop products with less environmental impact potential. A wide-ranging programme with these objectives has already been initiated as a major step towards integrated thinking, a concept that is assuming growing importance.'

In a section of that 1987 annual report entitled 'After Schweizerhalle', Sandoz admitted that the disaster had cast doubt on 'the competence and credibility of the chemical industry as a whole.' But it also noted that one positive result for the environment had been the establishment of a new set of 'ecological markers', which would force industry to further tighten its safety and environmental standards.

A number of other chemical companies immediately instituted reviews of their operations to ensure that they had not overlooked similar risks. **ICI** was one such. 'ICI had already recognised the serious environmental con-

sequences which can arise from the escape of contaminated fire-fighting water in such circumstances,' the company explained in its 1986 annual report. 'Nevertheless, a further review of ICI's practices has been initiated in the light of the lessons to be learnt from this incident.'

In that year, outgoing chairman Sir John Harvey-Jones wrote to all ICI senior executives to ensure that they were aware of their personal responsibilities for implementing ICI's corporate environment policy. The annual report contained a potted summary of the company's policy, which is 'to manage its activities so as to avoid causing any unnecessary or unacceptable risk to the safety and health of its employees, customers and members of the public who may be affected by its operations.'

There were also prominent mentions for such 'clean' products and technologies as ICI's 'Aquabase' solvent-free paint-spraying and 'Tempro' protective coating systems for the motor industry. Both had recently won a Pollution Abatement Technology Award, a fact mentioned in the report. In common with most annual reports, however, there was no mention of specific environmental problems which ICI and its affiliate companies (including Tioxide) had experienced.

By contrast, a company like **Fisons** thought it sufficient to drop in a photograph and short caption on its voluntary conservation policy for the restoration of worked-out peat land. And **Boots,** despite the fact that it is developing a new business based on environmentally acceptable biocides (page 60),

BUSINESS ENVIRONMENT

made no mention of the environment at all.

Expensive

While **Hoechst UK's** annual report also made no mention of the environment, concentrating almost entirely on the company's financial performance, German chemical companies operating on their home ground had a great deal more to say on the subject. **BASF,** for example, mentioned in the editorial introduction to its report that it was developing environmentally compatible products, including printing inks and low-solvent car painting systems.

In common with other companies, BASF stressed the scale of the environmental expenditure it was making. Sandoz pointed out that it had spent over 500 million Swiss francs (around £200 million) on environmental, safety and security systems in the decade to 1976, with the running costs totalling 194 million Swiss francs (around £78 million, an extraordinarily high figure) in 1986 alone. BASF reported that environmental protection accounted for 7% of its total 1986 capital expenditures of DM 2,657 million (around £886 million).

Ciba-Geigy devoted a few short paragraphs to health, safety and environment, focusing on a number of audits and environmental impact assessments undertaken during the year. In addition, the company had carried out a survey of waste materials, to assess the potential of high temperature incineration.

Clean

The 1986 annual report produced by the Belgian chemical company **Solvay** was unusual in that it included six pages on safety and environment. Solvay also itemised some of the 'clean technology' recently fitted to plants to improve their environmental performance, including:
- mercury stripping units at the Matorell (Spain) and Povoa (Portugal) plants;
- new units for the steam-stripping of aqueous effluents of chlorinated organic compounds, and new investment in the recovery of by-products in the company's Jemeppe (Belgium) and Tavaux (France) plants;
- incineration of residual gas from chlorinated organic compound units in the Tavaux and Rheinberg (Federal Republic of Germany) plants; and
- biological purification of aqueous effluents in the Netherlands and the United States.

This investment in the cleanest technologies available represented about 10% of total costs, the company said. In the build-up to European Year of the Environment, Solvay also stressed the fact that many of its chemical products are used in effluent treatment and other areas of environmental protection.

Some French companies, like **Total** (which produces oil, coal,

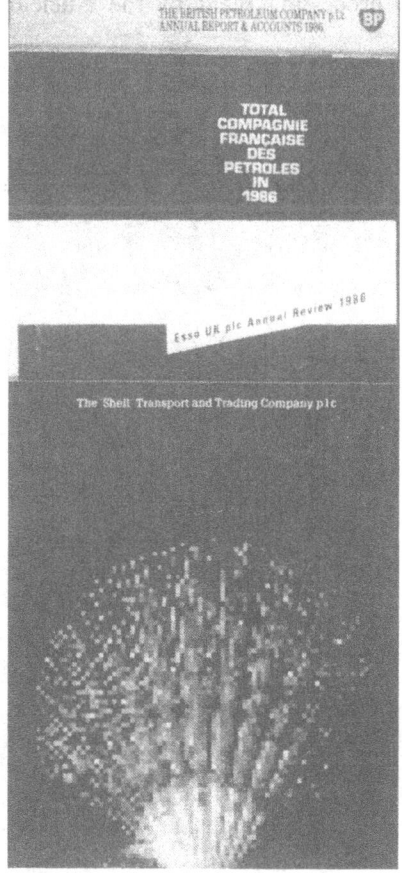

uranium and other energy products), had nothing to say about their environmental performance. The company's annual report did, however, mention continuing work in the solar energy field – although it noted that the fall in oil prices had made this area of business more difficult.

Newly-privatised **British Gas** confined itself to a few lines accepting that gas pipelines sometimes have to run through some of Britain's most attractive countryside. In such cases, the company said, 'we make every effort to restore the scenery to its former beauty. Just one of the ways in which British Gas cares for the countryside.'

Unleaded

Esso, on the other hand, had much to report. On the product side, Esso was the first company to introduce unleaded petrol to the UK market and by the end of 1986 there were 100 stations selling unleaded country-wide. Considerable space was also devoted later in the report to Esso's links with such environmental regeneration groups as the British Trust for Conservation Volunteers (BTCV), Groundwork and UK 2000.

Both **BP** and **Shell** also devoted considerable space to environmental issues. BP noted that its reputation for environmental protection was high and reported that 'in order to maintain our good standing, we have issued an updated set of principles which will apply worldwide to BP's project developments, operating sites, acquisitions and closures.' As an example of BP's policy of co-operating with environmental organisations, the company mentioned the nature conservation guidelines (page 30) it had helped to prepare with the Nature Conservancy Council and John Elkington Associates. The health, safety and environment section of the 1986 annual report highlighted the increased awareness of such issues in society as a whole. 42→

Indeed, Shell featured its environmental activities in a short section under the heading 'Shell in society'. Among the initiatives mentioned was the provision of advice to customers on the use of unleaded petrol with, in West Germany, a guarantee against engine damage. Given the company's long-running Shell Better Britain Campaign, however, it significantly underplayed the positive side of its environmental performance.

Chairman Peter Holmes did note, however, that 'the public is always understandably concerned about the way in which industrial activity can affect the environment, and also about health and safety. For very many years,' he stressed, 'Shell companies have attributed great importance to these aspects of their businesses, and they will continue to do so.'

'Traumatic'

Still in the energy field, the **Central Electricity Generating Board (CEGB)** has given a high profile to environmental issues in its 1985–86 and 1986–87 annual reports. Noting that 1986–87 marked a turning point for the CEGB, with a resurgence in power sales after years of over-capacity and low investment, CEGB chairman Lord Marshall accepted that 'the Board has a duty to develop its own policies in tune with the move towards higher environmental standards, and this cannot be done cheaply.'

The accident at Chernobyl on 26 April 1986, the CEGB reported, 'was the most traumatic event in the history of civil nuclear power.' Although it stressed that Britain does not use reactors of the Chernobyl type and that the operators of the Chernobyl reactor ignored safety guidelines, the CEGB accepts that 'without public acceptance (the electricity industry) could not have nuclear power, and that is why it must continue striving to win public confidence.'

The CEGB's 1986–87 annual report devoted a fair number of pages to the environment and to the Board's clean-up activities. Among the key issues addressed were acid rain and radioactive waste management. In addition, the report mentions charitable assistance the Board has given to such conservation organisations as the World Wildlife Fund and the British Wildlife Appeal (launched by the Royal Society for Nature Conservation).

At **British Nuclear Fuels,** meanwhile, the 1985–86 and 1986–87 reports showed a distinct change in the company's stance on the public's right to information on the nuclear industry's environmental performance. 'If I have one objective,' said incoming chairman Christopher Harding (page 134) in the 1985–86 report, 'it is for the Group to combine business success with public acceptability.'

The 1986–87 report was published in the wake of a safety audit of the Sellafield nuclear fuel reprocessing plant by the Nuclear

Installations Inspectorate. Once again, the Sellafield site was castigated for various failures and continuing poor performance in some areas. BNF immediately undertook to meet all the NII's requirements. Meanwhile, the company's 'open door' policy continued, with thousands of visitors passing through the Sellafield exhibition centre and a total of over 84,000 people visiting the company's various sites during the year. Although most environmentalists remain hostile (page 18), the impact on public opinion has been positive (page 223).

Monergy

Companies in the energy efficiency sector reported mixed results. In its 1985–86 report, glassmakers **Pilkington** noted that demand for insulation products had been soft. By the following year, however, during which the Pilkington Energy World House was featured at the Milton Keynes Energy World exhibition and the Department of Energy invested considerable effort in its 'Monergy' campaign, sales of insulation products exceeded projections. Interestingly, Pilkington glass features in the energy-efficient Princess of Wales Conservatory at Kew Gardens, which houses 10 different climatic habitats.

Pilkington has put a great deal of energy into job creation programmes, particularly in the St Helens area of Lancashire, working with groups like Business in the Community and Groundwork. Pilkington is very active in the defence technology sector, as are a number of other companies which have reported major environmental advances or initiatives. Examples include **Rolls-Royce,** the aero-engine manufacturer, which developed the quiet, fuel-efficient and much less polluting RB211-535E4 engine, and **Hawker Siddeley,** which helped sponsor 'The Green Designer' exhibition at London's Design Centre – as a green contribution to Industry Year 1986 (page 72).

BUSINESS ENVIRONMENT

In France, glass-makers **Saint-Gobain** reported that its insulation products division accounted for 20% of its 1986 cash flow. Both Pilkington and Saint-Gobain are heavily involved in research and development on new materials, such as those used to make optical fibres, optical data storage discs and energy-saving industrial ceramics.

Competitive

With the continuing quest for the 'clean car', the motor industry will eventually be a major consumer of such ceramics, which will help engines burn hotter, cleaner and more fuel-efficiently. In its 1986 report, Sweden's **Volvo** noted that since 1977 more than 700,000 of its cars had been fitted with catalytic converters. Indeed, since 1985 engines fitted with catalytic converters had become standard equipment in Volvos delivered in Austria, Switzerland and other countries. In Sweden and West Germany, catalytic converters are optional in all Volvo models.

West Germany's **Volkswagen** also had a fair amount to say about the environment. It noted, for example, that the number of new car registrations was hit in 1986 by the controversy over car exhaust emissions. 'The share accounted for by new low-pollution vehicles being registered showed a constant increase in 1986,' the company reported. 'Of the passenger cars newly registered in West Germany, 56% were fitted with low-pollution engines. Half of them were diesel vehicles. Against a background of the phasing out of full tax exemption for new low-pollution vehicles on December 31, 1986, there has been an increase in demand for catalytic converters since September.'

British companies have been much slower to pursue the 'clean car', however, except when building luxury cars for export to pollution-sensitive markets like the United States. Paradoxically, one company which welcomed European Year of the Environment with open arms was **Johnson Matthey**, the British company which pioneered in the development of catalytic converters (page 116). These devices, which purify exhaust emissions, were first introduced in the United States in 1975 and have since played a key role in cutting petrochemical smog problems in major cities such as Los Angeles and Tokyo.

Johnson Matthey has long lobbied legislators and their advisors on the role which its products can play in environmental improvement. The catalytic converter market is increasingly mature and competitive in established markets like the United States, but is likely to open up substantially in Europe in the wake of concerns that car exhaust emissions are a major contributor to acid rain problems in countries such as West Germany.

Among Johnson Matthey's competitors in Europe is the US company Engelhard, whose 1986 report lists such customers as Alfa-Romeo, BMW, Daimler-Benz, Fiat, Peugeot, Renault, Rolls-Royce, Saab, Volvo and Yugo. Engelhard has a joint venture in this area with West Germany's Kali-Chemie.

Radioactive

With well over 10,000 companies now operating in the environmental business across Europe, it is impossible to give more than an impression of the major trends. But there is certainly continuing interest in overseas markets for environmental systems, including sewage and industrial effluent treatment equipment.

Babcock International is among the companies operating in this sector, reporting its share of the UK sewage and water treatment market continued to expand in 1986 and that it was securing repeat business even in the Middle East, where there had been a distinct economic downturn. Babcock also reported major contracts for British Nuclear Fuels and AWRE focusing on the treatment of radioactive liquid effluents.

In a project for Blue Circle, Babcock installed a system to extract, transport and use gas generated by a landfill site in Kent. **Blue Circle** itself noted that the Swanscombe landfill gas project – the largest in Europe – had been commissioned, and mentioned the 'Clariflow' process it had developed for sewage treatment. But it had little else to say on the environment, surprisingly given the scale of impacts associated with the quarrying and cement production sectors. It did note, however, that it had applied for planning permission to turn a 200 acre quarry at Dartford into a shopping and leisure centre, Blue Water Park.

Bugs

The only annual report of all those reviewed here actually to sport, perhaps coincidentally, a green cover (with pink bars) was **BioTechnica** (now known as **BTL**), a leading agricultural and environmental biotechnology company based in Cardiff.

44→

BioTechnica's 1987 report mentioned the launch of a new subsidiary, **BioTreatment**, to provide environmental services in the areas of land decontamination, landfill energy and industrial waste treatment (page 116).

BioTreatment has been working with companies like the US Occidental Chemical Corporation, which now owns Hooker Chemical (responsible for the infamous Love Canal toxic waste site), to identify micro-organisms which can break down such toxic materials as polychlorinated biphenyls (PCBs). The same approach has been used by BioTreatment to clean up contaminated gasworks sites in Blackburn and Doncaster. 1987 was BTL's third year of operation and saw it break into the black for the first time, with a profit of £200,000.

Food

Other companies which are either using biotechnology in the agribusiness sector – or planning to do so – include **BAT Industries, Lonhro** and **Unilever.** None have much to say on environmental issues. Lonhro, as an aside, mentions that its printing division produced a number of series of stamps featuring wildlife for countries such as Senegal, the Seychelles and Togo. Unilever mentions its Scottish fish farming operations, but there is nothing on the concern about the ecological impact of such projects which has led the Nature Conservancy Council to launch a major research programme at the University of Stirling.

Indeed, when one considers the scale on which such companies operate, it is surprising that they have not yet picked up on the need for regular reports on environmental management and sustainable development.

The green thread is also conspicuous by its absence in the annual reports produced by **McDonald's** (1986) and **Sainsbury's** (1987). There is not a whisper on the rain forest or ozone depletion in McDonald's report, both issues where the company has been targeted as a representative of the fast food industry generally.

Money

But they are not alone. If you check through the annual reports of most major banks and building societies, it soon becomes clear that they have a very different understanding of what the word 'environment' means. For the **Midland Bank,** for example, the 'environment' in 1986 was the 'Big Bang', the technological revolution which shook the financial institutions of the City to their very roots. For the **Abbey National,** 'environment' is what it offers to customers, in the way of comfort and personal service, when they come through the door of the branch office.

Leaf through the reports produced by the **Halifax, Lloyds,** the **National Westminster Bank,** or the **Royal Bank of Scotland,** and there is no mention of environment, sustainable development or the longer-term implication for either of the Third World debt problem. Again, this is somewhat surprising given the level of sponsorship already given to projects developed by conservation organisations. The NatWest, for example, spent a total of £8 million on charitable sponsorships in 1986, helping 5,500 organisations – including a number with green objectives.

Even the **Prudential Corporation,** which has advertised its contributions to conservation projects in magazines like *BBC Wildlife,* was mute on the subject in its 1986 annual report – despite the fact that such environmental sponsorships are part of the new 'identity' which the Prudential is seeking to establish.

Turn to the reports produced by the computer and telecommunications companies which have provided the momentum behind the 'Big Bang', and you will again find no mention of environmental issues. The closest that **British Telecom** comes is when it discusses the redesign of phone booths to minimise the risk of vandalism.

Sustainable?

In this context, **IBM's** 1986 annual report was all the more surprising. Not only did it talk about environmental sponsorships which the computer company was developing with groups like the World Wildlife Fund, Groundwork, the Council for Environmental Education and CEED, but it also had a short 'Sustainable Development' heading – perhaps the first time a company had ever taken this step.

Why did IBM decide to start a sustainable development programme? Not because there is any automatic link between such sponsorship and the likelihood that the computer user will buy an IBM PC next time around. Nonetheless, as IBM UK chief executive Tony Cleaver pointed out early in 1987, the idea is to capitalise on the company's technology. As the 'Computers' section of *Green Pages* illustrates, information technology will have a key role in the transition to more sustainable forms of development.

'In the late 1960s a book was published called *The Limits to Growth,*' Tony Cleaver recalled. 'The picture on the front cover depicted the world encircled by chains which represented the absolute limit to growth that could be achieved before our resources are exhausted. I am not that pessimistic, but I do recognise that ultimately our business growth might be constrained by the world's inability to manage its resources. Hence it is clearly in our interest to do what we can to assist in managing these resources better.'

It will be interesting to see whether this sort of enlightened self-interest begins to colour the thinking and annual reports of other major companies as we move towards the business opportunities – and inevitable environmental problems – of the 21st century. ☐

- IS DEMAND FOR ELECTRICITY INCREASING?
- DO WE NEED NEW POWER STATIONS?
- WHAT ABOUT ALTERNATIVE SOURCES OF ENERGY?
- HOW DO POWER STATIONS AFFECT THE ENVIRONMENT?
- WHY DO WE NEED NUCLEAR POWER?
- IS NUCLEAR POWER SAFE?
- WHAT ARE WE DOING ABOUT ACID RAIN?
- ARE WE AT RISK FROM LOW LEVEL RADIATION OR NUCLEAR WASTE?
- COULD A CHERNOBYL-TYPE ACCIDENT HAPPEN HERE?

Why not discuss these issues with the people who can give you the answers?

The CEGB welcomes invitations from societies and organisations to answer questions and discuss the various issues concerning the production of electricity, and has a team of scientists and engineers available to give illustrated presentations throughout England and Wales.

Further details of this free Energy Talks Service and a copy of the latest CEGB free film and video library catalogue can be obtained by completing this coupon or by telephoning 01-634 5456.

CENTRAL ELECTRICITY GENERATING BOARD

Send to: Energy Talks Service, Central Electricity Generating Board, Sudbury House, 15 Newgate Street, LONDON, EC1A 7AU.
(Please tick)
I would like to invite a CEGB speaker to address my group (or group discussion). ☐   Please send me further details of your free Energy Talks Service. ☐
Please send me the latest CEGB film and video catalogue. ☐   I would like to arrange a visit to a power station. ☐

Name _____   Organisation _____
Address _____   Postcode _____   Telephone Number _____

Greener Growth

The Brundtland Commission's report called for a new era of 'sustainable' growth. Later sections of *Green Pages* focus on key sectors of the European economy which can help deliver 'sustainability'. But what is it?

Gro Harlem Brundtland.

A New Era of Growth

'Many of the development paths of the industrialized nations are clearly unsustainable,' concluded Norway's Prime Minister, Gro Harlem Brundtland, after completing several years' of intensive work on *Our Common Future,* the report of the World Commission on Environment and Development. 'And the development decisions of these countries, because of their great economic and political power,' she stressed, 'will have a profound effect upon the ability of all peoples to sustain human progress for generations to come.

'Many critical survival issues,' she continued, 'are related to uneven development. They all place unprecedented pressure on the planet's lands, waters, forests, and other natural resources, not least in the developing countries. The downward spiral of poverty and environmental degradation is a waste of opportunities and of resources. In particular, it is a waste of human resources.'

Her overall conclusion? 'What is needed now is a new era of economic growth – growth that is forceful and at the same time socially and environmentally desirable.' A tall order, but as later sections of *Green Pages* demonstrate, an increasingly achievable one.

What sort of picture does the phrase *the environment business* conjure up in your mind? Most people tend to think of pollution control and waste management *technology*. This is hardly surprising, given that there are now over 9,000 European companies active in the pollution control sector alone (page 108). But, as later sections show, the 'green growth' sector of the European economy also now embraces a rapidly expanding range of service activities.

Business and industry have a key role to play in the transition to more sustainable forms of development. The sections which make up the remainder of Green Pages *report on progress in key sectors of the green economy. Green growth is now a reality and, as CBI President Sir David Nickson argues on page 48, environmental excellence can give exporters an important edge.*

Nor should we forget the potential contributions which the green consumer (page 71), the green investor (page 186) or the green tourist (page 166) can make, consciously or unconsciously, to the transition to an ecologically sustainable Europe.

The real challenge will be to transform global prescriptions like the *World Conservation Strategy* not only into national conservation strategies, which is now being done, but also into new business concepts which enable the ordinary consumer, investor or tourist to contribute towards the broader goals of sustainable development.

While many early pioneers in this field have been deeply, emotionally, committed to environmental protection and sustainability, and prepared to make significant personal sacrifices as a result, most people are not. Indeed, short of a series of massive disasters which force people to sit up and take note, the only effective way to change the behaviour of the bulk of the population is to make sustainable development 'user-friendly'. Convenience, in short, is likely to be as important a factor when persuading people to help save the world as it is when persuading them to use a particular bank or shop.

Desirable – but what is it?

Before you can make something convenient, however, you have to know what it is. Paradoxically, while no-one who knows anything about environment and development doubts that 'sustainability' is a desirable goal, even those who have long worked in these fields may have difficulty in pinning down precisely what the word means in particular cases (page 50). As usual, it is often easier to say what is *not* sustainable.

'Sustainable development,' the Brundtland Commission suggested, 'is development that meets the needs of the present without compromising the ability of future generations to meet their own needs.' In fact, as long as we can develop suitable techniques to accurately forecast potential future problems and the legislation necessary to ensure that they can increasingly be prevented, then there is no reason why many forms of growth should not continue – and be actively promoted.

Even though the Bhopal and Chernobyl disasters happened durings its life, the Brundtland Commission left readers of its report, *Our Common Future* (page 21), in no doubt that a new era of growth is now needed to move the world's industrial and industrialising nations from 'their present, often destructive, processes of growth and development onto sustainable development paths.'

Key objectives, the Commission stressed, must include:

- reviving economic growth, but a new type of growth, 'less material- and energy-intensive and more equitable in its impact';
- meeting essential needs for jobs, food, energy, water and sanitation;
- ensuring a sustainable level of population;
- conserving and enhancing the resource base;
- reorientating technology and managing risk; and
- merging ecological and economic considerations in decision making.

A daunting challenge

One example of an environmental service industry which aims to help merge ecological and economic considerations is the environmental research and consultancy sector (pages 84–93). This now provides such services as environmental impact assessment (EIA) – together with linked environmental accountancy, auditing and training skills – to a growing array of clients, both in the industrialised nations and in the Third World.

The basic idea underlying EIA, which draws on a wide range of specialist disciplines, is to identify potential adverse impacts before they appear, so that remedial measures can be taken at the *design* stage (page 72). Reassuringly, EIA and related techniques are now finding applications in many different sectors, from energy supply (page 128) to farming and forestry (page 138).

But the long term challenge remains daunting. For if new development is to be environmentally sustainable in the longer term, then such techniques will be needed not simply when products or projects are designed, but also when government policies or corporate business strategies are first put together.

Sustainability, the Commission suggested, also 'requires the enforcement of wider responsibilities for the impacts of decisions. This requires changes in the legal and institutional frameworks that will enforce the common interest.' Sustainable development, it added, also presupposes:

- a political system that secures effective citizen participation in decision making;
- an economic system that is able to generate surpluses and technical knowledge on a self-reliant and sustained basis;
- a social system that provides for solutions for the tensions arising from damaging development;
- a production system that respects the obligation to preserve the ecological base for development;
- a technological system that can search continuously for new solutions;

149→

TREES, WOODS & THE GREEN MAN

6 new beautifully illustrated postcards have been designed to encourage paper recycling as well as a greater caring for old trees and orchards, garden and street trees, hedgerow and field trees. Available as mixed or single sets of 6 @ £1.50 incl. p&p.

Order them from us now!

Common Ground

45 Shelton Street · Covent Garden · London WC2H 9HJ

PERSPECTIVES

Exporting Environmental Excellence

Companies looking for a competitive edge in international markets should pursue environmental excellence. *Sir David Nickson*, President of the CBI, on the environmental factor in business success.

'Let me start by giving a warm welcome to *Green Pages*. We share a common goal, to ensure that adequate attention to the environment is given in all our businesses. I am sure that *Green Pages* will contribute greatly towards this.

The staleness in British business is ending. There is a wind of optimism blowing, born of the realism that survival depends on long term competitiveness which in turn trades on the excellence and reliability of goods and services. Providing traditional goods to traditional standards by traditional methods is no longer good enough. We need sustainable wealth creation which means we must:

- invest in our workforce, their inventiveness and enthusiasm;
- consider our neighbours and the quality of life that they expect;
- understand our potential and existing markets, and provide goods and services to satisfy them.

In all of these the environment is fundamental to our chances of success. Environmental excellence gives a competitive edge which has to be recognised and incorporated from the start.

Local solutions

Employees are important. For too long they have been the forgotten people of the environment. However, it is local solutions to local problems inside and outside the factory, which gives real environmental progress and helps to build confidence and encourage positive environmental attitudes. It is workers who build environmental excellence into products and processes. The 3M company's 'pollution prevention pays' strategy may be an overused example but it is still classic: a continuing search by all members of the company for small operational improvements which reduce environmental impact and hence the base cost of product, serving to enhance competitiveness worldwide.

Neighbours are important. Giving time to them and to their needs reduces the prospects of unnecessary worry and hence the resources which might otherwise be diverted to ease it and to repair the company image. Again, this helps to keep basic costs down and allows the skills of the workforce to be directed fully towards the company's real target, the market place.

Customers are important. They decide the company's ultimate success. At home and abroad their wants are increasingly more sophisticated, more knowledgeable about the environmental impacts of goods and services and the wastes that are eventually generated. It is vital to understand the attitudes and needs of the people in the prospective market-place and to assess the likelihood of new standards and conditions: these determine what the company should provide.

Increasingly, environmental factors are a key to sales potential, for example:

- cadmium content may determine the products which can be sold in Sweden;
- emission controls affect the sale of motor vehicles throughout the developed world;
- ease of construction and transport is important in deciding which water purification units are suitable for isolated communities.

Rewards are high

No company understands the significance of the environment better than Johnson Matthey, a world beater in catalytic technology, or Castrol, pollution abatement technology award-winner for its oil for outboard motors used on Swiss lakes. Nor UK consulting firms who, according to the World Bank, are competing in a potential overseas market of £250 billion to provide the world's population with clean water and sanitation.

Motor vehicle catalysts by Johnson Matthey.

So at home and abroad environmental excellence will give business opportunities for sales and services. British companies cannot sit back and wait for business to come to them but must now go out and compete forcefully and with foresight in the markets of the world. Disregard of environmental factors leads to inefficiency, misuse of valuable resources and inattention to the needs of the customer – a recipe for failure.

The lesson is hard but the rewards are high for those companies willing to take the initiative and care of the environment. They must be under no illusion. The competition is fierce and growing and so far Britain's main rivals seem to have more consistently recognised the significance of the environmental factor. But we can, must and will improve and thereby gain a larger share of world markets. **'**

SIR DAVID NICKSON, CBE *has been President of the Confederation of British Industry (CBI) since 1986 and Chairman of Scottish & Newcastle Breweries plc since 1983. His recreations are listed in* Who's Who *as 'fishing, bird watching, the countryside', and he was Chairman of the Countryside Commission for Scotland from 1983 to 1985.*
The Confederation of British Industry, *Centre Point, New Oxford Street, London WC1A 1DU. Tel: 01 379 7400.*

---

147 ←

- an international system that fosters sustainable patterns of trade and finance; and
- an administrative system that is flexible and has the capacity for self-correction.

Many of the organisations and companies now making the running in this field are small. Even the Body Shop (page 70), whose commercial success has ensured a regular airing for green issues in the pink pages of the *Financial Times,* is small by comparison with mainstream cosmetic companies. The structure of the environmental business is probably going to be somewhat different to that of other industries for some time, partly because of the personal objectives of those who have set up these organisations and companies. This fact may make it rather harder for financial analysts and investors to come to terms with such new business sectors, although ultimately they will have no option.

The emerging generation of 'inner-directed' people, predominantly aged between 20 and 45 (page 52) has already had a profound impact on business – and the chances are that this is only the beginning. But many of the new environmental entrepreneurs and 'green capitalists' now recognise that they will need to scale up their activities if they are to compete effectively in the market-place, let alone have any chance of turning our economic leviathan in more sustainable directions.

Selling sustainability

This extraordinarily ambitious and far-reaching 'shopping list' suggests that environmental lawyers (page 28) are not going to be the only benefactors. Indeed, short of a world-wide recession, the prospects for Europe's emerging environmental business seem almost unimaginably bright.

But if Europe is to capture a major share of the new markets which are likely to evolve from these inter-linking needs, it must move beyond the stage of simply thinking and talking about sustainability to *marketing* sustainable development.

As Keith Brunt of Boots points out on page 60, there is no point in developing cleaner or more energy-efficient technologies and products if they are not going to be sold at least as aggressively as their more polluting or wasteful competitors. And, as Paul Harrison notes (page 68), these approaches will also need to be carefully tailored if they are to appeal in Third World markets.

The annual reports of many European companies are increasingly addressing green issues in one way or another (page 40), and a growing number are now also focusing on the opportunities opening up in the green economy. Selling sustainability will not be the same as selling the latest washing powder, but the time is not far distant when we may find ourselves wondering how we ever did without it. ☐

PERSPECTIVES
What *is* Sustainability?

Sustainable development, suggests *Lloyd Timberlake*, may prove to have been one of the most seminal ideas produced by the twentieth century.

'Sustainable development' has become the new rallying cry of the environment/development movement. Like most such cries ('Liberty!', 'Power to the People!') its meaning is not absolutely clear.

Examples of *un*sustainable development, like examples of distinct shortages of liberty, abound and are obvious. Cropping steep Ethiopian hillsides year after year, an activity engaged in by illiterate peasants, soon brings disaster. Clearing rainforests over poor soil to create cattle ranches which soon turn into pastures of poisonous weeds, a practice encouraged by some of the world's best educated and highest paid development experts in various governments and development banks, is another activity which brings short-term profits and slightly longer-term environmental bankruptcy.

But what development activity is sustainable over the long haul on a small planet of five billion souls, the resources of which may well have to support eight to twelve billion? The World Commission on Environment and Development, also known as the Brundtland Commission after its chairman, Norwegian première Mrs. Gro Harlem Brundtland, spent three years and $7 million researching this question on five continents. The best its 1987 final report, *Our Common Future,* could do was to opine that an activity is sustainable when it 'meets the needs of the present without compromising the ability of future generations to meet their own needs.' It added that the exploitation of resources, the direction of investments, the orientation of technological development and institutional change must all be bent towards this goal. It also says – bluntly for such a group – that this generation steals from its children 'because we can get away with it; future generations do not vote; they have no political or financial power; they cannot challenge our decisions.' It has called upon the United Nations to produce a Universal Declaration and a Convention of Environmental Protection and Sustainable Development and also a UN Programme of Action on Sustainable Development.

The Brundtland Commission did not invent the term 'sustainable development', but by recommending that it become the goal of every ministry in every government and of every international agency, it put

After the band aid, sustainable development?

the concept on a much bigger political map. And about the time that the Brundtland report was released, the International Institute for Environment and Development (IIED) was bringing together frontline development workers in a London conference to offer examples of projects which actually enhance rather than squander environmental resources: certain people-led soil and water conservation and tree-planting activities.

At the opposite end of the spectrum from the experts, the BBC and television networks in other nations produced an 11-part TV series, *Only One Earth* – also at the time of the Brundtland report publication. The series and the book which accompanied it hammered away at the idea of sustainable development by pointing up what it is not (Inter-American Development Bank loans to Panama to clear forest for cattle on hilly, erosive ground) and what it is (eight separate, detailed studies of ordinary people using their local resources sensibly and sensitively). Around the world, many other books, conferences and TV series have been examining the ideal.

Even the grim science of economics has been getting involved, trying in activities loosely dubbed 'the new economics' to find ways of getting onto a balance sheet the values of ecological processes underlying economic development. And some of the best of these 'new economists' are working in development banks and think-tanks.

It is easy to poke fun at the vagueness of the idea of 'sustainability', but then other powerful concepts – such as 'liberty' are vague and in need of constant redefinition to meet different and changing situations. Sustainable development may turn out to be a seminal idea of the century. It is a shorthand way of pointing out that the Emperor has no clothes on, that the motivation for some of the grandest development schemes are criminally short-sighted. As one African development worker pointed out, there is a great difference between a 'successful' project and a 'sustainable' project, i.e. an irrigation system that works well one year after the ribbon-cutting but fails after five due to lack of maintenance, spares, expertise and consultation with the farmers using the system.

Perhaps the most exciting aspect of the notion is that it unites the concerns of different constituencies. Environmentalists and developmentalists are being brought together by the recognition that development which destroys the environmental resources upon which it must be based is futile. Thus the World Wildlife Fund, an 'environmental' group, is concerned over the 'development' issue of national debts which encourage governments to destroy wildlife habitats for short term cash crop profits. And Oxfam, a 'development' group, is concerned over deforestation which leads to both environmental and eventually agricultural and financial bankruptcy of villages with which it is working. And both groups agree with the disarmament crowd that the perfecting and stockpiling of potentially planet-destroying weapons is hardly a 'sustainable' way to seek security.

The concept is also politically exciting generally, in that all writers on sustainable development, from the Brundtland Commission to the economists, agree that it is a goal which must be pursued at the grassroots level. The Commission even notes that this pursuit requires 'a political system that secures effective citizen participation in decision making'.

Thus the cry of sustainability may be heralding a new renaissance in the ways in which humans order their political and economic affairs. Or it may offer only a new vocabulary with which the converted can continue to preach to the converted. It is still too soon to tell.

Further Reading
Only One Earth: Living for the Future, by Lloyd Timberlake, BBC/Earthscan, London, 1987.
Our Common Future, the report of the World Commission on Environment and Development, Oxford University Press, Oxford, 1987.
The Living Economy: a New Economics in the Making, edited by Paul Ekins, Routledge & Kegan Paul, London, 1986.

LLOYD TIMBERLAKE *is writer-in-residence and senior editor at IIED. He is an American living in London, where he worked as science editor and in other positions at Reuters news agency. He was an editor at Earthscan for five years, and is the author of several books on environment and development issues, including the award-winning* Africa in Crisis.

The International Institute for Environment and Development, *3 Endsleigh Street, London WC1H 0DD. Tel: 01 388 2117.*

PERSPECTIVES
The Emergence of Inner-Directed Europe

Inner-directed Europeans are well on their way to constituting a third of the
continent's population. And, says *Sheila Moorcroft*, since they are often among the trend-setters,
their activities deserve close attention.

'A new breed of European is emerging. At Taylor Nelson Applied Futures we carry out regular, national surveys of attitudes in Britain – and our associate companies monitor trends in many parts of Europe, in North America and Japan. The trends we are identifying suggest a major shift in the way people think and act, a shift which has major implications for each of the market sectors covered in *Green Pages*.

It is all too easy to forget that societies are created and shaped by people, by their aims, priorities and approach to life. As people change, so too do institutions, legislation, technologies and markets. Most Euorpean countries are currently undergoing a period of significant change as new priorities, aims and objectives challenge the established order. Many of these new priorities we describe as 'inner-directed' and later on we will look at how inner-directed people behave as consumers, at work and at play.

But first, who *are* the inner-directeds?

Three broad groupings are emerging across Europe – and in other developed regions of the world (page 56). These are the 'sustenance-drivens', the 'outer-directeds' and the 'inner-directeds'.

The group which has been with us longest are the 'sustenance-driven', whose main objective is to survive in the face of adversity. They have been the dominant group ever since we were hunter-gatherers. During the Industrial Revolution, however, a second group began to emerge, the 'outer-directeds'. Although they have many other characteristics, they are perhaps best caricatured as the 'corporation man' and the 'conspicuous consumer'. The inner-directeds, by contrast, are a very new group, part of the move towards a 'post-industrial' society. And they are the group which is likely to have the most profound influence on European markets into the early decades of the 21st century.

The central feature of the inner-directed approach to life is 'holism', a desire to be aware of the wide picture and of implications, coupled with a growing interest in the real costs and benefits of actions, products, services and technologies. For inner-directeds, the primacy of the individual is fundamental; the freedom to be yourself, to achieve your maximum potential as a human being, both mentally and physically.

Health, in its widest sense, is therefore a top priority (page 78), resulting in an active pursuit of quality of life – although this may not be measured in any traditional, material sense. There is a strong inclination to make decisions on the basis of informed choices, rather than the dictates of class, cohort, job, fashion, age, sex or any other stereotype.

Openness and honesty are highly valued, resulting in a high sense of personal integrity and raised expectations of integrity from institutions of all kinds. Information, in fact, is seen as a route to better choices and communication, rather than as a route to power.

An invisible trend?

Education is a key factor fuelling the spread of inner-directed values, with these people tending to be concentrated among the professional, management and skilled sections of the population, with a fairly even split between men and women.

One of the 'problems' in identifying the inner-directed within society, however, is their almost invisible quality. Their emphasis on individualism means that they can be found in almost every walk of life, involved in a wide range of activities and jobs and living wherever suits them best. This 'invisibility' has resulted in the many analysts completely missing one of the key social changes of the post-war years.

But this is a real-world trend with real-world implications – and implications across the board. So how do the inner-directed behave as consumers, in the work-place and at play?

Consuming . . .

As consumers, the inner-directed are confident and well informed. They set great store by convenience and service, and look for products and services which are well matched to their needs. They will tend to buy according to their own priorities (which may include performance, energy efficiency or noise levels), rather than accepting 'special offers' or advice that a particular product is 'the' top model.

In clothing, they are distinctly more likely to be setting the fashion by pursuing their own highly quixotic and individual style, rather than following fashions *per se*. But they will want comfort, style and reliable quality. If clothes are simply a 'uniform' for the task in hand, the focus will be on suitability and durability. This may result in them buying traditional brands, where the reputation for genuine quality is well established, or going to mainstream stores for convenience. Their level of expenditure will often be quite high as a result.

Quality is also important in food, with convenience and variety among other prime requirements.

The polarization of food markets between commodity products, where branding has almost disappeared, and the delicatessen and specialist areas, where choice is paramount, is typical of their needs. The food industry has responded with new technologies to ensure freshness, has enhanced the range of products available (e.g. by using flexible programming to produce different varieties of traditional sausages) and promoted healthy eating, to very great effect.

The inner-directeds actual pattern of shopping has also been an important force for change, since they wish to be able to fit shopping into their own timetable. The flexibility of late night opening, mail order and shopping from home all appeal, as does the convenience of cash dispensers. They are happy to try new approaches where there is a definite perceived advantage.

...at work...

In the work-place, not surprisingly, inner-directeds do not suddenly undergo a metamorphosis, but bring their own priorities and approaches with them. Work, as an integral part of their lives, is therefore to be enjoyed if at all possible, and is likely to be a major source of fulfillment. They are quite likely to be successful – without necessarily pursuing success, since they are independent spirits, willing to take risks and setting store by doing whatever comes to hand as well as possible.

Their expectations of the organisations for which they work will reflect their own personal priorities. Their desire for flexibility and openness in terms of structure and communication, rather than tradition or status, may for many be threatening and disruptive, since it will seem to disregard 'the rules'. This trend also shows up in their preferred method of communication, 'networking'.

Another focus, epitomised by such 'green capitalists' as Anita Roddick of the Body Shop (page 70), is responsible profit-making, with a duty to all stakeholders, from the lowliest employee and occasional customer to the community and society at large. They put a high priority on:
- achieving community involvement;
- honesty and consistency in communications with their staff and the outside world;
- sourcing and purchasing policies that reflect a long-term perspective rather than a drive for short-term profit; and on
- adequate investment and research.

Their own personal independence will make them more likely to work independently, which can again present problems for larger organisations – unless they are able to decentralise and give genuine responsibility to wider groups of employees.

...and at play

At play, the inner-directeds place a premium on personal development. This goal extends to creativity, acquiring new knowledge and skills, getting fit, seeking out new experiences which enable them to confront themselves – all these are seen as important and desirable. These interests are translated into an active and busy lifestyle, including individual and competitive sports, an interest in food and traditional crafts, and learning through classes and special interest holidays (page 174).

Examples of where their leisure priorities have influenced markets is the growth of interest in Yoga and the martial arts, the increasing autonomy of travellers to more unusual parts of the world, the development of retreats and the personal growth movements, and the growth of self-help groups on almost every topic imaginable.

A force for change

In summary, the inner-directeds are a force for change both directly and indirectly. Their approach to life ensures that they will seek out new ways of doing things. The ideas which they espouse and generate in the process are often picked up by other groups and become mainstream concepts and driving forces in the market-place. Some of them are also willing to be extremely vociferous to achieve their objectives, and are strongly attracted by the idealism and action-orientation of campaigning groups like Greenpeace, although in the main they take a personal approach to change.

From sex to self-actualisation

The very first evidence of inner-directedness on a reasonably large scale was probably to be found among the Beatniks of the mid-1950s. The Beatnik phenomenon was pretty extreme and faded quickly, but they held many inner-directed ideas – and these ideas really bloomed among the Flower Children of the 1960s. A visit to the Sather Gate at the University of California is a sobering experience today, because the place is filled with ageing, down-and-out flower children who never made it through the Sixties. Most people did, however, and inner-directedness has matured and mellowed as it has become the mainstream emerging social trend of the 1980s.

What began as protest and rebellion has matured into a realignment of ideas. But is is not simply a question of the Sixties generation moving on, even though the main demographic focus for these new ideas is certainly among the under-40s. There has also been a considerable growth in inner-directedness among the under-25s since 1980, particularly in the UK.

Although the research carried out by Taylor Nelson Applied Futures on the trend towards inner-directedness has other roots, it is interesting to consider the research results in the context of Maslow's 'hierarchy of needs', which is summarised in Figure 1.

Table 1: The spread of inner-directedness

	Inner-directed	Outer-directed	Sustenance-driven
Europe	28	41	31
USA	19	49	32
Japan	10	55	35

According to Maslow, all human beings have the same hierarchy of needs which motivate their behaviour. These needs range from the basic biological needs present at birth to the more complex needs of later life, such as self-fulfillment – which Maslow saw as the ultimate goal. The nesting of the hierarchy reflects the fact that the needs of each level must, to a greater or lesser degree, be satisfied before those of the next level can be attained.

The seven levels of the hierarchy combine to give three core groupings: sustenance-driven, outer-directed and inner-directed. These three, in turn, reflect the dominant values of the main phases of historical development to date (Figure 2).

Just as personal development towards new priorities and approaches to life is rarely trouble-free, so a society's progression and change in response to the cumulative growth of new priorities is often turbulent and problematic. Many of the conflicts of modern day society, in fact, are the result of the confrontation and threat posed by new ideas for representatives of vested interests, and those embedded in traditional, established values.

Inner-directed ideas are challenging the *status quo* across the whole of Europe. Neither the rate of

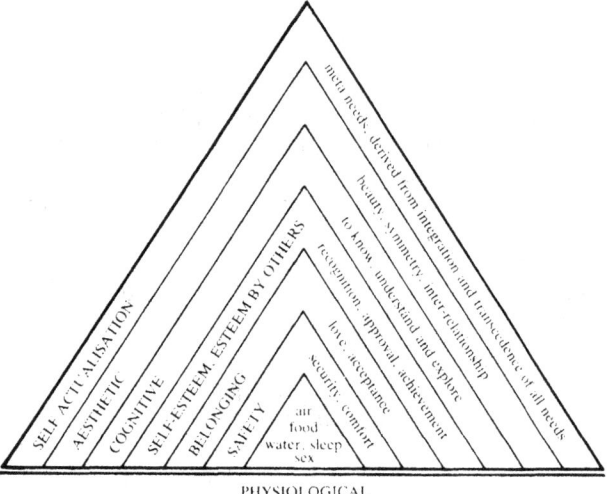

Figure 1: Maslow's hierarchy of needs

change, nor the manifestations of the different groupings, are consistent throughout Europe. Table 1 shows the penetration of inner-directed ideas across Europe, and in the United States and Japan, as of the early 1980s. Inner-directed Europeans are well on their way to constituting a third of the continent's

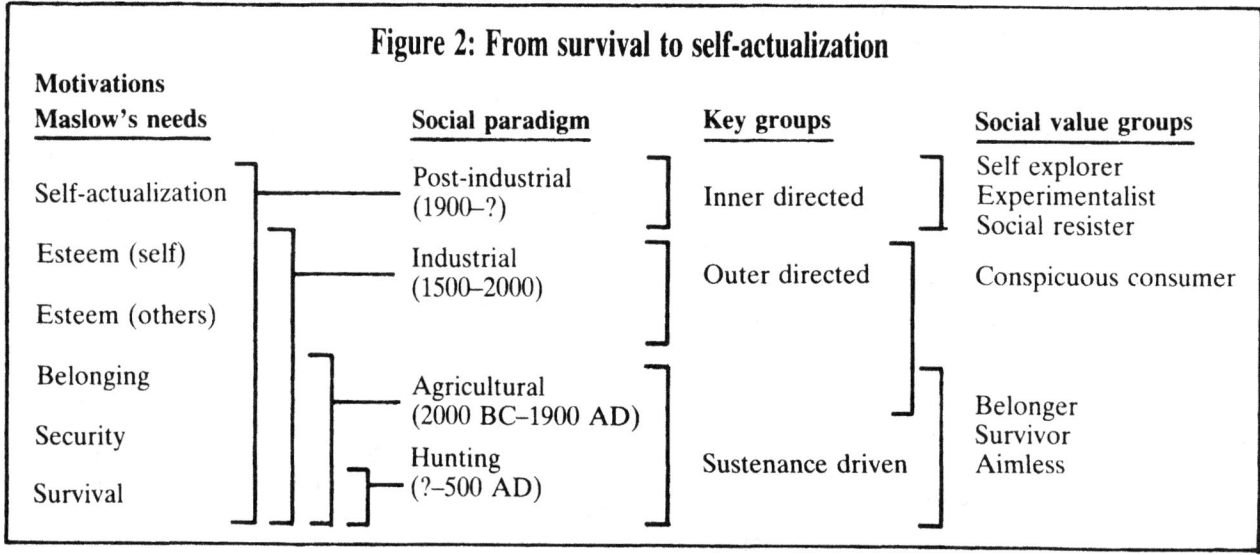

Figure 2: From survival to self-actualization

population – and, since they are often among the trendsetters, their activities deserve close attention.

How green are the inner-directeds?

Environmental concerns, while by no means the exclusive domain of the inner-directeds, are nonetheless an area of active interest. Indeed, the increasing acceptance of Green movements and concepts by business and political parties has coincided with the growth of the inner-directed slice of the population. Inner-directeds usually raise issues because they are of genuine concern, although in some cases the movements come under the control of outer-directeds, who see the opportunity to gain personal power.

Inner-directed consumers will tend to consider the environmental dimensions of their lifestyles even if they live in cities. They will often respond positively to – or possibly find themselves at the forefront of – initiatives to build up a community spirit or to green the urban environment (page 152). The sort of approaches to urban renewal and design which Prince Charles has supported are very much along inner-directed lines.

Their emphasis on personal health and well-being is in many respects a natural extension of, or alternatively the starting point for, environmental concern. Food chains provide one obvious link between the two. The growing demand for organic produce and mineral waters, and the explosion of health food shops are all strong indicators of the spread of that concern.

The development of wellness and healthy eating is a prime example of how specific ideas generated by one group, the inner-directeds, move into the mainstream as time passes, and are assimilated and changed as they are repackaged to appeal to the outer-directed and sustenance-driven.

Ten years ago, those who determinedly followed their own beliefs about healthy foods were regarded as 'cranks'. But the interests of the 'brown rice brigade' translated into lean cuisine and new-style takeaway foods; the nut rissoles and organic food of 'veggies' spawned an entire industry of vegetarian restaurants and food suppliers; and the interest in healthy exercise triggered the boom in aerobics and other fitness pursuits.

As a result, a new generation of 'conscious' or 'green' consumers is beginning to flex its muscles. And it is worth noting that their interest in shaping the world by their consumer decisions is likely to extend well beyond the food they buy.

The car, for example, has long been under attack from environmentalists – and this situation will undoubtedly continue. Even within the constraints of the market, these concerns have already translated into significant improvements in the environmental performance of the latest models, and the pressure can only continue to build. Technological breakthroughs, such as the potential for achieving 'superconductivity', may eventually give rise to the long-awaited, much-debated – but extremely evasive – electric car. But, whatever happens on this front, the car industry has some fairly difficult years ahead of it.

Packaging is another area where there have been major changes in response to environmental pressures, although much remains to be achieved (page 78). Pump sprays, recycled paper and glass, re-usable bottles, and fewer layers of packaging – all find favour among inner-directeds.

Inner-directed consumers are also likely to respond favourably to products which offer enhanced energy-efficiency (page 136), including time switches, low-temperature washing powders, short-wash programmes, quiet lawnmowers and vacuum-cleaners, better window design and easy-to-use insulation materials. Durability and easy maintenance will also be welcomed.

SHEILA MOORCROFT *is a Senior Consultant with Taylor Nelson Applied Futures, one of the founder companies of the International Research Institute for Social Change (RISC). She assists clients in incorporating the implications of social change into their medium and long term corporate strategies. Before joining Taylor Nelson, she spent 10 years with SRI International, providing research services for strategic planning. She is the author of several publications on consumer markets, social statistics and European business issues.*

Taylor Nelson Applied Futures, *44–46 Upper High Street, Epsom, Surrey KT17 4ZS. Tel: 03727 29688.*

SECTION 1

Targeting the Green Consumer

It's not enough to slap a green label on a product and wait for
the customers to roll in. The markets for green products and services need to
be properly researched – and effective marketing is as essential in the emerging green
economy as in any other business sector.

Market research, if you believe Anita Roddick of the Body Shop chain of stores (page 70), is like 'looking in the rear-view mirror.' You are looking at what has gone. No enthusiast for market research, her views are worth listening to, since she turned a £4,000 overdraft in 1976 into a public company with profits of £7.9 million in 1986–87. But not everyone has Anita Roddick's business flair.

Green Cuisine, for example, was an excellently produced publication focusing on health foods, in addition to covering many parts of the emerging green economy. Launched with much enthusiasm, and to considerable critical acclaim, it never really caught on. It shut up shop in 1987.

In a period of extremely rapid change, with consumer preferences increasingly shaped and reshaped by environmental concerns, it can be extremely difficult to predict which existing markets are going to be affected, let alone what new market opportunities may open up. Those of us without the Roddick touch cannot afford to forget the importance of well-targeted market research and marketing.

The opportunity spotters

While there is an entire industry which describes what it does as 'market research', lateral thinker Edward de Bono prefers to think in terms of an 'opportunity search.' He points out that many prime commercial opportunities have been totally overlooked by companies which have too narrowly focused on a particular definition of what business they were in.

For the small sum of $100,000, he recalls, Alexander Graham Bell offered to sell his telephone patents to the giant Western Union Telegraph Company. 'He had no choice,' Dr de Bono noted, 'because his backers had run out of funds. Without any hesitation, William Orton, then President of Western Union, turned the offer down.'

Most industrial executives, de Bono argues, 'are trained for maintenance, for efficiency and for problem-solving. Opportunity thinking is quite different. An opportunity is not there until after you have seen it. Seeking, recognising and designing opportunities requires a different set of thinking skills. These are skills of perceptual and conceptual thinking; the skills of creativity and lateral thinking.'

We are all surrounded by opportunities, most of which will be seen only if we go out and look for them. To help steer his clients towards some of these opportunities, de Bono has distinguished between many different types of opportunity – some of which are highlighted on page 57. 'In a corporation,' he stresses, 'the search for opportunities should be everyone's business, for everyone is directly concerned with what tomorrow will be like.'

No-one doubts that new commercial opportunities are opening up in the green economy – but how can one spot them? Edward de Bono recommends what he calls 'opportunity thinking'. Contributors, including Anita Roddick of the Body Shop (page 70), look at the way in which green products and services can be developed and sold.

As later sections of *Green Pages* show, the green economy is bursting with what de Bono would describe as 'real opportunities' (e.g. pollution control, energy efficiency, organic farming or ethical investment), 'hidden opportunities' (e.g. the buying power of the Green Consumer) and 'opportunity rich areas' (e.g. green publishing or tourism).

It is also possible to think of examples of 'shallow' or 'false' opportunities – and of markets where established companies or environmental entrepreneurs have made a 'wrong entry.' It is all too easy to misjudge the rate at which markets which are driven by regulation or ethical concerns are going to develop. Companies which select markets with a strong political dimension, like the catalytic converter market in which Johnson Matthey has long been a leader (page 116), may find that the slow pace of political progress injects a good deal of uncertainty into the market. But environmental entrepreneurs should not give up too soon: some areas, such as renewable energy, are likely to prove not 'wrong entry' markets but areas where they should be thinking in terms of 'late rewards'.

Gauging the market

Once you have a product or service which you think is going to meet a real market need, the next stage is to come up with a properly targeted marketing strategy.

MARKETS

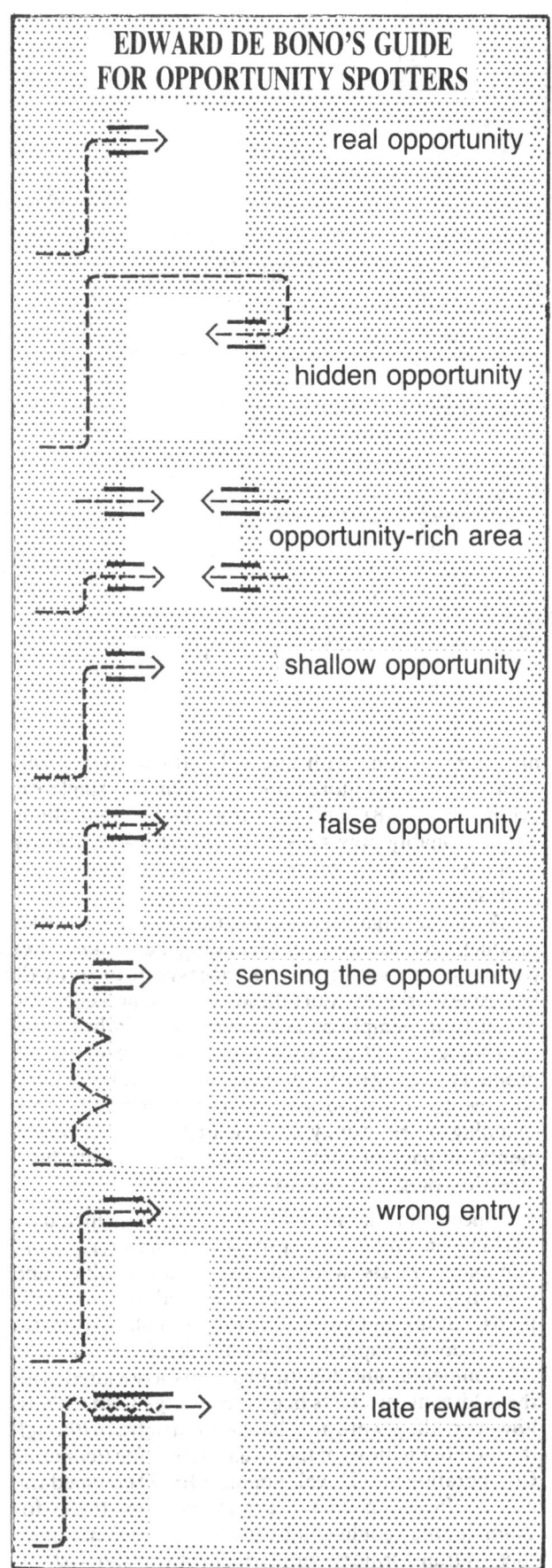

Not long ago, marketing was left to second- or third-rate managers, but the 1980s have seen a radical re-evaluation of the importance of marketing people. 'Their patch takes in market research, sales promotion, advertising, public relations and general management jobs with a marketing bias,' explains Dorothy Venables, a senior consultant with Hoggett Bowers Search and Selection, 'in fact, every discipline that boosts the selling of goods and services.'

The golden rule of market success remains the same: you need a detailed knowledge of what the customer really needs and wants. If you are selling consumer products, perhaps you should be talking to a specialist research company like Taylor Nelson Applied Futures (see page 52). If you operate in the environmental equipment market, on the other hand, you may want to buy a market assessment produced by a company like Frost & Sullivan.

The global market values you will be presented with will often sound impressive. Frost & Sullivan forecast in 1986 that the West European market (in a total of 18 countries) for all the mechanical equipment used in water and waste treatment, worth $1.3 billion in 1985, would reach $1.8 billion by 1995 (in constant 1985 dollars).

Such global figures are of little value on their own, however. You need to know who will want to buy what sort of equipment when – and at what sort of price. In this area, at least, West Germany turns out to be the largest national market, with about a 25% share, followed by France and the UK with fairly equal but lower shares, and then Italy. Taken together, these four countries represent two-thirds of the European market, leaving the remaining third spread across the remaining 14 countries, including Sweden, Norway, Finland, Austria and Switzerland.

But it may be a mistake for a company wanting to move into this area to simply target the biggest market: it may already be sewn up by well-established producers. Another tactic is to look for the national markets whose share of the overall market is likely to grow most rapidly. This might then place the spotlight on such countries as Italy, Spain, Belgium and Greece.

The next stage would be to look at specific technologies and applications which are most likely to produce buoyant demand. Frost & Sullivan, to stick with this particular example, expect rapid growth in demand for equipment for the tertiary processing of liquid effluents, for the chemical filtration of fresh water and for waste sludge dewatering. While public sector demand may tend to come from the need to increase treatment capacity as populations expand and older systems are upgraded, industrial demand is more likely to be driven by such factors as the need for ever-cleaner production processes or the introduction of new effluent controls.

It would also be a mistake, however, to imagine that such markets are ready and waiting to embrace

Market forces brought these tuna to Tokyo . . .

innovative new technologies. Some are, of course, but the water and waste treatment sectors tend to be rather conservative in their approach to innovation, not least because of the political sensitivity of public health and the sheer financial impact of any failure to provide a system which works to increasingly stringent standards.

Since there is no point in biting off more than you can chew, the next stage might be to ask which equipment users are likely to be easiest to sell to – either because you already have a track record with them or because their needs are not unduly sophisticated. As in most areas of business, it is important to start out by picking areas where you have a reasonable chance of succeeding and then build on that success.

Fingers on the pulse

Once you have broken into a market, particularly in the green economy, it is essential to keep a close watch on the way the market is developing. There are a growing number of options here, but it makes sense to subscribe to an information service which regularly monitors the regulations, decisions and other factors likely to have a major market impact.

Many companies, for example, now subscribe to the *ENDS Report* (page 34), to keep their finger on the environmental pulse. Other options include linking up with some of the environmental networks which are now emerging or joining one or more of the relevant environmental organisations.

There is also a growing interest around Europe in a new approach to public relations, in which the process of communicating with internal and external constituencies becomes more important than any single PR event (page 218), and environmental organisations unquestionably now rank high on the list of priority contacts for any self-respecting PR company or professional.

As those organisations zero in on product after product, technology after technology, company after company, it will often be necessary to provide intensive market support. In some cases, however, the product may simply be beyond support. Polychlorinated biphenyls (PCBs) have been a prime example of a product reaching such a point of no return. It is vital to be able to recognise such a transition point, since spending more money on research on the environmental impact of such a product may simply be a diversion of scarce resources.

Once found in all kinds of equipment, including washing machines, aircraft and computers, non-flammable PCBs were also used for cooling and insulating electrical equipment, and as hydraulic fluids, cutting and lubricating oils, and plasticizers (in paint, copying paper and printing ink). Even when the environmental and health problems associated with these 'dream' products began to emerge in the 1960s, however, they were not banned outright. Although the member nations of the Organisation for Economic Co-operation and Development (OECD) banned the use of PCBs in many applications in 1973, for example, they could still be used in 'closed' systems – such as transformers, industrial heat transfer systems and hydraulic equipment in underground mines.

MARKETS

. . . and these smuggled macaques to Belgium.

Less than seven years later, PCB manufacturing had fallen by 60% in the OECD area and its use had practically stopped in 10 out of the 24 OECD member countries. The final stage came in 1987, when the OECD Council imposed a total ban on PCBs. The manufacturing, importing and exporting of PCBs and of any equipment containing or requiring PCBs must cease from 1 January 1989.

In other words, it took 14 years to achieve a total ban on this range of hazardous chemicals. During that time, the producers and suppliers came under increasingly stringent controls and were required to restrict the marketing of their products to a rapidly shrinking number of approved applications.

In hindsight, perhaps it would have been better to go for a total ban much earlier on, but the situation is rarely simple enough to permit such action. Many products – like the chlorofluorocarbons implicated in atmospheric ozone depletion (page 88) – have major advantages which offset, to a greater or lesser extent, their environmental and health implications. Another example of a product which has come under fire from environmentalists is the thermoplastic PVC.

A friendly plastic?

The perfect plastic. That, in a nutshell, was what the environmentalists who attended the European Conference on Plastics in Packaging in 1986 were looking for. Why, they asked, could industry not make do with just one plastic, a plastic which met every need without causing environmental problems in the process?

The answer was not long in coming from the industrialists present: there is no such plastic. Whatever the facts of the matter, however, the environmentalists came to Brussels because they believed (and believe) that plastic packaging causes real environmental problems. From an industrial point of view, this type of environmental challenge is always unwelcome, but particularly so when the product under threat does not enjoy a buoyant market. PVC is one such product and the plastics industry has therefore been worried by the environmental question marks which have clustered around what it sees as one of the most versatile and cost-effective thermoplastics.

Apart from early concerns about the health impact of vinyl chloride monomer, the PVC industry has also had to respond to other issues, including worries about the safety of PVC in fires, the possible contamination of food by plasticizers in PVC clingfilms, and the contribution of PVC packaging to the littering of town and country. The latest concern, however, is not about the behaviour of PVC in normal use, but about its contribution to air pollution problems, caused by hydrogen chloride emissions produced when it is burned in municipal waste incinerators.

The pressures on the industry have been most intense in Switzerland, where the Migros supermarket chain decided to abandon the use of PVC packaging – and to publicise the fact in a major advertising campaign. The company's vice-president, Mr Gugel-

61 →

PERSPECTIVES

The Commercial Environmentalist

Keith Brunt offers some advice on marketing for the supplier of cleaner, quieter or more resource-efficient technology.

KEITH BRUNT *is Manager of the Boots MicroCheck Group at The Boots Company plc. Having worked for Parke Davis, G.D. Searle (including two years for Searle in Zambia) and Samuel Banner & Co, he joined Boots in 1977 to market speciality chemicals.*

He founded the Boots Biocides Group in 1981 to develop new, safe and environmentally acceptable biocides. The products are used to control microbial fouling in industrial processes, air conditioning plant, cooling towers, oil wells and other sensitive areas, bringing major health and energy efficiency benefits. The group, which won a Pollution Abatement Technology Award in 1985, changed its name to Boots MicroCheck in 1987 and is now the fastest growing and most innovative business in microbial detection and control systems in the world.

The Boots Company plc, *Nottingham, NG2 3AA. Tel: 0602 592584.*

'With the growth of intensive farming and with industrial activity accelerating everywhere, public concern about potential hazards and the ensuing legislation are creating a rapidly expanding market for both pollution-prevention systems and environmentally 'soft' industrial processes. Private enterprise is already responding to this challenge and an increasing variety of appropriate products are appearing.

This is fine, just as it should be, but we must not be lulled into thinking that the job stops with basic innovation. It is absolutely essential that the invention and production of 'environmentally suitable systems', which I shall hereafter abbreviate as ESS, are effectively marketed and fully supported. The necessity for such professionalism can be summarised as follows:

- The purchaser of an ESS will often be relatively ignorant of environmental science. If we are to establish our credibility as suppliers of ESS, our potential customers must be confident in our products and recommendations without the need to take expensive independent specialist advice.
- The consequences of using the wrong system in the wrong place may be much worse than using no system at all. Ignorance on the buyer's part, coupled with incompetence, indifference or even dishonesty on the manufacturer's part, will greatly increase the chance of this happening.
- Technical innovation may be copied. Once we have invented and marketed our exciting new ESS, all manner of wily characters will come up out of the woodwork to copy it. We must remember that in many parts of the world patents are held in scant regard. Our only defence against this activity (short of doing physical violence to the miscreants, a practice usually frowned upon by the local authorities) is to ensure that our ESS is more readily available, and easier to use.

Service wards off competition

So there are three aspects of the problem. How do we approach their solution? We have found that the main elements of a successful marketing and support package are:

- A properly planned product launch, timed to take place only after sufficient field trials have been carried out to provide data on product performance in each potential market. Data collection from systems already in commercial use should be

encouraged. This approach should ensure that the product is not sold into the wrong market.
- Where possible, acceptance trials should take place before the final sale is closed. In this way the purchaser will be sure he has bought what he needed, enhancing the vendor's reputation.
- Technical advice and service must be available to purchasers of our products. Good service is a prime way of warding off competition.
- All of the foregoing points necessitate a highly trained and motivated marketing and sales team. It will generally be impossible to meet the objectives laid out above unless all personnel who will have the job of presenting products to the market are: (1) technically competent; (2) properly selected and trained as salesmen; and also, preferably, (3) trained in the necessary marketing functions.

In our experience at Boots MicroCheck, where we develop (and market globally) systems to detect and control industrially troublesome bacteria, we have formed the dual policy of close integration of marketing and technical teams, coupled with a very high level of technical and sales training for the people concerned.

This approach has proved to be highly rewarding and motivating for the sales teams involved, and extremely successful in generating business. Most customers will not buy an ESS simply because it is environmentally acceptable. We are convinced that this sort of highly professional approach is going to be essential for long-term success in this new ESS industry. **'**

---

59 ←

mann, explained that it had taken action not because it was disappointed with PVC as a packaging material, but because there was concern that it might be contributing to 'acid rain' and the destruction of forests. Migros, he said, felt 'obliged to use packaging materials which are friendly to the environment.'

Forced into a voluntary agreement to restrict the use of PVC in the packaging sector in Switzerland, the industry had been looking for ways on ensuring that its own case was heard – hence the Brussels conference. The event helped to disseminate the results of the latest research, which showed that materials like PVC are environmentally acceptable, provided they are used in an environmentally sound way.

According to the results reported in Brussels, the incineration of PVC is not contaminating the environment with dioxin and the resulting emissions are not killing Europe's forests. But materials like PVC remain acutely vulnerable to environmental challenge and the industry must be prepared to react to that challenge. Increasingly, that means meeting environmentalists on their own ground and talking in their own terms.

An alarming wedge

Some companies, like Castrol, have gone a very long way to ensure that environmental concerns do not nibble away at their markets, even relatively small ones. When the Swiss began to complain about oil pollution in the country's lakes, for example, and proceeded to ban large outboard motors on some lakes, the oil companies thought they saw the thin end of an alarming wedge.

Even though research showed that outboards were not the main source of the pollution, Castrol, always loath to lose market share, decided to make its outboard fuels more biodegradable. Because the resulting two-stroke oil was 150% more expensive than a normal can of two-stroke, Castrol also worked out a way of halving the amount of oil needed in two-stroke fuel, making sure its product, Biolube, was price-competitive.

'This isn't just a question of ecology, of a nice warm feeling in your breast,' explained Mike Beggs, the company's engineering manager. 'It's a question of politics. The Swiss police were soon requiring boat owners to have their outboards tested every year. If they produced smoke, they failed. In many cases, the police were telling people that if they used Biolube 100, our oil, they would pass. Obviously that helped us.'

Green boycotts certainly can hurt product sales, but generally involve punishing industry for damage already done. Combined with regulatory pressures outlawing some products and restricting the use of others, however, these boycotts have prodded manufacturers to develop less damaging products – including 'soft' detergents, unleaded petrol, biodegradable plastics, recycled paper products and organically grown foods.

Increasingly, however, it is impossible to ignore the question of how well a product performs in environmental terms. Let's stick with cars and look at the paints which are used in the car industry. 'The key point to remember,' says Dr Brian Letchford, motors director of ICI Paints, 'is that we are selling products in the *world* market. The motor industry is now a world industry, with world standards. We must come up with world products. Around the world, pollution issues are increasingly important for the paints industry, so we have to achieve improved product quality and higher environmental standards simultaneously.'

And that is precisely what ICI managed to do with its 'Aquabase' water-based paints and 'Tempro' water-based protective coatings, which sidestep the need to use potentially polluting solvent-based products. Such market breakthroughs rarely come easily: ICI spent £2 million on these two products between 1980 and 1985, and tested them thoroughly for toxicity

63 →

PERSPECTIVES
The Alternative Traders

From a turnover of less than £500,000 in 1970 to more than £30 million in 1987,
alternative trading organisations are taking off.
Richard Adams explains their approach and potential.

'What's different about alternative trading? This was the question that 50 organisations from all around the world tried to answer at the fifth bi-annual conference of Alternative Trading Organisations (ATOs) held in Berlin in October 1987.

Only eight ATOs were established before 1970 and in that year they had sales of less than £500,000. By 1987 more than fifty ATOs were trading with a turnover exceeding £30 million. The common thread that runs through the ATO group is that they all aim to benefit the poor in developing countries. Most import handmade products and foodstuffs and have education programmes to inform affluent consumers about injustices in world trade.

Consumer power

The ATO movement has grown rapidly, often exploring areas of trading practice that now reflect the concerns of the 'green consumer'. This process has been helped by the growing disillusionment with the ability of conventional aid to the Third World to really make changes. ATOs, albeit in a small way, offer consumers the chance to use their spending power on behalf of the disadvantaged. They also offer a different relationship to the relief and development organisation. Buying from an ATO involves an exchange of money for goods, often for products reflecting the artistic and cultural heritage of a country, but always representing skilled work.

The producers do not feel like objects of charity and they can retain their dignity whilst developing their skills and earning a living. The purchasers are not providing a 'hand-out' but buying something they want; the transaction puts the coffee farmer in Tanzania or the basket maker in the Philippines, in the same category as the smallholder growing carrots in Cambridge or the car assembly worker in Cowley.

500,000 catalogues a year

All ATOs work hard at ensuring they only deal with producers who are working in reasonable conditions, get good pay for the locality and have some share in their organisation and participate in its decision making processes. Such groups are not easy to find and need encouragement and support if they are to make their way in an increasingly competitive world.

Many ATOs recognise that justice in trade also has to start at home. Shared ownership, participative management, progressive personnel policies and openness and accountability are features that also have to be reflected in the ATOs themselves. In Britain, Traidcraft is probably the best known ATO and the only one which is a public company. More than 3,000 individual shareholders join with a linked charitable Trust to provide capital and ensure accountability. More than 500,000 mail order catalogues are distributed each year offering a very wide range of products including foodstuffs, crafts, clothing, furniture, recycled paper, toys and carpets. 150 people work at Traidcraft's Gateshead headquarters. Bringing work to one of the country's unemployment blackspots has paralleled providing jobs for more than 3,500 people in the Third World.'

RICHARD ADAMS *is Managing Director of Traidcraft plc. Prior to founding Traidcraft in 1979 he was an Industrial Development Officer in the North East of England, and then in Scotland. He started a vegetable importing business for products from the Third World in 1973, subsequently founding Tearcraft Ltd in 1975. He was Managing Director of Tearcraft for four years. His qualifications include a Master's Degree in Business Administration.*

Traidcraft plc, *Kingsway, Gateshead, Tyne & Wear NE11 0NE. Tel: 091-487 3191.*

and ecological effects to ensure that they were environmentally acceptable. The UK car industry has not been easy to win over to the new approach, however, which perhaps suggests the need for carefully focused environmental campaigns designed to encourage such industries to adopt 'clean technologies'.

The interesting spin-off benefit for the environment is that the logical next step for a company like ICI or Castrol is to advertise the environmental acceptability of their new products – putting pressure on their competitors to play 'catch-up'.

The green consumer

The next logical step for business is to ask the question: 'Is there such a thing as the Green Consumer – and, if so, how can we target Green Consumers in our advertising and other forms of product promotion?'

Various indicators do indeed suggest that the 1990s could be the decade of the green consumer. A number of environmental organisations are now beginning to think about how 'consumer power' might be effectively harnessed to the twin causes of environmental conservation and sustainable development. Several books have appeared in this area (see page 214) and more are in the pipeline.

The signs are that the ground could be surprisingly fertile for initiatives such as Friends of the Earth's *Good Wood Guide,* designed to enable consumers to switch to tropical hardwoods grown in plantations managed with sustainability in mind (page 64). When the Consumers' Association surveyed readers of *Which?*, for example, 90% said that they were concerned about environmental pollution.

According to surveys carried out by Taylor Nelson Applied Futures, over a third (36%) of Britons now subscribe to attitudes which make them potential green consumers – and the firm reports that they are the fastest growing group in the population (page 52).

Marketing experts like Dorothy Venables recognise that ever-increasing quantities of brain power are needed in marketing generally, 'because markets have become more complex and more segmented. For example, consumers are increasingly being classified into narrower bands of income level, age, lifestyle and buying behaviour. And all kinds of companies are making gains by identifying these segments of the market more accurately, and then targeting swiftly to meet their needs.'

Anita Roddick's Body Shop, in fact, was an early business concept targeted almost entirely on environmentally-concerned consumers. The company, which has consciously steered away from animal toxicity testing and profligate packaging, has associated itself closely with campaigns by groups like Greenpeace and Friends of the Earth, in the belief that these links will not only help the environment but will also help shift 'green' products.

The challenge for the emerging generation of green entrepreneurs is to carry their philosophy deep into the heart of the high street – and thence into the City and other bastions of traditional business thinking.

'We can't see any distinction between commercial advantage and being a concerned business,' as the Body Shop's head of environmental projects, Nicola Lyon, put it. 'But what we are trying to do is to steer ourselves away from the "cranky fringe". In the early days, I am quite sure that there were people who wouldn't have shopped at the Body Shop because they felt it belonged only to people who ate lentils, lived in North London and read the *Guardian.* Increasingly, however, we are moving into the mainstream.

Real dividends

At first these products were developed either by small, poorly funded companies or by larger firms which were essentially backing into the green marketplace as they were forced to abandon environmentally unacceptable product lines. There have been an increasing number of cases, however, where industry has worked with environmental interests to ensure that a particular product is acceptable, is manufactured and is used.

In Britain, for example, the Nature Conservancy Council (NCC) and the Royal Society for the Protection of Birds (RSPB) have worked closely with firms which produce non-toxic alternatives to the lead shot and fishing weights which have poisoned so many swans and other wildfowl. When the NCC convened a committee to work out ways of speeding the introduction of alternatives, it attracted support from such companies as Anglers Snapshot, Dynacast, Johnson-Matthey Metals, Lammiman Fishing Products, Plansee Metals, Saturn Shot and Thamesly Fishing Tackle.

This example illustrates a number of the alternative strategies available when a product comes under fire. The Lead Development Association wanted to keep this outlet for lead open and therefore looked at ways in which it might organise the collection of surplus lead weights for safe disposal. The problem was that the minimum quantity which it would be worth collecting was thought to be of the order of one tonne! Thamesly Fishing Tackle also came up with a plastic, non-spill container designed to stop accidental loss of lead weights. In the end, however, the best solution will probably be for anglers to switch to the non-toxic alternatives made by such companies as Anglers Snapshot, Saturn Shot or Thamesly.

Participation in such exercises can pay real dividends for companies making more environmentally acceptable products. The *Daily Mirror,* for example, became so enthused with the idea of getting

PERSPECTIVES

The Good Wood Guide

There is growing interest in the potential impact of the ethical, conscious or Green consumer. Charles Secrett explains the background to Friends of the Earth's Good Wood Guide, *designed to bring consumer power to bear on the problem of tropical deforestation.*

'For environmentalists concerned about problems as serious, and as far away, as tropical deforestation, using community purchasing power on an international scale is one potentially powerful way of directly affecting what goes on in the rainforests themselves.

This conviction underpins Friends of the Earth's newly launched *Good Wood Guide* campaign. The campaign's purpose is to persuade the tropical timber trade in both consumer and producer countries to manage tropical forests on a sustainable, ecologically sound basis. This means logging forests without destroying them – something that, believe it or not, is almost unheard of in the tropics. On top of lobbying political and industrial leaders, we are trying to generate market forces strong enough to change production methods through consumer demand for the 'right' sort of tropical hardwood products.

The *Good Wood Guide* lists all those retailers and manufacturers who sell the 'right' sort of product, namely, sustainably produced tropical woods. It will also list architects, local authorities and interior design companies who have made conscious decisions not to use tropical woods unless they are sustainably produced.

Creating a market gap

It is important to remember that the High Street shopper is the most visible but not the only consumer – every trade link in the buying chain from forest tree to finished product purchases something. All of them are influential. Our aim is to persuade as many traders as possible at every stage to buy with environmental priorities in mind. The *Guide* is our way of directly involving the first tier of trade consumers in ethical decision-making. Thus, by creating a strong demand for sustainable woods, we expect suppliers to fill the market gap as news of what is wanted filters down the chain. Publicity, direct appeal and economic sense, we hope, make our arguments for change convincing.

Our 220 local groups, who helped to compile all the campaign information, nominate candidates for inclusion in the *Guide* on a yearly basis, according to a simple set of criteria. These include pressing suppliers for sustainable woods until they arrive, stopping selling non-sustainably produced tropical woods, lobbying their trade representatives to support reforestation efforts in producer countries and so on.

Every approach to stores or other procurers is done by letter with a colourful explanatory leaflet, and then by a personal follow-up. Each successful applicant receives a 'Seal of Approval' to display for one year, including a framed wall charter, window stickers and labels for individual products. The World Wildlife Fund (WWF) have very generously given us a grant to ensure the highest quality design and production of the *Guide* and Seals.

Accompanying the *Guide* is another booklet, the Tropical Hardwood Product List (for want of a better name!), which identifies those retailers, from DIY to Department stores, by name and address, who sell tropical woods that come from forests severely degraded by logging. If you like, these are the 'baddies', the outlets that the conscious shopper could avoid.

Regularly updated

To help people make an informed choice, the List also catalogues the tropical wood products on sale by item and brand name, as well as by type of wood. There is information about suitable and unsuitable logging methods, origin of the wood, the role of the timber trade in tropical deforestation, and solutions for the future (material also contained in the trade leaflet). And it provides information about alternative temperate woods and wood products. Both the *Guide* and the List are regularly updated and are used by Friends of the Earth local groups and central office to advertise the respective merits of each group of retailer/procurers as widely as possible.

We believe that this approach works. It certainly has in other similar campaigns that we have run, although they had a simpler message – BOYCOTT! A crucial element of the hardwood campaign is that we are *not* trying to stop the trade in tropical hardwoods. Tropical governments need the revenue too badly and, in any case, unless the forests earn revenue as forests they will simply be cleared for some other purpose.

Many of the companies and individuals whom we have approached, and explained the problems of deforestation to, are sympathetic. Our local groups also report an enthusiastic response from shoppers. Although the campaign has only been running for a few months, a recent national opinion poll, conducted

MARKETS

by MORI (page 22), showed that 25% of the population would stop buying tropical hardwood products unless they came from protected forests.

Code of conduct

The National Association of Retail Furnishers have formally endorsed the *Good Wood Guide*, and the Timber Trade Federation have approved in principle a Code of Conduct drawn up by FOE that would ensure all tropical hardwood imports came from sustainable, ecologically sound sources.

The trade are interested because they are beginning to realise that unless something is done to protect the forests, they are going to be out of business in a few years' time. According to the World Bank (hardly an environmentalist group), the thirty or so major exporting nations of tropical woods will be reduced to under ten, and the value of the trade will shrink from $7.5 billion to less than $2 billion, within a decade because of over-exploitation by loggers.

Commercial loggers work over five million hectares of tropical forests every year, and are the second largest cause of destruction. If they get their house in order, not only will they save their business, but they would go a long way to saving the forests too.

Although Britain is the third or fourth largest consumer of tropical woods (for plywood, household and office furniture, sawn timber, panels, joinery etc), a campaign like this has to be run on a global basis. Japan is the biggest consumer of tropical woods by far, and the US and EEC are the other main markets. Action by Britain to encourage trade in sustainably produced woods has to be followed up abroad. FOE campaigns are now gearing up in these countries.

The ITTO

Tracing sustainable supplies and checking logging operations, agreeing international standards and labelling systems, and involving Customs can only be done properly by governments co-operating with one

66 →

another. One of the main efforts of groups like FOE and WWF has been to encourage the setting up of the International Tropical Timber Organisation (ITTO) with the active participation of the producer and consumer countries. A principal aim of the ITTO is to conserve and sustainably use tropical forests. It would be the ideal body to run this scheme, and monitor the trade by a licensing system.

The 80-plus nations which support the Convention on International Trade in Endangered Species (CITES) already implement a more complicated version to regulate the much larger trade in wild animal products. If governments can do this for animals, plants, birds, insects and reptiles numbering many thousands, and distinguish between banned, licensed, ranched or farmed and freely traded goods of these species, they can surely do it for trees.

Consumer campaigning was crucial in persuading governments and industries using whale products in a wide variety of goods to stop doing so. That campaign ended up with an EEC Trade Directive banning the sale of all such goods. The tropical hardwood campaign is more subtle. It involves much more sophisticated information, and depends upon a truly discerning response from the consumer. The *Guide* and the Seal of Approval should enable them to make the right consumer choices. Until individuals become committed at this level, the prospects for tropical forests will remain bleak.

CHARLES SECRETT *has worked at Friends of the Earth for eight years. He ran FOE's Wildlife and Countryside campaigns for several years, before initiating and launching the FOE International Rainforest Campaign in 1985. One of his principal concerns has been to involve individuals at every level of environmental campaigning, and to design campaign tactics around community action. He has been responsible for developing the tropical hardwood consumer campaign, based around the* Good Wood Guide *(Friends of the Earth, 1987). He has written extensively on environmental issues – and is author of* Rainforest: Protecting the Planet's Richest Resource.
Friends of the Earth, *26-28 Underwood Street, London N1. Tel: 01 490 1555.*

ALTERNATIVE TRADING: Putting People Before Profit

CUT OUT THE MIDDLE PERSON!

Traidcraft deals directly, in more than 30 countries, with producers of crafts, clothing, tea and coffee, recycled paper and food products.

Traidcraft also offers to organisations, overseas and in the UK, design and development facilities for products and literature and has a substantial contract sales section offering a complete merchandising service for socially concerned organisations.

For further information about Traidcraft's products and services please write to:

 Traidcraft plc Kingsway
Gateshead Tyne & Wear NE11 0NE
Telephone 091 487 3191

MARKETS

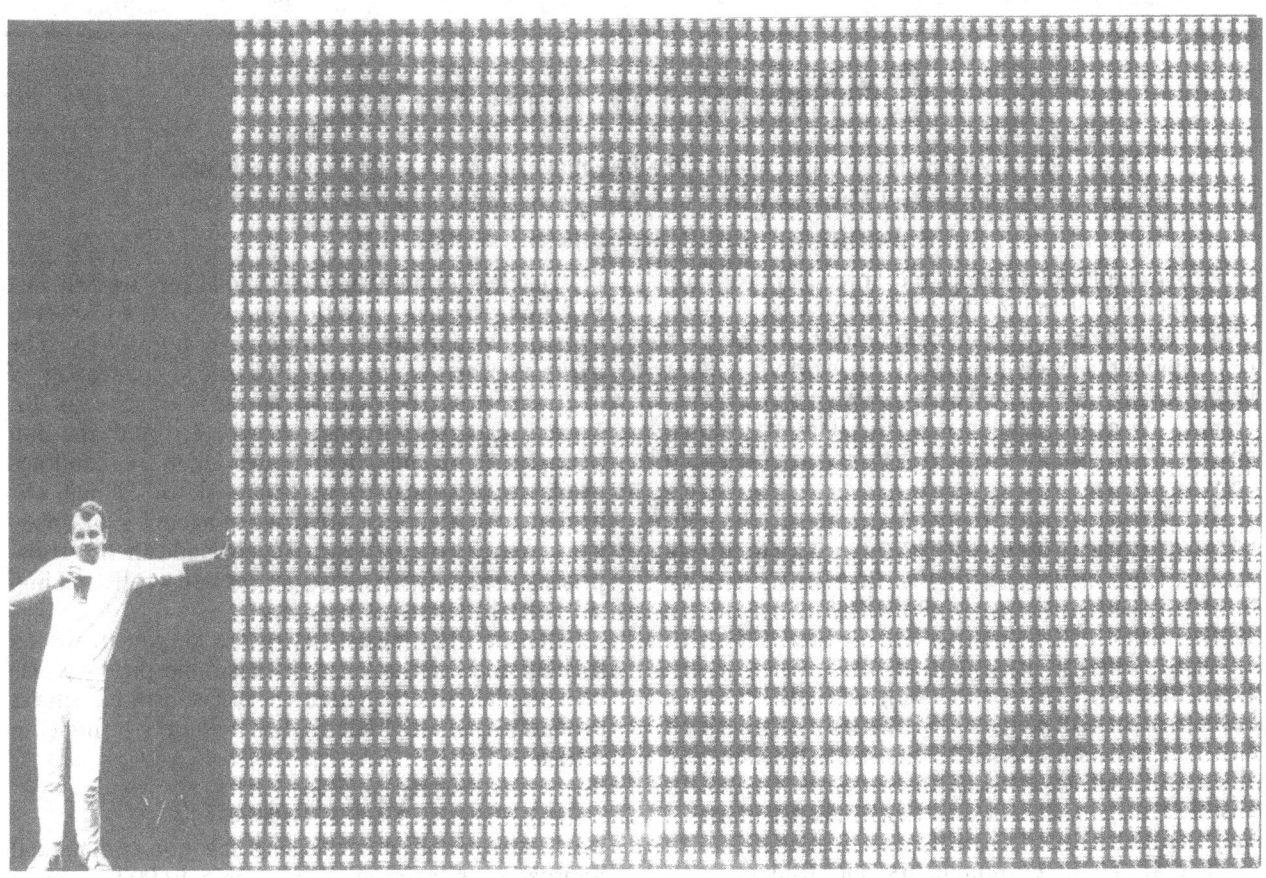

A lifetime's supply of baked beans (2,000 cans for the average Briton) hints at the potential impact of greener consumption patterns.

anglers to switch to the alternatives that it set up a series of angling competitions, with a final held at Longleat. All the events were fished with the non-toxic alternatives. The top prize was worth £5,000, with the other prizes worth a total of £20,000. This level of prize money, a quarter of which was contributed by the NCC, ensured the sort of publicity which such small companies can rarely – if ever – afford.

It is perhaps worth pointing out that many products, perhaps most, are greened without the consumer ever being aware of the fact. Legislation imposes new standards which all new models or product generations have to meet. And industry tends to be happier that way. Car manufacturers, for example, would prefer it if people did not choose their next car on the basis of its pollution output per mile: they want to talk about horsepower, styling, colour and optional extras.

Baby boomers

But will green consumers be significant outside niche markets? There are those who would probably advise caution. According to a market forecast prepared by John Naisbitt, whose book *Megatrends* sold over seven million copies and was translated into 22 languages, one of the most far-reaching changes in lifestyle in the impending (and long-heralded) Leisure Age will be the emergence of the 'global lifestyle.' Prepared for McCann-Erickson Advertising in 1986, the Naisbitt leisure futures report forecast that the 'New Wave' generation, aged 21 and under, will spurn the liberal, permissive attitudes of the 1960s in favour of a new conservatism that is pro-technology, environmentally unconcerned and less worried about health and fitness. The main concern, Naisbitt concluded, would be employment.

But at the same time there is an underlying demographic trend which means that those in their teens and 20s will no longer rank as the biggest spenders either in Europe or North America. The lower birth rates of the 1960s and 1970s, coupled with the unemployment of the 1980s, mean that the New Wave generation will be overshadowed by the 'baby boomers', born in the 1940s and early 1950s. Exactly those who were most influenced by the Environmental Revolution of the 1960s and 1970s.

It is also worth noting that one of the 'megatrends' identified by Naisbitt himself was the growing shift from short term to longer term thinking in industry. This trend, he noted, has been accelerated by the debate over the environment and non-renewable resources. The scene is set, in short, for the entry of the Green Consumer. Begin your opportunity searches. □

PERSPECTIVES
Coming to the Boil

Many Third World stoves waste most of the fuel they use. More appropriate technologies are available, as *Paul Harrison* points out, but green products like fuel-efficient stoves and contraceptives also need appropriate marketing.

'Attempts to develop and spread appropriate technology in the Third World have so far been overwhelmingly non-commercial. Usually, a development agency like UNICEF works together with a small number of villages to design a new stove, granary or grain grinder – or to adapt traditional designs. And usually such innovations do not spread very far.

In a few cases, some system of dissemination might be set up – perhaps a voluntary group with nationwide membership, or the government network of agricultural extension workers. Often the technology fails to spread because consumer testing was not thorough enough. Many projects to introduce fuel-efficient stoves foundered because cooking pots failed to fit, or because nights are cold and the new stove does not let any heat out. Sometimes dissemination is artificially aided with a subsidy, which induces people to adopt an unsatisfactory product which they would not accept if they had to pay the full cost.

Yet all along entrepreneurs and traders were spreading new and often quite appropriate technologies. To do so, they used a distribution network that was already in place, reached out to the most remote villages, and needed no extra government employees or expenditure: in short, the market. They were charging the full cost and making their own profits too.

Riding the market

The bicycle is a perfect example of a 'green' resource-saving and labour-saving technology spread purely by the market. Others include the kerosene lamp and the steel hand maize-grinder.

The development agencies, however, are only just beginning to wake up to the potential of the market to spread environmentally appropriate technology. The earliest efforts came with the social marketing of contraceptives. Population Services Europe, in Sri Lanka, Bangladesh and elsewhere, used the full panoply of business techniques to make condoms available in almost every village shop. Though the dealers, shopkeepers, advertising agencies and market research companies involved made their normal profits, the main organisation was non-profit making, subsidised by outside funding.

Recently the idea of using the market to spread socially and environmentally desirable products has been applied to other spheres. It has inspired what is probably the most successful stove programme in Africa so far.

Ask the consumer

Most stove programmes using the non-commercial approach can claim no more than 5-10,000 stoves in use in African homes. Kenya's improved charcoal stove programme set out an equally modest goal, yet within three years of its launch it had created a new industry which had sold 250,000 fuel-saving stoves – at a profit.

Managed by Energy Development International (EDI) on behalf of the US Agency for International Development, the project did not, unlike so many others, set out to design a new stove from scratch. Instead, it aimed to provide an alternative to the 'jiko', a cheap, short-lived little stove, made of scrap metal, which wastes 81% of its heat.

The final design was perfected after consumer testing in 600 households across Kenya. Basically, the traditional cylindrical jiko was given a waisted shape, and the top half was lined with an insulating ceramic inset to reduce heat loss. The base of this inset was pierced with holes to make a built-in grate. The new stove lights faster, uses 30-50% less charcoal, cooks faster and lasts longer than the old jiko. Now that production is in volume, the new stove costs only 12% more than the old. At prevailing charcoal prices, it pays for itself within one month in Nairobi, and in less than three months elsewhere.

An irresistible investment

Such a return on investment is virtually irresistible, so it is scarcely surprising that virtually everyone who can afford the slightly higher price of the new stove buys it instead of the old jiko.

Having picked a winning design, the choice of dissemination method was equally crucial to the project's success. Instead of setting up their own separate distribution network, EDI decided to use the existing network of metal artisans, dealers and stallholders who were making and selling the old jiko. The artisans were trained to make the cladding out of scrap metal, and pottery firms were trained to make the ceramic liners and loaned start-up capital. Once started, the programme soon became totally self-financing. The original USAID project is now over, but the new stove is continuing under its own steam, making no demands on government or aid budgets.

Marketing, whether fully commercial or 'social', cannot solve all environmental problems in developing countries. It is probably not the best channel for spreading new techniques of farming that do not involve any purchased inputs – such as agroforestry, windbreaks or terracing for soil conservation. Nor can it go very far in the poorest areas or countries where people have no spare cash to spend and where markets are rudimentary.

That still leaves many fields where commercial approaches could achieve rapid results, however. Nitrogenous fertilisers, for example, are little used in sub-Saharan Africa, not only because farmers are short of cash, but also because their effect in increased production often does not cover their cost, especially in drier areas. But phosphate fertilisers produce a massive yield increase for a small outlay, especially in the drier parts of Africa. Farmers in Niger who tested them for a research centre on a small part of their farms were so impressed by the results that they got a local trader to supply them. Within three years they were using them on 60% of their land.

Forget the plough

Low cost farm equipment for minimum-tillage or no-plough farming is another area where marketing could achieve rapid results. Research at the International Institute for Tropical Agriculture at Ibadan, Nigeria, has shown that many African soils erode even more rapidly than normal if ploughed. Minimum tillage, which involves killing weeds and stubble with herbicide and planting the crop through the killed sod, cuts erosion by 99% and raises long term yields by 100-200%. There is a huge potential market here for low cost sprays, planters and herbicides.

Biogas is another obvious field where a commercial approach could pay off. Digesters costing as little as $20-$50, made of PVC or polythene, would be far more attractive to farmers than the costly models being promoted by national programmes such as India's.

Another big potential market is in labour-saving devices for women, from maize or cassava grinders to tanks for collecting rainwater from tin roofs.

These are areas, it seems to me, where private companies, Western or Third World, could gain not only opportunities for modest direct profits, but perhaps more importantly, political openings, public goodwill, market experience and market presence. At the same time they would be helping to conserve the often fragile tropical environment and spreading appropriate technologies faster and with far less cost to aid and government budgets than can the conventional non-commercial approaches. Any volunteers for a trust to test out the potential?

PAUL HARRISON *is a freelance writer and consultant on development who has worked for the World Bank, the Food and Agriculture Organisation, the International Planned Parenthood Federation and others. He has masters degrees from Cambridge and the London School of Economics. His books include* Inside the Third World, The Third World Tomorrow *(Penguins) and* The Greening of Africa *(Paladin).*

PERSPECTIVES

The Beauty of Green

With 88 shops in the UK and 180 overseas, the Body Shop has emerged as the leading 'green' company in Europe. *Anita Roddick* explains the philosophy which has underpinned the company's phenomenal success.

'Green Marketing' is a fashionable phrase at the moment, but it's nothing new in The Body Shop. Right from the beginning we have taken a strong and consistent attitude towards the environment which shines through in everything the company does. The shops have always attracted customers who are well-informed and environmentally aware. They have always bought, and will continue to buy, Body Shop products because they want natural biodegradable cosmetics, manufactured without cruelty to animals and minimally packaged. They want our refill service which saves them money and enables them to reuse bottles.

But those customers alone could not account for the company's rapid growth from one shop in 1976 to our international network of over 270 in 1987. In High Streets all around the world other customers, particularly the young, are drawn into Body Shops because they are vibrant exciting places, always full of colour and new ideas. Many of these customers have never read an environmental magazine or joined an environmental organisation. Yet we do not sacrifice our own strong environmental conscience to the need to reach this other market. Instead we educate those new customers to our own way of thinking. Clear labelling and our Product Information Files tell shoppers all about our raw ingredients. All our staff are trained to answer questions. Some of our shops have huge lighted information boards with changing displays, and we use our windows to inform the public not just about our products, but about the philosophy behind them.

We don't duck the issues either. We are producing a range of free information leaflets on such subjects as animal testing in the cosmetic industry, recycling, and acid rain. We also join with environmental organisations like Greenpeace and Friends of the Earth, in joint projects that give them a presence on the High Street and access to new markets.

We also tell the customers that it's not just the products: the company is 'green' through and through. We pack their goods in biodestructible plastic bags. We use only recycled paper and card. We've set up an office waste-paper retrieval scheme. One way and another, customers leave the shops with our message ringing in their ears. And they come back for more. All the time they are asking questions, and they know that from us they will get clear honest information as well as environmentally benign products.

Strong selling point

This approach to green marketing works all over Europe. Different aspects appeal in different countries. For example, in Belgium people expect and value honesty and information in retailing, and The Body Shop fulfills this need. In The Netherlands, a nation of animal-lovers, customers can use our products with a clear conscience. The Germans are becoming more and more aware of environmental

MARKETS

issues in general, and find shopping in Body Shops entirely consistent with this concern. They feel they can apply their green principles in a practical way without the need to be 'cranky'.

The West German government has recently passed legislation against the use of animal testing for cosmetic purposes. The Body Shop has always fulfilled those conditions voluntarily. In Austria, one of Europe's most beautiful countries, The Body Shop's responsible approach to the natural world is a strong selling point. We're now trading in 22 European countries, and there's no doubt that the Body Shop idea works from the Mediterranean to the Arctic Circle. In each country sales are rising because, to quote one of our German franchisees, 'The Body Shop is like a green oasis in a chemical desert'.

In 1987 the world is at a crucial stage in the attempt to develop a more concerned attitude to our environmental problems. Awareness is growing, but commitment is still fragile. Companies dedicated to better environmental practice must produce the whole package. It's not enough just to put a green product on the shelf. Consumers today want style and they want good presentation. Above all they want to be fully and honestly informed. Get all this right, and you are not just selling an environmentally-benign product, you are marketing the whole green idea.

ANITA RODDICK *is Managing Director of The Body Shop International plc. Founded in 1976, offering 15 products in simple plastic bottles with labels hand-written by Anita, the original shop in Brighton has since expanded into a group of 88 shops in the UK and 180 shops overseas. It operates in 28 countries and will be building up its US operations from 1988. The Body Shop went public in 1984 and has since consistently impressed the City with its financial performance. In 1986–87 its turnover was £17.4 million, with profits of £7.9 million.* **The Body Shop International plc, Dominion Way, Rustington, West Sussex BN16 3LR. Tel: 0903 717107.**

The Green Consumer Guide

Consumer power has scored some notable successes. A new initiative aims to provide the information needed by the Green Consumer.

The news that McDonald's planned to abandon the use of chlorofluorocarbons (CFCs) in fast-food cartons was one of the environmental milestones of 1987. The threat that consumers might boycott Big Macs because of the contribution of CFCs to ozone destruction in the upper atmosphere (page 88) was a deciding factor in the company's decision. Competitors like Wimpy Restaurants promptly started talking to their carton suppliers, explaining: 'We don't want to be left behind.'

McDonald's are probably not out of the woods yet, however. Various environmental groups are focusing on the 'hamburger connection', whereby tropical forests are cleared to provide land for unsustainable ranching – with much of the meat produced going to hamburger chains in the North.

Whether the target is deforestation or aerosol propellants, there is now strong support in the environmental movement for more product boycotts, as the *Green Pages* survey shows (page 14). But boycotts alone are unlikely to be sufficient. Groups like Friends of the Earth are now developing more sophisticated initiatives, like the *Good Wood Guide (page 64)*.

On a broader front, *The Green Consumer Guide*, pulls together information on a wide variety of products which are environmentally unsound or sound.

The aim of the 1988 edition of the Guide is not to be totally comprehensive, but to look at what consumers can do to cut down their contributions to priority environmental problems. The plan is that future editions will broaden the range of products covered.

Rather than trying to promote a 'hair-shirt' lifestyle, the *Guide* is pitched at a 'sandals to Saabs' spectrum of consumers. The information provided is designed to ensure that whatever lifestyles people choose to adopt they know where to find attractive, cost-competitive products and services which are environmentally acceptable and – as far as possible – a pleasure to use.

Compiled by John Elkington and Julia Hailes of SustainAbility, *The Green Consumer Guide* is published by Victor Gollancz, 14 Henrietta Street, London, WC2E 8QJ.

SECTION 2

Designs with a Future

'Any colour, so long as it's black,' was Henry Ford's answer to a pressing design question of the day. In today's world, however, green is increasingly the colour which sells products in Europe.

Even in our shrinking world, the main limits to economic growth are not energy shortages nor are they raw material shortages. They are shortages of imagination, innovation and enterprise. Happily, however, there are growing signs of a renaissance in design throughout Europe, with many industrial clients now acutely aware that they need products designed for the environment-conscious world of the 1990s and beyond.

Consider Italy. One of the fastest growing Italian companies has been the Feruzzi Group, which operates in the agricultural sector. Its chairman, Raul Gardini, lists the development of environmentally acceptable technologies as one of the group's top priorities.

Europe, says Gardini, must create new horizons for its people. 'We have our houses, cars, comforts. Now we must begin to think of the environment. In Paris, in Rome, Venice and London, almost everywhere, you can detect the need felt for making the world beautiful again, as it was 30 years ago.' And the interesting conclusion to be drawn from recent developments in the field of environmental design is that we now have the skills, the materials and, potentially, the political will to design a future which is both economically and ecologically viable.

Useful fiction

Two products which neatly encapsulate these trends are the EcoSphere and Biosphere II, described on pages 76–77. Indeed, a pair of EcoSpheres occupied pride of place when Britain's Design Council launched 'The Green Designer' exhibition as its contribution to Industry Year 1986.

The 'green designer', however, is no more than a useful fiction. Even in today's environment-conscious markets, very few designers earn their living solely by designing environmentally acceptable products. Too often, too, we tend to talk of the 'designer', in the singular, when we are really talking about an interdisciplinary team. But, as the exhibition demonstrated, the progressive greening of the world of design is no fiction.

Industrial and engineering designers are increasingly finding that the environmental performance of their products and technologies counts. Indeed, in a growing number of businesses it is proving to be a case of make or break. Many of the companies whose products and technologies were spotlighted by the Design Council had learned the importance of environmental excellence the hard way, when earlier products ran headlong into environmental road blocks.

Even so, at a time when the importance of design is increasingly recognised, it is easy to forget how earlier generations of environmentally unacceptable products helped fuel the 'anti-design' movement of the late 1960s and early 1970s. Just a few short years ago, in the opening stages of what Max Nicholson (page 162) dubbed the 'Environmental Revolution', environmentalists saw design – and designers – as the enemy.

The aim of the green designer is to do more with less. In a world where the environmental performance of a technology or product can be a question of make of break, the designer has a key role to play in the pursuit of sustainability. Keith Grant, Director of the Design Council, argues the case for green design on page 80.

The design profession was accused of being obsessed with styling and surface decoration, concentrating on what a product looked like rather than on what it was meant to do – or on any unintended side-effects. Frequently, it must be said, these accusations by environmentalists were justified, not least because industry saw designers as the people who were drafted in at the eleventh hour to discuss packaging and presentation.

Essentially, the designer's job was – and still is – to help sell the client's products. What designers and their clients often failed to consider, however, was the impact of successful products when in widespread use. One car, one aerosol, one squeeze-pack of washing-up liquid: none of these could be described as a threat to the environment. But when millions of them turned up on the roads or in the kitchen, they often proved to have totally unforeseen consequences. Photochemical

DESIGN

Big noises in green design: Rolls-Royce's ultra-quiet engines and (inset) British Aerospace's 'Quiet Trader' aircraft.

smog shrouded major cities like Los Angeles and Tokyo, while London's sewage works disappeared under mountains of foam.

What's appropriate?

Throughout the 1960s, growing concerns about the environment resulted in many young people rejecting technology out of hand. By the early 1970s, indeed, many of the fundamental assumptions of design were being challenged even by professional designers. Addressing the Royal Society of Arts in 1970, Michael Tree of the Council of Industrial Design – which became the Design Council in 1972 – contrasted the extreme efficiency of many products with their extreme inefficiency in terms of their social or environmental effects.

'We praise and admire a well-designed product,' he noted, 'and then discover that the manufacturer's packaging or his servicing arrangements fall sadly below its high standard. We welcome the introduction of mechanical safety factors into the manufacture of modern cars and then lament the pollution coming from their exhausts.'

But while some attempted to turn their backs on technology, others consciously set out to develop what they variously called 'alternative', 'appropriate', 'intermediate' or 'soft' technologies. Their bible was E.F. Schumacher's book *Small is Beautiful* and the world was soon dotted with communes sporting windmills, solar roofs and biogas digesters. Most, sadly, were not a technical success. But the work of pioneers like the Intermediate Technology Develop-

74→

ment Group (ITDG), established by Dr Schumacher, has produced some remarkably successful technologies, particularly for use in less developed countries.

Most of the Third World's population, for example, depends on fuelwood as its main source of energy for cooking and heating (page 68). More than a billion people are already facing hardship because of growing fuelwood shortages. For many, in fact, the fuelwood crisis is over: they cannot get any. One answer, of course, is to plant more trees, but, while important, this is clearly a long-term solution. To produce more immediate benefits, ITDG started work on improved stove designs for use in the Third World.

Working with countries like Sri Lanka, Nepal and Indonesia, ITDG has produced a range of stoves which are safer, cleaner and more fuel efficient. They also cut the cooking time required. Many tens of thousands of these new stoves, which are simple enough to be made by local skilled artisans, are now in use, helping to slow the pace of deforestation – which many scientists rank as the world's most pressing environmental problem.

Most designers, however, did not begin to think about the environmental implications of the products they were working on because they were enthusiastic disciples of Schumacher's. They did so because they were required to do so by law.

Once they started looking at the environmental dimensions of their brief, however, the pace of innovation accelerated. Soon there was talk of 'non-waste' or 'low-waste' technologies, then of 'clean' or 'cleaner' technologies. Studies carried out around Europe showed that many of these processes were economically viable and attention switched to ensuring that they were adopted by industry (page 113).

Brand X or brand Y?

The green designer, meanwhile, has an increasingly important role to play in the transition to more

Solution on a Stick

One of Europe's largest chemical companies, ICI also stands out as the only company to have won more than one Pollution Abatement Technology Award. To date it has won three. Of these, the award for the Electrodyn sprayer most elegantly demonstrates the way the company constantly tries to 'do more with less.'

Although most environmentalists would rather see crops which were grown organically, perhaps even being genetically engineered to resist pests and disease (page 183), pesticides are often necessary. But the sprayer, developed by ICI's Plant Protection Division, dramatically cuts the amount of pesticide needed to defend crops.

The Electrodyn consists of a 'stick' to which is attached a 'Bozzle', a combination bottle and nozzle, which contains ready-to-use, specially formulated pesticide. The Bozzle generates electrically-charged droplets of pesticide solution. These wrap around the crop target, ensuring all-round, relatively rainfast coverage of leaves and stems. Virtually all the spray is deposited on the target plants, while the fact that the drops are mutually repellent ensures a uniform coating.

The system enables a farmer to treat a hectare of crops with one litre of pesticide, or less, compared to the 200–400 litres needed when using conventional spraying

systems. And because the farmer does not need to measure out the pesticide and dilute it, he is less likely to make errors.

The Electrodyn sprayer is also unusual in that it has been tailor-made for hand spraying of pesticides in the tropics. It is not something adapted from an invention originally intended for European or American agriculture. The spray stick has no moving parts to wear out or break down, which means that it should give trouble-free service season after season.

Used with improved varieties of cowpea, the Electrodyn can multiply food output ten-fold even in the semi-arid regions of Africa which have been hit so hard by drought and famine.

The entire system is astonishingly light, at 2.5 kilograms, and because one 750 ml Bozzle will typically treat up to 1.5 hectares, which can take four hours to cover, the operator can readily carry enough spray for an entire working day. The Electrodyn, says its inventor, Dr Ron Coffee, 'is a highly appropriate technology, with the potential to help transform food production levels in many developing countries.'

sustainable forms of economic development. A growing number of mainstream industrial products are having to be designed (or redesigned) to meet new environmental standards. Industry's markets are changing and many consumers are becoming more discerning about the environmental performance of particular types of product.

The 'green consumer' – who switches from brand X to brand Y because brand X may be a risk to the environment, or, even more ominous, stops buying this type of product altogether, regardless of brand – is a threat that business can no longer afford to ignore (page 56).

The number of industrial products that have lost market share or have been removed from the shelves completely because of the pollution they caused – or were suspected of having caused – is legion. 'Hard' detergents had to be replaced with 'soft', biodegradable detergents. Aerosol sales fell when chlorofluorocarbon propellants were found to be eroding the planet's vital ozone layer, high in the atmosphere. Some of the noisier passenger aircraft have been squeezed out of the skies – and so the list goes on.

There is a natural inclination to relax environmental standards during times of economic recession, in an attempt to spur recovery. But a report by Britain's Royal Commission on Environmental Pollution stressed that 'a country that can maintain a position in the vanguard of pollution control will have considerable opportunities for the export of appropriate technology and equipment, provided other countries follow suit with similar abatement policies.'

The designer is a problem solver. The design process involves an element of 'lateral thinking' which, as Edward de Bono explained, involves 'changing perceptions and finding new ways of looking at things.' As designers have begun to consider the environmental implications of their work, they have found that sometimes the environmental cloud over a particular product line may have a silver lining. Today's crisis, viewed in the right light, may represent tomorrow's commerical opportunity. The green designer spots such opportunities and exploits them.

Doing more with less

Time and again, considering the environmental facets of a design problem leads on to an unexpected – but effective – design solution. But any problem may have a number of possible design solutions.

The landscape designer faced with mountains of ash from coal-fired power stations would think of ways of softening their lines and of greening their flanks with hardy strains of grass and other ground cover. But the lateral thinking green designer might also ask: What can we do with this ash which will help us tackle other long-term problems? Thermalite asked this question and now sells its answer by the tonne. Even further down the line, we might ask how we can heat our homes without having to burn so much coal in the first place?

One answer is to build more 'intelligence', in the form of computer hardware and software, into buildings, machinery and products. The rapid evolution of industrial technology, from microchips to superconductivity, is affording the designers a broad new range of tools and materials to work with, enabling us to do more with less. Scattered throughout *Green Pages* are examples of new products and technologies which display the unmistakable hallmark of the green designer.

'Our most important task,' as Sir John Harvey-Jones put it while chairman of ICI, 'is to get more and more out of less and less. That is the industrialist's mission. And actually we are getting pretty good at it.' ICI's Electrodyn sprayer is an excellent example of this trend at work (page 74). The sprayer achieves a much greater degree of crop protection – and a sharply reduced level of spray drift – for any given quantity of pesticide.

Design sells wholefoods, too.

To take another example, environmentalists may not like tin cans, because they use relatively scarce resources in a profligate way, but the green designer has already been at work on the tin can to make it somewhat more acceptable. The weight of steel used in tin cans has been steadily reduced, as has the weight of the tin coating. Between 1957 and 1985 there was a 30% reduction in the average body plate thickness and a 50% reduction in the thickness of tin coatings. This approach, known as 'light-weighting', is also bringing material and energy savings in other areas.

Hearing the light

Not so long ago, environmentalists worried that metals like copper would soon run out as rapidly growing consumption out-ran limited worldwide supplies. That prospect now looks more remote, thanks to some of the advanced materials now beginning to emerge from the laboratory. Consider fibre optic technology, increasingly being used to carry voice, data and video traffic which previously would have been routed via copper cables.

Within urban areas, six-inch copper cables can now be replaced with half-inch fibre cables which carry the same amount of information. The message is carried in light signals rather than as an electrical current. This helps designers do away with many of the problems caused by the heat generated in conventional electrical systems. Also the fibre optic cables are made from glass – whose raw materials are effectively inexhaustible.

But, like all tools, these new materials and technologies can be used in good ways and bad. A microprocessor which is used to monitor and control fuel consumption on a trans-Atlantic 747 might just as easily have been programmed to detonate a terrorist bomb and blast the aircraft out of the sky. The same chip which helps a 'reverse vending' recycling machine distinguish between metals in the incoming cans might also be used to sort out targets for a 'smart' missile.

The green designer does not reject technology out of hand, however, but moulds and remoulds it to ensure that its environmental performance is not only

Worlds within Worlds

Seal a crew of shrimp or humans into a miniature world and you can learn a great deal about life on Earth.

The brief: design a world which, as far as possible, is self-sustaining. Two early results: the EcoSphere and Biosphere II.

A small glass sphere, made in America, the EcoSphere strikingly illustrates the meaning of the phrase, 'Spaceship Earth'. One sits alongside the computer into which these words are being tapped. It is just over six inches (16.5 cm) in diameter and is inhabited by several bright red shrimp from the Pacific Ocean, small green tufts of algae rooted on a branch, and a cloud of invisible micro-organisms. Like the Earth, it is a closed ecosystem, requiring only an external source of light for its continued existence.

On a considerably larger scale, Biosphere II is being built in the foothills of Arizona's Catalina Mountains and should eventually cover 2.25 acres (just under a hectare). Apart from microcosms of rain forest, desert, savannah, and marshland, it will also include a miniature ocean – which alone will contain some 150 species. Biosphere II's human crew will be made up of eight volunteers, who will be very much part of the system during its two-year 'flight'. They will leave only in the event of an emergency.

Both the EcoSphere and Biosphere II are designed to be self-sustaining ecosystems. The EcoSphere was developed at NASA's Jet Propulsion Laboratory at the California Institute of Technology. The JPL scientists, who were interested in the possibility of long-duration manned space flights, were looking for ways of assembling enclosed ecosystems able to maintain plant and animal life for periods measured in years.

Biosphere II.

Not only is the EcoSphere a prototype of future space colonies, but it also turns out to be an extraordinary symbol of the delicate ecological balances which maintain life on Earth. Some of the earliest EcoSpheres, permanently sealed over seven years ago, continue to thrive as their inhabitants produce all the necessities of life, working together to break down wastes which would otherwise poison their environment.

As long as the system receives light, the algae produce oxygen via photosynthesis. The shrimp breathe the oxygen and graze on the algae and bacteria, in the process producing the carbon dioxide needed by the algae. The bacteria decompose the shrimp waste into the basic chemical nutrients used by the algae for growth, and also help boost the sphere's carbon dioxide level. The life expectancy of the shrimp, the only organisms which do not produce in the system, is estimated to be up to 10 years.

The EcoSphere has received rave reviews. 'The world arrived in the mail,' reported astronomer Carl Sagan. 'Our big world is very like this little one,' he mused, 'and

acceptable but becomes an important selling feature in its own right. The challenge, as with the pollution produced by motor cars, is not simply to design in pollution control equipment, such as catalytic converters — but also to design out such problems, for example by switching to 'lean-burn' engine technology (page 117).

A key technique in most types of design will be environmental impact assessment (EIA). Originally developed to evaluate the likely impact of major development projects such as dams, airports or motorways, EIA techniques are being adapted to serve in designing industrial processes and even consumer products.

The green designer's ultimate impact will depend on what the client — and the customer — want. In a market economy (and, for that matter, in any of the socialist or communist states) the designer who works on an environmentally desirable project one year may be switched to another project which reflects other dimensions of the world we live in.

But the green consumer is likely to be an increasingly important influence in the world of industrial and product design. Designers who ignore the fact, or who allow their clients to ignore it, risk losing out on some of the most exciting market opportunities of the 1980s and 1990s. They also risk losing their jobs. □

---

we are very like the shrimp. But there is at least one major difference: Unlike the shrimp, we are able to change our environment. We can do to ourselves what a careless owner of such a crystal sphere can do to the shrimp. If we are not careful, we can heat our planet through the atmospheric greenhouse effect, or cool and darken it in the aftermath of a nuclear war. With acid rain, ozone depletion, chemical pollution, radioactivity, the razing of tropical forests and a dozen other assaults on the environment, we are pushing and pulling our little world in poorly understood directions.'

The man behind the EcoSphere is Joe Hansen, a JPL ecologist now working on more complicated versions, with over 150 variations being tested. 'We've developed versions with fish and small snails,' reported Hansen's colleague Loren Acker. 'We even foresee terrestrial closed ecosystems in the future.'

Meanwhile, the Institute of Ecotechnics, which specialises in biospheric research, has already laid the foundations for Biosphere II (the Earth itself being dubbed Biosphere I). Whereas you can buy an EcoSphere for $250, the price tag for Biosphere II is likely to be at least $30 million. Space Biosphere Ventures (SBV), the for-profit company behind the project, has raised much of the money needed from Texas oil billionaire and philanthropist Edward Bass.

SBV hope to make money on the venture eventually, with possible sources of income including patents on such inventions as Biosphere II's air purification system or new crop varieties emerging from the cloning programmes the resident scientists will undertake. Smaller biospheres might eventually be marketed as laboratories for testing genetically engineered microbes or to study the links between atmospheric carbon dioxide and plant health.

Because the system will recycle almost everything, the 'Biospherians' must scrupulously avoid

The EcoSphere.

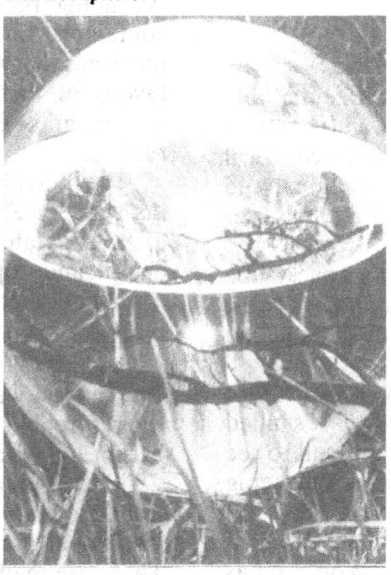

pollution. Pesticides, for example, will be banned on the 20,000 square foot (1,858 square metre) farm, in favour of biological pest control methods. The potential pitfalls are illustrated by the Soviet experience with a facility called Bios, located at a Siberian research institute, whose human inhabitants have logged 'flights' of many months. When the catalysts used to clean the air failed to work as planned, noxious gases began to build up in the Bios atmosphere — and were only spotted when the growth of potatoes slowed and potato leaves started to curl.

To keep track of such problems Biosphere II will contain some 5,000 sensors, measuring everything from trace gases to the temperature of individual leaves. Even so, the design team are having to be extraordinarily careful in choosing the species for this latter-day Ark.

To pollinate the rain forest plants, for example, you need bats or hummingbirds. But some hummingbirds zoom skyward during mating, which sets a premium on low-flying species. In the savannah areas, meanwhile, the termites needed to break down the tough grasses can also digest some of the sealants used to make this manmade habitat airtight. However careful the designers, the crew can be sure of one thing: this bold new voyage of discovery will be full of surprises.

PERSPECTIVES

Conspicuous Consumption

Simple packaging in recyclable materials can be stylish, denote quality and help both our pockets and the environment, says *Adrian Judd*.

'With 'convenience' at the top of everybody's shopping list, designers are not wholly to blame for the fact that we are currently seeing the worst 'throwaway' period in packaging history. Returnable bottles are almost a forgotten memory, combinations of plastics (making them totally unrecyclable) have never been more popular and shameless over-packaging with multi-layers never more common.

It is estimated that we throw away £750 million worth of 'rubbish' a year. Furthermore, it costs £720 million a year to remove this rubbish. Of the 56 million tonnes of waste generated in the UK about 15 million tonnes are recycled. The rest goes mainly to landfill sites. Unless we are keen to adopt the Japanese method of waste disposal and build great hills of rubbish around our major cities, we are going to have to rethink fast. By the year 2000, the UK will have filled its present dumping sites.

Of course we could burn the rubbish (page 120), but unless we separate out the reclaimable materials, we will be guilty of wasting our resources and, possibly, polluting the atmosphere with the toxic fumes produced when plastics are burned. A great deal more can be done to ensure that potentially useful materials are extracted from the waste-stream and that our landfill resources last well into the next century. But it is also increasingly important to convince industry, designers and consumers that much of today's packaging is an inelegant and unsustainable answer to the problem of making products appetising.

Dubious packages

Designers can potentially play a highly influential role in halting this profligacy. Their aesthetic and construction skills can be combined with sound ecological sense to produce packaging which is functional and environmentally acceptable before, during and after use.

By looking at some examples of dubious packaging and contrasting them with some sounder alternatives, maybe it will be possible to provoke some thought and consideration for this problem.

The first is Honey in a Tube by Ratcliffes of Oxford. The question here has to be 'why?' It's billed as 'Honey in a convenient way' but it's difficult to see how it really is more convenient. Apart from being more expensive than the old fashioned (and reusable) honey pot beloved of Pooh's paw and generations of children, it looks like a hair conditioner. Worse, it has two different types of plastic, which means that if the plastics are not separated at source – that is, in the home – there is little chance that the plastic collected will be sufficiently pure for any recycling process.

Push-button cream

697 million aerosols were produced in Britain in 1985, and you won't be surprised to hear that Friends of the Earth are none too keen on them. Aerosols first appeared as a sales promotion gimmick in the 1950s but their use is now almost universal. The version for Anchor Real Dairy Cream, costing £1.30, has many environmental drawbacks and is probably sold to promote the 'fun aspect' of cream – spray it on kiddies' food. Or the kiddies. The tin-plated can is non-recyclable after use: it can't be punctured or burned because it contains a nitrous oxide propellant that may well also be harmful to the ozone layer in the atmosphere.

A good alternative is a glass container with a mechanical pump which uses air pressure and needs no added propellant.

These problems aside, who really wants cream from an aerosol? Can you think of anything that looks a more unnatural way of storing natural country produce? It is just as well that the cows don't get to see where the fruits of their gentle labours wind up.

Staying with dairy produce, Kerrygold's Cream for Coffee is enough to make one despair. One cannot help but think that this is convenience gone truly mad. It consists of 10 small plastic cups each with a metal foil lid, all in a plastic dish and covered with a card top. Assuming that the cream is required in separate containers, simple adjustments could be made to use materials that would be less wasteful. The argument in favour of these things is probably that they save wasting milk. But at what cost with all this additional rubbish?

The individual containers could be joined together (as with some yogurt cartons), eliminating the need for a separate base and top. Promotional graphic design and copy should be put on the top of the containers themselves.

Grecian urn

By contrast we have the Grecian Urn of packaging, the returnable milk bottle. What more needs saying – except long may it survive?

Next, the problem of the egg. There is a growing trend to use plastic egg boxes rather than the traditional and perfectly adequate cardboard version. These are made from waste paper recycled to create cardboard, which is ideal for this use.

DESIGN

Plastic egg boxes not only refuse to biodegrade but also, surely, are uglier receptacles. They might be slightly cheaper and let you see the eggs, but people would pay an extra 1p or so if they knew what damage they could save. More expensive, free-range eggs are often packaged in cardboard boxes to give them a more wholesome appeal. Friends of the Earth do actually sometimes get called by designers for advice on good-looking recycled paper for a 'natural' look, and we are only too happy to oblige.

Kerrygold's Cream for Coffee, says Adrian Judd, 'is enough to make one despair'. The ordinary milk bottle, by contrast, is 'the Grecian urn of packaging'.

Tony Hutchings, Creative Review

ADRIAN JUDD *is Recycling Information Officer at Friends of the Earth. Previously, as a graduate geologist, he had worked for a large construction firm as an exploration geologist.*

Friends of the Earth, *26 Underwood Street, London N1. Tel: 01 490 1555.*

Polmark: Key to a £20 Billion Clean-Up Market

If you want to find out what is going on in the pollution control markets of Europe, Polmark can plug you in. *Dr Richard Haines* looks at how a computerised database could help you clean up.

The European pollution control market is valued in excess of £20 billion per annum – and is growing at a rate of 6–11% per annum. The principal driving force is the implementation and enforcement of increasingly stringent legislation. As a result, new opportunities are opening up – for those with access to up-to-date market information.

Polmark is a new database, one of a range of environmental services offered by Ecotec. The database contains information on the markets for pollution control, waste treatment and environmental monitoring equipment, and for environmental services. It is aimed at four main types of user: equipment suppliers, equipment users, public waste regulatory agencies and research organisations.

With its ability to link 37 separate fields of data, Polmark can offer much more than a standard literature search. The user can ask a series of interlinked questions, gaining instant access to information on:

- market trends in pollution control and waste treatment markets;
- government policies and any schemes offering financial incentives or other forms of support for those wanting to develop or buy environmental technology;
- the best available clean and pollution control technologies; and
- the principal suppliers of environmental technology and services to European markets.

Polmark covers such fields as water and effluent treatment, air pollution, noise, land contamination, and municipal, industrial and hazardous waste collection and treatment. The system has taken four years to develop and is now available on-line.

Dr Richard Haines, Director, Ecotec Research and Consulting Ltd, *Priory House, 18 Steelhouse Lane, Birmingham B4 6BJ. Tel: 921 236 9991.*

PERSPECTIVES
Designed for Sustainability

Keith Grant, Director of the Design Council, considers the designer's role in making industrial processes and products more resource-efficient.

'Designers have not just one but three crucial roles to play in helping to improve the quality of life, reverse the despoliation of the world's environment and move towards an economy that is sustainable in the long-term.

First, designers have a major influence on the use of the world's resources of materials and energy. Within the necessary constraints of designing products that are competitive in performance, quality, and price, it is the designer who decides what materials are used, how energy-efficient the product is in manufacture and use, how repairable and long-lasting the product will be, and even the ease with which it can eventually be recycled.

At one extreme, a furniture designer can specify a rare wood that depletes a disappearing species or he can specify a wood that is being satisfactorily replenished. At the other extreme, it is the engineering designers who have achieved such remarkable improvements in aircraft engine fuel efficiency, noise performance and the reduction of exhaust emissions.

Second, designers have a key role in creating the products that could reverse the despoliation of our environment and ensure the improvement of living standards in a sustainable manner. British designers have led the way in the development of commercial wind-powered electrical generation, in designing efficient cookers for a Third World desperately short of fuelwood, in finding ways to clean up oil spillages, and in developing crop-sprayers that dramatically reduce pesticide usage. It is this creativity and design skill that is essential for solving many of the problems which will confront us in the future.

The third role for designers in assisting the creation of a more environmentally-sensitive and sustainable world lies in the influence that they can, up to a point, have on the way in which people live. It was, after all, designers who created the proliferation of throwaway products of the 1960s. It is designers who can help to make recycled paper more acceptable; and design played a not inconsiderable part in making The Body Shop (page 70) fashionable and successful.

Tomorrow's opportunity

But designers do not work in isolation. Their work is useless unless manufacturers not only accept it but profit from it. And designers and manufacturers alike are constrained by national and international legislation. This is important not just because it can act as a spur to better standards but because, without it, irresponsible companies can undermine the viability of the responsible.

Fortunately, there are ample signs that industry in general and an ever-increasing number of specific companies are now recognising that the world-wide pressures for an improved environment are not a threat to industry but an opportunity. Significantly, the President of the CBI, Sir David Nickson, has endorsed the view that 'Today's crisis, viewed in the right light, may represent tomorrow's opportunity'.

There are plenty of examples from Britain, Europe, the United States and many other parts of the world to illustrate this thesis. For example, a recent issue of the American magazine *Design News* carried a major review of the way in which designers are tackling the problem of finding uses for plastics waste. Successful businesses have been developed manufacturing items as varied as cushion flooring, fence posts, playground equipment and urinal screens. The magazine concluded its feature by repeating a point that the Design Council made in its recent 'Green Designer' exhibition, that some major potential industrial developments – such as the all-plastic car – are being

held back waiting for scientists and designers to solve the problem of how such products can be recycled at the end of their life.

Anti-industry culture

The challenges and opportunities facing designers are manifold. But there is a need to better equip designers for their role in this changing world. For example, they need easy access to information about the environmental implications of using particular materials and processes; again, techniques for designing products for easy recycling need to be developed and made available. And, of course, not all new technologies and new products prove to be beneficial in the long run, so designers also need better training to help them to identify and forestall potential risks.

The potential for commercial success from exploiting the growing international demand for environmentally-benign products and processes is clear. But there is another potential advantage for Britain. It is now generally recognised that, while we continue to rely on industry for the products and services on which our quality of life largely relies, we still live in an inhibiting anti-industry culture. This is at least partly due to the environmental damage caused by industry in the last hundred and fifty years, and it can therefore be most readily reversed by the kind of new, environmentally-benign industries that are being built on the skills and talents of our scientists and designers.

KEITH GRANT *has been Director of the Design Council since 1977.*
The Design Council, *28 Haymarket, London SW1Y 4SU. Tel: 01-839 8000.*

TIM MOORE ASSOCIATES · GRAPHIC DESIGN CONSULTANTS
74 LEIGHTON ROAD LONDON NW5 2QE · TELEPHONE 01 267 1254

FRIENDS OF THE EARTH

ONE OF THE U.K.'S LEADING ENVIRONMENTAL PRESSURE GROUPS IS NOW INVOLVED IN EIGHT MAJOR CAMPAIGNS

ACID RAIN POLLUTION
•
RECYCLING
•
CITIES FOR PEOPLE
•
PESTICIDES
•
TROPICAL RAIN FORESTS
•
COUNTRYSIDE & U.K. FORESTRY
•
NUCLEAR POWER & RENEWABLE ENERGY

THE EARTH NEEDS ALL THE HELP IT CAN GET!

☐ I would like to become a member of Friends of the Earth (Membership fee £12)
I enclose a donation of:
£10 ☐   £25 ☐   £50 ☐   £100 ☐   other ☐

Please fill in and return to: Friends of the Earth Ltd., Membership Department, Freepost, Mitcham, Surrey CR4 9AR (no stamp needed)

BLOCK LETTERS PLEASE

Name ....

Address ....

.... Post code (please) ....

HELPING THE EARTH FIGHT BACK

10 Questions for the Green Designer

Held at London's Design Centre, 'The Green Designer' exhibition ran for six weeks before transferring to Glasgow. It posed ten key questions for designers, which are summarised below.

1. Is There a Risk of Disastrous Failure?
In the wake of the Chernobyl and Rhine disasters, this is obviously a critical question. Among the products highlighted were new electronic sensors developed by Thorn EMI to pick up potentially hazardous concentrations of a variety of pollutants before an explosion or gassing can occur.

2. Could the Product be Cleaner?
Consider the ubiquitous motor car. There has been a 50% reduction in the amount of pollution by cars over the last ten years, but with more than 20 million cars on Britian's roads – and with major markets like West Germany increasingly concerned about the contribution of car exhaust emissions to acid rain problems – the pressure for cleaner exhausts continues to mount. One exhaust-cleaning technology in the spotlight was the catalytic converter developed by Johnson Matthey Chemicals (page 116).

3. Is it Energy-Efficient?
When Energy Efficiency Year was launched, the Department of Energy calculated that energy worth £7 billion is wasted every year in Britain alone. However we produce the energy we use, economic, social and environmental considerations dictate that we should learn how to use it more efficiently (page 136). Among the energy-saving ideas on display at the exhibition was a computerised 'energy exam' for houses, developed by the Milton Keynes Development Corporation. Fuel-efficient stoves developed by the Intermediate Technology Development Group (ITDG) for use in the Third World were also featured.

4. Could it be Quieter?
Public complaints about noise have been rising, according to UK statistics. Among the products discussed in the exhibition catalogue were quieter oil drilling rigs and road breakers. In Sweden, meanwhile, the Conjet system developed by Atlas Copco uses water jets as a faster, quieter way of demolishing concrete structures. Silent products could enjoy a golden future.

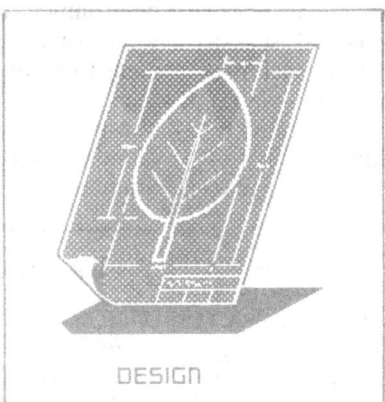

5. Should it be More Intelligent?
Many of the technologies and products featured incorporate programmed microchips. As a result, the Warren Spring Laboratory waste separator can sort out high-value metal wastes, for example, or the Intermediate Technology Development Group's micro-hydropower schemes can increase or reduce the flow of water through the generator, to ensure a steady output of electricity. Such a power source can be an enormous boon in regions of the Third World which risk losing their forest cover because of fuelwood collection – or their soils because of the burning of dung.

6. Is it Over-Designed?
Some remarkably simple design solutions were highlighted, including an effluent treatment plant devised by cider-makers H.P. Bulmer. Using bugs which thrive in extremely hot conditions, the plant cost £24,000 – and saved the company £30,000 in its first year of operation.

7. How Long Will it Last?
Generally, the longer a product lasts, the better the return on the raw materials invested in its construction. Thorn EMI's energy-efficient 2D lamp bulb, for example, lasts at least five times as long as an ordinary bulb.

8. What Happens When its Useful Life Ends?
Even the longest-lived product is going to wear out eventually, unless it ends up in a museum. Every year, each Briton throws out four times his or her own weight in rubbish. Among the innovative solutions endorsed by the green designer were Rockware Reclamation's VEND-A-CAN 'reverse vending' scheme for recycling aluminium cans and projects designed to convert waste dumps into 'bioreactors', producing useful biogas.

9. Could it Find an Environmental Market?
A growing number of products and technologies, some developed for other purposes, are now finding environmental applications. Vitrifix, for example, redesigned an existing furnace to convert asbestos wastes into harmless glass. ICI has taken an idea from plants and is marketing enzymes which break down cyanide. And BTL's silage additives cut down on pollution from silage clamps.

10. Will it Appeal to the Green Consumer?
With many millions of Europeans now belonging to environmental organisations, the emergence of the green consumer is an increasingly significant trend. The Body Shop's various products and programmes were featured by the Design Council – and a growing number of companies are following in their wake.

SECTION 3

More Questions Than Answers

With European environmental policy entering a vital new phase, the emerging research agenda for the 1990s is going to provide employment for tens of thousands of scientists and other research workers.

What went wrong? Why did it go wrong? What else might go wrong? How can we stop it? Where are things going right? Why are they working? What can we learn from their success? Scientists are paid to ask questions and they certainly provide value for money in the environmental field. As fast as the answers come in, it often seems, they produce new questions – and new proposals or grant applications. But there is no end in sight to the information we will need if the world is to move towards more sustainable forms of development.

We need to know, for example, how seriously we should take the latest crop of environmental issues; whether new policies or regulations are really tackling the priority problems; when commercially viable technical solutions are likely to appear; how quickly markets for environment-friendly technologies, products and services are likely to emerge, and who else is going to be competing for them.

Not an optional extra

The European Commission's Fourth Action Programme for the Environment, described on page 26, identifies ten main issues for further research and action in the 1990s. The Commission's overriding goal, however, is to ensure that environmental policy is integrated into all other Community policies. Environmental protection, in short, is now increasingly seen as an integral part of economic and social policies rather than as an optional extra.

Meanwhile, a growing amount of national and international research is now focusing on the potential for sustainable development – and on the obstacles which stand in the way of the quest for sustainability (page 50).

In 1986, for example, the International Institute for Applied Systems Analysis (IIASA), based in Laxenburg, Austria, published a 490-page report entitled *Sustainable Development of the Biosphere*. IIASA is particularly interesting because its membership pulls together countries from both sides of the Iron Curtain. The biosphere project was supported by Canada and the German Marshall Fund of the United States.

Thinking globally

The basic idea was to 'think globally while acting locally'. Regional, international and global issues were studied to see what specific actions and policy choices might be needed at the level of individual countries. The project also set out to check whether any emerging environmental issues could inhibit (or promote) development in particular regions of the world – and to identify the long-term research needs likely to be generated by any worldwide drive towards more sustainable forms of development.

One of the interesting points which emerged from IIASA's review of the history of environmental science was that the sort of questions asked by environmental researchers over the last 100 years were very strongly influenced by the kinds of measurement techniques available to them. Indeed, one reason why scientists are asking so many questions today about the environment is that the range of instruments available to them has increased dramatically.

We have unwittingly embarked on a gigantic experiment with our planet. For example, we are now triggering changes in the global climate, a process whose implications are almost incalculable. Dr John Bowman of the Natural Environment Research Council (page 88) and Florence Fisher of ERL (page 90) look at the role of environmental researchers.

Some, like the gas chromatograph, able to measure toxic chemicals like chlorinated hydrocarbons at the parts per billion level, provide astounding analytical sensitivity. One part in a billion is equivalent to one minute in 2,000 years or a drop of water in a swimming pool measuring 3 metres × 3 metres × 6 metres. Yet some chemicals may affect our health even at such vanishingly low concentrations. Other instruments, like the sensors carried on orbiting remote sensing satellites, give us a god's-eye view of our planet which would have been almost unimaginable a generation ago. And powerful supercomputers increasingly enable us to pull all this information together and begin to identify meaningful patterns and trends.

Around the world, environmental scientists are now using satellites to monitor the interplay between the land, oceans and atmosphere. Such 'high' technology, however, is not foolproof, as the 'ozone hole' example illustrates (page 88). But, wherever it comes from, the resulting information will be critically important when it comes to answering whether particular industrial or agricultural activities are likely to be sustainable in the long term.

Eyes in the skies

Satellite remote sensing has certainly proved one of the most important tools in research aimed at developing an understanding of how the global ecosystem functions. It is even possible to track the 'living atoms' of this vast interlinked system from orbiting platforms.

The Argos satellites, for example, orbiting the Earth every 101 minutes, are helping research teams like the Sea Mammal Research Unit, based in Cambridge, to track individual tagged seals and whales over distances measured in hundreds of kilometres. Combined with ever-smaller and more powerful transmitters, it is possible not only to monitor the position of marine mammals, but also their heart-beat, temperature and activity rate.

Given the accusations in the late 1970s that seals were eating 120,000 tonnes of fish a year, valued at £15–20 million at 1976 prices, the attempted renewal of the seal cull was inevitable – even if public pressure forced it to be abandoned. The sort of monitoring now possible, however, could well show once and for all whether seals and other marine mammals are having a significant impact on offshore fish stocks.

But new research techniques are by no means the whole story. The 1970s and 1980s, in fact, have been full of surprises, from the oil shocks of 1973 and 1979, through the commercialisation of recombinant DNA techniques to the emergence of the 'acid rain' phenomenon in Scandanavia and now across Europe. While environmental research aims to ensure that there are no unpleasant surprises, the pace of developments often outruns our ability to keep up – and we are reduced to playing catch-up.

Fingers on the pulse

The Chernobyl disaster, which occurred on 26 April 1986, was a case in point. Environmentalists may have been expecting something of the sort for some time, but the accident still took most people by surprise. But for some scientists the accident proved an opportunity in disguise. Taking advantage of the Institute of Terrestrial Ecology's widely dispersed research stations, for example, ITE scientists took simultaneous samples of ground vegetation across Britain.

One result was a map of the resulting fall-out, showing peaks of radiation where there had been heavy rainfall while the Chernobyl cloud was overhead. But the 'pulse' of radiation also provided a way of measuring the passage of radionuclides through the environment, whether they ended up in the sea or in the Sunday roast.

The Torrey Canyon *disaster showed how little we knew about the ecological impact of oil – and of oil dispersants.*

The real challenge, however, is not in responding to such outright disasters – although that is challenge enough. When a problem has hit the headlines the political impetus is generally available to ensure that whatever needs to be done – and can be done – is done. A much more difficult task is to mobilise the resources needed to investigate effectively some of the less dramatic, more insidious environmental processes, such as 'acid rain' problems or the climatic effects of tropical deforestation and the global build-up of atmospheric carbon dioxide.

An inter-disciplinary affair

One key to unlocking such complex processes is the use of inter-disciplinary research teams. In fact, environmental research has long been recognised as an inter-disciplinary affair. It is also increasingly international in complexion with close co-operation between national or international research agencies.

In Britain, for example, the Agricultural and Food Research Council (AFRC), Economic and Social Research Council (ESRC), Medical Research Council (MRC), Natural Environment Research Council (NERC) and Science and Engineering Research Council (SERC) set up a committee in 1984 to promote better co-ordination between them on pollution research. And AFRC, ESRC and NERC later set up a joint working group focusing on the environmental consequences of agriculture.

Internationally, one of the key organisations synthesising environmental research results has been the Scientific Committee on Problems of the Environment (SCOPE). Currently working on such issues as the environmental consequences of nuclear war, ecotoxicology and global environmental change, SCOPE has produced a bookshelf of important interdisciplinary publications since the early 1970s.

As awareness of transfrontier pollution problems has grown in Europe, so the need for international co-operation has increased. This is true whether one thinks of research on European seas like the Baltic, Mediterranean and the North Sea, or about some of the international collaborative research programmes now getting under way – like the World Ocean Circulation Experiment (WOCE).

The expense of such programmes is increasingly beyond the resources of any one country, even the United States. But they are increasingly important if we are properly to come to grips with such issues as the climatic implications of atmospheric carbon dioxide build-up.

Living in a greenhouse

There is no question that carbon dioxide levels are increasing in the atmosphere, largely because of the dramatically increased burning of fossil fuels since the Industrial Revolution. Scientists like Frank Woodward at Cambridge University's Department of Botany have shown that some species of plant (including the oak, the sycamore, the bilberry and tomato) have responded to this trend over the last 200 years by reducing the number of stomata in their leaves – since fewer are needed to extract the carbon dioxide the plant needs from the surrounding air.

Programmes like WOCE are now critically important to find out how these rising levels of carbon dioxide are going to affect the planet's climate. Will they trigger the so-called 'greenhouse effect', for example, trapping incoming solar radiation in the atmosphere like a transparent blanket? Recent research in the United States suggest that the oceans may be able to absorb more carbon dioxide than was originally expected, because they do so not only when the ocean water is cold, as was originally believed, but also when it is warm.

The vital importance of such research is demonstrated by the fact that meteorological models suggest that the mid-latitudes of the northern hemisphere – including Britain and the rest of Europe – will be most affected by the impending climatic changes.

Totting up the cost

As our impact on the planet becomes more pervasive, so the cost of remedial measures is rising rapidly. Indeed, one reason why Britain's Central Electricity Generating Board (CEGB) decided to carry out further research on its contribution to 'acid rain' problems elsewhere in Europe and Scandinavia, for example, was the fact that the cost of cleaning up its emissions comes to around £200 million per power plant – and the CEGB has over 60 of them.

But the acid rain issue had been around at least since 1972, when the Swedes raised it at the Stockholm Conference on the Human Environment. There is no question that early 'wash-out' models, which suggested that airborne sulphur alone were to blame, was over-simplified. Subsequent research has shown that sulphur emissions are not the only source of acidity – and that acidity itself does not kill fish directly, but leaches toxic aluminium out of soils.

With the research results we already have, it will certainly be possible to focus environmental spending programmes to ensure that there is a real environmental return. Forestry, it turns out, can have an important effect on environmental acidification, with trees like Norway spruce able to 'scavenge' sulphur from the air, amplifying the acid rain effect. But the need for a much faster response to emerging environmental problems is now abundantly clear.

Industry's role

Whether the issue is the impact of aerosol propellants on the ozone layer or the damage caused by the anti-fouling paints used by yachtsmen and fish farms, industry has a central role to play in assessing whether such damage is real, identifying the causes, drafting any necessary regulations and standards, and developing and marketing less damaging processes or products.

Many of the companies mentioned in *Green Pages* have significant environmental research programmes, from giant chemical companies like Bayer or BASF (page 41) to small, but fast-growing, green companies like the Body Shop (page 70). Some companies, like ICI with its Brixham Laboratory and other resources, do much of the work in-house, while smaller companies may rely to a greater extent on external consultants. In the UK, a *Directory of Environmental Consultants* is available from Environmental Data Services Ltd.

Industry's research facilities represent a major resource which can increasingly be harnessed to the cause of sustainable development, provided that industry can be persuaded of the desirability of that goal. In fact, a number of environmental organisations are now devoting increasing effort to research programmes designed to identify ways in which they can work more closely with sympathetic industrialists.

The World Resources Institute, for example, has been working with the biotechnology, information technology and hazardous waste treatment industries in the United States, while a number of European organisations are developing their own programmes. As new technologies like genetic engineering, microelectronics, advanced materials and superconductivity begin to transform major sectors of industry, environmentalists must aim to be at the forefront of change. The ten research areas identified by the European Commission's Fourth Environmental Action Programme (page 26) provide a useful guide to areas where environmentalists and industrialists must increasingly work together to achieve more sustainable forms of development. □

A Green Framework For Research

A 10-point research agenda was put forward in the EEC's fourth Environmental Action Programme.

'People throughout the Community have come to see the importance of a vigorous environment policy,' explained Mr Stanley Clinton Davis, Commissioner responsible for environmental affairs, introducing the fourth Environmental Action Programme late in 1986.

'We cannot ignore the continuing threat posed to the quality of life in Europe – and elsewhere in the world,' he continued, 'by pollution, urban decay, the deterioration of the natural environment and the effects of new scientific developments. Our new programme lays down the basis for real progress into the 1990s. We need to ensure that protection of the environment is an integral part of policy development.'

Given the public demand for improved environmental standards and environment-friendly goods, the Commission emphasises that successful manufacturers will be those who gear themselves to meeting this demand. Stricter European standards, it believes, will put industry in a stronger competitive position.

The five-year fourth Environmental Action Programme stresses the employment creation potential of environmental investments. Indeed, the Commission plans a parallel programme of demonstration projects designed to examine the job creation potential of such investment.

The Commission put forward a number of priority themes for environmental research in the Action Programme. These include:

- further action to reduce *air pollution* (including the sulphur and nitrogen oxides responsible for Europe's growing 'acid rain' problems);
- intensified efforts to deal with *water pollution* (focusing on inland, coastal and marine waters);
- strict controls on *chemicals*, particularly in the wake of the Seveso, Bhopal and Rhine disasters;
- new measures to govern *biotechnology* developments (covering the classification, containment, accidental or deliberate release, and ultimate disposal of potentially hazardous organisms);
- the safer use of *nuclear power* (with a growing emphasis on the harmonisation of national safety criteria and work on radioactive waste management);
- a new emphasis on the *conservation of natural resources* (moving on from the protection of, say, birds to the protection of bird habitats – and of the habitats of wild animals and plants generally);
- the protection of the *soil* (against erosion and losses caused by urbanisation or the construction of major infrastructure projects such as motorway networks);
- the regeneration of decaying *urban areas* (with Community initiatives under way in such cities as Belfast and Naples) and the multi-purpose management of *coastal and mountain zones;*
- the disposal and recycling of *waste;* and
- the control of *noise* (whether this involves zoning laws, noise emission standards or noise-labelling for equipment and household appliances).

These themes combine relatively well-known agendas, such as the question of what to do with the more than two billion tonnes of waste the Community produces each year (80% of which is potentially re-usable, or could be recycled for raw materials or energy), and the completely new – such as the questions raised by the proposed release into the exotic new organisms produced by genetic engineering (page 92).

Since its launch fifteen years ago, in 1973, the Community Environmental Action Programme has been supported by a succession of Environmental Research Programmes. The programme for 1987–1991 covers four broad areas:

- general environmental research, focusing on such areas as the health and ecological effects of pollutants, testing of chemicals, the quality of air, water and soil, and work on waste management and emission reduction;
- climatology and natural hazards, addressing such long term problems as possible climate changes caused by the build-up of carbon dioxide in the atmosphere;
- major technological hazards, such as the accidental release of dangerous products from industrial processes; and
- remote sensing from space.

In short, although there have been cuts in environmental research budgets in a number of EEC member states in recent years, the longer term demand for research in the areas identified by the Commission is likely to grow very considerably indeed.

PERSPECTIVES

Asking Difficult Questions

Do we have the wit to avoid self-imposed extinction? Environmental science, says *Dr John Bowman*, asks difficult questions and is coming up with some interesting answers. The need for planet management has never been greater – and sound information will be the key to success.

'There are those who estimate that the planet's maximum human carrying capacity is several times the 11 billion figure projected for the year 2000. But even today there is widespread concern that human activities are undermining key ecosystems and other environmental resources. Even if 11 billion people can be fitted in, our environmental management skills are going to be tested to the limit.

How can we learn to use our environmental resources in a sustainable way? There is very little time for the environmental scientist to find answers to the difficult questions now being asked. Often the answers will be demonstrated in the real world before we have had time to predict them. Wherever possible, however, we must ensure that we have a much fuller appreciation of the way the planet works and of how we can feed, house and employ those extra billions.

Confusing signals

Environmental research involves many different elements. To start with, there are the observations needed to build up a picture of the physical structure, biology and chemistry of the planet. The fourth dimension of time is critically important in building up an accurate picture of the way that environmental systems work.

Over relatively short periods of evolutionary time – hundreds or thousands of years – the earth's environment has varied widely around fairly stable mean values of physical parameters and biological content. Over longer time periods – hundreds of thousands or even millions of years – the variations have been more dramatic. If we are to understand how our activities are affecting the environment, it is essential that we understand this natural background of variation and change.

This is easier said than done. In fact, it is very difficult to dissociate natural from man-made changes, not least because the natural variations already contain a great many competing 'signals', some of them short term, some very long in time-scale.

Using computers and mathematical models, it is possible to extrapolate the likely future state of the earth's environment. The possible perturbations to all the parameters can be built into the models, although verifying such models can be extremely difficult. As a result, their value is often questioned.

A hole in the sky

These problems can be illustrated by a topical piece of environmental research. Ozone is the only constituent of the atmosphere present in sufficient quantity to serve as an effective screen against solar ultraviolet (UV) radiation. This radiation can harm many living organisms, including man, and damage a wide range of materials. The amount of ozone present in the atmosphere is determined by a series of competing processes and reactions, some of which create ozone and some of which destroy it.

A major step forward came with the realisation that the major processes of ozone destruction are

Dr JOHN BOWMAN, CBE, FIBiol *has been Secretary of the Natural Environment Research Council since 1981. Originally, he read agriculture at the University of Reading and then carried out genetics research at the University of Edinburgh for his PhD. From 1958-66 he was Chief Geneticist for Thornber Bros Ltd. In 1966 he was appointed Professor of Animal Production in the University of Reading, where he was also responsible for the university farms. As a result of a major grant from the Nuffield Foundation in 1975, he also became Director of the Centre for Agricultural Strategy. He has travelled widely, publishing over 70 scientific papers and four books.*

RESEARCH

activated by compounds which may only be present in trace amounts – but which acts as catalyst. For more than a decade, chlorofluorocarbons (CFCs), widely used as refrigerants, foam-carriers and aerosol propellants, have been regarded as a potential danger to the ozone layer. Indeed, it is now known that, as a direct result of their emission, the abundance of 'total chlorine' in the stratosphere has doubled since 1965.

The next question: how significant was this trend? Scientists of the British Antarctic Survey have, for the past 30 years, measured the total amount of ozone in the atmosphere at Halley Station, on the Weddell Sea coast of Antarctica. In the last decade, a dramatic change has taken place in the annual variation of ozone. Now, each spring (September and October), a very rapid depletion of ozone is observed. In 1985 and 1986, the thickness of the ozone layer was halved in just 40 days. Satellite maps show that the severest depletion – the so-called 'ozone hole' – occurs in the very cold air trapped in the core of the polar stratospheric vortex.

Completely unexpected

This depletion, the first unequivocal systematic change in ozone climatology to be identified, was completely unexpected and has not yet been satisfactorily explained. Many scientists have sought to relate it to the growth of stratospheric chlorine; others have attributed it, purely or in part, to natural atmospheric processes.

The results of measurements of several trace gases by the US National Ozone Expedition, from August to November 1986, show that chlorine chemistry is indeed implicated. It appears that chemistry in the core of the vortex is now chlorine-dominated, in contrast to that at lower latitudes, which is nitrogen-dominated.

Much further research is needed to clarify the causes and implications of the 'ozone hole'. More observations of trace constituents are clearly needed, together with laboratory studies of chlorine chemistry and other reactions. We can have little confidence in predictions of the effects of future CFC emissions until the ozone depletion in Antarctica is fully explained.

Though our species has travelled the surface of the earth and into space, there is much we still do not know. For example, we have yet to properly explore areas such as the deep ocean, the deep earth and ice-covered regions such as Antarctica. These areas may hold important clues to how the earth, in the absence of man, maintained such a comparatively stable environment over millions of years.

We need to investigate these areas to be able to predict whether 11 billion people will be able to live on this planet without changing its environment to such an extent that it is irreversibly altered – and in a manner which may cause not only the destruction of much that we value but also our very extinction as a species. ,

A British Antarctic Survey balloon goes up at Halley Bay, Antarctica. US satellites had been picking up evidence of the 'ozone hole' for years, but NASA's computers, programmed to discard data outside certain limits, ignored the phenomenon. Instead, BAS balloons uncovered the hole, which can reach the size of the continental United States.

PERSPECTIVES

Trends in Environmental Consulting

Why does industry turn to environmental consultants?
Florence Fisher considers the role of the independent expert.

'While it is not a new issue, public interest in chronic health risks from the hazardous by-products of industry, energy and agriculture – including chemical and radioactive waste, chemicals in the workplace, pesticide residues in food, and pollutants from combustion fuels – is spreading quickly throughout Europe. This issue is currently gaining momentum for several reasons:

- highly publicised debates over the location of hazardous waste sites;
- fallout from the Chernobyl nuclear accident;
- a sudden increased interest in food additives and healthier lifestyles;
- pressure on national health services to detect, treat and prevent chronic illnesses; and
- improvements in scientific capabilities, such as new technology which can detect ambient residues at levels of 'parts per billion' or less.

These trends are starting to present serious difficulties for the responsible industrialist, who must somehow balance: (1) the need to keep costs down and productivity high; (2) a general commitment to do whatever is necessary to protect public health and the local environment; and (3) the opinions of customers and investors who are constantly gauging public confidence in the company.

Building public trust

Before taking action, the industrialist needs to understand the situation fully, to see what options are available, and to compare their costs and benefits – costs in terms of profits and productivity, and benefits in terms of both enhanced environmental safety and increased public and business confidence. It may be difficult for industrial managers to get this information from inside their own companies – whether for lack of specialist skills in environmental and risk assessment, the sheer pressure of work on in-house environmental staff, or the understandable bias among company scientists to discount the importance of seemingly unfounded public concerns. Business managers, however, do understand the importance of building public trust – and many are turning to independent specialist consultants for the clarification and analysis of their options.

In the sixteen years since I founded Environmental Resources Limited (ERL), many major industrial companies around the world have turned to us for independent and authoritative advice on their environmental problems. What is gradually changing is the degree of sensitivity and uncertainty in the issues we are asked to address: in 1973 we were being asked about the ecological effects of phosphates in detergents; in 1987, we are being consulted on the chronic human health risks of trace residues from hazardous waste disposal sites. Companies now turn increasingly to consultancies because – to deal with the new, more sensitive environmental issues – decision-makers feel a greater need for objective expertise external to the corporate framework.

A wealth of experience

By their nature, consultants have far broader experience than any one company, having assessed and mitigated risks for dozens of clients. This experience gives each client access to a much larger repertoire of technical or management solutions than they might otherwise have to hand. Where appropriate, consultants can apply standardised environmental auditing procedures, so that the company can be told how their practices compare with others in the industry. And because specialist consultants deal with these issues every day, they are already fully familiar with the techniques and language of risk assessment and mitigation, enabling them to communicate the ins and outs of the issue more effectively with scientists and technicians, contractors, government bodies, and the public or the press.

As risk assessors, environmental consultants can provide a scientifically sound and politically neutral evaluation of the extent and nature of the risks caused by industrial activities. These evaluations may include:

- the review and management of existing scientific information;
- laboratory testing to establish, where possible, dose-response relationships;
- environmental fate studies which trace the movement and chemical transformation of pollutants;
- field monitoring and other measurements to determine current levels of exposure;
- rigorous probabilistic analyses of the resulting risks; and
- sound engineering and technical advice on how exposures or releases of pollutants can be minimised.

Where further scientific information is required, expert advice will be provided on setting standards and priorities for research.

As communicators, consultants can help companies clarify and communicate information and technical data about their operations to government agencies and regulators. They can also help bridge the gap between various parts of the client company which speak in different terms – for instance, between business managers, scientific staff, factory technicians, and the legal department. Many consultants are prepared to help companies communicate with the public on the issue – in such a way that it does not inflame the issue or antagonise opposing interests. In all communications, consultants are adept at putting across the full complexity of what is known, while making perfectly clear what is not or cannot be known for certain.

Support for the decision-maker

Lastly, as decision-support experts, consultants can help their clients identify and compare alternative actions and policies. A number of new analytical tools – many utilising recent advances in micro-computing software – have recently become available to help consultants create for their clients an 'interactive' rather than 'static' approach to examining the implications of alternative actions. For instance, ERL has set up an online computer system to help the European Commission analyse the costs and environmental benefits of alternative 'acid rain' control strategies. Instead of producing the usual cost/benefit analysis with foregone conclusions, ERL's system allows the user to simulate the effects of various combinations of assumptions, values, and actions – while incorporating differing expert opinions in the form of probabilities. Similar new approaches to decision-support will be equally useful in analysing alternative policies on chronic health risk issues in coming years.

In summary then, from now on and well into the 1990s, industry will be confronted increasingly with the difficult issue of chronic health risks from industrial practices, waste and environmental pollution. By providing independent expertise, and by integrating the scientific, communication, and decision-support aspects of issue management process, consultants can help guide their clients smoothly through the coming storm.

FLORENCE FISHER *is Chairman of the international consulting group Environmental Resources Limited, which she founded in 1971. The company's expertise spans the full spectrum of economic and government activity relating to environment and resources, including: environmental planning, management, and impact assessment; waste management and resource recovery; pollution control and risk mitigation; the development of natural resources and energy; and law, policy and market studies. Clients include major industrial companies, national governments, the United Nations, the European Commission, and the World Bank.*

Mrs Fisher is American, but resides in London where Environmental Resources Limited is based. She is a Fellow of the Royal Society of Arts and founding member of the International Association for Environmental Affairs (IPRE). She is also currently a Trustee of The Environment Foundation, and was involved in establishing their Pollution Abatement Technology Award Scheme.

Environmental Resources Ltd., *106 Gloucester Place, London W1H 3DB. Tel: 01 486 1211.*

Jiri Polacek, Panos Pictures

A Disruptive Technology

Biotechnology will have its disasters, as has every other sector of industrial activity before it. A great deal of research will be needed to ensure that the environmental damage caused is minimised – and that the environmental benefits are maximised.

Even in straightforward commercial terms, biotechnology promises (or threatens, depending on your viewpoint) to be a highly disruptive technology. The commercialisation of bovine growth hormone could open up major new markets for biotechnology, for example, but the result will be to aggravate existing milk production surpluses – triggering further restructuring in an industry already undergoing major change in Europe.

The *environmental* implications of biotechnology, meanwhile, are unclear: they may be positive overall, they may – although on current evidence this is less likely – be negative. Environmentalists are aware of the generally reassuring messages which have emerged from major reviews of the health, safety and environmental implications of biotechnology. But a growing number of European environmental groups – including Les Amis de la Terre in France and Friends of the Earth, the Green Alliance and Greenpeace in the UK – are staffing up to keep an eye on this rapidly emerging new industry.

After three years of difficult and intensive work, 80 experts pulled together by the **Organisation for Economic Co-operation and Development (OECD)** concluded that the risks associated with genetically engineered organisms are mainly of the same nature as those found with traditional, non-recombinant organisms. The OECD's report, *Recombinant DNA Safety Considerations,* argued that international guidelines covering the deliberate release of recombinant organisms would be 'premature at this stage', but some member states disagreed.

Two European countries, Denmark and West Germany, pressed ahead with their own legislation. The Danish Parliament passed a law banning all releases of recombinant organisms unless prior clearance had been obtained from the authorities, while the Germans published a set of guidelines and began to talk in terms of a 5-year moratorium.

The reactions of UK environmentalists to the world's first deliberate release of a genetically marked virus (destined for use as a pesticide in forestry plantations) early in 1987 were muted. In part this was because the **Institute of Virology** had taken great pains to explain that the test would not be hazardous, but it was also partly because environmentalists had not yet decided how they should react to biotechnology.

Various networks are now keeping a close watch on the latest developments in biotechnology, including the **International Coalition for Development Action.** ICDA's long-running seeds campaign has now been broadened to take account of the impact of biotechnology on Third World agriculture. Campaign co-ordinator Henk Hobelink has produced a short ICDA book on the subject, *New Hope or False Promise: Biotechnology and Third World Agriculture.*

Environmentalists, meanwhile, are worried that most biological impact assessment techniques are still fairly rudimentary. The scientific base for prediction is patchy, with the behaviour of truly novel organisms unlikely to mimic that of introduced conventional species. And some critics of biotechnology point to the impact that Dutch elm disease has had on the landscape, or the introduced Myxoma virus on rabbit populations, as an example of the rapid change which even conventional introductions (accidental in the first case, deliberate in the second) can cause.

Among the official agencies which have been looking into the environmental implications of the deliberate release of recombinant organisms is Britain's **Royal Commission on Environmental Pollution.**

Research projects focusing on the environmental applications of biotechnology have been fewer and far between. One relevant report published late in 1986 by the **World Resources Institute** was *Double Dividends? The US Biotechnology Industry and Third World Development.*

But it is clear that some of the early deliberate releases of recombinant organisms will test applications which could help solve other critical environmental problems. Already, some European biotechnology companies are using non-recombinant organisms in such fields as environmental clean-up and biological pest control.

For example, **BioTreatment** is exploiting new microbial techniques to clean up abandoned and highly polluted industrial sites in the North of England. **ICI**, meanwhile, is developing its Cyclear enzymes, used to break down waste cyanides. In Holland, too, **Gist-Brocades** is one of a number of European companies now

RESEARCH

Today, we worry about biotechnology.

working on biological methods of treating effluents and wastes, often producing useful quantities of biogas in the process.

Novo Industri (page 118) is developing biopesticides based on a toxic protein produced by the bacterium *Bacillus thuringiensis*. Such pesticides should be much safer than the chemicals they replace, because they are specific to a narrow range of pest species. In Belgium, meanwhile, **Plant Genetic Systems** is working with the US company Ecogen to develop insect resistant lettuce – and plans to extend this approach to other crops.

In short, the environmental potential of biotechnology is very considerable. Environmentalists now face the difficult task of ensuring that the environmental implications of such technologies are fully considered, without damaging the commercial prospects of environmental biotechnology companies.

 Natural Environment Research Council

The Natural Environment Research Council, established under Royal Charter in 1965, is uniquely able to provide governments, industry and commerce with highly trained personnel backed by the most modern equipment, data-banks and other facilities for contract work across the spectrum of environmental science. NERC's institutes undertake work on an individual and collaborative basis, and can offer either projects or integrated programmes in areas such as resource exploration and evaluation, environmental management and impact assessment.

NERC's CAPABILITIES ENCOMPASS:

Consultancy and Advisory Services on all Aspects of Environmental Studies · Mineral and other Natural Resources, Assessments and Surveys · Feasibility Studies · Environmental Impact and Land Use Surveys · Pollution Pathways and Effects · Conservation and Wildlife Management · Training and Research Services

RESEARCH ESTABLISHMENTS
Throughout the UK, European Office in Brussels, Representation in South East Asia and in North America

ENQUIRIES SHOULD BE ADDRESSED TO:
Research Marketing Group, Natural Environment Research Council, Polaris House, North Star Avenue, Swindon SN2 1EU Telephone: (0793) 40101 Telex: 444293 ENVRE G.

SECTION 4

Wheels for the Brain

Apple Computer described its machines as 'wheels for the brain'. *John Elkington* and *Jonathan Shopley* visited a number of leading US computer companies when writing *The Shrinking Planet*, a report for the World Resources Institute. They consider the potential for information technology in sustainable development.

Information is perhaps the ultimate renewable resource. New technologies are constantly being devised to collect, transmit, store, process, package and display it. As we move deeper into the 'Information Age', with a rapidly growing proportion of global GNP produced by the emerging information economy, one result has been that we have become increasingly aware that our planet is 'shrinking.' And it is shrinking in several different ways simultaneously.

First, and most obviously, new transport and telecommunication technologies are bringing geographically far-flung areas much closer together. Modern air travel brings the other side of the Earth within a few hours' flying time. Place an international telephone call and the electronic signals encoding your voice streak at the speed of light through hair-thin optical fibre links or bounce off orbiting satellites. Satellite dishes sprout from offices and homes alike.

As a result, Ethiopians starve in our living rooms, terrorist victims bleed 'live' minutes after the bomb explodes, and the roar of bulldozers moving into virgin rainforest rattles television sets several continents away. Predictably, different parts of the planet are 'shrinking' at different rates, with the industrialised regions increasing their lead over the less developed regions. But in what Marshall McLuhan dubbed the 'Global Village' it has become increasingly difficult to ignore the widening disparities between North and South, between rich and poor.

Under strain

The Live Aid concerts in 1985, linked by satellite and organised to help drought victims in Sahelian Africa, exemplified strikingly how some of these new communication technologies are helping to bring home the other ways in which the planet has been shrinking – as population growth, often coupled with rising living standards and non-sustainable forms of economic development, puts the world's natural resources under increasing strain. But how far can we expect the information technology industry, which looks set to be the world's biggest industry by the early years of the 21st century, to help in the international drive for more environmentally sustainable forms of economic development?

The environmental impact of this industry's 'wheels for the brain', and the impact of other forms of information technology, will depend on the objectives and abilities of those who use them. For example, the same computer used by the defence industry to launch and target intercontinental ballistic missiles could, in the hands of 'nuclear winter' researchers, help model the impacts of the resulting explosions on world climate.

Information may be the ultimate renewable resource, but it needs to be collected, processed, transmitted, stored and packaged if it is to be useful. We look at some of the ways in which computers are already helping conservationists, while Jeremy Cherfas reports on his experiences with the Ecodisc (page 106).

Marshall McLuhan, who immortalised the phrase 'the medium is the message' in the early 1960s, argued that the spread of electronic communications technology 'establishes a global network that has much of the character of our central nervous system.' McLuhan's conviction that this developing global network represented, in effect, 'a single unified field of experience,' enabling industrial man to experience in depth the consequences of all his actions, led him to the conclusion that the all-embracing reach of communications technology was shrinking the world into a Global Village.

The mechanisation of the Industrial Revolution extended the reach and power of the human body without a corresponding adjustment in the reach and sensitivity of the human nervous system. With the development of electronic sensing technologies, this adjustment has now begun to take place. Whereas the early reactions to the Industrial Revolution were stimulated by what the nose could smell, the eyes see, and the ears hear, many of today's emerging environmental problems are being picked up by equipment that can measure pollutants in concentrations as low as parts per billion or trillion.

Brains on a pinhead

Ironically, some of this environmental monitoring

COMPUTERS

Sponsored computers open up new horizons for nature conservationists.

equipment has shown that the computer industry, like every other industry before it, has sometimes been a significant source of pollution. Most controversially to date, solvents leaking from underground tanks have contaminated groundwater supplies in some parts of California's Silicon Valley, landing companies such as Fairchild Camera and Instrument in the courts.

'The industry that can mount an electronic brain on a pinhead,' one newspaper observed, 'cannot stop its tanks from leaking.' Once the problem had been identified, Fairchild spent over $14 million trying to clean up, though test wells remained contaminated. A leak-proof tank and leak detection equipment would have cost just $100,000.

The semiconductor and computer industries represent the heartland of the 'sunrise' sector. In the public mind, their image is often derived from magazine pictures of the highly sanitised 'clean rooms' in which microchips are assembled. State pollution officials in Silicon Valley also tended to think of the industry as 'squeaky clean,' as 'not so much factories, but something like insurance company offices.' But, while they may be orders of magnitude cleaner per unit of output than most 'sunset' or 'smokestack' industries, they do use chemicals and other hazardous materials. To take just one example, by 1979 Silicon Valley was already using 64,000 cubic feet of arsine each year, a toxic gas used as a weapon in the First World War.

Recent research has also suggested that there are potential health hazards in the 'clean rooms' themselves. Advanced Micro Devices, AT&T, Intel, National Semiconductor and Texas Instruments are just some of the companies that have removed pregnant employees from microchip production areas following concern, originating with Digital Equipment, that exposure to such materials as nitric and sulfuric acids may trigger miscarriages. A five-year study of pregnant women at Digital found that they had experienced a miscarriage rate of 39%, compared with a national average of roughly 20%.

Environmental applications

The other side of the coin is that computerisation, particularly where sophisticated monitoring and feedback loops are used, has generally improved performance standards in the related fields of health, safety, and environment. It has also increased energy and resource efficiency.

In Holland, for example, the Dutch environment ministry, VROM, has been using computer software designed by Technica and SIA, which speeds up the assessment of major process plant hazards in the highly industrialised region around Rotterdam. The package of some 50 programs, which takes account of such external variables as population densities and the weather, allows the effects of process modifications to be modelled to see whether they are likely to be both cost-effective and safe.

In the wake of the disasters at Flixborough (England), Seveso (Italy), and Bhopal (India), there has also been growing interest in the use of field-effect transistors (or Chem FETS) as sensors. When exposed to a particular pollutant or hazardous chemical, the electronic characteristics of the semiconductor

Keying In To Disaster

What is it like to live in a world which is unsustainable? There's no way that simply playing with a computer can reproduce the full horror of seeing your crops and animals die – and your children starve – as the desert creeps ever nearer. But educational software developed for the BBC microcomputer has been giving young people aged 11 and upwards a sense of how different factors combine to produce desertification in the Sahel region of Africa.

Sand Harvest, developed by the Centre for World Development Education (CWDE) and published by Longman, enables young people in the industrial countries to get involved through role playing. The focus is on desertification in Mali and the students can pick one of three different roles: Nomad, Government Officer or Villager.

Inevitably, each of these interest groups has a different perspective on the problems and the decisions they make during the simulation can affect other groups in unexpected ways. Role cards are supplied with the software, so that those taking part can understand the way in which each group views the world.

Although the level of feedback is not as great as with the Ecodisc (page 106), annual reports are provided throughout the simulation, to give those involved a sense of the impact their decisions – and the decisions of the other groups – are having on the environment and on the competing communities who depend upon it for their living. Copies of *Sand Harvest* are available in stand alone (£33, including VAT and postage and packing) or network (£44) versions from CWDE.

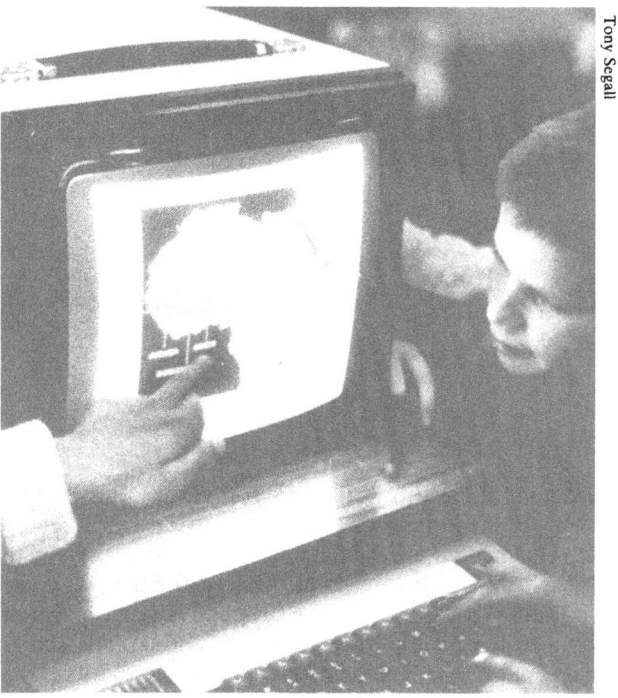

A hands-on lesson in interdependence.

component of the Chem FET change, stimulating a stream of electrons that can be used to activate a recording device or alarm.

Thorn EMI Security Systems, a British company, is developing an approach whereby the inside of cabinets or rooms containing electrical equipment are painted with a substance that gives off ammonia when heated. In the event of a fire, ammonia is detected by a sensor and the alarm sounded, with a strong indication of where the problem can be found. Such systems could well have averted many previous industrial pollution disasters.

Intelligent products

Another rapidly emerging applications area is computer-aided design (CAD). Using CAD techniques, process or product designers can test the performance of their design options on the screen, long before metal is first bent or concrete poured. Subsequently, computer-aided engineering (CAE) or manufacturing (CAM) methods help to ensure high standards of quality control in the production or implementation stages.

As the cost of microprocessors tumbles, so new product generations become increasingly 'smart' or 'intelligent.' Pollution control requirements helped spur the introduction of microprocessors in auto engines, a trend initially resisted by the auto industry – until it recognised the performance and other benefits that could follow.

Presumably, however, since computers are far from infallible, it is only a matter of time before computer failure or 'human error' embodied in software precipitates a major industrial disaster. The experience of computer failures during the NASA Space Shuttle missions shows how vulnerable such complex systems can be, even when the computer components are duplicated or triplicated. Even on a small scale, as when the Somerset Nature Conservation Trust lost most of its membership records (see page 98), such failures can be fairly devastating.

Thinking the unthinkable

But knowing that a certain proportion of cars or aircraft crash every year does not stop people from driving or flying, and computerisation will ultimately touch almost every part of our lives. Computers not only enable us to store extraordinary volumes of data,

COMPUTERS

Computers help synthesise the seawater used in Sea World's 'Living Seas' Pavillion, dubbed 'the world's sixth ocean'. It holds 5.7 million gallons of seawater and more than 200 species.

but increasingly also help us to 'think the unthinkable.' Some of the problems and opportunities that are now emerging in the field of sustainable development will require both abilities.

So far, however, the information technology industry has tended to back into the markets being created by the growing demand for environmental protection and sustainable development. US computer companies, because they continue to dominate the world information technology market and some of their products are inevitably used in environmental research or management applications, also find themselves increasingly involved in some of these new market niches.

IBM, for example, has been looking for future market niches and has considered both remote sensing and environmental management as possible large-scale consumers of computing power. The US industry also produces many of the world's most powerful computers, some of which have found environmental applications.

When Britain's Science and Engineering Research Council wanted a supercomputer able to store and process the voluminous data needed in analysing the circulation of the atmosphere and oceans, for example, it chose a Cray machine.

Given that environmental management clearly is (and sustainable development is likely to be) an information-hungry activity, more European computer companies should be investigating the commerical potential in the fields of environmental protection and sustainable development.

The interesting point about the results of the *Green Pages* computer survey, meanwhile, was that so few environmental lobbying organisations are currently exploiting the full potential of information technology (page 94). Very few, for example, are making use of the computerised databases now available or of the modem, which opens up the possibility of 'networking' computers in different buildings, towns or even continents. In fact anyone looking for a career in the environmental field might be well advised to get a qualification in information science rather than in environmental science.

The Green Computer Survey

Although there have been one or two disasters along the way, environmentalists and conservationists find computers a great help in saving the world. So interested were they in the subject that SustainAbility's questionnaire achieved a better than 70% response rate.

Anyone who has worked with computers can imagine the reactions of the Somerset Nature Conservation Trust when a software 'bug' effectively wiped two-thirds of the Trust's membership data from the memory of a Commodore. But most Green Computer users have been pleasantly surprised by the impact that computerisation has had on their operations.

When we mailed out nearly 130 copies of our Green Computer questionnaire to environmental and conservation organisations around Britain in 1987, we expected something like a 20% response. In the event, over 70% of those contacted returned completed forms – and 70% reported that they were already using computers. Most have found information technology increasingly helpful, although teething problems have been legion.

The overwhelming majority of respondents (91%) were using their computers for wordprocessing, although other applications also achieved high rankings: address databases (84%) and direct mail applications (60%) were favourites, with accounting (41%) and scientific processing (41%) lower down the pecking order. A quarter (26%) of computer users were using their machines for graphic purposes and almost as many (22%) were already using them for networking. Desktop publishing (14%), very much in the headlines recently, is also beginning to make an impact.

A number of innovative applications were reported, including the following:

- The British Trust for Ornithology is using computers to keep track of its bird ringing activities – and to crunch the numbers produced by nest surveys.
- The British Trust for Conservation Volunteers is using them to take reservations for its conservation holidays (page 175).
- The Countryside Commission for Scotland has developed its own computer-based 'geographical information system', able to copy new information accurately onto base maps.
- Earth Resources Research is using computer models to link energy supply options and pollution effects, and to get a feel for the effects of a nuclear attack.
- The Game Conservancy is using computers to help it with the radio-tracking of gamebirds and the simulation of animal populations.
- Groundwork has developed landscape management and environmental networking programmes.
- And, by no means finally, the Zoological Society is developing animal databases to help with breeding programmes for rare breeds and zoo animals.

Diversity backfires

One of the golden rules of ecology, if you happen to be an ecosystem like a forest or coral reef, is that species diversity is the key to success. On this basis, the extraordinary range of different types of computer used by those who took part in the SustainAbility survey suggests that Britain's green lobbyists should be sweeping the board.

From Acorns, Apples and Apricots through to rather more obscure machines such as a Chinese Tsunghen and a Zilog, diversity ruled. At least 33 different types of computer were in use and it also soon became clear that, in computing at least, such diversity could be the stuff of nightmares.

Nine types of computer took the top five positions in our computer census: Comart came top, with 19 mentions; Amstrad second with 14 mentions; IBM third with 12; Apricot fourth with 5; and fifth place was shared by Apple, BBC, Compaq, Digital Equipment and Prime, each of which got 4 mentions.

The Comart system won hands down largely because it was adopted by the Royal Society for Nature Conservation (RSNC), following a joint feasibility study with the Nature Conservancy Council in 1984. A four-year programme was launched that year to ensure that the Nature Conservation Trusts not only got computers but got compatible systems.

The Trusts have been offered 50% of the cost of the Comart system in grant aid, with the remaining 50% often raised from such sponsors as the World Wildlife Fund, BP and Shell. Over half of the Trusts had got at least one computer by the time of our survey.

Overall, our respondents had 316 microcomputers with a total of 642 terminals. Some also had much more powerful minicomputers: the Countryside Commission for England and Wales had 9 Cifer machines, for example; the Nature Conservancy Council 9 Primes; the Wildfowl Trust and the Forestry Commission 2 Data Generals each; and the World Wildlife Fund 2 IBMs.

Most of these machines had been bought outright (67%) or bought with grant aid (20%). A further 5% had been donated. The RSNC had been the main source (28%) of external consultancy advice when the decision on which computer to buy was being taken, with other consultants (14%) and universities (9%) also chipping in with advice.

Epson dominated the printer scene (34% of mentions), followed by Brother (16%). Only 14% of respondents had modems, however, and laser printers were used by just 6%. As far as software was concerned, the chief operating systems used were MS-DOS (the IBM standard), CP/M (for the Comarts, Amstrads and others), and DOS (for Apples and others). Interestingly, the next generation of operating system, UNIX, is beginning to be used on some of the non-Prime minicomputers.

Wordstar 'fiddly'

Wordstar (38% of mentions) was the most used wordprocessing software, although far from the most popular. It was criticised for being fiddly and difficult to learn. Wordperfect, which we used for *Green Pages,* is seen as more user-friendly – but is three times more expensive. Other wordprocessing packages reported included Volkswriter, Superwriter, Neword and Superscript, while all the Amstrads use inbuilt Locoscript software. Locoscript, while being updated at the time, was roundly criticised for its slow speed and over-complicated manual.

The most popular database packages, mentioned by 30% of those developing this type of application, were dBase II and III, marketed by Ashton Tate. Smaller users, mailing to a shortish list of members, seem to be using cheaper packages like Cardbox, Cambase and Delta 4 (for Amstrads and Comarts) or Foxbase (on MS-DOS systems).

No clear favourite emerged in the accountancy field, although brands mentioned included Pegasus and Paxton (for Comarts and Amstrads) and Jarman and Revelation (for IBM-compatibles). Spreadsheet favourites are Supercalc and Lotus 1-2-3. Supercalc got the most mentions, probably because it is significantly cheaper and adequate for the needs of many smaller users.

Keeping abreast

When it comes to keeping up with the extraordinary pace of developments in IT, however, the pattern was rather different: only 8% of respondents reported using the RSNC, compared to 45% who used the computer press to keep them abreast – and 25% who felt they needed no further updates. 'IT moves very fast for smaller organisations,' as the Woodland Trust put it. 'You have to run to keep up.'

For those reading up about computers, a number of general publications *(The Guardian, New Scientist* and *What to Buy for Business)* are read regularly, while enthusiasts tend to rely also on the specialist literature – including such publications as *Byte, Computer Weekly, Mico Decision, PC User, Personal Computer World, Practical Computing* and *Prospectus.*

The Comart Communicator.

Although there was a feeling that the RSNC and NCC (working with Wildlife Link) have been making useful progress, three quarters (74%) of the sample felt that the conservation movement is ignorant of the full potential of IT. More than two-thirds (68%) of those who have not yet computerised felt that they would benefit from doing so, naming membership databases as the most pressing priority.

Half (48%) of those who had computers reported that there had been significant changes in their working habits, with increasing familiarity with computers helping to remove pockets of resistance to their use. Those who felt that there had been no change in their styles of working had either been using computers for many years, like the Forestry Commission ('computers are part of the office environment'), or had only just computerised, like the Flora and Fauna Preservation Society ('too early to say').

A high 80% reported that computers had boosted their efficiency, with the rest feeling that they were still too low on the 'learning curve'. Many felt, like the British Trust for Conservation Volunteers, that computers had enabled them to do more in existing areas and had 'opened up previously impossible areas.' Or, as one Nature Conservation Trust noted: 'The previously unthinkable is now possible at little extra cost.'

Don't expect to save money

A typical breakdown on capital costs for a Comart system would run as follows: a Comart micro, Epson FX 80 printer, Wordstar and RSNC software would cost in the region of £5,300. Another £1,100 would probably be needed for: delivery and installation (£100), a maintenance agreement (£250), 'consumables' such as disks, ribbons and paper (£250), and staff training (£500). For those organisations which do not appoint additional staff, a rough rule of thumb would be that annual operating costs would amount to perhaps 10–25% of the initial capital cost.

At the top end of the range, on the other hand, groups like the World Wildlife Fund, BTCV, the Wildfowl Trust and the Zoological Society have systems valued in the range £50,000–£100,000. The really big systems, costing more than £100,000, are confined to organisations such as the Nature Conservancy Council, the Royal Society for the Protection of Birds, the Institute of Terrestrial Ecology or the Countryside Commission. Here it is quite usual for computer users to spend 100–200% of the total system cost each year on operating costs.

Because computers tend to open up such new areas, their ability to actually save an organisation money is limited. The general consensus was that computerisation increases running costs since, as the British Trust for Ornithology explained, 'any savings are offset by expanding programmes.' Earthlife reported that, 'while hardware is becoming cheaper, the cost of expertise to run the systems is getting more expensive.' Another problem, underscored by Scottish Conservation Projects, is that 'the computer system makes the organisation more vulnerable to the loss of trained staff.'

Generally, however, computer users felt the investment had been necessary and was proving very effective. 'It's an exciting time,' noted Groundwork. 'When all the systems are up and running, the payoffs in terms of information availability and control start to come through. The boost to Groundwork's development potential has made the investment well worthwhile.' The Royal Forestry Society also pointed out that computers can benefit the conservation movement by allowing volunteers to work more flexibly in time and space, with some able to work from home.'

There were warning voices, however, that form should not overwhelm substance. Dr Meg Game of the Greater London Ecology Unit suggested that: 'There is a dangerous trend which has developed over the past few years to worry more about computer availability and compatability than about original information. Providing large quantities of computer equipment would solve few problems,' she concluded,

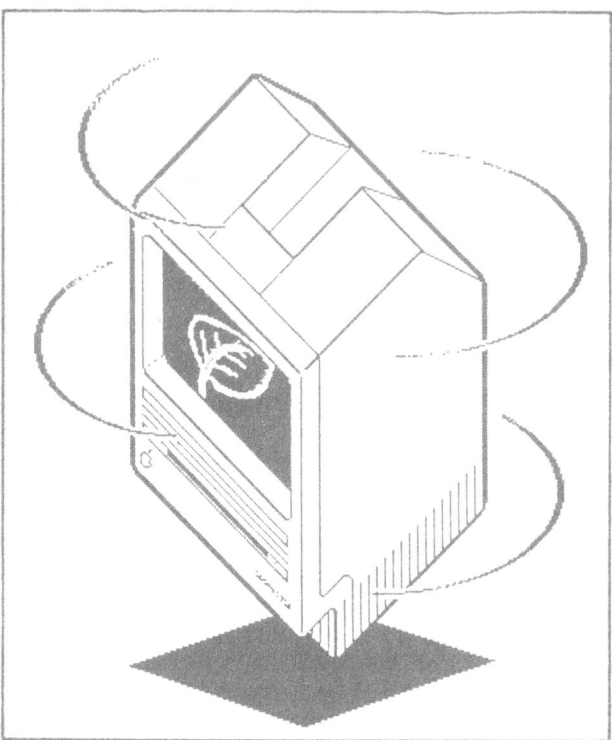

'since useful base information to input to such systems is usually lacking, as are the staff to manage and use such data.' The real need, she felt, 'is for someone – for example Local Authorities – to have a statutory duty to collect information on habitats and species, or to see that such data are collected.'

Very few organisations were willing to sell their data. Those that were included the British Lichen Society (species lists), the British Trust for Ornithology (ornithological data), the Greater London Ecology Unit (data on London wildlife habitats available on a case-by-case basis), the Institute of Terrestrial Ecology (data is free to research organisations, but commercial users are charged) and the Wildfowl Trust (research data). The Royal Society for the Protection of Birds will co-operate with fund-raising mailings, but like almost all other organisations will not give away or sell its membership lists.

Expansion plans

Computers were used most intensively in the smaller organisations, although nearly two-thirds (64%) of respondents felt that their systems were not operating to capacity. This was largely because of staff shortages and a general lack of expertise. Nonetheless, fully 70% of those replying said that they planned to expand their systems.

But if there is one echoing gap in the market it is in the training area. There is a considerable need for training and other forms of support for computer users working in the smaller end of the market. One respondent, the British Deer Society, noted that its computer was still in the box in which it had arrived. No-one knew quite what to do with it. □

COMPUTERS

Information at the Touch of a Button

The idea is seductive. Tap in a few words to your computer and you
can link into a growing network of databases. But who is offering
what – and how much should you expect to pay?

Ask environmentalists what they use their computers for and a high proportion (84%) mention membership address databases. But, so far at least, they make relatively little use of external databases, free or commercial. With growing numbers of green computers fitted with modems, however, it is probably only a matter of time before the use of online environmental databases becomes a matter of routine. So what do they have to offer the user?

Ashton Tate, producers of the ubiquitous dBase II and III software packages, have given countless small and large organisations the ability to construct their own databases. But over the years data have been stored in very different formats, on a wide range of computers, with the result that many organisations are unable to exploit the full potential of computer technology. A number of initiatives have been launched to try and help them tackle this problem.

A computer Esperanto?

The *National Federation for Biological Recording* was formed in 1986 to act as a forum for the many organisations involved in biological recording. Working with the *Nature Conservancy Council NGO Data Handling Group*, they aim to standardise procedures for biological recording so that local and national survey and monitoring will be practicable.

The NCC, according to Dr Ian Baugh of the NCC, having learnt from its own experiences in standardising systems for all its regional offices, felt confident enough to begin liaison with organisations like the World Wildlife Fund UK, Marine Conservation Society, Royal Society for Nature Conservation, Royal Society for the Protection of Birds, Mammal Society, Joint Committee for Conservation of British Insects, National Federation for Biological Recording, Institute for Terrestrial Ecology, Biological Records Centre, Linnaean Society, and the National Trust to develop common database standards for the conservation movement.

European survey

A Europe-wide questionnaire survey on 'Databanks and other information systems in the field of Nature Conservation' is also being conducted by the *Environment Protection and Management Division of the Council of Europe*.

Another database of nature conservation importance, and one which has a European-wide application is the *CORINE (Co-ordinated Information on the European Environment) Biotopes Register*. In 1985 the Commission of the European Communities embarked upon the project, starting with a four year development programme. Designed as a means of harmonising environmental data collection in the EEC, and as a source of information to guide environmental policy-making in the European Commission, CORINE has a number of constituent programmes of which the *Biotopes database* is one.

The database is co-ordinated from the Bangor office of the *Institute of Terrestrial Ecology (ITE)* which is where the *Ecological Data Unit* is based. A computer-based geographical information system has been developed on the ITE VAX computer and data for over 4,500 sites have been entered for the 31 data fields which are used to characterise the sites. Other aspects of the CORINE project include the use of remotely sensed environmental data, and there is a particular focus on atmospheric emission modelling, and water quality monitoring in the Mediterranean region.

The standardised system developed by Bernard Chandler, director of environmental studies at Hatfield Polytechnic, for the Royal Society for Nature Conservation (RSNC) and the 48 Wildlife Trusts has paved the way for the unification of the local area databases held by those Trusts which have developed biological databases on the Comart system. This programme of work has been sponsored by British Petroleum (BP), the World Wildlife Fund and the Nature Conservancy Council. Well over half of the Trusts now have Comart computers, but not all of these have yet established biological databases.

A standardised species diversity database system for biologists, *ALICE*, has been developed by the Biology Department of the University of Southampton. The database has been specially developed for IBM-compatible PC microcomputers and for biologists with little or no computer knowledge who wish to establish species diversity databases.

The University of Southampton also hosts *ILDIS (International Legume Database and Information Service)*. This is an international collaborative project aimed at generating a database of the world's legumes in support of research into plant development and germplasm conservation programmes. The main centres of data collation are at the Royal Botanical Gardens, Kew, and the Missouri Botanical Gardens, St. Louis.

The *Biological Records Centre* is drawing together written and computerised records from 60 plus National Biological Recording Schemes and a variety of other sources, and operates a national compute-

102→

rised databank of information about the occurrence of plants and animals in the British Isles. Most of the data are recorded on a voluntary basis. The database is used to publish distribution atlases for various species, and can be accessed to provide data for research, monitoring, education, planning and conservation. The data are processed by the mini-computer at Monks Wood, and then stored on the Natural Environment Research Council's mainframe computer at the British Geological Survey, near Nottingham.

More generally, the Economic and Social Research Council Data Archive's *Rural Areas Database* (RAD) unit has been established to provide a centralised information resource for rural research and policy-making in the UK. It is drawing together and integrating the wide variety of data relating to social, economic and environmental aspects of the British countryside. The Archive itself holds some 2,500 socio-economic data-sets, including the 1981 Census, the General Household Survey and the Family Expenditure Survey. Services offered range from information searches to full research contracts.

Although the power of computers generally allows the archiving of all available data, the *Greater London Ecology Unit* has used its IBM-based *ADABAS/NATURAL database management system* to hold selected data about sites of urban wildlife habitats, which are of particular use in drawing up local structure plans and in long-term monitoring.

Data held on the Greater London Ecology Unit's database feeds into two more general databases held by the *London Research Centre. Acompline* and *Urbaline* cover complementary areas of urban planning and management and local government affairs. Together they access over 150,000 records of books, reports, journal and newspaper articles held on an IBM mainframe computer. Funded by the London boroughs, the London Research Centre won the Aslib/ISI award for innovation in information management in 1985. Although the database's primary role is to service borough staff with information required for management, the databases are sold to outside users through two host organisations – *Pergamon Orbit Infoline* and the *European Space Agency.*

Infoline and Dialog

Pergamon Orbit Infoline acts as a host to about 70 individual databases. The individual databases originate in a variety of sources. For example, the *Aqualine* database is compiled by the Water Research Centre and covers aspects of water quality management and control, while the *NIOSH* database is compiled by the US National Institute for Occupational Safety and Health Technical Centre in Cincinnati, Ohio.

Although there are a large number of host organisations, *Dialog Information Service Inc* is by far the largest, with distribution rights for over 280 individual databases. Dialog is a subsidiary company to the Lockheed Corporation, and is headquartered in Palo Alto, California. The European distribution office is in Abingdon. Dialog has fifteen databases in its Energy and Environment section. Two of the better known are *Enviroline* (compiled by *EIC/Intelligence Inc.* in New York, containing over 119,600 records of abstracts from more than 5,000 international sources of environmental intelligence) and *Energyline* (also by EIC/Intelligence).

These two databases can be accessed online, using computer communication packages at a rate of around £1.20 per minute, or around 23p per record printed in response to a written search request. Although all the Diaolog databases are interrogated using one standard system, efficient use would normally require some operator training and knowledge of the database being used (Dialog offer short training courses for about £90).

While a large amount of computerised data originates in the United States, *Longman Cartermill* won a government contract to compile a UK national database, *B.E.S.T.* (British Expertise in Science and Technology) to cover publicly funded research in the UK. The database covers all scientific and technical disciplines in the UK's university, polytechnic, and government research establishments and has recently been extended to include the social sciences. It is interesting to note that the principal divisions within the database do not include any on topics such as pollution control, acid rain, waste technology or environmental management.

It is difficult to predict the cost of accessing a particular database service. However, as the costs of the hardware involved (PC microcomputers, modems, computer storage) decrease, lowering the entry threshold for a larger body of users, the cost of commercially available data tends to rise, offsetting any net decrease in overall costs to the end-user.

Updates on CD-ROM

One computer development to watch, and one which tends to put an upper limit on data costs, is the deployment of CD-ROM discs for data storage. CD-ROM discs operate on a similar basis to compact disc players. One 4.72 inch diameter disc can store up to 600 megabytes of digital data. The British Post Office's Postcode Address File, which contains every postal address in Britain, fits easily onto a single disc.

Many database producers are now offering CD-ROM discs containing whole databases, or even sets of two or three on one disc. With a CD-ROM disc drive attached to a microcomputer, a disc-based database can be interrogated at will. Such disc drives with microcomputer interfaces currently cost about £1,000.

One organisation which has previously dealt mainly in printed information, but is now offering databases on CD-ROM discs is *Microinfo Ltd.* For

COMPUTERS

example, a one year subscription to the CD-ROM version of the *Cambridge Science Abstract's* Life Sciences Collection costs £960, including quarterly updates. Cambridge Science Abstracts also produce the *CSA Pollution, Ecology and Toxicology* database, which consists of some 25,000 abstracts related to environmental pollution, the interaction between organisms and their environment, and toxicology studies of industrial chemicals, pharmaceuticals, food, agrochemicals, cosmetics and other products. However, this database is not yet available on CD-ROM through Microinfo. The *NTIS* database from the US National Technical Information Service (NTIS) of the Department of Commerce, which includes data on air pollution, noise pollution, radiation, toxicology, and water pollution, is available on disc at an annual subscription of £2,750 (including records from 1982 onwards, and quarterly updates).

Microinfo, Pergamon and Dialog are but three hosts out of a total of about 90 public access hosts in Europe. These 90 hosts provide access of one sort or another to over 600 publicly accessible databases.

In the light of this veritable flood of digital information, it is not surprising that very few of the environmental organisations in the *Green Pages* survey were making any of their data available on a commercial basis. With the co-ordination efforts now underway, however, it is conceivable that an organisation may emerge from the environmental movement to provide a commercial host service in UK environmental data.

ECHO is free

One host which offers access at no charge to a number of environmentally orientated databases is ECHO, an acronym for European Commission Host Organisation. ECHO was set up in 1980 under the umbrella of the Directorate General for Information Market & Innovation (DG XII/B) of the Commission of the European Communities to encourage and support the use of online data in Europe. ECHO currently supports seven databases, all driven by the same 'common command language'. Access is free to all databases except one. *ENDOC* is a directory of over 500 environmental information and documentation centres in the member states, detailing the services they are able to provide. *ENREP* contains information on environmental research projects in the members states. The *DUNDIS* database would tell a user how to access information within the UN network, in particular, for example, the *United Nations Environment Program's (UNEP) International Register of Potentially Dangerous Chemicals* (IRPDC) or the UNEP Industry and Environment Office's *LNWT* (Low- and Non-Waste Technologies) database.

Potentially the most useful is DIANE GUIDE, a database of databases, database producers, and host organisations. DIANE is an acronym for Direct Information Access Network for Europe, and DIANE GUIDE gives details of all the 90 hosts and the 600-plus databases accessible through the network.

Aslib, the Association for Information Management, provides a range of services, including advice on accessing online databases. It published *Databases suitable for users of environmental information* (by Gerda Yska and John Martyn) in 1978, and although this has not been updated, the annual sourcebook *Going Online* provides an overview of its online activities (£10.00 plus VAT to non-members of Aslib).

Zoos byte back

There are, in addition to the commercial databases and those held by the variety of environmental organisations mentioned above, examples of task specific databases which have been compiled to address a particular need.

At the *Zoological Society of London,* for example, staff have compiled a database on the almost 700 species there, as well as those at Whipsnade zoo, 40 miles away. Each entry gives details of an individual animal, covering species, age, parentage, place of birth, and then information about any diseases, blood tests, pathological and post-mortem findings. The £20,000 project is in its first stage, which concerns the London and Whipsnade zoos' own animals. This information will then be made available to other outside bodies, such as veterinary staff at other zoos. Ultimately, it will become the repository of similar data from a much wider collection of zoos. In this way it is hoped that information about animal diseases will reach a level where 'preventative veterinary medicine' can be practised.

A computerised NOAH

Alongside the veterinary database is another called *NOAH* (National Online Animal History), which is being specifically developed to help with captive breeding programmes. It holds data on the pedigree of animals and allows zoo personnel to design breeding programmes which will help to prevent inbreeding and maximise genetic diversity.

In the case of NOAH, the software used is that written by the International Species Inventory System in Minneapolis. The *ARKS* (Animal Records Keeping) software is used by a zoo to maintain their animal records on an IBM PC or compatible microcomputer. Synchronicity Ltd, a computer software consultancy based in London, is developing an online version of ARKS so that records held at individual zoos can also be held on a central database at London Zoo. The project is being developed by the *National Federation of Zoos'* which has a membership of 55 out of the 260 registered zoos in the UK and Ireland. At the moment, UK data are posted to the ISIS centre in Minneapolis, but in future computer links may begin the first global captive animal database.

104→

The International Union for the Conservation of Nature (IUCN) established the Conservation Monitoring Centre (CMC) in 1983 to provide an information service on global conservation. CMC is also IUCN's contribution to the Global Environmental Monitoring System (GEMS), established by the United Nations Environment Programme (UNEP). CMC's primary function, however, is to continuously collect, analyse, interpret and disseminate data as a basis for conservation.

CMC integrates four monitoring activities covering the status of animal species (Species Conservation Monitoring Unit), plant species (Threatened Plant Unit), the wildlife trade (Wildlife Trade Monitoring Unit) and protected areas (Protected Areas Data Unit). The data come from organisations and specialists all over the world, including:

- the network of IUCN members, including governments, government agencies and non-governmental organisations;
- the international network of scientists affiliated to IUCN and its six commissions;
- the researchers under contract for over 300 IUCN/WWF field projects annually;
- The IUCN Environmental Law Centre and the IUCN Conservation for Development Centre, which maintains a roster of consultants able to undertake environment and development projects;
- The IUCN Environmental Law Centre and the IUCN Conservation for Development Centre, which maintains a roster of consultants able to undertake environment and development projects;
- the network of TRAFFIC (Trade Records Analysis of Flora and Fauna in Commerce) offices; and
- international organisations with which IUCN co-operates. These include the International Council for Bird Preservation (ICBP), the International Wildfowl Research Bureau (IWRB), the UN Food and Agricultural Food (FAO), the UN Environment Programme (UNEP), and the UN Educational, Scientific and Cultural Organisation (UNESCO).

Red data books

CMC makes extensive use of computers. A minicomputer based at the Threatened Plant Unit at Royal Botanical Gardens, Kew, holds a database of over 40,000 taxa of plants, for example, and is used to monitor their conservation status. The *Red Data Books,* which are produced by the Species Conservation Unit at CMC, Cambridge, draw on a number of such databases.

Partly because of funding cutbacks, CMC has increasingly been marketing services related to its databases. It sells services to the CITES Secretariat, which operates the Convention in Trade of Endangered Species (CITES). CMC, for example, provides data used in controlling the ivory trade. Under CITES, every ivory producing country receives an annual ivory quota, and each tusk receives a CITES reference number. It is CMC's task to keep track of all ivory imports and exports within the CITES system.

Meanwhile, the Kew database of plants is being selectively sifted by Dr G. Wickens to extract information on plants which may provide a useful role in desert encroachment control. The database, which is being compiled with support from Oxfam and the Clothier's Foundation, now contains information on over 5,000 plants. However it is the 500 with potential for arid and semi-arid areas of the Third World which are being targeted for bulk seed production programmes.

By no means finally, the *Warmer Campaign* holds an extensive computerised library of information relevant to energy-from-waste from a wide range of international sources. The information is regularly updated, and publicised in the *Warmer Bulletin.*

GreenNet and JANET

The computer revolution has seen two major developments. The first is the almost exponential growth of computerised data, and the second, linked to the development of microcomputers, is the dispersed nature of these data.

Computer communication using modems, and online information databases are now the order of the day. There are a number of commercial 'electronic communication' services, of which *Telecom Gold* is the best-known. Besides communication services like electronic mail and telex, it gives access to commercial information databases covering financial statistics, weather, entertainment and many more.

Of particular interest to environmentally oriented users are *GreenNet* and *JANET*. GreenNet provides communications services particularly for non-profit and voluntary organisations working in environment and related areas. GreenNet provides a UK point of contact to a number of similar networks in the US and Europe. Greenpeace is one of the organisations which uses GreenNet to co-ordinate its international lobbying activities.

JANET (*Joint Academic Network*) is a communications network specifically set-up to link research institutions in the UK. It is co-ordinated from the Rutherford Appleton Laboratories, and also provides a 'gateway' to the European academic network – EARN (European Academic Research Network), and the US equivalent – BITNET.

General advice

Two organisations which operate as general centres of information on computing matters are the subscription funded *National Computing Centre Ltd.* and the DTI funded network of *Microsystems Centres.* □

COMPUTERS

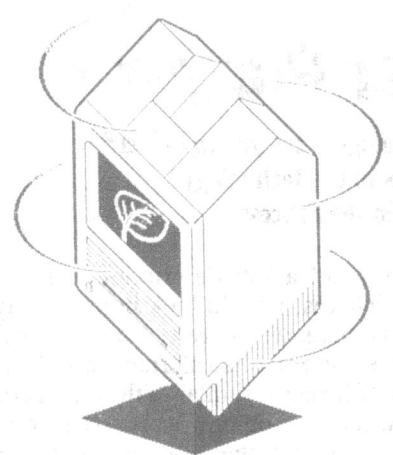

The Environment Online

Aslib (Association for Information Management), Information Resources Centre, Information House, 26–27 Boswell Street, London WC1N 3JZ. Tel: 01 430 2671. Contact: M S G Turpie.

Biological Records Centre, c/o Institute of Terrestrial Ecology, Monks Wood Experimental Station, Abbots Ripton, Huntingdon, Cambridgeshire PE17 2LS. Tel: 0487 3381.

Conservation Monitoring Centre (CMC), 219c Huntingdon Road, Cambridge CB3 0DL. Tel: 0223 277314. Contact: John Caldwell or Jonathan Barzdo.

Dialog Information Retrieval Service, PO Box 188, Oxford OX1 5AX. Tel: 0865 73 0275. Contact: Brian Collinge.

ECHO (European Commission Host Organisation), ECHO Customer Service, 177 Route d'Esch, L-1471 Luxembourg. Tel: +35 2 488041. Contact: Mr C Van der Venne or Mrs B Sweeney.

Economic and Social Research Council Archive, University of Essex, Wivenhoe Park, Colchester, Essex CO4 3SQ. Tel: 0206 872139. Contact: Jean Shearman for Rural Areas Database.

Environment Protection and Management Division of the Council of Europe, B.P. 431 R6, 67006 Strasbourg, Cedex, France. Tel: +33 88 614 961. Contact: Jean-Pierre Ribaut.

Greater London Ecology Unit, 4th Floor, Berkshire House, High Holborn, London WC1. Tel: 01 633 5686. Contact: Dr Meg Game.

GreenNet, 26–28 Underwood Street, London N1 7JQ. Tel: 01 267 0188. Contact: Mitra or Jeremy Mortimer.

Institute of Terrestrial Ecology, Bangor, Gwynnedd, Wales LL57 2LQ. Tel: 0248 364001. Contact: Barry Wyatt for the CORINE Biotopes database and G.L. Radford for the Ecological Data Unit.

JANET (Joint Academic Network), Rutherford Appleton Laboratories, Chilton, Near Didcot, Oxfordshire OX11 0QX. Tel: 0235 21900. Contact: Dr Ian Smith.

London Research Centre, Research Library, County Hall, London SE1 7PB. Tel: 01 633 6713. Contact: Annabel Davies for ACOMPLINE and URBALINE.

Longman Cartermill Ltd., Technology Centre, St Andrews, Fife KY16 9EA. Tel: 0334 77660. Contact: Sandy Shaw, for B.E.S.T.

Microinfo Ltd., PO Box 3, Omega Park, Alton, Hampshire GU34 2PG. Tel: 0420 86848. Contact: Carol Brown or Roy Selwyn.

Microsystems Centre Headquarters, Erick House, Princess Square, Newcastle on Tyne NE1 8ER. Tel: 091 232 2353.

National Computing Centre Ltd., Oxford Road, Manchester M1 7ED. Tel: 061 228 6333.

National Federation for Biological Recording, c/o The Museum Documentation Association, Building 0, 347 Cherry Hinton Road, Cambridge CB1 4DH. Tel: 0223 242848.

National Federation of Zoos, Regents Park, London NW1 4RY. Tel: 01 586 0230. Contact: Dr Peter Bennetto.

Nature Conservancy Council, NGO Data Handling Group, Information Technology Branch, Northminster House, Peterborough PE1 1UA. Tel: 0733 40345. Contact: Dr Ian Baugh or Chris Goody.

Pergamon Orbit Infoline, 12 Vandy Street, London EC2A 2DE. Contact: Susan Inglis.

Royal Botanical Gardens, Kew, Surrey. Tel: 01 940 1171. Contact: Dr G Wickens.

Synchronicity Ltd., 1 Shelton Street, London WC2H 9JN. Tel: 01 240 3118.

Telecom Gold, 60–68 St Thomas Street, London SE1 3QU. Tel: 01 403 6777.

United Nations Environment Programme (UNEP), Industry and Environment Office, Tour Mirabeau, 39–43 Quai Andre Citroen, Cedex 15, 75739 Paris, France. Tel: +33 1 45 78 33 33.

University of Southampton, Southampton SO9 5NH. Tel: 0703 55 9122. Contact: Dr. F. Bisby, Department of Biology, for ALICE and ILDIS.

Warmer Campaign, 83 Mount Ephraim, Tunbridge Wells, Kent TN4 3BS. Contact: Philip Evemy.

Zoological Society of London, Regent's Park, London NW1 4RY. Tel: 01 722 3333. Contact: Dr James Kirkwood.

PERSPECTIVES

Nature on a Silver Platter

The BBC's Ecodisc is a miracle of modern technology, says *Jeremy Cherfas*.
It will help young people work out ways to use technology
without wrecking the environment in the process.

'I don't know when I last had such fun. For a whole afternoon I was in control of a Nature Reserve. I surveyed the various habitats, wandered around the place looking it over summer and winter, heard the wishes of various people who use the place, and came up with a ten-year management plan. As a result, I managed to wipe out the local otters. Never mind, though; nobody ever saw the otters anyway.

All this without having to pull on my green wellies or trusty Barbour, thanks to the BBC's latest interactive videodisc. The Ecodisc is a miracle of modern technology. On the shiny silver platter is a vast amount of information about Slapton Ley, a real nature reserve in Devon. My mission, which I was glad to accept, was to manage the reserve. The disc, along with a computer to control it, let me mess up the habitat in a fraction of the time it normally takes.

My first task was to acquaint myself with the reserve. To do this, I elected to ramble around on my own. (I could have chosen a preset walk.) The ramble took me round the reserve, including a sail up the lake itself, in steps of roughly 100 metres. At every point, I saw still photographs of my surroundings, and I could look in each of eight compass directions. With a press of the button the seasons changed, summer to winter and back again in no time.

Everywhere on the walk I could choose to see what was there in more detail. Short films introduced me to the animals and plants, told me a bit about the different habitats, explained some of the methods I might use to study them further.

The next task was to discover what on earth I was supposed to do. A couple of clicks of the button and a presentable TV presenter appeared to tell me, in general terms, that I was on probation as a reserve manager, my task being to formulate a ten-year plan. Then came a very clever bit; the Ecodisc chose, at random, four special topics that I might like to keep in mind. Two concerned money. The local Sailing Club wanted to lease the lake to teach youngsters, and the Shooting Club wanted to clear the woods and introduce game birds. Less easily quantified, birdwatchers were concerned that any changes in management might disturb their feathered friends, and scientists hoped that I would not do anything to disrupt their studies. The presenter suggested I might like to go to my office and check it out. I did.

This was a real revelation. In the office were a television, a pile of newspapers, an in-tray, a computer, and a job description, and all of them worked. That is, I could look in my in-tray and read the letters there, which were from the special interest groups the presenter had alerted me to. The television presented film clips, similar to the ones I could choose to see while out on my walk. The computer had information about the reserve, information that I could manipulate to see how things were changing. There was even an answering machine. The local eel poacher, currently in the nick, had called to let me know that everybody had to make a living, and eels were his, and could I do my best not to wipe them out.

DR JEREMY CHERFAS is *Life Sciences Consultant at New Scientist. He is the author of a number of books, including* Man-Made Life: A Genetic Engineering Primer *(Blackwell, 1982) and* Zoo 2000 *(BBC, 1985). The Ecodisc (priced at £169, plus VAT) is available from BBC Enterprises.*
BBC Enterprises, *Woodlands, 80 Wood Lane, London W12 0TT. Tel: 01-576 0339/0340.*
New Scientist, *New Science Publications, Holborn Publishing Group, Commonwealth House, 1–19 New Oxford Street, London WC1A 1NG. Tel: 01-829 7777.*

Time, then, to find out a bit more about the ecology of Slapton Ley. The Ecodisc simulates many of the things ecologists normally do. In the woods and reedbeds you can perform proper transects, laying down quadrats and counting the plants in them. Do enough of these, and the computer back in the office will show you a classic kite diagram, the abundance of each kind of plant at each point along your survey line.

Or you can go out birding. Decide where you want to be and the Ecodisc will present you with brief pieces of film of birds. The computer chooses these by knowing how many of each species you are likely to encounter in different habitats. You have to identify the birds, and you can look them up in a reference file if you need to. But there are no right or wrong answers, no nasty bleeps from the all-knowing computer if you count Cetti's warbler as a reed warbler. You may discover your mistake when you come to check your results against the office computer's database, but then again you may not, just like a real ecologist.

One of my favourite tasks was the mammal survey. To do this, you can set out up to eight cameras. These are triggered by any mammals that pass by, again sent there by the computer according to its knowledge of how and where the mammals of Slapton really spend their time. Cameras alone will survey the mammals for you, presenting a nice activity graph too, of when each picture was taken. But you can follow up on the photographic pilot work, with a trapping program.

Traps, like cameras, catch the occasional mammal. You can then put a radio-collar on the animal and track it as it moves about the reserve. After a few minutes of this, you discover that badgers, for example, have large territories that overlap, while mink have much smaller territories that are much more fiercely defended. I never did trap an otter, so I can't tell you how they range about the reed beds, though I did manage to snap one who passed by one of my cameras.

Cameras don't work so well underwater. Instead, you can set nets and examine the haul. The Ecodisc encourages you to measure the pike, and will produce a graphic of how many pike you have of each size. It will also let you mark each pike with a spot of dye. Once you have done that for all the pike in one set of nets, you release the marked fish back into the lake. Set the nets again, and some of the pike you catch will be marked with the dye spot. Count them, and like a real ecologist you can work out roughly how many pike there are at large in the lake.

The basic field techniques of ecology are thus all simulated in the Ecodisc, but as with the birding, there are no right or wrong answers. You have to decide whether the results make sense or not.

Another excellent facility allows you to see what happens to the various habitats if you do nothing. The Ecodisc contains models that simulate events over a 50 year period, often with neat little twists thrown in from real life. The birds, for example, decline even if you do nothing. Why? Check the pike, and there seems to be a cycle, with peaks every 15 years or so when there are lots of big pike, but fewer roach and rudd. Again, the answers are there in the system for you to discover.

Finally, there comes the moment when you have to submit your plan. Up pops the presenter, who has miraculously remembered which pressure groups he warned you about at the start of the affair, to tell you what they think of the proposals. The items in the office change, again to reflect their views. You are free to modify your plan, but if you pig-headedly persevere with your scheme to spray herbicide on the reedbeds and allow local farmers to use water from the lake for irrigation, the Ecodisc ends up with a final tally, telling you what a disaster you have unleashed on the land.

I cannot praise the Ecodisc too highly. I got fully caught up in the reality of the reserve, spending far too long radio-tracking mink and badger, hoping against hope to trap an otter, measuring pike, counting trees, the whole thing. Perhaps the most frightening aspect of the process is how hard it is to do anything right; almost every plan one can submit has some bad effects on Slapton Ley, and even doing nothing is not an answer.

Given a good teacher, I feel sure pupils will get even more out of the Ecodisc than I did. But there is one point that we should not lose sight of. The Ecodisc simulates a real nature reserve, and it does so by calling on the talents and results of the people who have worked there. As the producer of the disc stresses, it prepares students for field work, shows them how hard and how satisfying it can be, but can never replace the real thing.

SECTION 5

Cleaning Up

Environmental protection is now big business, with export earnings booming. Over 9,000 companies are involved in Europe alone and the growing worldwide demand for sustainable development could open up important new commercial opportunities.

There has been a growing trend in recent years to justify any new piece of environmental legislation by pointing to the beneficial impact it is likely to have on the pollution control industry. Although this argument can easily be over-done, the fact is that millions of people are now employed worldwide in the environmental protection industry. In Europe alone, it is estimated that around 1.5 million are employed in this sector – and the evidence suggests that the figure will reach two million some time in the 1990s.

It is also important to remember that the pollution control 'industry' is now a major foreign exchange earner. By 1985, overseas trade in air pollution control and wastewater treatment equipment was earning European companies more than 10 billion ECU (around £5 billion) a year worldwide, with the main environmental export markets being in the United States, Japan and the newly industrialising countries. Among the technologies in which European companies have excelled are:

- catalytic converters used to control car exhaust emissions (page 116);
- high efficiency electrostatic precipitators used to control grit, dust and fume emissions from the chimneys of power plants and factories (page 109);
- ion exchange systems for removing toxic metals from industrial effluents or wastes;
- and anaerobic digestors for the treatment of effluents with a high biochemical oxygen demand (page 110).

European technology for wastewater treatment alone is now exported to over 130 countries, with the major companies involved exporting between 25% and 35% of their sales. Overall, there are more than 9,000 companies actively involved in the development, manufacture and supply of equipment for air, water and wastewater pollution control and waste management. These firms are achieving total equipment sales of over 30 billion ECU (around £15 billion) worldwide, although they are facing increasing competition, particularly from the United States and Japan.

'PABCO Inc'

The scale of the US pollution control industry was demonstrated by a recent report by Management Information Services (MIS). In 1985, MIS noted, US capital and running expenditures for pollution abatement and control (PABCO) amounted to $70 billion. Alvin Cook, Jr, an economist with MIS, pointed out that 'if PABCO were a controlled corporation, it would rank near the top of the Fortune 500'.

States during 1985. MIS found that these investments resulted in total US sales of $19 billion, that they generated business profits of $2.6 billion and provided jobs for 167,000 people.

Even high technology companies like Denmark's Novo Industri (page 118) can find their future growth plans constrained by environmental pressures. As a result, whether the goal is cleaner power generation or cleaner cars, the environment business is now big business. And the evidence suggests that the market opportunities will continue to grow.

And Cook had an answer for those who argued that environmental investments are economically 'non-productive', like building pyramids in the desert. The public now demands environmental quality, he pointed out, and investments in plant and equipment that produce this strongly desired public good are as productive as those that produce the cars, television sets, golf balls or defence systems which we pay for privately or through taxes.

Analysts at Kidder, Peabody, a US stockbroking firm, estimate that simply cleaning up America's one million industrial storage tank (35% of which may be leaking into underlying groundwater) could grow into a $1 billion-a-year business by 1990. That represents an average annual growth rate in spending of 35%, with Kidder, Peabody also forecasting a 25% growth rate in the business of removing waste from sites earmarked for treatment and 30% growth in the business which analyses the make-up of hazardous wastes.

A costly business

As far as PABCO's European (we might call it

POLLUTION & WASTE

Air pollution hits the elderly and young hardest.

'PABCO SA') or British ('PABCO plc') counterparts are concerned, however, it is not easy to find out how well environmental technology companies are performing in terms of return upon capital and other standard financial indicators. One useful source of financial information on UK companies is the ICC Information Group. Among the annual surveys published by ICC are *Pollution Control* (the 1987 edition reviewed 253 companies) and the even larger survey of *Waste & Scrap Dealers & Merchants*. But it would take a fair amount of time to extract a coherent overall picture of the performance of this sector from such data.

Overall, the 1980s have been a difficult period for industry generally and the pollution control sector has not been immune from the problems that have hit the European economy as a whole. But many companies, including Johnson Matthey (a striking omission from the ICC survey of the pollution control industry), have done well in the environmental protection sector.

Care should also be taken in assessing the profitability of broadly-based companies which also happen to be in the environmental sector. Johnson Matthey, for example, reported group profits up 67% after taxation in 1987. However, although the company welcomed European Year of the Environment, in the belief that it would help boost sales of pollution control equipment like it's catalytic converters, used to make cars more 'environment-friendly' (page 116), the profits reported by its catalytic systems division rose just 2%. The bulk of that profit increase came from the company's precious metals, materials technology, colours and printing businesses.

Acid test for clean-up firms

The problem with many of these emerging clean-up markets is that they are a product of environmental politics, the outcome of which is often unclear until the eleventh hour. One area where there will certainly be growing demand, following rising concern across Europe about 'acid rain problems', is in power station clean-up technology. The ideal solution for British power stations would be to burn low-sulphur coal, but because British coal contains relatively high levels of sulphur, a technical solution is essential.

There are a number of options, including treating the coal before it is burned to remove much of the sulphur. In fact some biotechnologists are working on microbial desulphurisation methods. But the option preferred by the Central Electricity Generating Board (CEGB) is the chemical treatment of the emissions following combustion. This approach is unlikely to be cheap, however: a figure of £1 billion has been given for the next wave of power station anti-pollution controls, mainly at three of the CEGB's existing 2,000 megawatt power stations and two new ones planned for the south coast and Nottinghamshire in the 1990s.

This price tag includes £170 million for controlling nitrogen emissions from all coal-fired stations and a £600 million programme to cut sulphur emissions from the three 2,000 megawatt stations. Because of the dearth of new power station construction orders,

111→

PERSPECTIVES

Stepping on the Gas

The idea of converting animal manures and wastes into fertilizer and energy sounds appealing. But firms operating in this market have had to overcome the resistance caused by early failures. *Tim Clarke* says anaerobic digestion is bubbling again.

'Justus von Leibig invented artificial nitrate fertilizers after he realised that large quantities of agricultural nutrients were being irretrievably lost to rivers and the sea by the careless disposal of sewage wastes from the rapidly growing urban populations of the early nineteenth century.

In the early 1840s, von Leibig visited London twice in order to try and persuade the authorities to recycle sewage wastes to land. Although he failed to get his message across then, it is just as relevant today as Europe struggles to come to terms with such interrelated problems as water pollution from organic wastes, the nitrate contamination of water supplies and deteriorating soil structures caused by the loss of organic matter.

The natural recycling processes have proved too slow to cope with the scale and pace of human activities, with the result that the environment often clogs up with our waste products. By failing to recycle such wastes when dealing with sewage disposal and agricultural waste problems, and by artificially compensating for the lack of nutrients returned to farmland, we have created a new set of problems. One emerging solution: anaerobic digestion.

Light from the sewers

Often regarded as a recent innovation, anaerobic digestion has been used for waste treatment and energy production for many years. In the late nineteenth century, for example, street lamps were fuelled by methane produced from city sewers, and large concrete digesters have been treating sewage sludge from large towns and cities since the turn of this century.

Where it occurs in Nature, in the anaerobic (low oxygen) conditions of marsh and estuarial muds, anaerobic digestion is a slow process. Its rate can be greatly increased, however, by creating in a digester the optimum conditions for anaerobic bacteria to grow and reproduce. This allows large amounts of organic wastes to be processed in a relatively short time – and produces considerable quantities of biogas, a mixture of methane and carbon dioxide which can be used for cooking, heating or the production of electricity.

After the price of oil rose dramatically in the early 1970s, interest in digestion as a means of producing renewable energy grew rapidly. During the following decade, there ensued a boom period of digester construction, mainly on intensive livestock farms. Several hundred farm digesters were built, often with the aid of large capital grants.

Problems

Unfortunately, this rush of enthusiasm out-ran the necessary engineering and process expertise, with the result that a large number of digesters have failed to operate to specification. Not surprisingly, anaerobic digestion has come to be regarded as uneconomic and unreliable. The main reasons for this poor image include the following factors:

- practical difficulties in matching energy use to the constant production of gas;
- the low net energy yield from dilute slurry wastes; and
- the lack of specialised equipment and accessories, such as separators and generators.

In short, the sort of problems one might expect with any new technology. After a promising start, though, these problems have greatly slowed the rate of farm digester installation in Europe. In marked contrast, there is the rapidly expanding use of anaerobic digestion for the treatment of domestic sewage in the UK. This trend accelerated in 1981, when Farm Gas Ltd supplied the first prefabricated sludge digester to a Water Authority. The system of construction pioneered by Farm Gas has dramatically cut installation and operating costs, and has been adopted as the standard for the increasing numbers of digesters being installed.

PATAS awards

A key factor underlying this growth has been the recognition that anaerobic digestion is not simply a renewable energy source, but is also an effective means of treating organic wastes – and of reducing their often considerable pollution potential. For example, digestion can cut the biological oxygen demand (BOD) of organic wastes by as much as 80%.

This change of emphasis has caused renewed interest in the economics of digestion, with other advantages including the destruction of most weed seeds and pathogens, odour control, the stabilisation and conservation of nutrients in the wastes, and the production of high-value fertilizer. With the technology now on the rebound, the fact that Farm Gas won both an award and a commendation in the 1986

POLLUTION & WASTE

Pollution Abatement Technology Awards came as a considerable boost.

The award was for a particularly interesting scheme at Bethlehem Abbey, near Porthglenone, Northern Ireland. An anaerobic digestion system and fibre separation plant produce biogas for the Abbey's central heating and for grain drying, while the fibre separated from the digested sludge is composted, bagged and sold. Finally, the separated liquids from the digester are returned to the land and form the basis of the Abbey's new organically-grown wheat enterprise. Details are given in the *Pollution Abatement Technology Award 1986* booklet (contact: Royal Society of Arts, 8 John Adam Street, London WC2N 6EZ or on 01 930 5115).

TIM CLARKE *spent his early years in Sri Lanka, received his BSc from St Andrews University and then taught science in New Zealand. After several years with a family business, he helped build a prefabricated Farm Gas sludge digester system at Saintfield, Ulster. In 1982-83 he travelled to India, Australia, New Zealand, Papua New Guinea and the United States to investigate anaerobic digestion technology. From 1984 to 1986 he was Project Manager, Research and Development, at Farm Gas. Since then he has worked for the company in a range of development, sales and consultancy capacities.*

Farm Gas Ltd, *Industrial Estate, Bishops Castle, Shropshire SY9 5AQ. Tel: 0588 638577.*

Tim Clark (right) and Michael Chesshire (centre) of Farm Gas received a Pollution Abatement Technology Award from Environment Minister William Waldegrave.

---

there has been intense competition between major engineering companies for this business. There are three main technologies contending for this market: the limestone-gypsum process, the spray-dry system and the regenerative method.

The first, to be installed at the Drax power station in North Yorkshire and the new stations, will consume massive quantities of limestone – which is used to mop up the sulphur in the stack emissions. The end-product is gypsum, which is suitable for use in plasterboard production, but which will be produced on such a scale that is certain to flood the market. The second produces a waste product which is only suitable for tipping. The third, which uses much less limestone, produces sulphur products which might find markets in the chemical industry.

By late 1987, eleven consortia were busy producing design studies for the CEGB based on these technologies, some offering their own technology while others have licensed foreign technology from Japanese, US, Swedish or West German companies.

For investors wondering whether and where to invest in the green economy, the *Financial Times* reported that those offering the limestone-gypsum process were SimChem (with Deutsche Babcock); Lodge Cottrell (with Saarberg-Holter of West Germany); John Brown Engineering (with General Electric of the US); NEI International Combustion (with Mitsubishi); Babcock Power (with Babcock-Hitachi); Foster Wheeler Energy (with Peabody Process Systems of the US); and Davy McKee (with Research Cottrell). Spray-dry technology is offered by Foster Wheeler (with Flakt of Sweden) and Lodge-Cottrell, while regenerative systems are available from SimChem (with United Engineers of the US) and Davy McKee Wellman Lord.

Sir David Nickson of the CBI (page 48) has stressed the export potential of environmental technology, products and services, but strong environmental pressures on domestic industry are generally a pre-requisite for healthy export sales of environmental technology. Most foreign customers like to see at least one working example of a technology in the producer's domestic market. In fact, given the relatively slow pace of progress to date in the UK, Davy McKee has done remarkably well overseas, selling some 30 flue gas desulphurisation (FGD) overseas without a single domestic sale.

The scale of the UK pollution control industry as a whole was indicated in 1987 by Environment Minister William Waldegrave, who reported that in 1985 the industry had included about 1,500 firms. The 335 firms for which figures were available had reported a combined turnover of £2.2 billion, twice that of the UK pharmaceutical industry.

A quieter TNT

However profitable or unprofitable environmental technology companies may be, there is no question that pollution control expenditures can impose a considerable financial burden both on major utilities like the CEGB and on mainstream companies, as Novo Industri's experience shows (page 118). But, such experience also shows, there may be significant

Systems for a Cleaner World

Clearwater offer a complete range of sewage and effluent treatment systems providing economic solutions to most waste water problems — from mini package plant for an individual dwelling to systems capable of serving a complete town or industrial complex.

Clearwater's technical staff can advise on all process, engineering and operating problems associated with water and waste water treatment. For full details contact: **Clearwater Systems, Riverway Estate, Portsmouth Road, Guildford GU3 1LZ. Tel: (0483) 33831 Telex: 859356**

CLEARWATER
Sewage and Effluent Treatment Systems

economic benefits to be had from installing cleaner, quieter and more energy-efficient technologies. In some cases, these benefits can more than offset the costs incurred in cleaning up.

Novo may eventually move into effluent treatment enzymes, for example. Less speculatively, a company like British Aerospace which develops an ultra-quiet aircraft such as the 146-QT 'Quiet Trader' will be much better placed to win major sales in noise-sensitive markets. In 1987, British Aerospace won a £700 million contract from the global transport company TNT for up to 76 of the freighters – for use in overnight services.

In many cases, however, the main benefits will be environmental, rather than commercial. In these circumstances, many obstacles can slow or prevent the spread of such technologies. In the absence of tough new regulations, there may be no immediate advantage to a company which installs such technology and therefore no incentive – other than the possibility of environmentalist campaigns – to 'do the right thing'.

Even those companies which have made major progress in cleaning up their operations, as Monsanto has with its waste reduction programmes find the costs soaring as they work their way through the easier targets to some of the more intractable pollution problems.

At the same time, too, many of the companies that most need to hear of such technologies either fail to learn of their existence or, where they do find out about them, lack the funds to proceed to the next stage. As a result, some countries have been using a range of 'carrots', in addition to the regulatory stick, in their attempts to induce industry to move faster.

Barriers to progress

When the Organisation for Economic Co-operation and Development (OECD) looked at the reasons why clean technologies have not spread rapidly, it identified the following barriers which need to be overcome:

- low levels of environmental awareness and training in pollution control, which result in industry seeing environmental regulations simply as an imposition;
- an unwillingness among industrialists to consider themselves as waste managers as well as waste producers;
- a general reluctance to alter production processes and introduce new technologies;
- a lack of confidence that such technologies, even if adopted, will prove technically and economically feasible;
- lack of the technical expertise needed for successful implementation, including dealing with the inevitable initial teething problems;
- a lack of independent advice, leading to an over-dependence on the suppliers of pollution control equipment for advice; and
- lack of access to the financial resources needed to support the necessary capital investment.

The Quiet Trader.

A number of new initiatives have been launched in these areas. Take the first point, for example. One scheme designed to increase industrial awareness of pollution control issues and options is the 'Open Tech' distance learning package put together for British industry by a consortium led by Leicester Polytechnic.

Working with Imperial College and Loughborough University, and funded by the Manpower Services Commission, the 'Open Tech' team have produced learning materials which enable people in industry to learn about such areas as the control of air pollution, water pollution, and noise and vibration when they like, where they like and at their own preferred pace.

EEC initiatives

Since the European Community's fourth environmental action programme lays great stress on the promotion of clean and low-waste technologies, such barriers will need to be effectively tackled and, wherever possible, removed. One relevant initiative under development by the European Commission is Polmark, an advanced database and information service on pollution control and waste management technology and markets.

Another initiative is NETT – the European Network for Environmental Technology Transfer. An array of networks is helping drive the transition to more sustainable forms of development, but most are highly informal and relatively few have been set up by national or international government agencies. NETT is an exception and will speed the exchange of know-how between companies and organisations across Europe.

When Polmark and NETT are fully operational, manufacturers of environmental equipment, to take just one example, will be given better information both on existing markets and on the new opportunities which will open up as subsequent EEC regulations are implemented.

There is now growing evidence that cleaner technologies are a practical option. Ecotec, for example, has produced case studies of such companies as Gist Brocades of the Netherlands, Dornier-System of West Germany and ICI of Britain for the Commission of the European Communities (CEC).

The conclusion, again and again, has been that government agencies must do more to disseminate information about the best available technologies. Polmark and NETT will help achieve this goal, while the CEC's regulation on 'action by the Community relating to the environment' (ACE) provides financial assistance for clean technology demonstration projects.

Seven industrial sectors are currently eligible for CEC support on clean technologies:
- Surface treatment, including scouring, lacquering, galvanizing and cadmium-plating.
- Leather processing, particularly tanning.
- The textile industry.
- The cellulose and paper industries.
- Mining and quarrying, including the recovery and processing of wastes.
- The chemical industry, with a particular focus on organo-chlorine compounds, solvents and sulphurising processes.
- The agri-food industry, including sugar refineries, oil mills, margarine production plants and abattoirs.

A key objective of ACE-funded demonstration projects is to overcome the 'not invented here' syndrome. The environmental industry is developing on such a broad front that it is inevitable that different countries will innovate in different areas, in different ways and at different speeds. It is essential to achieve effective environmental technology transfer both within Europe and between Europe and the rest of the world.

A good example of such transfer is the use by the Anglian Water Authority of the 'root zone bed' for low cost, low maintenance effluent treatment method pioneered by Professor Reinhold Kickuth of West Germany's Kassel University. The basic idea sounds simple, involving the use of artificially created reed beds to treat sewage effluents. The effluent is broken down by bacteria which live in close association with the reeds and the reeds themselves provide the oxygen needed by the 'process'. A visit to West Germany in 1985 by a team from the UK water industry led to the construction of a root zone bed at Anglian Water's Acle sewage treatment works later that year.

Green carrots

Individual member states have developed their own programme to promote the development and deployment of such technologies. Britain, with its traditional emphasis on voluntary approaches to environmental protection, has long been one of the pioneers. The Department of the Environment, the Confederation of British Industry, the Royal Society of Arts and the Environment Foundation, for example, have co-operated on the Pollution Abatement Technology Awards scheme since the early 1980s.

Some of the technologies and products which had won PATA awards over the years were also featured in the 'Green Designer' exhibition, which ran for six weeks at London's Design Centre during Industry Year 1986, before transferring to Glasgow (page 83). For EYE, the scope of the awards was broadened considerably to include four separate award categories:
- The original *Pollution Abatement Technology Award* continued, promoting the development and adoption of cleaner, quieter and more resource-efficient technologies.
- To encourage the incorporation of environmental considerations, such as resource recovery and waste reduction, into the earliest stages of product design, the *Green Product Design Award* was introduced for the first time.
- The *Good Environmental Management Award* aims to promote the pursuit of 'environmental excellence' (see page 226) in industry.
- And the *Export of Appropriate Environmental Technologies Award* from Europe of environment-related technology specifically adapted to the needs of developing countries.

BIOTREATMENT LTD

Microbiological Expertise and Conventional Engineering Solving Environmental Problems On Site

BioTreatment Ltd provides a fully integrated package of services covering design and implementation of programmes for:

- DECONTAMINATION OF LAND
- LANDFILL MANAGEMENT
- INDUSTRIAL WASTE TREATMENT

For a full assessment contact:
BioTreatment Ltd., 5 Chiltern Close, Cardiff CF4 5DL.
Tel: (0222) 766716 Telex: 497244 Fax: (0222) 766945.

POLLUTION & WASTE

Feeling Guilty – But will they Recycle?
How recycling cans plants a tree in the Third World

Ultimately, some of the biggest potential business opportunities may be found in recycling, despite the fact that many parts of the recycling sector have been plagued by a boom-and-bust syndrome. The political pressure for recycling is likely to increase in the longer term, not least because the European Community imports over half of its energy and three-quarters of its raw materials.

The Community also produces over 6 million tonnes of municipal and industrial waste every day, 90% of which is landfilled – resulting not only in the loss of valuable materials but also in groundwater pollution. Less than a third of all this waste is currently recycled, according to European Commission estimates, although the potential exists to more than double the volume recycled.

Recycling wastes can yield reusable alternative materials like tin, glass and paper and provide alternative energy sources, such as refuse-derived fuel (page 110). Several European countries, for example, have a recycling rate for glass bottles of about 30%, up from next to nothing in the 1970s. There is a growing need to consider the potential for recycling right at the outset of the product design process (page 83), however, because products which use a number of non-compatible materials may prove extremely difficult to recycle cost-effectively.

Throwaway lines

Britain, which generates more than 100 million tonnes of waste each year, has not been among the leaders in recycling, despite the environmental and energy benefits recycling can bring. We recycle only 28% of our waste paper, compared to 41% in West Germany – and a Community average of 35%.

The cost savings potentially available are illustrated in aluminium recycling. It takes about 15,000 kilowatt hours (kWh) of electricity to produce one tonne of aluminium from its raw material, bauxite, compared with only about 550 kWh for one tonne produced from recycled aluminium. Recycling technology is constantly progressing, so that the secondary materials produced are purer.

When the Department of Energy asked the Warren Spring Laboratory (WSL) to look at the potential for recycling aluminium scrap, WSL concluded that technology could be developed for the economic recovery of over 30,000 tonnes of aluminium scrap currently discarded in the UK every year. It also estimated that increased use of secondary aluminium could save industry around £15 million a year in energy costs alone.

Alcan's Cash-a-Can scheme, abandoned in 1984, was relaunched in 1986 and extended throughout the Midlands in 1987. When it folded in 1984, it had achieved a peak annual recovery rate of 14 million cans, a small fraction of the two billion aluminium drink cans then consumed annually in Britain. The relaunched scheme should have a better chance of survival, being sponsored not only by Alcan but by Alcoa, Pechiney and VAW. In an interesting incentive scheme, for every 20 cans delivered by Britain's 26,000 primary schools, the industry will pay for a tree to be planted in the Third World – at a cost of 10p per tree.

Unfortunately, WSL's Recycling Advisory Unit failed to attract significant financial support from industry. Members of the UK Reclamation Council, representing the main material recovery industries, said they were not prepared to contribute any of the £100,000 a year which the Government had asked for to match its own funding of the Unit.

Clearly, a great deal more will need to be done to stabilise prices in the recycling industry before companies can enter this field with any great confidence. But there is no doubting the public's enthusiasm for recycling. When kitchenware (and dustbin) manufacturer Addis surveyed housewives, for example, it found that only 43% felt guilty about the amount of domestic rubbish they threw away, with younger housewives (under 34) least likely to worry – only 33% reported guilt feelings. Strikingly, however, 89% of the sample felt that local authorities should play a much more active role in recycling waste materials.

A somewhat surprising 94% also said that they would be happy to help with recycling programmes. For those wishing to boost their personal recycling rate, one of the most useful guides is *The Recyclers' Guide to Greater London*, the second edition of which was published in 1986 by the London Energy and Employment Network (LEEN). Every major region or city should have such a guide.

Most of the projects described in such guides, however, are small in scale and depend on a considerable input of voluntary labour. Eventually, the environmental business as a whole must become financially self-sustaining. And to do so it must build up to the point where it can benefit from some real economies of scale. Small may be beautiful, but big can be better if you are selling into a competitive market.

Overall, the scale and complexity of the world's environmental problems, coupled with the short time-scale over which ecologically and economically sustainable solutions must be developed, make continued public sector funding essential for the foreseeable future.

Not an easy option

Although 'environmental' markets can be increasingly rewarding, they demand at least as much market research, investment in research and development, and professional marketing and post-sale service skills as any other technology-based market. They are not, as the refuse-derived fuel example shows (page 110), an easy option. But their central role in the transition towards more sustainable forms of development suggest that they represent a reasonably attractive commercial proposition for companies prepared to take the long view.

Another commercial opportunity is emerging in the clean-up of contaminated sites. One British company which is pioneering in this field is BioTechnica Ltd (now BTL). Based in Cardiff, Wales, BTL is a start-up environmental biotechnology company which employs more than 50 people and broke into profit for the first time in 1987 (page 43). The company is exploiting microbes to help produce saleable methane from landfill and municipal solid waste sites, for the on-site decontamination of highly polluted sites and for the removal of toxic chemicals from solids and sludges.

At the Greenbank gas works site in Blackburn, Lancashire, for example, BTL's BioTreatment subsidiary has been treating a 10 hectare derelict site, of which something more than half is contaminated with tars, phenols and cyanide. The £760,000 total project cost shows a significant saving – of about £70,000, compared with conventional processes requiring the removal of contaminated soil to distant landfill sites and the importation of clean soil.

The rolls or the mini?

However, even if companies like Monsanto succeed in cutting back still further on the amount of waste that they generate, there is always going to be a need for properly run and cost-competitive waste collection, treatment and disposal services. But Monsanto's problems in identifying environmentally acceptable

Roads to Cleaner Motoring

The demand for cleaner cars is a worthwhile trend. But the nature of the resulting market opportunities will very much depend on whether Europe opts for 'lean-burn' engines or catalytic converters.

Fifteen years ago, with the world reeling from the shock of the first OPEC oil crisis, the motor industry's main concern was to produce more fuel-efficient cars. The success of the resulting research and development programmes is reflected by the fact that, while the number of cars in the world's major car-producing countries jumped by a third between 1972 and 1982, the total consumption of vehicle fuels actually fell by 4%.

The challenge today, however, is to maintain (and improve on) those fuel efficiency achievements, while also producing cars which are considerably less polluting. Motor vehicles are one of the main sources of air pollution in the industrialised countries. Although the motor industry may point to a 50% reduction in noxious emissions from the average car over the last decade, the European Community is now moving towards stricter standards for exhaust emissions, although different countries have been moving at different speeds. West Germany and Denmark, for example, have sought to impose the toughest Community standards, while Britain, France and Italy have tended to drag their heels.

Ironically, a British company, Johnson Matthey Chemicals, is now the world's largest manufacturer of the catalytic converters which have been used to clean up car exhaust emissions in countries like the United States, Japan, West Germany, Sweden and Australia.

A catalytic converter consists of a catalyst-coated ceramic honey comb inside a steel casing, the whole assembly being slotted into a car's exhaust system. So-called 'three-way' catalytic converters, based on such catalysts as platinum, palladium and rhodium, can convert more than 90% of three major exhaust pollutants, nitrogen oxides, carbon monoxide and unburnt hydrocarbons, into water, carbon dioxide and nitrogen. The cost of fitting such a system has come down to around £200–£300, although companies like Fiat, Volvo, Mercedes and Nissan have begun to offer catalyst-equipped cars at no extra cost.

To begin with, the markets for catalytic converters were exclusively export markets. The photochemical smog problems experienced by cities like Tokyo and Los Angeles in the 1960s led to new legislation, such as the 1970 US Clean Air Act, which introduced tough new vehicle emission standards. Indeed the US imposed such tight emission standards that catalytic converters became compulsory and it is currently Johnson Matthey's biggest market. The company, which now produces some 15 million autocatalysts a year worldwide, supplies over 50% of US requirements.

POLLUTION & WASTE

waste disposal options underscore the problems which the waste industry faces in Europe.

Meanwhile, the cost of waste disposal, both in the industrial and municipal waste sectors, continues to climb. The wealthier industries may club together to establish purpose-built treatment and disposal facilities, like those at Indaver, but there will be many opportunities for well-run private sector initiatives designed to serve demand in this area. Companies currently active in this field in Britain include Cleanaway, Leigh Environmental, Ocean Environmental Technology and Re-Chem International.

The lesson which waste disposal companies have learned fairly painfully, like Berridge Incinerators, which was forced to close a hazardous waste incinerator near Nottingham, is that environmental excellence is as essential in this field of individual endeavour as in any other.

The waste industry has long been plagued by 'cowboy' operators, with fierce price competition between different disposal options, and between different companies in the same sector. This has made it difficult for the more forward thinking companies to develop commercially viable, environmentally sound approaches. But the pressure on companies like Re-Chem International, which incinerates chemical wastes and has long been the focus of controversy, continues to grow. Indeed, Re-Chem broke with industry precedent early in 1987 by hiring Graham Searle, the founding executive director of Friends of the Earth in the UK, as an environmental consultant.

With the pressures for a total ban on waste incineration at sea intensifying, Searle believes that land-based incineration is an essential alternative to land or sea dumping of toxic wastes. 'I have been saying for 20 years that chemical waste is better disposed of in a Rolls-Royce rather than in a clapped-out Mini sort of way,' he noted.

Clearly, however, stringent legislation and a willingness on the part of the regulatory authorities to take the cowboys to court are going to be essential if the better-intentioned waste disposal companies are not to succumb to cut-price, corner-cutting competition.

But markets have now begun to open up in Europe, too. The growing concern about the health of West Germany's forests has led to an expanding market for catalytic converters there, with Johnson Matthey second only to West Germany's own Degussa in terms of market share.

The British motor industry, however, has tended to argue that for smaller-engined cars, up to two litres, so-called 'lean-burn' technology provides the best answer, both environmentally and economically. By using sophisticated electronics, improved engine management and modified cylinder heads, lean-burn engines burn fuel more leanly, with a thin air/fuel ratio of up to 24 parts of air to one part of fuel. Among the companies working on improved fuel injection systems, which help save fuel and cut emissions, is West Germany's Bosch.

Apart from cutting the output of carbon monoxide and nitrogen oxides, lean-burn engines are typically between 10% and 15% more fuel efficient. Fuller combustion results in the destruction of potential pollutants, although groups like Friends of the Earth have argued that lean-burn engines still produce hydrocarbons, which may cause cancer.

Recent years have seen a spate of announcements about lean-burn technology. But American car manufacturers abandoned lean-burn technology in favour of 'three-way' catalytic converters. One problem with catalytic converters is that they can be 'poisoned' by leaded petrol, with the result that their ability to clean up exhaust emissions is reduced. Clearly, the trend towards unleaded petrol will help on that front.

'A clean air wave is moving over Europe as exhaust emission control and unleaded petrol are the object of pending legislation in more and more countries,' observed Volvo. Although Volvo

NOVO INDUSTRI

In a Ferment About Pollution

One of Europe's leading biotechnology companies, Novo believes it may have to cut its discharges of nitrogen and phosphorus by as much as 50% over the next 5–6 years. It is trying out a number of innovative ways of encouraging its various units to clean up.

Novo Industri, the Danish pharmaceutical and enzyme producer, is not generally thought of as a polluter. But Denmark's ever-tightening pollution control legislation is putting increasing pressure on all industries to cut back on their discharges of nitrogen and phosphorus into rivers and the sea.

'Personally I think that when we get to the year 2000, we will hardly be allowed to discharge anything at all,' says Niels W. Holm, Novo's chief operating officer, 'unless it is in the form of a product serving a useful purpose, such as a fertilizer – or in the form of waste water that is so clean that it may, literally speaking, be used as drinking water. Some innovative thinking is clearly needed.'

The pressures on companies like Novo have intensified since oxygen levels were found to be depressed in some areas of the sea north of Zealand, during 1981 and 1986. These findings gave rise to a heated debate in the Danish parliament and an action programme to improve the marine environment was passed into law in 1987, to take effect from 1 January 1993.

Who is responsible?

Suspicion had focused on two main pollutants: nitrogen and phosphorus. According to a study carried out in 1984 by the National Environment Agency, agriculture is responsible for nearly 90% of nitrogen discharges and municipal purification plants for around 50% of the phosphorus discharges. Industry, by contrast, was estimated to account for 2% of the nitrogen and 23% of the phosphorus.

But because agricultural discharges are much harder to tackle – and because industry is generally better at cleaning up its discharges than are local authorities – the pressures on industry are likely to be particularly intense. Indeed, notes Holm, the new action programme marks something of a break with Danish precedent, in that it is no longer a question of how much pollution the environment can safely absorb, but of how clean industry and other potentially polluting operations can become.

The programme aims to cut nitrogen discharges by 50% and phosphorus discharges by 80%, at an estimated total cost of Dkr 12–13 billion – or well over £1 billion. The cost to Danish industry with separate discharge lines is likely to be around Dkr 1 billion, plus annual operating costs to the tune of some Dkr 240 million. Industries connected to municipal sewage systems will have to pay Dkr 3-4 billion, plus annual operating costs.

'From its Kalundborg plant, Novo discharges on an annual basis some 400 tonnes of nitrogen and 75 tonnes of phosphorus,' observes the company's environmental affairs manager, Torben Schjoedt Jensen. 'The establishment of the necessary purification facilities at our Kalundborg plant will amount to approximately Dkr 200 million and annual working expenditure to some Dkr 40 mil-

---

has pioneered in 'clean car' technology (including catalytic converters) since the 1970s, when it received an award for 'Cleanest Car in the USA' from the California Air Resources Board, it is increasingly trying to design clean engines rather than opting for strap-on converters.

'In general', it notes, 'catalytic emission control systems are expensive, require more maintenance and suffer damage if run on leaded petrol. By contrast, the newly-engineered and non-catalytic Volvo engines achieve their low emission levels at little extra cost and with no significant reduction in performance and fuel efficiency.' One technique used by the company is exhaust gas recirculation, with the exhaust stream passed back to the cylinders via the intake manifold, reducing the levels of nitrogen oxide in the eventual exhaust emissions.

There has been concern that if lean-burn engines are used on cars of 1.4–2.0 litres, they might actually *increase* the output of nitrogen oxides and hydrocarbons at higher speeds. A test programme run by the West German motoring industry on a lean-burn Peugeot 1.6 GTI and a VW Golf GTI equipped with a US-standard catalytic converter found that at 30–40 mph the Peugeot produced 5 times more nitrogen oxide and 30 times more hydrocarbons, while at 55 mph it produced 240 times more nitrogen oxides and 25 times more hydrocarbons.

If all European vehicles of this size were to be equipped with such engines, Johnson Matthey has estimated that emissions of nitrogen oxides would increase by 1.5 million tons a year, hydrocarbon emissions by 500,000 tons and carbon monoxide by 2.2 million tons. The conclusion: even if lean-burn technology does become widely available, catalytic converters will still be needed on many models. □

lion. On top of this, we envisage an increase in the fee we pay to the municipal purification plant at Copenhagen, where Novo's effluent from the Copenhagen plant is discharged.' The discharges from Kalundborg go into Jammerland Bay.

How are the fish?

The nitrogen in a typical Novo effluent originates partly from cell residues and nutrient medium from the fermentation tanks, and partly from the salts, such as ammonium sulphate, which are added to the fermentation broth as a dietary supplement. The phosphorus compounds come mainly from these salts.

Although there has been some concern that the resulting pollution might hit fish catches in Denmark's coastal waters, substantial increased in catches have been reported in recent years. 'A survey has been conducted among the fishermen of Jammerland Bay,' reports Schjoedt Jensen. 'This survey does not lend substance to the assertion that the fishing industry is suffering a decline, nor that the general health of the fish population has changed. Furthermore, Novo has conducted an extensive survey of Jammerland Bay ecology.'

Whatever the facts of the matter, however, Novo recognises that environmental pressures will continue to intensify. In fact, all the company's departments and units are now making a concerted effort to find new methods to cut nitrogen discharges.

'Four to five years ago we told our production people to produce away,' says Holm, 'as much as Novo could sell. A purification unit would take care of the effluent. This has worked fine and we have a competent and efficient purification unit. However, if we have to observe the narrow limits I envisage for the near future – perhaps a 50% reduction of the discharge within the next 5–6 years at increased production levels, that is – then we have to start thinking differently.'

A silver lining?

'We have to find methods to reduce our consumption of raw materials,' he observes, 'we have to substitute nitrogenous raw materials, reuse and recirculate raw materials, and investigate the possibilities of purifying effluent at individual production units, before it is mixed in Novo's central purification plant at Kalundborg.'

From 1988, each production unit has been charged Dkr 70 per kilo of nitrogen discharged into the central purification plant. For comparison, the nitrogen used in production processes costs around Dkr 5–10 per kilo. This 'duty' is seen as an incentive for the individual units to find alternatives to their present discharge practices.'

Meanwhile, on the basis that there are few dark clouds without a silver lining, Carsten Ravn of Novo's Technician's Association has suggested that Novo should start developing enzymes for use in effluent purification. Torben Schjoedt Jensen accepts that enzymes can speed up the reaction rate in certain types of effluent treatment plant, but notes that this 'isn't an area we are active in currently. But it is quite possible,' he concludes, 'that it may one day become another business area for Novo.'

Novo Industri A/S, *Novo Alle, 2880 Bagsvaerd, Denmark. Tel: +45 2 98 23 33.*

Fuels from Waste

Two new processes for turning waste materials into useful fuels have recently gone commercial. But, although the UK is among the world leaders in these technologies, *Mike Flood* argues that serious legal, financial and institutional obstacles are slowing market penetration – and in one case could sink a technology completely.

'Britain's 18 million households throw out around 14 million tonnes of refuse a year containing useful quantities of ferrous and non-ferrous metals, glass, plastic, paper and board. Commerce and industry generate another 16 million tonnes. All this represents a major resource which could, in principle, be recycled.

Over the years, many attempts have been made to recover some or all of these materials – even the rotting vegetable matter which can be composted and used as a soil conditioner. However, one of the most promising options is to recover combustible materials for use as fuel.

Two very different energy-from-waste technologies are now emerging onto the market. One harnesses natural bacterial decay in landfill sites to produce a combustible gas; the other converts raw refuse into a light flock fuel which can either be burnt directly in conventional solid-fuel boilers or squeezed into hard fuel pellets which can substitute for coal in a wide range of applications.

Landfill gas

Landfill gas is a mixture of methane and carbon dioxide with a heat value around half that of natural gas. It can be recovered by sinking wells into specially prepared landfill and used on site to generate electricity or exported to nearby factories to provide process heat. In the US the gas is also 'scrubbed' and fed into local gas utility networks. The technology was originally developed to overcome serious environmental problems associated with gas migration. At some sites gas was found to cause vegetation to die back. It also led to fire risks and even dangerous accummulations in nearby buildings. In 1986, a bungalow in a village near Ripley, Derbyshire, was demolished following a methane gas explosion and the occupants of several hundred houses on the neighbouring estate were put on 24 hour evacuation alert.

Landfill gas extraction is now becoming big business. It began in California in 1975, and already there are over 140 schemes in operation in more than a dozen countries. Nearly 20 schemes were in production in Britain by the end of 1987, saving a total of around 125,000 tonnes of coal equivalent per annum. More are planned. A recent survey of licensed landfill sites in the UK has indicated that as many as 330 may be suitable for landfill gas extraction. Experiments are also under way to see whether gas production can be increased by recirculating leachate or pumping nutrients (such as sewage) into the landfill. It may ultimately be possible to double or even treble the yields.

But landfill gas has not had an easy time over the last couple of years as a result of the fall in the price of oil. Producers have also been forced to operate on slim profit margins because of cut-throat competition from British Gas. The pay-back time on some projects is around four years – double what it was a couple of years ago. Moreover, those contemplating using the gas for electricity generation have had to think twice because of the low buy-back tariffs offered by the generating boards. A number of proposals for small schemes (1 MW and below) have actually been put on ice. Predatory pricing by large monopolies is a very real fear amongst producers.

The second resource-conserving technology that is facing even greater problems is refuse-derived fuel (RDF).

Refuse derived fuel

The practice of burning refuse to provide useful heat is not new – a refuse incinerator in Oldham, Lancashire, was being used to raise steam for electricity generation as long ago as 1896. Since then waste incinerators in many parts of the world have been used to supply steam for industrial process heat and group heating, as well as generating electricity. Today there are over 350 energy-from-waste schemes in operation, mostly in Continental Europe and North America. A few are in Britain.

Many of the early UK incinerators were batch-fed and burnt screened and sorted municipal wastes. In addition to providing useful heat, they reduced the volume of material requiring disposal by *two thirds* or more, and produced an innocuous residue that was more easily disposed of in landfill. More sophisticated 'mass burn' incinerators were introduced in the 1960s, but these proved less reliable and earned the technology a bad name.

The new installations were highly automated and involved very much more complex (and expensive) machinery. They took raw refuse (without pre-treatment) and burnt it on continuous rather than stationary grates. But raw refuse turned out to be a rather awkward fuel because of its variable composition, high moisture content, and low

POLLUTION & WASTE

calorific value, and the fact that it produced copious quantities of fly ash. Expensive modifications were necessary at many installations as a result of poor design and, as often as not, maloperation by inexperienced staff. Some local authorities got their fingers badly burned.

RDF Flock: A more successful process was developed by private industry in the early 1970s. Associated Portland Cement Manufacturers (now Blue Circle) was one of the early pioneers. The company undertook trials on burning shredded and screened refuse at its Shoreham cement works as early as 1973 and later adapted the process for a full-size commercial plant at Westbury. One fifth of this plant's energy now comes from refuse derived fuel (RDF), the rest from coal. The Westbury cement kilns consume around 60,000 tonnes of Wiltshire's refuse each year.

RDF Pellets: Pelletized RDF is a potentially more useful fuel than flock because it can be burnt in a far wider range of industrial appliances. It is equivalent in size to washed coal 'singles'. Demonstration plants to produce pellets were completed in 1979/80 at Byker (Newcastle), Doncaster and Eastbourne. The first two were supported by generous government grants, the third by private finance. The Byker plant was the biggest of the three, and designed to produce around 12,500 tonnes of RDF a year from 50,000 tonnes of household and commercial waste. More recently, two larger commercial RDF plants have been built, one at Huyton on Merseyside and the other at Castle Bromwich in the Midlands. Two more are planned (at Newport, on the Isle of Wight, and at Hastings). A small pilot plant is also operating in Glasgow.

Experience suggests that such plants can provide an economically viable disposal route for authorities with high waste disposal costs. The plant operator would normally require a 'gate fee' of £8–10 per tonne of waste handled (for reducing the volume of the waste requiring disposal). It is not possible to make a profit on pellet sales alone.

There have been materials handling problems at both Huyton and Castle Bromwich, which have delayed the operation of the plants and restricted station output. Merseyside Waste Derived Fuels, who operate the Huyton plant, have actually taken the main contractor, Tollemache, to court claiming damages for none fulfilled contractual obligations. But given time (and money) the technical difficulties and teething problems will be overcome. It is marketing the fuel that is turning out to be the real headache.

Marketing headaches

Early indications were that there would be a major industrial market for refuse derived fuel amongst solid fuel users provided the price was right. It was on this basis that Merseyside and West Midlands County Councils invested in the technology. Huyton and Castle Bromwich cost around £3.5 million each (including generous grants from the Government and EEC, respectively). But, by the time the first fuel pellets were coming off the production lines (in 1986), many of the old 'smokestack' industries had closed down because of recession, coal prices had slumped (in sympathy with oil), and the market for new and replacement boilers had virtually dried up.

Moreover, industrialists appeared to have had second thoughts about converting to RDF because of the added handling and storage problems, the costs in-

volved in modifying their boilers, and fears that burning the new fuel could lead to reduced boiler availability through corrosion and fouling. (Recent studies indicate that, with some types of boiler, these fears are not entirely groundless.) The growth in public concern about possible links between burning refuse and the release of dioxin also made potential users nervous. Many considered that there was simply insufficient of a price advantage to outweigh the added inconvenience and risk, and there was little scope to reduce the price of pellets.

Worse still, the operators of the Castle Bromwich plant came up against a major legal problem: while the plant was under construction, Birmingham became a Smokeless Zone which meant that only *authorised* fuels could be burnt in the region. And RDF was not an 'authorised' fuel under the terms of the Clean Air Act. Now, before companies in the Midlands can convert to RDF, they have to get special clearance, which involves extensive testing of their equipment – a complication Birmingham City Council (the current owners of the plant) could well do without.

One highly innovative authority (not burdened with the Smokeless Zone problem) has managed to get round the marketing difficulties by selling RDF to *itself*. East Sussex is burning pellets produced in the small Eastbourne plant in three of its Colleges of Further Education. The Council, through its company East Sussex Enterprises, has also found a lucrative market amongst glasshouse horticulturalists, and has even sold fuel on the domestic market, although this practice has now been officially discouraged.

Avoidable mistakes

There are some important lessons to be learned from the experience with landfill gas and RDF concerning the difficulties that new biofuel technologies can face. While the technical problems are well on the way to being solved, some of the more intransigent legal, institutional and marketing problems remain.

All new technologies face an uphill battle to gain acceptance. Invariably, there are financial risks, because the technologies are less well understood, and high unit costs, because of small scale production. There may also be problems in establishing a market for the product, especially when no established distribution network exists.

New energy technologies are also prone to uncontrollable sea-change events in the market (such as the collapse in oil prices), and often face fierce competition from powerful and well established fuel industries, and unsympathetic treatment from generating boards. Landfill gas and RDF are no exception.

But mistakes have also been made. With RDF, for example, most of the effort went into 'technology push' without testing adequately for 'market pull'. And the combustion characteristics of the new fuel were not fully investigated before critical decisions were taken to invest in large scale production plant. It was simply assumed that RDF would replace coal. In practice, it has turned out to be a very different kind of fuel. The fact that the producers were geared more to *production* than to sales did not help: they have had to learn about marketing the hard way.

Earlier discussions with boiler manufacturers and users might well have anticipated some of the technical and institutional problems that have now arisen. For the future, the answer may lie in specialist heat supply or energy service companies taking over from local authorities or small private concerns. They have the necessary financial backing, more appropriate marketing skills, and better access to potential users.

DR MICHAEL FLOOD *founded Natural Resources Research in 1985 to carry out work on new and renewable energy technologies. NRR has carried out a series of studies on non-technical barriers to policy implementation and is also interested in the assessment of the social and environmental impact of new technologies. Having obtained a First in chemistry at Leeds University in 1968, he focused his PhD on organic chemistry – following which he switched to study science policy at Bath University and nuclear terrorism at King's College, London.*

A consultant to Friends of the Earth during the early stages of the nuclear debate (1976–82), he has given evidence to a number of official commissions, including: the Royal Commission on Environmental Pollution (1976); the Australian Ranger Uranium Inquiry (1976); the New Zealand Royal Commission of Inquiry into Nuclear Power (1977); and the Parliamentary Select Committee on Energy (1980, 1983). He is a member of FoE's Energy Advisory Panel. His books have included Nuclear Prospects *(1976),* The Pressurised Water Reactor *(1981) and* Solar Prospects *(1983), and he edits* Solar News, *published by the UK Section of the International Solar Energy Society.*

Natural Resources Research, *15 Church Lane, Loughton, Milton Keynes MK5 8AS. Tel: 0908 666275.*

POLLUTION & WASTE

Rechem is committed to a cleaner, safer world.

Rechem plants are licensed under the Control of Pollution Act to process virtually the entire range of industrial wastes.

Facilities include high temperature incineration, chemical treatment, waste disposal consultancy and hazardous waste emergency response.

Rechem recognises public concern regarding waste disposal facilities. An on going programme of research and development is geared to ensure the Company's operating and safety standards maintain Rechem's reputation as a world leader.

Industrial societies produce a wide range of chemical products and by-products that must be destroyed safely. They are generated by almost every industry: transport, household furnishings, electrical equipment – even food and medicines.

However they arise they must eventually be destroyed. Without threatening the environment or the health of people and animals.

Rechem employees share the concern of "the Greens" about society's need for safe waste disposal. Only by utilising scientific methods can people be certain of preserving a safe environment for ourselves – and future generations.

If the standards Rechem are pioneering were attained by every industrial enterprise, we could all be sure of leaving a cleaner and safer world to our children.

Rechem is committed to a cleaner, safer world.

RECHEM
ENVIRONMENTAL SERVICES

RECHEM INTERNATIONAL LIMITED
CHARLESTON ROAD HARDLEY HYTHE SOUTHAMPTON HAMPSHIRE SO4 6ZA TEL SOUTHAMPTON (0703) 898915 TELEX 477733 FAX 0703 897282
PONTYVELIN INDUSTRIAL ESTATE NEW ROAD PANTEG PONTYPOOL GWENT NP4 5DQ TEL PONTYPOOL (04955) 56231 TELEX 497781 FAX 04955 57019
Registered Office: Madeley House 8 Packhorse Road Gerrards Cross Bucks SL9 7QE Registered in London No 934787
Tel (0753) 880077 Telex 848079 Fax 0753 887292

PERSPECTIVES

Clean Technologies?

Clean – or cleaner – technologies are generally agreed to be a good thing.
But, as *Ernst von Weizsäcker* notes, different countries have very
different ideas on what a clean technology is.

'Pollution prevention pays,' said Joseph T. Ling of the American 3M Company, adding a new environmental principle to the existing one, the 'polluter pays' principle.

Because pollution fines were rising sharply at the time, as were energy and raw material costs, it was only natural that pollution prevention would become a high priority, and sometimes profitable, objective for industrial companies. At 3M, some 1,900 projects proposed as part of the Pollution Prevention Pays (3P) Programme had been approved by 1987, bringing savings of $300 million.

How 3P works

In environmental terms, the Programme now eliminates annually 110,000 tonnes of air pollutants, 13,200 tonnes of water pollutants, 275,000 tonnes of solid wastes and sludges, and more than 1.5 billion gallons of waste-water.

The basic thrust of the 3P Programme has been to reformulate products, modify production processes, redesign equipment and recover waste materials for re-use. More specifically, 3M has concentrated on:

- using waste materials as inputs to its manufacturing processes;
- reducing water consumption by switching to a closed water cycle and by segregating drains;
- cutting energy consumption by selecting suitable processes and process conditions, by integrating heating and power systems, and by grouping plants in such a way as to reduce energy loss;
- improving yields by collecting spillages and by segregating and re-using by-products;
- and, finally, on choosing the right clean, low-energy and long-life process routes and products.

Comparable developments have been reported in Japan since the early 1970s. The cost of energy was artificially inflated in Japan, well beyond world market prices, and polluters were taken to court by their victims and convicted – even on *statistical* evidence of cause-and-effect chains. As a result, Japanese industry was forced into cleaner technologies faster than many of its competitors.

What is a clean technology?

'Clean technologies' have also been a central objective in European policy-making for years. In 1980, for example, the EEC arranged a major international congress on clean technologies and several countries gave them priority attention. Unless one assumes that it will become cheaper to pollute in future, which on current trends seems unlikely, there is no conceivable reason why clean technologies should disappear once they are developed – unless they are replaced by even cleaner ones.

But there *are* significant constraints on the development and deployment of such technologies, not least being the question of cost. Whatever the 3M experience may suggest, there is no automatic linkage between the cleanliness and cost-competitiveness of a technology or product. If anything, such technologies and products are likely to be more expensive, because of the necessary investment in R&D. And there are a number of non-cost constraints, which will need to be tackled if clean technologies are to achieve their full potential (page 113).

Nuclear 'clean technologies'

First, for example, it is far from universally clear what

PROFESSOR Dr ERNST von WEIZSÄCKER *is Director of the Institute for European Environmental Policy.*

The Institute for European Environmental Policy *has offices in Bonn (Aloys-Schulte-Str 6, D-5300 Bonn 1, Federal Republic of Germany or on 21 38 10), London (3 Endsleigh Street, London WC1H 0DD or on 01 388 2117) and Paris (55 rue de Varenne, F-75341 Paris Cedex 7, France or on 4222 1234).*

'clean technologies' are. For France, the transition from fossil fuel-burning power plants to nuclear reactors was held up as the symbol of clean technology. In Germany, meanwhile, the focus was on desulphurisation and denitrification systems. For many environmentalists, however, only conservation and renewable-resource technologies qualify. So the trend is not as simple as the facts might at first suggest.

Second, the pace of development and deployment of such technologies is profoundly influenced by the rate at which new legislation is introduced and the vigour with which it is enforced. Rapidly introduced, stringent legislation may be popular, but can lead to more costly, less efficient 'end-of-the-pipe' solutions, rather than to clean technologies proper. The most effective approach, at least as far as the promotion of clean technology R&D is concerned, is likely to be based on strict, predictable long-term legislation.

Third, the definitional problem has hampered clean technology support programmes. Several countries have introduced fiscal incentives in this area, but the 3M experience also suggests that many thousands of ordinary process innovations could hypothetically qualify for such support. So, to fend off a possible avalanche of doubtful borderline cases, the tax incentives have been restricted to clearly separable and identifiable technologies – and that, ironically, has again favoured end-of-the-pipe solutions.

ICI's waste brine treatment plant, Runcorn.

POLLUTION & WASTE

The International Biochemicals Group

Develops, manufactures and markets high-performance products that put naturally-occurring microbes to work.

Our range of environmentally safe products has applications ranging from industrial and municipal waste water treatment, domestic sewage treatment and the enhancing of agricultural processes, to the tackling of drainage-associated problems in the Catering and Food Processing Industries.

These products are safe, simple and effective, solving problems currently being solved by less acceptable methods.

Product range includes:

The Biolyte Systems
A range of microbially based products developed to improve efficiency of biological waste water treatment plants.

BioFree
A biological product developed to prevent the problems caused by grease and food waste accumulation in drainage sytems.

Septaplan
A scheme that keeps septic tanks/cesspits working effectively, preventing common problems.

Forager
A biological additive to improve silage quality.

Life Force at Work

 The International Biochemicals Group
Group Marketing
Aldine House 9-15 Aldine Street London W12 8AW
Telephone: 01-740 4422 Telex 295978 INTBIO G
Fax: 01-749 2534

Head Office: Dublin

PERSPECTIVES

Don't Expect Instant Fixes

An old Yorkshire saying holds that you 'don't get owt for nowt.' If industrial development is to become more sustainable, says *Mike Flux*, we must beware of expecting overnight success.

'From the point of view of someone who makes his living promoting environmental excellence in a major European company, there have been some quite remarkable developments in business attitudes to the management of environmental issues in recent years.

The trends have been developing for some time. The World Industry Conference on Environmental Management (WICEM), held at Versailles in 1984, just weeks before the Bhopal disaster, concluded that world-scale environmental problems would not be resolved without the co-operation of the industrial sector.

And this theme was picked up and underscored by the Brundtland Commission's report, *Our Common Future*. Economic development, we were told, is essential if the world's most pressing environmental issues are to be tackled with any hope of lasting success.

Dangerous stereotypes

These conclusions may not please some of the more extreme environmentalists, but they should not dismiss them out of hand. The popular stereotype of the 'good guys' of the environmental movement ranged against the 'villains' of commerce and industry has always struck me as dangerously simplistic. For one thing, it downgrades the important contributions which industry makes to our everyday quality of life.

Whether one thinks of our relative freedom from hunger, disease and drudgery, or of our ability to travel and broaden our education, I cannot believe that these are aspects of modern life which most people would willingly surrender.

Of course, none of this is to deny that our technology, and in particular the scale on which we now deploy that technology, has brought major environmental problems in its wake. But we should not develop massive guilt complexes about these problems unless we are failing to address them. Just as the need to improve nutrition, health and living conditions were a key part of the agenda for previous generations, so the need to develop new styles of industry and new lifestyles which are better fitted to life on a smallish planet represent the challenge both for us and for future generations.

Sidestepping disaster

Environmentalists reject what they dub 'technological fixes', but they should beware of dismissing technology outright. Indeed, the only way we are likely to combine the ability to sustain and improve the quality of life, whether in the world's industrial economies or in the developing countries, while at the same time recognising the new environmental imperatives, is to develop better technologies. Any failure to do so will result not only in environmental disaster but in heightened political tensions. The ultimate manifestation of political conflict is war, the ultimate environmental disaster.

'Sustainable development' is increasingly recognised as a natural meeting ground for industrial and environmental interests. Indeed, industry's experience in practical resource management has a great deal to offer – not least by ensuring that the search for Sustainable Development does not prove as elusive for us as the search for the Philosopher's Stone or the Elixir of Life proved for the medieval mind.

Inappropriate development or poorly designed products can certainly help speed the transmutation of environmental resources into dust, but beware slogans. Faced with a simple slogan, one is tempted to believe that the solution to our problems will also be simple. Nothing could be further from the truth.

Doing more with less

If a new technology can be developed that enables industry to extract more value out of a given quantity of raw materials and energy, with less pollution, clearly we would be foolish not to adopt it. The fact that such 'clean' or 'low-waste' technologies are not adopted overnight suggests that either they do not exist – or that where they do there are other obstacles in the way of progress.

There is a wealth of difference, for example, between a technology which has been shown to work on the laboratory bench or at the semi-technical scale and a robust, reliable commercial process. Inventions cannot be made to order, as the quest for a cure for AIDS painfully demonstrates, nor can success be guaranteed when a possible product or technology is identified. The history of technical development is littered with the financial and institutional ruins left by grand failures.

An elusive goal

There is something approaching a fundamental law in the old Yorkshire saying that you 'don't get owt for nowt'. All too frequently, progress in one area produces undesirable results in another. The political row over where to get the limestone needed to feed

POLLUTION & WASTE

the flue gas desulphurisation (FGD) plants needed to clean up the emissions from CEGB power plants is a case in point. Yet it had previously been impossible for lateral-thinking industrial environmentalists to raise such issues without being branded as 'reactionary' by the acid rain lobby.

Even if the path towards more sustainable forms of development will be slow, uncertain and difficult, however, industry has a great deal to contribute, not least by developing new, more environment-friendly technologies, products and modes of operation. Note that I say 'more', because I believe that we are unlikely to find complete solutions to all our problems within a reasonable timescale. Indeed, we should not ignore those 'less than complete' solutions which nevertheless may have an important contribution to make.

The process of developing more sustainable technologies is likely to be a challenge for as long as our species exists on Earth. A great deal is being achieved and, in the longer term, today's near-miracle may well become commonplace. But in the meantime the search for perfection could well lead us off in the same fruitless quests which diverted the talent and resources of Europe's alchemists for centuries.

MIKE FLUX *is a chemist who has worked for ICI for 30 years in a number of technical and managerial roles. For the past nine years, as Group Environment Adviser, he has been responsible at ICI's head office for the co-ordination of the group's environmental activities.*

Imperial Chemical Industries plc, *Imperial Chemical House, Millbank, London SW1P 3JS. Tel: 01 834 4444.*

ICI's FM21 Chlor-alkali cell

SECTION 6

Finding the Energy

The omens are mixed, but the 1990s could well see another oil shock of the kind which severely dented economic growth in the 1970s. At the same time, environmental concerns constrain a growing number of energy supply technologies. So what are the prospects for 'green' energy technologies like renewable energy and energy efficiency?

In the ten years prior to the first OPEC (Organisation of Petroleum Exporting Countries) oil shock of 1973, when oil prices quadrupled, primary energy demand in the non-communist countries grew at around 5% a year. By 1986, however, demand was growing at an annual rate of only around 1%, reaching 98 million barrels a day of oil equivalent that year. Various indicators suggest that the growth in energy demand will remain relatively low for the rest of the century, but energy issues are likely to remain high on the political agenda.

Oil is still by far the largest energy source, accounting for some 47% of total primary energy demand in the non-communist world in 1986. The opening up of non-OPEC oil production areas since the 1970s helped buffer the impact of the long-running Iran-Iraq war, but the longer-term prospect is not particularly good. At the time of the first OPEC oil price hike, OPEC members provided the industrial world with two-thirds (67%) of its oil. By 1987, they provided well under half (38–40%), although estimates prepared by the International Energy Agency suggest that the proportion will be back to around 63% by the year 2000. The potential for future oil shocks is clear.

Coal provided 20% of non-communist primary energy needs in 1986 and natural gas 17%, with the remainder supplied mainly by nuclear and hydro-power sources. Britain is well endowed with coal resources, with coal consumption accounting for a third (34%) of primary energy use in 1986.

None of these energy sources is without its environmental problems, however, which may seriously constrain their ability to stand in for oil.

Oil tops poll

As far as oil itself is concerned, while the super-spills of the 1960s and 1970s may seem to be a thing of the past, accidental spills and chronic pollution will continue to pose problems as long as we continue to extract, ship, process and use oil. Overall, however, the industry has done remarkably well in cleaning up its operations. Indeed, although the burning of oil and other hydrocarbon fuels still contributes significantly both to acid rain problems and to carbon dioxide build-up in the atmosphere, the oil industry's achievements are recognised by many British environmentalists, who ranked it top in terms of environmental sensitivity in the *Green Pages* survey (page 14).

The most pressing of today's environmental problems are to be found in the electricity supply industry. These include concerns about the safety of nuclear power stations and continuing difficulties in ensuring the safe disposal of nuclear effluents and wastes. Also worrying, though, are the 'acid rain' problems which have appeared across Europe and Scandinavia (page 86), and the prospect of longer

---

Lower oil prices have lulled many Europeans into the false belief that the energy crisis is over, cooling interest in energy efficiency (page 136) and renewable energy. But future oil shortages and the environmental constraints on fossil fuels burning will guarantee long term success for companies that stay the course.

---

term carbon dioxide build-up leading to possible climatic changes. The main contributors to carbon dioxide build-up are the burning of fossil fuels and plant biomass.

Although nuclear power is possibly the most controversial energy supply option, coal burning is currently the most environmentally damaging of the major options. 'Coal,' as *The Economist* noted, 'is dirty and dangerous to mine; expensive to transport; and bad for the atmosphere. A large coal-fired power station produces enough ash in a year to cover an acre of ground to the height of a six-storey building. It also pumps out carbon dioxide, which turns the atmosphere into a greenhouse, and sulphur dioxide and nitrogen oxides, which turn rain to acid.' Cleaning up the sulphur and nitrogen oxide emissions from Britain's coal-fired power stations is going to be a major business opportunity (page 109).

Nuclear power, for all its admitted problems, at least has the advantage that it does not contribute to the build-up of atmospheric carbon dioxide, as Christopher Harding notes on page 134. Indeed, if the 'greenhouse effect' turns out to be as serious a long-term threat as some scientists contend it will be,

ENERGY

West German firemen wash down a truck found to be contaminated by radioactive fall-out from Chernobyl.

then the nuclear industry may well soon be using such environmental arguments in its own defence.

The nuclear future

Like it or not, the nuclear industry is likely to be with us for the foreseeable future. Some countries, however, are more dependent on the nuclear option than others. Some, like Sweden and Switzerland, have considered dispensing with the nuclear option altogether. In Europe, the two countries which depend most heavily on nuclear power are France (which gets over two-thirds of its energy from nuclear power stations) and Belgium (slightly over half).

The nuclear industry is – and will continue to be – highly controversial. While the electricity industry sees nuclear power as an insurance policy against rising world fuel prices and strikes in the coal industry, the nuclear industry is far from popular with the general public.

It is significant that, when asked to name the industrial organisation with the *worst* environmental reputation, the environmentalists in our survey (page 18) put British Nuclear Fuels in the 'top' slot (37% of those expressing an opinion) and the Central Electricity Generating Board in second place (20%). A total of 51% expressing an opinion specifically mentioned the nuclear industry in their answers to this question. Both BNF and the CEGB now recognise the need to be much more open in dealing with environmental concerns, although it remains to be seen how far they will feel able to go in meeting such concerns.

Even without the Chernobyl disaster, the long-running concerns about the quality of environmental management at the Sellafield nuclear reprocessing plant and the sheer volume of contradictory evidence given to the Layfield inquiry on the proposed Sizewell 'B' pressurised water reactor would have kept the industry in the public eye. And the issue of nuclear waste disposal has also stirred public concern in many European countries. When Spain's state-owned Empressa Nacional de Residuos Radioactivos (Enresa) began to investigate the possibility of storing high-level nuclear waste near where the River Douro forms the border with Portugal, for example, relations became fairly strained between the two countries.

Green energy?

If Britain's power supply industry is privatised, however, with the CEGB split into competing generating companies, it is not at all certain that those companies will want to build further nuclear power stations. Offered a stake in the industry, the new breed of popular capitalist created by Prime Minister Margaret Thatcher's successive administrations might well balk. And, given that CEGB chairman Lord Marshall has said that no fast breeder stations will be in operation for at least 50 years, it is also open to question whether private investors would be much interested in continuing research on the fast breeder reactor option.

So what environmentally acceptable options would be open to the power industry? First, it is worth noting that there is no such thing as a totally 'green' source of energy. Any form of energy supply, even renewable energy sources like wind or tidal power, can cause environmental damage. Tidal power sta-

130 →

The challenge with solar power is to move it out of the gimmicks market (inset: Solar Walkman) and into the mainstream. The main photograph shows a solar powered radio relay station in Algeria.

tions will be located in estuaries which, as the Nature Conservancy Council points out, are among the most productive – and vulnerable – habitats in Britain.

But renewable sources of energy have the advantage that they do not pollute, blow up or melt down. Unfortunately, however, they are also often diffuse, intermittent and, as a result, less reliable than the more conventional alternatives. Take these considerations into account and the environmental balance sheet begins to look rather less one-sided.

A 1,000-megawatt solar 'farm', for example, might occupy 5,000 acres, compared with less than 150 acres for a nuclear power station producing the same amount of power. If crops were grown for conversion into oil or gas, a 1,000-megawatt output would require plantations covering some 200 square miles (128,000 acres), and the use of considerable quantities of agrochemicals. Generally, it is a question of trading off the desire for an assured energy supply against the environmental problems associated with particular supply options.

Saving it

Environmentally, the most attractive energy option is unquestionably energy conservation – particularly the pursuit of increased energy efficiency. Indeed, enormous progress has already been made in this area. During the 1970s and 1980s, high oil prices combined with other factors to produce lower economic growth rates in the major industrialised countries. As energy conservation programmes built up and the shift away from energy-intensive heavy industry proceeded, the 'energy intensity' of the leading industrial economies fell sharply. In other words, less energy was needed to achieve the same level of production. Almost 20% less energy was needed in 1986 to produce a given unit of gross domestic product (GDP) than in 1973.

The initial response by energy consumers to the sharp increase in oil prices involved belt tightening measures, such as reducing the thermostat settings on central heating systems and avoiding unnecessary car journeys. Increasingly, however, and particularly once the second OPEC oil shock of 1979 had worked its way through, consumer attitudes relaxed. The main emphasis switched from energy conservation to energy efficiency, where the goal is to design plants, processes and products from scratch so that they use less energy (page 136).

Unfortunately, the incentives for energy efficiency have been significantly blunted in Britain by the discovery of North Sea oil and by the general fall in oil prices. But we have, at best, a precariously limited breathing space. Meanwhile, there are significant disagreements between the experts on how long North Sea oil will last. Even Kerr McGee's discovery of a major new oil field in a comparatively young Eocene formation, previously thought to be an unlikely oil prospect, does not alter the basic facts: North Sea oil production has already peaked and will, in all probability, progressively run down through the early years of the 21st century.

The peak production figure of 2.6 million barrels a

day, achieved in 1985, will never be achieved again – even though the North Sea may still contain more oil than the 7 billion-plus barrels extracted to date. Indeed, some estimates assume that there could be as much as 18 billion barrels waiting to be found, but the average size of find is falling.

In the early 1970s, the average discovery contained 300 million barrels of oil, whereas most of those found today contain 100 million barrels or less – and the average size is continuing to fall. The Kerr McGee field, thought to contain as much as 350 million barrels, is likely to be very much an exception. As a result, the very nature of the North Sea oil industry will change, with fewer large platforms and scores of small fields linked into existing pipelines.

As far as onshore oil exploration is concerned, the picture is not particularly bright. As BP points out, fields as small as 2–3 million barrels can be made economic onshore, because the costs of extracting oil on land are typically a twentieth of those for a marginal North Sea field. But, apart from the large Wytch Farm oil field in Dorset, most of the oil fields discovered around Britain in recent years contain less than one million barrels of oil.

Energy without end?

Admittedly, there are wild cards in the energy pack. In Sweden, for example, Professor Thomas Gold drilled one of the world's deepest holes to find what he believes will be enormous supplies of natural gas. In contrast to most scientists, who believe that natural gas was formed during the decay of organic matter (what Gold derisively dubs the 'squashed fish theory'), he argues that natural gas is a by-product of the formation of the earth itself, and that it exists in quantities sufficient to meet our energy needs for millions of years. His case is unproven.

But the dream of a world with limitless energy supplies is seductive. Another possibility here is fusion power, with the EEC announcing in 1987 that it would provide £700 million for the building of an experimental nuclear fusion reactor. Following initial successes achieved by a European team working on the Joint European Torus (Jet) experiment, Jet scientists believe that they may reach the 'energy break-even' stage by the time the Jet project ends in 1992. At the moment, megawatts of electricity are being pumped into the Jet machine to extract about enough power to run a few electric kettles.

The attractions of this form of nuclear reactor, which would need to operate at a temperature of around a hundred million degrees, include the fact that its fuel is, to all intents and purposes, limitless. To meet the world's current electricity demand, you would have to burn about 1,700 million tonnes of coal. You could do the same job, however, with just 135 tonnes of deuterium burnt in fusion reactors. Each cubic metre of seawater contains 35 grams of deuterium, so the total quantities available are potentially enormous.

BP's Wytch Farm onshore oil production site in Dorset.

But this is an extremely complex technology, whose ultimate role in meeting world energy demand is speculative at best. Fusion scientists, in fact, do not expect to see the first nuclear fusion demonstration plant, dubbed 'Demo', until around the year 2020. And commercial fusion reactors, according to current projections, are unlikely to come on-stream until about 2040.

The renewable options

So what about the genuinely renewable energy technologies? Although over 90% of the world's traded energy demands are currently met by non-renewable energy sources, renewable energy sources will become increasingly significant. By the early part of the 21st century, the world's population will have grown by another 2 billion, mostly in the Third World (page 244). As a result, the demand for energy will continue to grow – and more of our energy needs will be met by technologies tapping into such renewable sources as the sun, biomass, the wind, water, waves, and tides, and geothermal resources.

Biomass energy is enormously important in the Third World. About as much energy is stored in living plants at any time as in the world's proven reserves of coal. Over half of the world's population relies on biomass for cooking and heating. Indeed, since 1970 fuelwood consumption has risen by an average 2–3% a year. Some countries currently get around 90% of their energy from this source.

In rural areas of some developing countries, this heavy reliance on biomass – firewood and agricultural or animal wastes – has already resulted in severe deforestation and soil erosion. Apart from the difficult task of growing more trees to meet the demand for fuel, one area where considerable progress can be made is in the design of fuel-using equipment, such as stoves (page 68).

At the same time, there will be a growing need for appropriate, cost-effective solar energy technology. It

is estimated, for example, that every year the planet's surface receives about ten times as much energy from the sun as is stored in the whole of the world's fossil fuel and uranium reserves. This incoming solar energy, it has been calculated, is equal to 15,000 times world annual energy demand. But though thermal, photovoltaic systems are evolving fairly rapidly, only a small fraction of this energy is harnessed.

The most promising renewable energy technologies in Europe are probably hydropower (currently used to generate around 25% of the world's electricity), wind power and tidal power. In fact, a study published by the British Wind Energy Association (BWEA) early in 1987 concluded that, on good sites, wind energy turbines can produce electricity for around 2p per kilowatt/hour. This is 30% less than the cost per kilowatt/hour given by the Central Electricity Generating Board for the pressurised water reactor (PWR) power station it is building at Sizewell.

The BWEA's chairman noted that the Association 'is not anti-nuclear; we are not proposing that Sizewell be scrapped and replaced by wind turbines. We believe that the electricity boards are correct in following a policy of diversity of fuel supply, but consider that this should include coal, oil, nuclear and wind energy.' According to the BWEA, the main reason for the fall in wind power costs is a drop of 25% in the cost of wind turbines in less than two years. Given that the wind is free, the cost of wind energy depends almost exclusively on the cost of the equipment. The BWEA believes that 20% of Britain's electricity could come from wind – and argues that the government should be spending at least six times as much on the technology.

In fact government interest in renewable energy has been picking up. Apart from the long-heralded Severn tidal barrage scheme, the Department of Energy increasingly favours energy-from-waste schemes (page 120), biofuels and passive (but not active) solar power. Tidal and wind power, and geothermal energy, projects are also thought worthy of further investigation.

Solar demonstrations

The best UK source of information on renewable energy research and development is the Energy Technology Support Unit (ETSU), part of the Department of Energy. ETSU publishes a free newsletter, *Review* which is available to anyone with an interest in this field.

The *Directory of UK Renewable Energy Suppliers and Services* is produced by the Energy Equipment Testing Service at the University College, Cardiff. And two useful reviews of the prospects for renewable energy are *Synthetic Fuels and Renewable Energy,* an information brief from the Shell Briefing Service, and *Energy Without End: The Case for Renewable Energy,* a Friends of the Earth publication by Michael Flood.

In addition to the renewable energy projects undertaken independently by member states, the European Community is backing a growing range of demonstration projects for energy conservation and alternative energy technology. In France, for example, a solar tunnel dryer installed by the University of Perpignan has been used to preserve prime quality fruit and vegetables. Elf-Aquitaine has used solar

From Mileage Marathon to Formula One

Slow and fast routes to fuel efficiency.

If you are prepared to travel flat on your back in a vehicle which looks like a squashed toothpaste tube on wheels, you can squeeze an unbelievable 3,804 miles out of a single gallon of petrol.

This was the mpg rate achieved by a King's College team in the Shell-Motor Mileage Marathon in the summer of 1987. It is worth recalling that when the competition was opened up to machines designed simply to cover the greatest distance for a given amount of fuel, the contestants were thrilled to reach 450 mpg. Now the aim is to break the 5,000 mpg barrier.

'The competition has the value of drawing attention to the importance of fuel economy,' noted Bob Reid, chairman of Shell UK, 'and encouraging some of the country's liveliest talents to think seriously and practically about it.'

But most people are unlikely to want to drive to work or the supermarket in a mobile toothpaste tube. As far as increasing the fuel efficiency of the ordinary family car goes, Shell points to its involvement in Formula One motor racing as a much more significant test-bed for new fuels and lubricants.

Shell UK Ltd, *Shell-Mex House, Strand, London WC2R 0DX. Tel: 01 257 3000.*

PERSPECTIVES

The Nuclear Balance Sheet

British Nuclear Fuels, according to the *Green Pages* survey, has the poorest environmental reputation of any British company. But, says *Christopher Harding*, the nuclear industry may yet prove to be an environmental asset – and there may be room for developing common ground.

'I welcomed the editors' invitation to contribute to *Green Pages* as an opportunity to say something of the positive contribution which nuclear energy can make to the conservation of resources and the protection of our environment.

Many people, I appreciate, have yet to be convinced that nuclear energy represents a net benefit to man and his environment. We can expect the debate on this issue to go on for a long time to come. I would like to think, however, that in pursuing this debate we can learn to avoid the excessive polarisation of attitudes which for too long has bedevilled relations between the nuclear industry and environmentalists.

In some ways our relationship has tended to mirror that of rival political parties who acknowledge no merit in any statement or policy emerging from the rival camp. Sensible people find this ritual political antagonism rather stupid. Equally absurd in my view would be the prolongation of a ritual slanging match between the environmental movement and the nuclear industry. Of course there are significant differences between us. So there are between political parties. Such differences should be discussed. But we have much in common, as do rival political parties if they were prepared to admit it.

Balancing act

We have to recognise that the protection of the world about us, now and for the future, requires a continual balancing between cost and benefit. Industry will need to continue to develop and expand. New products and processes will emerge, and society as a whole will decide whether on balance these are beneficial. On occasion, as we have seen for example with some drugs, some agricultural processes, society will judge that there is no balance of benefit and will not permit the products and processes to be used. In other cases, legislation and regulation will impose expensive sanctions to ensure that people's health and safety are protected and the environment safeguarded from the adverse effects of development.

The nuclear industry I believe has nothing to fear from environmental cost/benefit appraisal, sensibly applied. Certainly there are entries which have to be made on the debit side. The process of nuclear fission creates dangerous materials which require to be handled with care and respect. They are potentially harmful to man and to nature and meticulous controls are needed to ensure that their impact is kept to a realistic minimum. Absolute safety can never be guaranteed but we need to demonstrate that we are at least as safe as alternative forms of energy and preferably much safer. This I believe we can do.

The credit side of the nuclear cost/benefit balance sheet outweighs the debits. The contribution to conservation is one of the most important entries. Coal and oil, our most important sources of energy to date, are finite and cannot be renewed. A sensible environmental policy for planet Earth demands that they be cherished and husbanded as a dwindling resource of steadily appreciating value. By contrast, uranium, the source of nuclear energy, has no other significant use in the world.

It is in abundant supply and, by use of fast reactors which breed fuel as well as consume it, the nuclear industry can convert uranium into virtually a renewable energy source, far outstripping all the other mineral sources of energy available to us.

Greenhouse effect

Nuclear power, unlike the burning of fossil fuels, does not contribute to the 'greenhouse effect', which is increasingly seen by environmentalists as a long term threat to life on earth (page 86). Its adverse effects on health, contrary to many people's perception, are far less than those from the atmospheric pollution caused by coal and oil-fired power stations. Its radioactive wastes are comparatively small in volume and their safe disposal presents no significant technical problems (as distinct from those of a political and public relations nature).

The price of safety assurance and of controlling and minimising the adverse environmental effects of nuclear power is a heavy one in financial terms. My own company, with capital investment of some £700 million in new plant and equipment to control pollution, can bear witness to that. Such expenditure is not grudged. What the nuclear industry can reasonably expect is that environmentalists will apply equal vigilance in monitoring the health, safety and environmental impact of competing sources of electricity so that like can be compared with like. I am confident that objective and dispassionate comparison will confirm nuclear energy as one of the most benign forms of electricity generation.

Renewable contenders

We can expect that new forms of energy will emerge as

ENERGY

serious contenders in the future. The wind, the waves, the tides, as well as geothermal and solar power, may eventually be developed to compete economically with the longer established sources of electricity generation. I very much hope that proves to be so.

No one I know in the nuclear industry is opposed to the search for alternative energy sources. If that search proves successful, nuclear power will then, as now, be required to justify its continuing role in terms of economic and environmental comparability. It will stand or fall on its own merits and those of the rest of the field.

Meanwhile nuclear power will continue as the most tightly regulated and closely monitored of the energy industries. The rigorous supervision by the regulatory authorities will no doubt continue to be complemented by intensive scrutiny by environmental pressure groups. In BNFL we necessarily maintain close liaison with our official regulators. I see value in establishing dialogue with our unofficial scrutineers too. When I became Chairman of BNFL I took an early opportunity of meeting with some of the leaders of the environmental movement and greatly value the exchange of views that took place then and has continued since.

I believe it is important that industry and environmentalists should recognise the ground we have in common as well as the points on which we differ. It is always possible that sensible discussion will help enlarge the former while diminishing the latter.

,

CHRISTOPHER HARDING *is Chairman of British Nuclear Fuels plc. Unlike most senior people in the nuclear industry, the bulk of his career has been non-nuclear. After receiving an MA from Corpus Christi College, Oxford, he worked for ICI from 1961 to 1969. From 1969 to 1974 he served as Director of various subsidiary companies of the Hanson Trust Ltd., following which he became Managing Director of Hanson Transport Group Ltd. He has been a Non-Executive Director of Hanson Trust plc since 1979. Joining BNF as a Non-Executive Director in 1984, he took over as Chairman in 1986. He is a Council Member of the Confederation of British Industry and of Business in the Community, and a Member of the British National Executive Committee of the World Energy Conference.*

British Nuclear Fuels plc, *Risley, Warrington, Cheshire WA3 6AS. Tel: 0925 835000.*

Safety First.

A pledge from Nirex.

Britain today is using more and more nuclear generated electricity. In our homes and in our industries one light in five is lit by nuclear power.

In addition, hospitals use radioactive materials for diagnosis and treatment.

And research laboratories and industry for monitoring, measuring and inspection.

But, if we are to take full advantage of the benefits of nuclear power and other uses of radioactivity, we have to make sure the waste is disposed of safely. And responsibly.

For this reason, UK Nirex Ltd have the task of implementing the Government's strategy for the safe and efficient disposal of these wastes.

So if you'd like more details of our plans, why not ask for our Fact File.

Simply by writing to UK Nirex Ltd, Information Office, Curie Avenue, Harwell, Didcot, Oxon OX11 0RH.

UK Nirex Ltd

PERSPECTIVES

A Rush to Profligacy?

Falling oil prices stalled energy effiency programmes in a number of European countries – and put them into reverse in others. *Andrew Warren* considers ways in which Europe can accelerate into an energy-efficient future.

'Between 1973, the time of the first Great Oil Shock, and 1985, the twelve European Community nations succeeded in improving their energy efficiency by 20%. They have now set themselves the target of doubling that effort, so that by 1995 the 'efficiency of final energy demand' will be down by at least 20% more.

It is accepted that a large part of the savings achieved to date have been via pressure from higher energy prices, and by structural changes in European industry itself. Attempts to measure just how much of this conservation has come from genuine investments in energy saving equipment have long floundered on a lack of comparable international statistics: however, a commonly accepted yardstick is no more than 30%.

The rest of the 'savings' have either come from changes from heavy to light industry, and from simply doing without (closed factories, cold homes). And the sudden fall in oil prices in 1986 cast severe doubts upon the ability of the Community to maintain its progress on energy efficiency.

Warning signals

The Energy Directorate of the EEC recognised the warning signals early, and expressed considerable alarm in many public fora as to the effect such softening of prices might have upon the capacity of individual governments to maintain the pressure towards reducing energy intensity. Even before the collapse of the dollar price of oil, from 1983 onwards the real price of energy was already falling – and the Community were monitoring worrying signs of an actual worsening (rather than the conventional gradual improvement) of energy efficiency in many countries.

Nation after nation was reducing financial support for conservation measures, and lowering the profile of their energy efficiency campaigns. This was particularly true of those countries which had long been in the vanguard of energy conservation activities, like Holland and France, but rather less true of those like Spain and the UK, which had come rather later to the topic. Perhaps fortuitously, the latter country's designation of 1986 as Energy Efficiency Year helped to blunt an otherwise precipitate rush to profligacy.

The Commission has identified a number of specific obstacles which impede progress towards their second 20% energy efficiency goal, and which may indeed be helping to erode the earlier gains recorded.

These are:
- Lack of knowledge about energy-saving items, particularly amongst householders, and smaller businesses.
- Disparity of rate of return expectations for investments on both the supply and demand side of the energy industry. A typical conservation scheme is given no more than five years to 'pay back' its capital, while a typical new power source is given 15 years.
- Separation of expenditure and benefit. Those who use the fuel frequently never see the fuel bill.

14-point plan

To counter this, the Commission has drawn up – and the Council of Ministers have approved with enthusiasm – a fourteen point plan. This plan is itself divided up into three sections: information; regulations; and stimulation of investments.

The *information* section naturally deals predominantly with means of spreading the message. It advocates publicising the overall message and appropriate new technologies; providing company energy audits; integrating the various energy saving measures as a synergised programme; targeting architects, planners and plant managers; promoting demonstration projects; and using government procurement policy as a pump primer. This latter initiative is probably the most novel, and possibly the most influential: it is estimated that around half the commercial building stock is publicly owned, and the critical role that good energy practice in public buildings can play cannot be over-emphasised.

The *regulations* section calls for all member states to provide an energy labelling system for household appliances. It also recognised the importance that setting minimum energy standards can have for new or rehabilitated buildings. Whilst acknowledgements are made to the importance of obtaining voluntary agreements with the relevant manufacturers, the Commission seems in no doubt that the patience some governments have with foot-draggers and filibusterers is out of place – and that some new regulation directives *will* be required.

The final section deals with the *stimulation of investments*. There are three main proposals in this sphere. The first is to seek to improve the assumed profitability of projects during periods of low fuel prices by continuing to provide project finance

ENERGY

ANDREW WARREN *is Director of the Association for the Conservation of Energy (ACE). Born in 1948, he was educated at Rugby School and the University of Exeter. Upon graduation, he worked in advertising for Saatchi and Saatchi Garland-Compton Ltd, before becoming the Secretary to the Movement for London Campaign. Upon the foundation of ACE in 1981, he was appointed its first Director. He was the co-author of the TV series* Fancy Saying a Thing Like That. *He is an underwriter at Lloyds.*

through the provision of grants, soft loans or tax incentives.

The second concerns the development of a third party financing industry (largely following work undertaken for the Commission by the Association for the Conservation of Energy), as a way of obviating barriers in expertise and capital non-availability.

Finally the Commission has fired a warning shot across the bows of the energy utilities, who 'should be encouraged to view themselves as energy service companies, and not simply producers and distributors of power'.

The Commission intends to examine with the electricity and gas utilities how *they* can provide, particularly for smaller business and private consumers, energy surveys (on demand), low interest loans, and load management techniques.

In summary, the trend towards greater energy efficiency in Europe has historically been acceptable; is currently rather worrying; but will in the future be extremely positive – provided that the blueprint provided by the European Commission becomes a reality. It is up to the member State governments to ensure that it does.

The Association for the Conservation of Energy, 9 Sherlock Mews, London W1M 3RH. Tel: 01 935 1495.

---

photovoltaic pumping to irrigate a test plot in southern France. In Italy, solar energy has been used by La Metalli Industriale to dehydrate waste cutting oil emulsions, used to lubricate and cool tools in rolling mills and machinery plants. And a wind turbine generator has been designed and built by Britain's Wind Energy Group, and installed near Ilfracombe, Devon.

But perhaps the most striking harbinger of the economy of the future is not a solar irrigation pump or even a windmill, for all these may find important applications. Instead, it is the Voyager aircraft which Richard Rutan and Jeana Yeager flew non-stop around the world in 1986. Made out of honeycomb-like composite materials, combining plastics and wood fibre, the strange aircraft took nine days to circumnavigate the earth without stopping or refuelling. Although the average speed was just 115.8 miles per hour, the achievement showed how energy resources can be stretched out by careful design, planning and operation.

Back on earth, energy efficiency gains are becoming somewhat harder to achieve. In 1986, Energy Efficiency Year, the UK continued to use the equivalent of 1.5 tonnes of coal for every £1,000 worth of gross domestic product for the fourth year running. That compares with the 1.7 tonnes used in 1979.

In straightforward commercial terms, however, Energy Efficiency Year was an important shot in the arm for the energy efficiency industry. A total of 71 companies in the energy supply market also incorporated the Monergy (combining money and energy) theme in their advertising, multiplying the Energy Efficiency Office's advertising spend seven-fold. According to the surveys, awareness of the Monergy concept rose from 4% in the run-up campaign to 68% over the year, with the general message reaching an estimated 31 million Britons.

Although it clearly takes time for such awareness and interest to convert into sales, there was a 50% increase in demand for energy efficiency survey grants in the last four months of 1986 compared with the same period in 1985. There was also a 10% increase in related products and services. Philips reported that sales of its energy-efficient lighting were up 84% on the previous year, while Thorn reported a 130% increase in sales of low-voltage tungsten halogen lighting in the six months ending March 1987.

During a period of relatively low oil prices, the incentives to save energy have relaxed considerably. But the companies represented by such organisations as the Association for the Conservation of Energy ACE know that it is only a matter of time before the pressures will come back in earnest. Given the political element in energy crises, however, it is far from clear exactly how long they will have to wait before the markets for their products and services open up again.

SECTION 7

Growing Pains

Throughout Europe, farmers and foresters are under increasing pressure from environmentalists and countryside campaigners. We can expect some major changes in policies and practices through the 1990s.

European agriculture has gone through a period of continuous intensification during the post-war period. Yields have improved dramatically, largely thanks to much higher inputs of agrochemicals, but also because of the achievements of crop plant breeders. Now that we are faced with problems of agricultural over-production in the European Community, however, there is growing concern not only about how farmers will make a living in future, but also about the impact of modern farming methods on the landscape and on other elements of the natural environment.

It is significant that the most-mentioned book in the Green Pages survey of the *Green Bookshelf* (page 208) was Marion Shoard's *The Theft of the Countryside*. Farming is now viewed in a very different light and an increasing range of organisations both in Britain and elsewhere believe that they should have a say in what happens to the countryside.

Field of battle

If you want to get a feel for the way that the pressures on European farmers may go, look at Denmark. As part of an ambitious programme for the reduction of the pollution of the seas surrounding the country, the government has imposed controls on discharges of nitrates and phosphates from agriculture, aquaculture and industry.

Companies like Novo Industri (page 118) may provide the easiest initial targets, but farmers are the main offenders – so the pressures are likely to build considerably through the 1990s. The Danish Ministry of Agriculture, meanwhile, is requiring all farms to submit field cultivation and fertilizer use plans for government clearance. Early casualties have been pig farmers and two of the country's largest slaughter-house and meat processing companies (Tulip and Steff Houlberg), which were forced to close several plants and lay off nearly 900 workers.

British farmers have also been coming under growing pressure on the pollution front, although to nowhere near the same extent. A 1987 report published by the Water Authorities Association and the Ministry of Agriculture, Fisheries and Food (MAFF) confirmed that farms are the main source of water pollution – with cattle farming the most serious source of pollution, followed by pig farming. Despite some positive moves in pollution prevention, the report concluded that farmers still find it cheaper to pay fines than to control pollution. Farm pollution incidents doubled between 1980 and 1986 and the problems will get worse if present trends continue.

The pesticide pollution problems of the 1960s and 1970s have been successfully tackled in many areas, so that the massive wildlife kills which led to the publication of Rachel Carson's book *Silent Spring*, a 1962 book which still enjoys a prominent position on the Green Bookshelf, are a thing of the past. But pesticide pollution problems, particularly those re-

---

Throughout Europe, farmers and foresters are coming under fire from environmentalists. David Baldock reports that the European Community's Common Agricultural Policy has caused widespread environmental damage (page 148), while Robin Grove-White looks at some of the impending changes in the way we use the countryside (page 150).

---

sulting from aerial spraying, continue to cause concern.

There are examples of farmers working in partnership with conservation interests, but to date they are few and far between. In Britain, for example, the Agrochemicals Association has been working with the Game Conservancy and the Nature Conservancy Council on a series of projects designed to protect farmland flowers and the bees which depend on them. Even so, the overall ecological balance sheet is still strongly negative.

If work under way in agricultural biotechnology institutes, like the Sainsbury Laboratory (page 183), achieves its targets, some crops may be grown without needing pesticides. The transfer of pest resistance into crop plants is beginning to move forward at quite a rate. For example, Plant Genetic Systems, a Belgian company, has conducted field trials with tobacco plants containing the gene coding for a natural insecticide produced by a microbe, *Bacillus thuringiensis (Bt)*. Tobacco was chosen simply because it is a well-tried experimental plant. Once introduced into the plants, the gene was passed on to successive

FARMING & FORESTRY

Mr Barry Wookey on his farm in Pewsey, Wiltshire, which has been farmed organically since 1972.

generations, producing levels of insecticide sufficient to kill caterpillars.

At the same time, other companies, including Denmark's Novo Industri, are now working on biological pesticides (see below). Like the Bt pesticides, these promise to be much more specific than chemical insecticides. And the growing move towards organic farming, described later in this section, will also help reduce the amount of agrochemicals used on some farms. But even if pesticides could be removed from the scene overnight, there would be no shortage of other environmental controversies in the farming and forestry sectors.

Manure mountain

These controversies are brought into much sharper relief by Europe's agricultural surpluses. The European Common Agricultural Policy (page 148) has been a success in terms of encouraging agricultural output, but – in addition to being extremely expensive to operate – has resulted in some major distortions of the EEC agricultural market.

Now, hot on the heels of the grain and butter mountains, comes the manure mountain. The intensive farming of livestock produces more manure than most farmers are able to cope with, particularly in the pig-farming areas of countries like Denmark and Holland.

In addition to the regulatory approach, where Denmark leads, various innovative technical approaches are being tried to deal with the problem, ranging from anaerobic digestion systems (page 110), which exploit microbes to break down manures and slurries into biogas and fertilizer, through to new soil injection techniques.

Spread on fields, manures or sewage sludge can cause major odour problems – and contribute to the pollution of nearby rivers. The idea of injecting manures and slurries into the soil is increasingly attractive because a high proportion of European farms are close to built-up areas. One tractor-drawn soil injection system, developed by the Cranfield Institute of Technology, enables some 140 cubic metres of slurry to be injected beneath each hectare of pastureland. This approach cuts down on the problem of highly polluting run-off into rivers. It also prevents the evaporation of the ammonia contained in the slurry into the atmosphere, where recent research results suggest that it may contribute to acid rain problems. But if the farmer uses the technique in spring, the evidence also suggests another problem, with grass yields cut by 10% to 15%.

Unless farmers change their ways, however, such compromises will increasingly be forced upon them. And there are many other areas where modern intensive farming is causing concern.

Nitrogen fertilizers are emerging as a pollution source in many parts of Europe. About one million tonnes of nitrogen fertilizer are used every year in Britain. While most of this fertilizer is taken up by plants, and while chemical companies are introducing new computer programmes to help farmers apply fertilizers more sparingly, considerable amounts can be washed out of the soil in the autumn or winter.

They end up either in the underlying groundwater (where they may represent a hazard to the health of people dependent on those aquifers for their drinking water) or in streams and rivers (where they can cause pollution). Nitrate concentrations in drinking water are rising in many parts of Europe, for example, particularly in areas of intensive arable farming, such as East Anglia.

Scorched earth

Another controversy revolves around straw burning, which causes extensive air pollution and damage to the country's shrinking heritage of field hedges. Changes in the pattern of arable production during the late 1970s and early 1980s resulted in huge surpluses of straw. Some 6 million tonnes, equivalent in calorific value to 3 million tonnes of coal, were burnt on one million hectares of land in 1986 alone.

This represents a significant potential energy resource when you consider that Britain's rural industries, such as maltings, breweries, sugar beet processing, and cement and brick manufacture use the equivalent of 8 million tonnes of coal each year.

But the main concern of groups like the National Society for Clean Air (NSCA), which has long campaigned against straw burning, is not the lost energy but the environmental damage caused. The NSCA has investigated alternative uses for straw, including its use as a fuel, as a fertilizer (when ploughed back into the soil), as animal feed or bedding, in horticulture, for paper and board manufacture, for thatching and for chemical production. In 1986, the NSCA co-sponsored a detailed Soil Survey map of Southern and Eastern England, showing which soils are suitable for the ploughing in of straw.

The Landscape Institute is the professional body for landscape practitioners. It promotes the highest standard of professional service in the application of the arts and sciences of landscape architecture and management.

The full potential of your landscape can be realised by employing the wide range of experience and expertise of a landscape practitioner.

For further advice contact the Landscape Institute.

12 Carlton House Terrace, London SW1Y 5AH.

Although the situation would be transformed by an outright ban on stubble and straw burning, most of these alternative uses face significant problems. On straightforward economic criteria, industrial applications, as in the board and paper industry, are a long way off. But such technical barriers are not slowing some other members of the European Community where the regulatory environment is tougher.

In 1985, for example, the Danish Parliament passed legislation which will effectively outlaw straw-burning by 1990. As a result, there are much greater pressures on farmers and on industry to make fuel-from-straw technology work. A single Danish power station, for example, should soon be using 40,000 tonnes of straw a year.

In West Germany, meanwhile, the Federal government has introduced a system of limited straw-burning permits which has made life so difficult for German farmers that most straw is now either baled or incorporated in the soil. By 1985, only 5% of the straw produced in Germany was burnt in the field, compared with 37% in Britain – excluding areas of stubble burnt after the straw had been removed. Even in France, only 2-3 million tonnes of the 22 million tonnes produced were burnt, with much of the remainder being used to fuel local grain drying facilities.

Warning shots

The much-vaunted efficiency of UK agriculture, it can be argued, is achieved at the expense of growing environmental costs which rarely turn up in the balance sheet. Nonetheless, a growing number of warning shots have been fired across the bows of the UK farming industry.

Indeed Prince Charles, one of Britain's largest landowners, noted that landowners and farmers 'have come to look on the land as an almost endless source of increasing income without too much regard for the old conventional view of giving back to the land.' Apart from the continuing barrage from the environmental lobby generally, there have also been highly critical reports from the House of Lords and the House of Commons.

As a result, albeit slowly, the agricultural industry is beginning to respond. The Agricultural and Food Research Council, for example, recognised in its second corporate plan, covering the period from 1985 to 1990, that it should be taking a stronger lead in research into the relationships between agriculture, land use and environmental protection.

There are also a growing number of initiatives designed to alert farmers to the need for effective conservation – and to ensure that they have access to the expertise and other resources needed to reduce their impact on the countryside. The Farming and Wildlife Advisory Group (FWAG), for example, has local groups covering the whole of England and Wales, and most of Scotland. FWAG, whose membership ranges from the Country Landowners' Association to the Royal Society for the Protection of Birds, provides advice on request. It covers the waterfront, from simple site management to whole farm planning.

In 1986, too, FWAG launched a joint initiative with the Agricultural Training Board designed to assess the needs within the UK agricultural industry for training in conservation. With backing from ICI Plant Protection, the brief given to Gillian Kerby, the ATB conservation development officer, was to develop new courses which would help farmers integrate conservation thinking into their day-to-day farm operations. After a successful start, the work was subsequently extended into a second year.

Many farmers may resist such advice, but many also now recognise that they have wider responsibilities than simply maximising production. They are increasingly aware, as FWAG adviser Eric Carter once put it, that they 'are regarded as a privileged class, free, with little or no restraint, to bring about major and often drastic changes in the countryside. Farming,' he noted, 'is supported financially in many ways, both directly and indirectly, and many taxpayers feel that they support agriculture to such an extent that they are entitled to a say in what farmers do in the countryside.'

Eroding confidence

While the agricultural industry has found it hard enough to come to terms with the demands of the landscape and wildlife lobbies, it could well find it even harder to come to grips with the demand for 'sustainable' agriculture. Although European agriculture does not face environmental problems on the scale of those which confront many Third World farmers (page 190), it is far from clear that current industrial farming practices are sustainable in the long term.

The sustainability of agriculture is becoming a major issue worldwide, representing a vital area for future research work. As Michael Dover and Lee Talbot put it in *To Feed the Earth: Agro-Ecology for Sustainable Development* (World Resources Institute, 1987), 'productivity without sustainability is mining.' Consider soil erosion.

When scientists from the Soil Survey of England and Wales studied 40 randomly chosen fields in south Somerset, they found that the mean soil loss from fields under cereal crops was 4.2 tonnes per hectare, compared with 2.3 tonnes per hectare under maize, 1.7 tonnes per hectare under potatoes and only 0.2 tonnes per hectare from bare ploughed land. Two of the cereal fields monitored lost a staggering 11 and 21 tonnes of soil for every hectare. The losses were heaviest on fields subjected to the greatest use of wheeled agricultural equipment.

The problem is aggravated on steeply sloping land and is found at its worst in the Third World, where population pressures drive farmers onto increasingly unsuitable land. When the Worldwatch Institute (page 240) published *Soil Erosion: Quiet Crisis in the World Economy* in 1984 it noted that, while proper terracing can control soil erosion even on intensively cropped slopes, cultivation of unterraced slopes can result in incredible soil losses.

Nigerian research, for example, has shown that land with a 1% slope planted with cassava loses an average of three tonnes of soils a year. On a 5% slope the loss leaps to 87 tonnes of soil per hectare, while on a 15% slope the loss runs at an extraordinary 221 tonnes per hectare. But, grave though the worldwide loss of topsoil may now be, Worldwatch's Lester Brown and Edward Wolf concluded that 'it is a quiet crisis, one that is not widely perceived. And, unlike earthquakes, volcanic eruptions or other natural disasters, this human-made disaster is unfolding gradually. What is at stake,' they stressed, 'is not merely the degradation of soil, but the degradation of life itself.'

Seeds of the future

Paradoxically, some of the crop protection chemicals which environmentalists so dislike may help reduce such erosion problems. Used in 'minimum till' agriculture, where the seed is drilled direct into the soil without ploughing, with the weeds held in check with herbicides, they can significantly cut the amount of soil lost from erosion-prone areas. 142→

Our policy is only to lend on properties which conserve resources, save energy or preserve communities. We have mortgage funds currently available. Telephone or write now with your requirements for further details

Ecology Building Society

8 Main Street, Cross Hills, Keighley, West Yorkshire BD20 8TB.

Telephone (0535) 35933

Longer term, as we have seen, some of the emerging trends in plant genetic engineering may help cut the amounts of agrochemicals needed by enabling crop plants to ward off major pests and diseases. The major agribusiness and agrochemical companies have been moving steadily into plant biotechnology. Unilever, for example, beat off competition from ICI and Booker to secure part of Britain's Plant Breeding Institute and the National Seed Development Organisation, both previously in the public sector, for a purchase price of around £60 million.

Chemical companies can see that longer term the demand for agrochemicals may shrink, while the market for seed of new pest- or disease-resistant crop strains could explode. Not surprisingly, they want a share in the action. In the meantime, however, a great deal more needs to be done to ensure that the pesticides which are still being used – and will continue to be used – are properly tested, that only such pesticides are used and that they are used in an acceptable way.

Major chemical companies now spend many millions of pounds and scores of man-years testing crop protection chemicals before they reach the market. Indeed, of the 10,000 chemicals screened as possible pesticides each year at ICI's Jealott's Hill experimental station, it is unlikely that more than one will ever reach the market place, so stringent are the tests now required. New technologies, like the Electrodyn sprayer (page 74), also offer the prospect of targeting pesticides much more precisely. But a great deal more needs to be done to ensure that pesticides are used safely, particularly in the Third World.

Biopesticides

Many observers have predicted that chemical pesticides would eventually be replaced by biological pesticides, including bacteria, fungi and viruses. First used over 50 years ago, biopesticides now achieve annual global sales of around $50 million, a tiny slice of the $16 billion market for agrochemicals. Part of the problem is that the very specificity of such products, which makes them so attractive to environmentalists, confines them to a handful of market niches.

The difficulties of breaking into the crop protection market with biopesticides were dramatically illustrated by the fate of Microbial Resources Ltd (MRL). Founded with £2 million of venture capital in 1984, MRL was Britain's first commercial biopesticide company, offering five products which had been largely developed by publicly funded research institutes.

To start with, the company's prospects looked good. Unfortunately, however, it was squeezed out of the potentially lucrative US market by competing products made by Abbott Laboratories, a multinational with much larger technological, marketing and financial resources. In the UK, MRL lost a large portion of its sales to the glasshouse sector when tomato growers switched away from water-based pollination induction systems. This resulted in failures of its whitefly control product, Mycotal, which needs a humid atmosphere to work effectively. Despite a further cash injection from RTZ in 1985, MRL finally went into liquidation in 1986. Its biopesticide business was taken over by Denmark's Novo Industri.

Given the growing problems of pest resistance to pesticides, however, and concerns about pesticide residues in water and food, there will be continuing pressure to develop safe biopesticides for use in integrated pest management programmes. These will combine a number of different pest control strategies, both biological and chemical, to slow or prevent the build-up of pest resistance.

Agrochemicals, in short, are likely to be needed for the foreseeable future. But however carefully tested such agrochemicals may be, and however sparingly applied, one underlying trend in European farming is towards chemical-free – or 'organic' – farming. And, on current evidence, it is likely to accelerate fairly dramatically.

Organic growth

Instead of using chemical fertilizers, organic farmers use animal manures and plough unwanted crop residues, including straw, back into the soil. To control pests they use a wide range of biological control systems, including the release of insects which,

DIGEST THE PROBLEM!

- Complete Turnkey contracts for cost-effective sewage sludge digestion plants, single or multiple stream, to serve populations of 100,000+ to less than 1,000, including CHP and sludge thickening if required.

- Backed by the experience gained in designing and building over 50 plants of all sizes, our range allows in-house sludge digestion to be a practical, economic option for every sewage treatment works.

- Our Award-Winning farm and abattoir waste treatment plants can often have a pay-back time of three years or less – turning an expensive problem into a valuable resource.

Prefabricated Anaerobic Digestion Plants
For Sewage Works, Farms and Abattoirs

FARM GAS LTD

Industrial Estate, Bishop's Castle, Shropshire, England. Tel: (0588) 638 577.

FARMING & FORESTRY

like ladybirds eating aphids, prey on crop pests, and the use of intercropping, with various different crops grown in preference to much more vulnerable monocultures. Organic farming also depends heavily on crop rotation, both to recharge soil nitrogen and to ensure that crop-specific pests do not have a chance to build up to problem levels.

Although some areas of organic farming have grown rapidly in recent years, they are typically doing so from a very small base. In the United States, for example, only about 1% of farmers used organic methods in 1980, although recent estimates suggest that the proportion has since grown considerably, with perhaps 10% of American farmers now growing some organic produce. In Britain, less than 1% of farmers can be called organic. Only some 450 farmers are certified to use the Soil Association's symbol for organically grown produce, with another 500 farmers waiting to have their farms certified.

In 1986, according to Soil Association figures, organic farmers in Britain produced 12,000 tonnes of cereals and 30,000 tonnes of vegetables and dairy produce. Altogether, this produce was valued at some £23 million. But such farmers are nowhere near satisfying domestic demand, which has grown rapidly with increasing interest in healthy eating (page 178). According to *The Economist*, around £11 million worth of organic produce is imported from other European countries.

West Germany has the longest tradition of organic farming, stretching back at least 50 years, although France, with its long-established interest in good food, probably has more organic farmers overall. There are still problems, however, in defining exactly what the word 'organic' means in different countries.

In America, for example, it simply means that a farm uses much less chemical fertilizer than its neighbours. As the trade in organically grown produce grows, so there will be increasing pressure for properly policed standards, to ensure that unscrupulous farmers do not label as 'organic' (thereby attracting a premium price) produce which has been grown in the normal intensive, high-yield fashion. The Organic Foods Production Association of North America has been trying to harmonise the situation by proposing an all-embracing definition, along the lines of 'organic foods are processed and stored without preservatives, radiation or pesticides'. That still leaves unresolved the question of whether artificial fertilizers have been used, however.

144 →

Going Organic

One of the most intriguing recent conservation victories was the acquisition by bodies like the Dorset Trust for Nature Conservation of 328 acres of the 606-acre Lower Kingcombe estate. The estate is like an ecological time-warp. Because pesticides and artificial fertilizers have never been used there, it is rich in wildlife which has all but disappeared from many parts of the country.

For anyone wanting to turn a mainstream farm back into an organic farm, however, there is a rather different time-warp to face. It takes anywhere between two to five years to allow the accumulated agrochemicals in the soil to disappear, a period during which the farmer is getting lower yields (because agrochemicals are no longer used), yet is unable to label the resulting produce 'organic' – and is thus unable to enjoy the premium which such produce can command.

The overall regulatory body for UK organic farming is the British Organic Standard Board (BOSB), formed in 1980 by the Soil Association, British Organic Farmers, the Organic Growers' Association, the Henry Doubleday Research Association, the Farm and Food Society, the Wholefood Trust, Organic Farmers and Growers, the International Institute of Biological Husbandry and the Organic Food Manufacturers' Federation.

Under the BOSB scheme, each organisation puts forward its standards for the BOSB to approve, with the result that there have been several different symbols for organic produce. These include the Soil Association symbol (no synthetic fertilizers, pesticides, growth regulators, antibiotics or intensive livestock systems); Organic Farmers and Growers (slightly stricter than the Soil Association, but offers a lesser label for farmers and growers 'in transition'); the Demeter symbol, used on foods grown according to the Biodynamic principles evolved by Rudolf Steiner and his followers); and the Conservation Grade standard, started by Jordans (producers of flours and cereals and Original Crunchy Bars), which permits the use of fertilizer compounds containing ground rock phosphate and rock potash.

If you are contemplating organic farming, a useful first step would be to read *Rushall: The Story of an Organic Farm*, by Barry Wookey (page 139). This is a first-hand account of the conversion of a 1,650-acre arable/beef farm in Wiltshire to an organic regime. Another useful publication, listing names and addresses of key contacts in organic farming, is the *Directory of Organisations and Training in the UK Organic Movement*, published by Working Weekends on Organic Farms. To see organic principles in action, a visit to the National Centre for Organic Gardening, near Coventry, is recommended.

Organic farmers always suffer a penalty when switching to low-input farming. In the United States, where many big farms use relatively low quantities of agrochemicals per hectare, however, the costs of switching are not so great as in Europe. The penalty is typically of the order of 5-15% less crop produced than on mainstream farms. In Europe, where inputs and yields are generally much higher, the organic farmer may end up producing around half the yield per hectare achieved by neighbouring farms.

More expensive

Leaving land fallow, or planting clover on it to fix atmospheric nitrogen, means it is unproductive, lowering the average annual yield. A study carried out by Organic Farmers and Growers in Britain in 1984 showed that conventionally grown wheat yielded 2.85 tonnes an acre, while organic wheat yielded 1.85 tonnes. Organic crops are generally more susceptible to pests and diseases, resulting in higher losses. And distribution costs also tend to be higher for organic produce, with small quantities needing to be shipped to specialist markets.

But, although would-be organic farmers have to wait between two and five years to clean pesticides and fertilizers out of their soils, a period during which they cannot label their produce as organic, when they do win the right to use the label their products can command a healthy premium. Although there are enormous differences in the mark-up charged in different outlets, a Food from Britain study estimated that organic food is, on average, 35% more expensive than non-organic. This premium is likely to fall, however, as more organically-grown produce comes on to the market.

The number of health food outlets is growing rapidly, and most sell organic food. At the same time, too, the major supermarket chains have been expanding into the organic market. Safeway, which began selling organic produce in 1982, sells everything from organic garlic to organic mangoes. Encouraged by Safeway's success, other chains, including Tesco and Waitrose, have been following suit. Indeed, according to *The Economist,* some 60% of organic food is now sold through supermarkets. While purists may feel this is a somewhat alarming trend, it could not have come at a better time for organic – and mainstream – farmers.

Fresh pastures

Many of Britain's 217,000 farms, which cover a total of around 40 million acres, are having to rethink their plans for the future in the wake of the milk quotas imposed by the European Community. And the productivity of Europe's dairy herds seems guaranteed to grow even further, with the introduction of bovine somatotropin (BST) to the European dairy industry. Produced by genetic engineering, BST is injected into dairy cows. It has no effect on milk quality, but can boost milk yields by 10-15%. Farmers, one can be sure, will want to use it to produce more milk from the cows they are allowed under the quotas.

Not surprisingly, 'diversification' is now a word often heard in the farming industry. Some farmers are branching out in unlikely directions, introducing 'war games' or carp farming, while others are looking to forestry as a possible alternative (page 146). Short of unforeseen disasters, the problems of over-production are likely to be with us well into the next century, and there are no major income-earning land uses which seem likely to quickly fill the gap. There is a limit to how many people want to play war games, for example, or to buy ornamental carp.

When the Centre for Agriculture Strategy at the University of Reading recently reviewed the options for farmers, it looked at alternative crops, alternative animal enterprises, forestry and a number of other possible land uses, including management for nature and landscape conservation purposes.

Among the Centre's conclusions: although there is

Table 1: Land use diversification options (source: *Countryside Commission*)

Land use with bias towards	Short term (up to 5 years)*	Medium term (5-10 years)*	Long term (more than 10 years)*
Agriculture	Rotational fallow	Alternative crops organic farming	Lower input farming including new permanent grassland
Landscape and wildlife conservation	Headland fallow Small-scale conservation planting and management	Integration of conservation into agricultural systems, including ESAs	New nature reserves New woodlands
Recreation and alternative enterprises	Picnic sites and other public access measures	Rights of way improvements	New country parks New woodlands Urban or urban-induced uses

* ie – length of time for which land would need to be allocated.

no single alternative crop enterprise which will use all the land likely to become available, candidates for smaller areas include flax, linseed, herbs and medicinal plants, essential oil crops, chickpea, lentil and salad crops. As far as animals are concerned, the Centre concentrated on the production of finer wool and milk (for cheese) from sheep, goat production and horses. It also suggested that the reduced pressures on land might lead to a de-intensification of some forms of animal husbandry, with possible increases in free-range poultry operations and in outdoor pig-keeping.

Organic farming, the Centre concluded, 'is increasing, but involves a substantial transition period and seems unlikely ever to occupy more than a small percentage of the agricultural area'. Among the possibilities in the forestry sector, the Centre identified the regeneration and extension of existing broad-leaved woodlands on lowland farms; the planting of new woodland, particularly on land currently growing barley; and the planting of trees on pasture land.

Table 1, which appeared in the Countryside Commission's report *New Opportunities for the Countryside,* published in 1987, highlights the timescales likely to be involved in a number of the most important diversification strategies. The Commission also wants to see important new restraints imposed on farmers, including a nitrogen tax (to curb the use of nitrogenous fertilizers), water protection zones in high nitrate areas, compulsory grass strips alongside vulnerable rivers and an enforceable code of practice to prevent pollution by silage and slurry.

Farming Nature?

The combination of over-production with a growing

Contrasting faces of forestry: mature beech in the Chilterns and (inset) a Norway spruce plantation in East Scotland.

public interest in countryside access and conservation is leading in a number of directions which would have seemed highly improbable even a few years ago. MAFF, for example, has been moving away from its long-standing focus on boosting food output to a rather broader agenda, which includes a growing emphasis on countryside conservation.

In 1987, MAFF began offering financial inducements to farmers in a number of areas of England designated as Environmentally Sensitive Areas, or ESAs, to farm at least some of their acreage in ways which contribute to the conservation of landscape, buildings and wildlife. The first nine ESAs, designated in 1984-85, included the eastern end of the South Downs, the Norfolk Broads, the Pennine Dales, the low-lying wetlands of the Somerset Levels, and sites in Cornwall, Wales, Scotland and Northern Ireland. Several more ESAs have since been named, including the western end of the South Downs, the Suffolk river valleys, Breckland in Norfolk, the Shropshire borders and the Test Valley.

The first group of ESAs covers an area of some 375,000 hectares and will affect between 5,000 and 6,000 farmers, while the second group will be at least as large. Although the initial budget of £5-6 million looked small against the total agricultural budget of more than £2 billion a year, it nonetheless marked a significant breakthrough in the Ministry's thinking.

One area which conservationists will be watching particularly closely will be the South Downs. The chalk hills of the South Downs represent one of the most distinctive English landscapes, created over the centuries by continuous grazing, in the absence of fertilizers. Unfortunately, although it is one of the richest habitats in England, it is also one of the most seriously threatened.

By 1966, less than 5,000 hectares of old chalk grassland remained in the South Downs, and since then more than a quarter of that figure has been lost. The purpose of ESA designation in this area will be to strengthen the protection of the 6% of the South Downs remaining as grassland – and to encourage the conversion of some ploughed land back to grassland. Such land cannot simply be left to nature, however. If that happened, the close-cropped, springy turf, with

---

Farm Foresters

Tree cover in the European Community averages about 22% of the total land area, with member states generally heavily dependent on timber imports. The Community's bill for imports of wood and wood products was 15 billion Ecus (roughly £7.5 billion) in 1985, while the average timber self-sufficiency of member states was 40% and falling. Britain is very much in the bottom rank.

In these circumstances, the idea of planting trees on some of the land no longer needed by agriculture seems attractive. But, while tree-planting is certainly appealing to policy-makers, past experience has shown that farmers and foresters need to be provided with realistic incentives. Capital incentives are not enough, with income support also likely to prove necessary in the early years after planting.

'Peddling the age-old argument that any forestry can be justified anywhere on the basis that we don't produce enough of our own wood is folly,' as one European Commission official told the *Financial Times.* 'A selective "horses for courses" approach is necessary, identifying those regions where there is demand for given wood products and potential for local economic production.'

The European Investment Bank has contributed many hundreds of millions of Ecus to forestry development in the last thirty years. Most of the EIB loans have gone to Ireland, while the bulk of the European Agricultural Guidance and Guarantee Fund since 1979 has gone to Mediterranean member states, where the problems of forest fires and soil erosion are widespread.

Forestry can unquestionably be a productive long-term investment. In Britain, for example, the attractions for the investor lie in increased land values, grants, tax reliefs and the tax-free income from the crop at the end of the growth cycle, some 40 to 50 years after planting. With forestry approval, land values can triple overnight. Sheep farming land worth £80 or £100 an acre can increase in value to between £250 and £350 an acre. For those paying the top rate of income tax, at 60%, the tax relief for forestry means that the investor is effectively given a 70% subsidy.

But there has been growing criticism of such investment. The National Audit Office issued a report in 1986 which questioned whether a national forestry programme could be economically justified. The basic argument was that forestry gives a relatively low return on government investment and creates little long-term employment. The report did distinguish, however, between upland and lowland afforestation, with planting on better quality areas in the lowlands likely to afford higher economic and amenity returns.

Foresters have also increasingly come into conflict with conservationists. In Scotland, the Forestry Commission and Fountain Forestry, Britain's largest wood-

its orchids and other wildflowers would rapidly be replaced by scrub.

Indeed, such landscapes will often need to be as intensively managed for conservation as for agricultural production. But the switch to conservation will bring many important benefits. Soil erosion, for example, is now a serious problem in the arable areas of the Downs, particularly where winter cereals are planted. Reversion to grassland would help protect the remaining topsoil.

Cost of millions

It remains to be seen whether the Government will fund such schemes at an adequate level, however. The idea of compensating farmers for maintaining wildlife sites is enshrined in the Wildlife and Countryside Act, 1981, but it is an expensive business. A single cereals farmer in North Kent, for example, had to be paid £1.6 million in exchange for not ploughing up 1,800 acres of marshes, and will need to be paid a further £320,000 a year to leave the land as grassland.

Interestingly, the annual figure of about a third of a million pounds is much less than the taxpayer would have had to find to pay the farmer to store and dispose of the corn he otherwise planned to grow on the land. The Nature Conservancy Council was expected to pay out a total of £7 million in 1987 to fund such agreements, a figure forecast to double within five years.

Whatever happens, it looks as though many farmers are going to have to rethink their purpose in life. A good deal of land will need to come out of intensive agricultural production and it is far from clear what will be done with it. Inevitably, different agencies are getting their bids in. The Countryside Commission, for example, wants to see a £320 million-a-year programme to convert some five million acres of surplus farmland to other uses, ranging from new housing to nature conservation. The Commission says that at least 150,000 new jobs could be created by the year 2000, enough to offset the annual loss from agriculture of around 9,000 jobs.

The many initiatives now being developed to redefine the relationship between farmers, the public and the land will continue to evolve through the 1990s. Europe-wide, they will also be spurred by the 18-month Council of Europe's Campaign for the Countryside, launched in Portugal during 1987. □

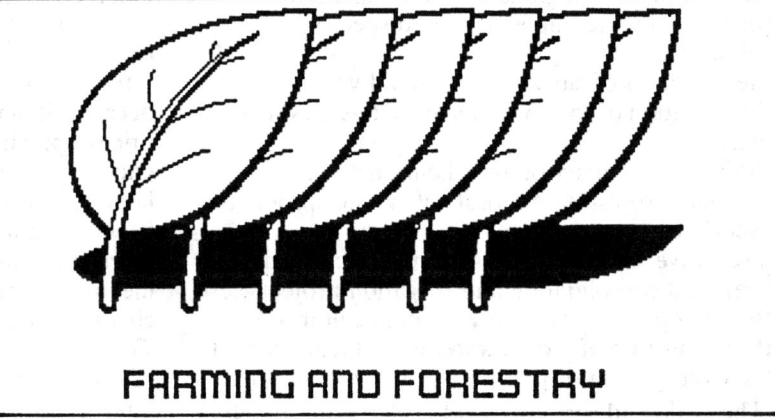

FARMING AND FORESTRY

land management company, ran into strong opposition from the Nature Conservancy Council and the Royal Society for the Protection of Birds, because of the proposed expansion of forestry in the so-called Flow Country of Caithness and Sutherland, which the NCC and RSPB believe could destroy a unique wilderness. The RSPB have argued that forestry operations already undertaken will cause a 50% drop in the number of golden eagles in several large areas of the Highlands.

The Institute of Terrestrial Ecology (ITE), meanwhile, has been conducting research for many years into the environmental impact of afforestation. One focus of the work has been on ways of modifying forestry techniques to improve the nature conservation value of commercial plantations. Recent publications on this theme include *Environmental Aspects of Plantation Forestry in Wales* and *Trees and Wildlife in the Scottish Uplands*.

While commercial conifer plantations do attract wildlife, they rarely provide habitat for endangered species. From a recreational point of view, too, they are problematic. Conifer plantations are frequently left unthinned and are, as a result, impenetrable. And their impact on the landscape often offends. But the low proportion of Britain's land surface devoted to trees must still be a matter of concern, particularly in the wake of the ecological devastation wrought by Dutch elm disease and storm (page 238).

Among the options the European Commision has been considering are traditional afforestation, producing large dimension timber and best suited to the sort of marginal, low-grade land found in Western Ireland, Wales, Brittany and Belgium's Ardennes; the rehabilitation of neglected farm woodlands; short to medium-term coppicing of oak, hazel, willow, chestnut, ash and sycamore, which is possible on most types of land; and 'agro-forestry', which involves a blending of grazing with tree farming.

The attraction of agro-forestry is that the rotation time is much shorter than in traditional high forest, with even hardwood species maturing in perhaps as little as 12-15 years. And the farmer can still use the land beneath the trees, so the land is not 'lost'.

PERSPECTIVES

Can the CAP be Made to Fit?

The EEC Common Agricultural Policy (CAP) has a profound influence on the European environment. *David Baldock* looks at some of the efforts now being made to produce a greener CAP.

'Agriculture is much the most important land use in the European Community, occupying about 60% of the total surface area. In some countries, such as the UK, as much as three-quarters of the land is farmed. Agriculture thus remains the primary activity shaping the environment.

While it is often pointed out that farmers were the main creators of the landscapes which we now want to protect, it is equally true that modern farming has a capacity to sweep away both cherished landscapes and valuable wildlife habitat and also to impose other environmental costs more usually associated with industry, such as water pollution. With scores of different farming practices in the European Community, the problems vary enormously, but currently the main concerns are as follows:

- landscape changes;
- destruction and degradation of wildlife habitats;
- practices threatening endangered species;
- soil erosion;
- the pollution of surface and ground waters;
- the pollution of soils with heavy metals, pesticides, etc.;
- the broader impact of agrochemicals;
- the inappropriate disposal of waste products, especially manure;
- insensitive infrastructure schemes, such as drainage, land consolidation and irrigation projects;
- the ecological vulnerability of monocultures;
- the exhaustion of groundwater in arid regions; and
- the over-grazing of pasture and forest land, etc.

The scale and seriousness of such environmental problems vary considerably and depends on local conditions. In general, however, many of the current environmental concerns stem from the recent trends towards agricultural intensification, specialisation and mechanisation, aggravated in some areas by increases in scale as well. Other problems, such as soil erosion, can also be found in areas where farming is less intensive, in Spain for example. It is probably fair to say that wildlife and landscape issues are pre-eminent in the UK, while pollution receives more attention in many other countries.

Advance and retreat

In addition to the changes taking place within agriculture, the extent and location of farming activities are also of importance environmentally. There are often environmental costs when agricultural advances onto 'marginal' areas such as wetlands or moorland, but important issues also arise when it retreats in the face of urban development, forestry or lack of economic viability. The consequences of agricultural abandonment are a major concern in many parts of the EEC and there are even signs of this debate growing in the UK as well. If land is removed from agricultural production on a large-scale, this could become one of the single gravest issues from an environmental perspective.

Since rural environmental issues are frequently local, the links with national and EEC policies are often indirect and complex and, in its simplest form, environmental opposition to the CAP can be no more than a general aversion to modern agriculture and the engine which appears to drive it. However, many environmental organisations have begun to subject the CAP to sophisticated forms of scrutiny in recent years and a substantial number of specific issues have emerged. Some of these can be set out briefly.

The CAP price policy, responsible for about 95% of the EEC agricultural budget (FEOGA), has attracted criticism from several quarters in the UK because it has been identified as raising farmgate prices, spurring further expansion and intensification, encouraging damaging new investment, forcing up land prices and raising the costs of compensation. Several commentators, such as John Bowers and Paul Cheshire, have seen lower prices as the principal means of halting the environmental destruction characterised by another author, Marion Shoard, as *The Theft of the Countryside* (page 209). The Ministry of Agriculture, Fisheries and Food, on the other hand, tend to join with the National Farmers' Union in regarding the prosperity of farmers as a necessary underpinning to environmental protection.

At a seminar held by IEEP and the Council for the Protection of Rural England (CPRE) in 1985 (the papers from which have been published as *Can the Cap Fit the Environment?*) a majority of participants seemed to agree that, while high CAP prices had contributed to many environmentally damaging developments, a simple cut in prices would not be a panacea. While prices should be curbed, compensatory measures would also be necessary, to protect certain vulnerable farmers and regions, to inhibit the development of large-scale prairie style farms, and to encourage environmentally positive forms of management, which might include low input systems and organic farming. Many environmental commentators also see the removal of farmland from production as representing an important opportunity to create new wildlife habitat, although there is considerable

FARMING & FORESTRY

opposition to the polarisation of the countryside into highly intensive productive areas on one side, and totally non-agricultural uses elsewhere. At present, schemes to remove land from production are only experimental but they could be adopted on a larger scale.

Inflexible

It is particularly regrettable that the CAP has relied on a single instrument, price policy, in pursuit of the many different goals of agricultural policy. This has resulted in an inflexible system in which conflicts are difficult to resolve. Environmental objectives are not easily inserted into such a narrow policy base.

The other and smaller section of FEOGA expenditure is the Guidance Sector, concerned principally with structural measures, marketing and food processing. While potentially a vehicle for encouraging environmentally sensitive farming in future, the Guidance Sector has not been used very much for this purpose in the past. Critics have pointed out that:

- the various systems of grant aid which have been established have often had insufficient environmental safeguards and failed to promote environmental investments;
- attempts to improve the rural infrastructure in poorer regions have often included substantial aid for environmentally damaging activities, such as land drainage in the West of Ireland or the uprooting of olives in Greece;
- the system of 'headage' payments for Less Favoured Areas, while ostensibly designed to help protect the countryside can, in some areas, be damaging, e.g. by encouraging over-grazing; and
- aids for forestry can also be damaging environmentally because of the methods of afforestation adopted in many countries.

Environmental arguments have received considerable attention in recent years, in North Western Europe and especially in the UK. Quite apart from their inherent merits, they have appealed to some governments and parts of the EC Commission because of the relationship between environmental improvements and reductions in the CAP budget. However, many environmental organisations favour a shift from price support to other forms of rural subsidy, rather than a drastic cut in CAP expenditure.

Environmentalists tend to agree on some aspects of CAP reform, such as the need to give more help to organic farmers, but there is less consensus about prices; the German Green Party, for example, argues that prices should be higher. However, aid for 'environmentally sensitive areas' is now allowed under the CAP and new schemes to link conservation and farming are beginning to appear.

DAVID BALDOCK *is a Senior Research Fellow at the Institute for European Environmental Policy, specialising in agriculture and the environment. He began environmental work at Earth Resources Research (ERR) in 1976 and also lectured part-time at the South Bank Polytechnic. He was on the Board of Friends of the Earth for many years and was Director of ERR when he left in early 1986. He has written reports and papers on many different environmental subjects, mostly concerned with agriculture, and a book* Wetland Drainage in Europe, *published in 1984.*

The Institute for European Environmental Policy, *3 Endsleigh Street, London WC1H 0DD. Tel: 01 388 2117.*

Hedge grubbing in Buckinghamshire.

PERSPECTIVES
The Changing Countryside

What sort of countryside do we want? *Robin Grove-White* suggests that we try to answer the question soon, because the pressures for change in the rural economy and landscape are building at an unprecedented rate.

'We are entering a period of major change in the countryside for which we are barely prepared. The crucial trigger will be the new situation for agriculture. Since the Second World War, the pattern of rural land uses has been dominated by the demands of agriculture and its powerful lobby. Food production almost without limit has been the policy of successive Governments. A web of guaranteed prices, freedom from planning controls and huge technical support and encouragement has transformed British farming, making it vastly more productive, but increasingly unpopular politically. That era of expansion is now coming to an end – a victim of its own excesses. The country can no longer afford an agriculture geared to more and more food for food's sake.

Agriculture's declining dominance coincides with other fundamental shifts.

The pattern of the rural population is changing. Over the past two decades there have been major movements of population out of the cities into more rural areas, reversing trends since the Industrial Revolution. Many of the old market towns and villages of lowland England have been transformed by newcomers drawn by what they can offer. As the agricultural workforce has declined, new populations have taken over dependent not on farming but interested in the recreational use of farmland.

What's more, there is huge and growing popular enthusiasm for leisure use of the countryside from *within* the cities as well as from outside. You can see it reflected most starkly in the soaring memberships of bodies like the Royal Society for the Protection of Birds, the National Trust, the Woodland Trust and the County Naturalists' Trusts. Other rural activities too are booming – everything from climbing to motor bike trailing to hang-gliding and war-gaming . . . The pointers are clear. The significance of the countryside for all of us, whether for frantic activity or for cultural and spiritual reflection, is increasing steadily.

Controversial

But these are far from the only new claims. There are also major tensions about new development, for housing and industry, in the countryside. Many historically rural areas are now experiencing unprecedented development pressures (who could ever have forecast the present housing boom in Dorset!) as mobility and housing markets grow and developers rush to stimulate and fill them. Rural house prices, especially in the South and along the motorway corridors, are soaring. And the process is spreading wider and wider.

Increasingly, too, the newer high tech industries have been seeking sites outside the cities, arguing that they too must go where their increasingly sophisticated work forces want to live. These days more new jobs are being created outside the conurbations than inside them.

These processes are highly controversial. The flow of people and development into rural areas challenges the needs of many of our cities, desperate for new investment and vitality. Recent political battles, some successful, by Council for the Protection of Rural England (CPRE) and others, aimed at maintaining planning restraints in Green Belts and the wider countryside have drawn on popular sympathy for the idea that, in a crowded island, the countryside should not be eroded away. If planning controls were significantly relaxed, large parts of the country – not just the South – could face sprawl of the 1930s variety (which our present controls were designed specifically to curb). But the tensions are real, notwithstanding the Government's new commitment to addressing the problems of the cities.

So how will the new state of agriculture affect this already volatile mixture?

Conservation again

Experts now talk of a drastically reducing need for agricultural land. The chairman of the Countryside Commission has suggested literally millions of acres of Britain's present farmland could become redundant for agriculture over the next decade, if the European Community is successful in imposing the limits on surplus production now thought necessary. Whatever the precise figure, it's clear that our land market will be affected profoundly.

Already, the pressures on many farmers to sell farmland for new housing or commercial uses are becoming intense. And the buyers are lining up. The question, 'What sort of a countryside do we want?', is going to face the nation with brutal starkness over the next few years.

Here are some pointers.

First, the role of the town and country planning system will be crucial – at precisely the time when it is facing growing political challenge from some quarters within the Government. Since the war, an underlying axiom for local authority planners has been that as much agricultural land as possible shall be protected. Planning *restraint* has been a watchword. Development has been concentrated as much as possible on existing settlements, big and small.

But as the case for protecting agricultural land for agricultural reasons erodes, any such restraint will have to be underpinned by new justifications, if it is to succeed. This will not be simple, particularly at a time when the strategic planning powers of county councils are about to be truncated by the Government. If we want an ordered transition to a new countryside, we shall need strong planning.

Second, the economic pressure for new land releases for housing and industrial development – and indeed for subtler adaptations of what the planners call 'permitted uses' – will be increasingly intense and controversial, particularly in the South. In some places, the pressures will succeed, perhaps rightly. But if this happens, the community as a whole is entitled to expect far greater public benefits from those who benefit commercially than it has obtained in the past from green field development. Huge profits will be made and this 'betterment' should be shared in some form. There is scope for major innovation here, in the pursuit of what one might call 'conservation gain' (rather than the old 'planning gain'). We might demand the creation of new common lands and rights of access on land separate from that about to be developed, if farmers and landowners are to benefit from new land releases. This would need new legal mechanisms and a new social contract between developers and the rest of us. It is for developers to offer the quid pro quo. And the community has the right to expect it to be a substantial one.

Third, it would be wrong to be fatalistic about future patterns of agriculture. Completely free markets should be resisted. They would be disastrous for the countryside, producing more intensification on the best farmland and corresponding decline, dereliction and even abandonment of farming on much of the rest (in the Midlands, for example). Few people want this. Instead, we should move towards new, perhaps more modest, patterns of agricultural subsidy, designed to sustain agriculture of a less intensive, more conservation-friendly character in much of the country. The financial supports in the new 'Environmentally Sensitive Areas' provide pointers to future possibilities. But they will need to be accompanied by stronger controls over production patterns if they are to command support more widely. In this context, the prospects for organic agriculture look increasingly promising. Of course, in much of the country there will continue to be highly intensive production; public opinion – and the recurrent pollution crises we may now confidently expect – will ensure that it comes under stronger controls as regards pollution and its impact on landscape and wildlife.

And fourth, we should look for alternative uses of land for, literally, non-productive purposes. Conservation bodies are themselves becoming major landowners in their own right. More power to them.

But less orthodox values have claims which must be met too. With the virtual certainty of high levels of unemployment continuing into the 1990s and beyond, more and more people will want to be able to use the countryside, drawing on its sacramental as well as its recreational potential. Conventional opinion recoils from the outsiders who comprise the Hippy Convoy or the Tipi People. But aren't such movements just the tip of an iceberg of radical alternative longing for the open sky and the freedom the countryside can offer? There must surely be room for us all.

There are tensions ahead, but the new possibilities for rural Britain have to be seized.

ROBIN GROVE-WHITE, *currently taking a two-year sabbatical at the Imperial College Centre for Environmental Technology, was Director of the Council for the Protection of Rural England (CPRE) between 1981 and 1987. He had previously been Assistant Secretary at CPRE from 1972 to 1980. He has contributed to a number of books, including* The Politics of Physical Resources *(1975) and* Future Landscapes *(1976), and co-authored* Nuclear Prospects *with Michael Flood (page 120).*

SECTION 8

Urban Revolutions

From massive garden festivals to small pockets of urban wildspace, the greening of Europe's cities is helping to rekindle the spirit of enterprise and attract new investment. Will this new approach to city planning and management be an exportable commodity?

Like it or not, most of us live in cities. 85% of Britons live in urban centres, so the 'environment' for most of us – and for most Europeans – is the urban environment. And many of our once-great cities are in deep trouble.

Simply driving through the outskirts of many major industrial towns in Northern Europe can be a profoundly depressing experience. While most European countries now have their 'golden corridors', 'sunbelts', or their counterparts of 'Silicon Glen', they also now suffer from the 'rustbelt' syndrome, with traditional industrial regions caught in a spiral of decline.

While the media may focus on the 'inner city', particularly those areas where there is a real prospect of rioting, the problem is developing on a much broader front. The economies of large cities and even entire urban regions are being undermined by the profound industrial changes now under way.

Faced with urban decay on such a scale, the first reaction is often to consider simply writing off large areas of the map as irretrievable. But the Liverpools of this world are not going to curl up and die – and the political pressures created by unemployment, poor housing, rising crime levels, vandalism and the constant threat of major disturbances generally make a 'hands-off' approach politically untenable.

Another possibility involves decanting urban populations into new towns or cities, built to higher environmental standards. Most European countries have adopted this strategy to siphon some of the population and development pressures away from their capital cities and other major conurbations, but this approach can have serious limitations – and is a very slow way of tackling the problems of the inner areas of existing cities.

Greentown

One interesting scheme which ultimately failed was 'Greentown', a project which grew out of a suggestion in 1978 by Lord Campbell, then chairman of the Milton Keynes Development Corporation (MKDC), that the Town & Country Planning Association should sponsor an experimental 'Third Garden City' on two of the large grid squares within Milton Keynes.

The idea, as Godfrey Boyle – one of the project's leading lights – recalled recently, was that Greentown 'would grow gradually according to ecologically-sound principles, encouragement would be given to renewable energy sources and energy conservation, and the development would include workshops, woodland and horticulture, as well as housing and public open space. To discourage land speculation, the freehold of all land in the village would be held by a company owned and controlled by the residents.'

Unfortunately, the Greentown Group found itself caught in a 'Catch 22' situation. Although various building societies had been prepared to offer mortgages, if MKDC would provide a written commitment that the scheme would go ahead, MKDC was unwilling to provide such a commitment unless it had firm evidence that there was solid financial backing

---

Most Europeans live in towns or cities, some of which are dying. Faced by a 'flight to the green', planners are trying to resurrect the inner city and other run-down areas. Meanwhile, urban greening projects, many run by Groundwork (page 159), show how even the worst-off areas can pull themselves up by their environmental bootstraps.

---

available for Greentown. In the end, MKDC pulled out of the negotiations and the idea of an ecologically sound new town went back on the shelf. The Greentown Group still hopes to create a co-operative green village, however.

'Not for the squeamish'

The third option is inner city regeneration. Even in the most favourable circumstances, however, such as in London's Docklands, urban regeneration can be an extremely controversial business. According to John Mills, deputy chairman of the London Docklands Development Corporation (LDDC), it 'is not for the squeamish. If you're not prepared to close businesses, demolish buildings, use compulsory purchase orders and persuade people to move, you will never get anywhere.'

The scale of redevelopment in London's Docklands beggars the imagination. The energy consumption of the redeveloped area will be such that it will increase London's power consumption by an eighth. A £77 million automatic light railway links the acres of new buildings with the rest of the city and, through the

URBAN RENEWAL

Green grows the industrial estate.

new short take off and landing airport, with the rest of Europe. Some new roads are being put underground, at a cost of £37,000 a yard (£65 million a mile). A quarter of a million new telephone lines are going in. Up to 40,000 jobs have been created and the LDDC forecasts that another 200,000 will come by the year 2000.

By the turn of the century, the LDDC estimates that £1 billion will have been invested by the government sector in new infrastructure for Docklands, with at least seven times that much coming from the private sector. Indeed, John Mills told *The Times* in 1987 that by the year 2000 'there will be approaching £2 million invested in every acre, a concentration of expenditure unrivalled anywhere in the world.'

But this solution can no more be applied to all Europe's inner city areas than heart transplants can be made universally available. The cost would be too great and, often, this sort of radical surgery is simply not appropriate. In some cases, for example, an improved pedestrian environment and the provision of cycleways may be a more appropriate response than the construction of another urban motorway or light railway.

Living magnets

Many European cities unquestionably need massive new investment if they are to survive and thrive. Surprisingly, too, urban greening programmes are proving an increasingly effective way of attracting such investment. Indeed, while previous generations saw the smoke which poured from factories as a powerful symbol of wealth creation, environmental quality is now recognised as a key dimension in a nation's wealth.

A healthy environment can serve as a living magnet for new investment. Many of today's industrial investors, in fact, insist on a high quality environment when deciding where to spend their money, build their factories, create new jobs, boost rate income and, ultimately, launch their products or services.

The new sources of wealth, whether they are microchips, microcomputers, microbes, Eurobonds or information, are strikingly different from most earlier industrial products. For a start, their suppliers are not bound by the location of energy and raw materials as were the major manufacturers of the Industrial Revolution.

Their most sought-after ingredients are highly trained people. The most successful companies have tended to move to – or start up in – areas near concentrations of brainpower (university cities like Cambridge or major research laboratories like MIT in the United States), transport nodes or networks (international airports like Heathrow or motorways like the M4) and environmental or leisure attractions (ski-slopes and golf-courses).

Spiral of decline

In the older conurbations, meanwhile, most city planners and many industrialists now recognise that a

The perfect breeding ground for high technology businesses.

Promoting the growth of high technology businesses involves much more than simply providing property with an up-market image.

Over the last five years we have developed half a million sq. ft. of premises specifically designed to to meet the needs of small and medium sized high technology firms. Each of the fifteen schemes is located close to a university, polytechnic or leading industrial company. This has opened the way to the transfer of ideas and expertise and the sharing of resources and amenities.

A case in point is the 167 acre Belasis Hall Technology Park. Here ICI and English Estates North, with support from central and local government, have joined forces in an initiative which will contribute significantly to the renewal of the economic base of Teesside. The first phase will provide the home for forty new and growing companies in a parkland setting adjacent to the Seal Sands Bird Sanctuary.

Although each of our high technology schemes has its own individual characteristics, all are helping the private sector to generate economic activity and create jobs in areas where they are needed most.

High Technology Developments at: Billingham, Bolton, Bradford, Cockermouth, Consett, Durham, Falmouth, Gateshead, Hull, Leeds, Liverpool, Middlesbrough, Plymouth (2), Ulverston.

English Estates, St. George's House, Kingsway, Team Valley, Gateshead, Tyne & Wear NE11 0NA. Tel: (091) 487 8941

spiral of environmental decline is not only a symptom of industrial collapse, but can actually accelerate that collapse.

Unfortunately, notes Groundwork chairman Christopher Chataway, himself deeply involved in the investment world as vice-chairman of the Orion Royal Bank, while 'industry is looking for attractive environments in which to operate, one of the problems is that the industries that have made the worst mess are those with least resources.' As a result, they are unlikely to be able to mobilise the sort of resources needed to effect major environmental regeneration programmes.

Yet all the available research suggests that people are extremely concerned about the state of the urban environment. When the consumer magazine *Which?* carried out a survey in 1987, for example, over three-quarters of the random sample of 1,250 people, said that they were unhappy with their local environment. Well over half wanted cleaner streets and half wanted to see waste ground landscaped.

With once-industrial cities now increasingly turning their eyes to tourism as a possible economic alternative, a career as a landscape architect is beginning to look more attractive. Coal tips and spoil heaps need to be reworked and planted, new industrial estates to be landscaped and greenspace to be introduced into the very heart of the concrete jungle.

One relatively new approach to urban regeneration, imported from West Germany, is based on garden festivals. The idea is to convert a large area of urban wasteland into the site for a festival, with the landscaping, facilities and much of the planting surviving beyond the festival's close, so the greening is permanent.

The first in Britain was in Liverpool in 1984, followed by Stoke-on-Trent in 1986. Next come Glasgow in 1988, Gateshead in 1990 and Ebbw Vale in 1992. The Liverpool festival made a £1 million operating profit in five months, but later became something of a white elephant. A leisure company took the site over in 1986, but subsequently went bankrupt. The Stoke site had an even harder time, with appalling weather and less media coverage, but the positive impact of the festival has probably been greater there than in Liverpool.

Meanwhile, growing numbers of smaller-scale projects aim to involve communities in the rehabilitation of their environment, encouraging them to take the task of urban greening into their own hands. 'Think Green', for example, has produced a series of publications, leaflets and fact sheets advising on how to clean up and green neighbourhoods. Copies of *Community Landscapes,* developed with Manchester City Council, are available from 'Think Green'.

The Green Leaf Housing Awards were established by the New Homes Marketing Board to encourage homebuilders to build on recycled, disused or derelict land, or to blend their developments into the existing landscape. There is no closing date for the competition, which includes Chris Baines, the popular wildlife gardener and landscape architect, among its judges. Entries are judged continuously and awards made to outstanding schemes. Baines, a professor at Birmingham Polytechnic, has used television as a powerful medium for promoting urban greening. In 1987, for example, he was responsible for the BBC series, *The Wild Side of Town.*

And other innovative new approaches are also now being developed. Some focus on the relatively simple – if important – objective of attracting wildlife back into cities (page 164). Others are attempting to green the urban environment on a much broader scale.

Environmental bootstraps

Groundwork (page 158), to take an example of the second approach, has been helping some of Britain's poorer industries and communities to pull themselves up literally by their environmental bootstraps. 'Caring for the environment is no longer seen as an obstacle to progress and the creation of jobs,' notes John Davidson, the Groundwork Foundation's chief executive. 'Quite the opposite. Businesses are now as aware as local government of the need to create a healthy social and physical environment for their enterprises to prosper.'

The original Operation Groundwork was launched at the end of 1981 in St Helens and Knowsley, as an extension of the Countryside Commission's urban fringe experiments. The aim was to show that neglected and forgotten countryside in and around urban areas could be brought back to life for recreation, food production and the benefit of the local community as a whole.

Unfortunately, because of the recession, industry was in no position to provide substantial funding for Groundwork's projects in St Helens and Knowsley. 'Companies like BICC and Pilkingtons were going through the most horrendous restructuring,' recalls Dr John Handley, director of Groundwork's local trust. 'They were shedding labour at a tremendous rate and were even questioning whether they should stay in the area.' But the trust did win many other kinds of support. David Pilkington, for example, a director of glass-makers Pilkington Brothers, helped Groundwork clarify its objectives and translate them into a business plan.

Indivisible

'The view in our company,' David Pilkington explained, 'is that, in the end, success is indivisible. If business is going to be successful, then the community has also to be thriving. The unemployment rate in St Helens is very high, about 20%. But the true unemployment rate among young people is around

155 ←

50%. This is one of the early industrial towns and, like an old garment, it is a bit threadbare. The key question is how do you go about generating a resurrection and achieving that sort of indivisible long-term success?'

He stressed that there are no quick solutions for such problems, but pointed out that the Groundwork formula has produced significant successes even in such difficult circumstances. 'I don't know who first thought of the idea,' he said, 'but Operation Groundwork was set up as a charitable trust. This is a very attractive way of operating, because you can have everybody involved in it: the Town Hall, the County Council, industry, the banks, schools and colleges, and so on. Once you are under way, it can all function with a minimum of red tape. It's a modern way of getting things done.'

An unexpected problem was that local people had become acclimatised to the local environment, so Groundwork had to work extremely hard simply to raise local expectations. It helped, for example, in the launch of a new amenity body, the Sankey Canal Restoration Society (SCARS). Later, as early successes were reported, other industrial sponsors began to back projects – and Pilkingtons also seconded storeman David Anders for two years. He proved a tremendous asset in managing the local Groundwork volunteers. Other companies, including Esso and ICI, together with the Central Electricity Generating Board, have also seconded people to Groundwork.

The attraction for industry, as Christopher Chataway explains it, is that 'any contribution we get from industry is multiplied by voluntary effort, by Government and by local government, so that you really do see, as a private donor, an awful lot of action for the few pounds you put in.'

Lowering the threshold

One thing such trusts can do, too, is to lower the threshold for environmental improvements, by pulling in funds from a variety of sources. The Rossendale Groundwork Trust, for example, secured a £20,000 Derelict Land Grant to help footwear manufacturers Lambert Haworth to turn an old coal-washing yard into a new car park, a scheme which involved demolishing buildings, relaying tarmac and clearing away waste.

Some very large companies, Ferranti among them, have commissioned similar landscaping work. ICI Pharmaceuticals, which was expanding its Macclesfield plant on the Hurdsfield Estate, is another case in point. The site borders the Macclesfield Canal and the new Macclesfield Way, and ICI took its environmental responsibilities very seriously. 'That site probably won't be developed until the next century,' noted Groundwork's Patrick Leonard, 'but ICI can see the advantage of planting trees which will be ready to screen the site when they do develop it.'

Such long-term thinking is ultimately what such projects are all about. They help local communities and industries to raise their sights, and can help foster a new kind of environmental enterprise. Many of the schemes which have resulted are small, but they can have an important catalytic effect.

Take Macclesfield again. Given the importance of transport technologies in shaping and reshaping our urban environment, for example, the conversion of the disused Macclesfield-Middlewood railway into a 12-mile 'greenway' designed for walkers, cyclists and

Michael Boddington & Associates

Specialists in rural planning issues, including agriculture, ecology, conservation, recreation and forestry. We undertake comprehensive land use and project planning and will represent your interests at public inquiries.

Windmill House, 37/39 Station Road, Henley-on-Thames
Oxfordshire RG9 1AT United Kingdom
Telephone: Henley-on-Thames (0491) 573818
Telex: 946240 CWEASY G (ref. 19019821) Fax: (0491) 579241

URBAN RENEWAL

horse-riders could have a much wider influence.

The local trust, with the aid of the Sports Council, also launched an experimental cycle-hire scheme, to provide low-cost access to the developing network of greenways. Initially, much of this work has been on the fringe of such towns and cities, but the hope must be that these green spaces and green links will eventually extend right into the heart of our urban environment.

One organisation which has long played a leading role in lobbying for more environmentally acceptable forms of transport is Transport 2000. While it almost certainly will be impossible to 'design out' the private car and heavy lorries for the foreseeable future, the London Docklands light railway shows that public transport will be at the heart of the city of the future.

'Flight to the green'

To date, most of the funding for greening projects has come from public sector sources or in the form of charitable donations from industry. Increasingly, however, greening projects will be set up as small businesses in their own right.

Some have already succeeded in attracting finance from some of the new green investment organisations, such as the Ecology Building Society (page 188) and the Financial Initiative (page 186), but this is a field which will need to open out very substantially if our cities are to provide an acceptable environment for life in the 21st century.

Some interesting experiments, meanwhile, are being carried out to see how city economies can be managed in such a way as to promote such small enterprises. When the New Economics Foundation (page 249) organised its 'Future City' seminar in Oxford in 1987, for example, there was considerable interest in a study being prepared for the Dutch government on ways in which five major cities – including Amsterdam, Rotterdam and The Hague – could encourage networks of small-scale enterprise against the cold winds blowing from the world economy.

Many of the trends, though, are towards what has been described as the 'spread city', a series of small, interlinked communities growing up around the shrinking cities of the past. Some observers predict, for example, that despite the investment that has gone into London's Docklands, the city will spread well beyond its traditional centres, ultimately extending from Cambridge to the south coast.

Professor Peter Hall, one of Britain's leading

161→

PERSPECTIVES
Livable Cities

It is five years since the publication of *The Livable City*, the urban component of the UK response to the World Conservation Strategy. *Joan Davidson*, one of the report's authors, and *John Davidson*, chief executive of the Groundwork Foundation, look at some recent initiatives.

'Not since the war have European cities faced such a crisis. For two decades they have been losing people and investment at an accelerating pace. These losses, together with cuts in public expenditure, have left many cities with jobless and disheartened communities, poorer services, neglected homes and decaying buildings, and much vacant land. All these changes have combined to destroy the quality of Europe's urban environments.

In Britain, especially in the north, the contraction of industry has left great tracts of land empty and derelict. There are more than 5,000 acres of wasteland on Merseyside alone. And there are other, smaller, pockets of urban desolation, born not just from the decline of economic activity, but from inappropriate measures to deal with urban problems. Many public housing estates have become environments of despair, bleak and dangerous. In Britain, more than 1.25 million families live on estates classified as 'run down'. Many local authorities, with budgets cut, have found it impossible to maintain the high-cost green landscapes of city parks and gardens.

Meanwhile 14 million Europeans are out of work. But what is significant is that some have seen this crisis of wasted land and wasted people in terms of opportunity.

Practical action

Indeed, the changed circumstances of cities in the 1980s have generated many innovative responses to problems. In the public sector, there have been garden festivals and reclamation schemes, but local communities have been especially innovative. New partnerships for action are now beginning to emerge – and much of the impetus has come from environmental groups. Many groups have been concerned to apply the messages of resource conservation and sustainable development to the city, and to move on from campaigning and fund-raising into *practical* action. In many cities, local groups are now involved in a whole range of environmental activities from greening drab and idle land, through the restoration of decaying buildings, to the recycling of wastes and energy-saving projects. Their work has become an important focus for community development and is creating much-needed employment, whether in the form of paid jobs or as opportunities for volunteering.

The signs are that practical environmental work of this kind offers scope for personal development and skills training and can also reach those who are often disadvantaged in the labour market – ethnic minorities, disabled people and women. Although the overall scale of such activity is presently small, new 'green' enterprises and community businesses are beginning to emerge.

City greening

The greening of towns and cities takes many forms, from the large scale reclamation of industrial dereliction to the small scale management of vacant plots. In Liverpool, for example, a local group, Landlife, has transformed some 30 inner city sites from wasteland to wild habitats since its 'Greensight Project' began in 1979. Building upon pioneering work in the Netherlands, Landlife has applied low-cost 'ecological' methods to the management of vacant urban land. It trains unemployed people and runs a business growing and selling wildflower seeds.

Here, and in other British cities where urban wildlife groups are active, the work is varied – with tree, shrub and flower planting, the restoration and care of woodlands, and the clearing of ponds and litter. Groups are involved in protection *and* creation, conserving the rich wild spaces that still remain and building new habitats for educational and community use. The British Trust for Conservation Volunteers is now a major agency for organising practical environmental action of this kind.

Thought for food

Food production is another use for wasted land in the city. Bristol's Windmill Hill, one of Britain's earliest city farms, has celebrated its tenth anniversary and a decade which has seen the movement grow from two farms in 1976 to more than 50. The National Federation of City Farms, a national co-ordinating and advisory body, has a widening membership of farms and community gardens and is busy helping them not only to extend their role as social and education centres, but also to develop new small businesses based on food production, horticulture and crafts.

The worsening social and environmental condition of many housing estates has stimulated some innovative neighbourhood renovations which combine work on land and buildings, with tenants involved in making murals, allotments and gardens. In Britain, schemes like these have been helped by a growing number of 'community technical aid centres' (CTACs), which provide professional advice on architecture, landscape and planning. CTACs, like Free Form in London's Hackney, have been highly successful at enabling local groups to design and implement their ideas, and raise the necessary funds.

A trout quarry

Protecting and improving the urban environment can become a valuable focus for urban regeneration, revitalising communities and attracting new investment. Already, some of the new green initiatives have grown into multi-purpose agencies which are not only transforming bad environments – turning liabilities into assets – but are responding to social needs and generating self-sustaining businesses. The Groundwork movement is a good example.

The twelve Groundwork Trusts are part of an expanding network of local partnerships between the voluntary sector, companies and local authorities, all working together to redeem derelict industrial and residential land. Providing technical expertise and help with funding, the Trusts have worked on many projects including the landscaping of ugly industrial sites, the building of school nature gardens and the

Who's Who in the Livable City

We asked the Davidsons to list some of the key people working on urban greening in Britain. Here are some of the names they mentioned.

The **Association of Community Technical Aid Centres** (The Royal Institution, Colquitt Street, Liverpool L1 4DE or on 051 708 7607) promotes and supports the development of community technical aid centres.

The **British Trust for Conservation Volunteers** (36 St Mary's Street, Wallingford, Oxon OX10 0EU or on 0491 39766) encourages and organises conservation action, using both volunteers and paid staff.

The **European Foundation for Living and Working Conditions** (Loughlinstown House, Shankill, Co Dublin, Eire or on Dublin 826888) recently completed *Voluntary Work in the Environment*, a study of initiatives, including environmental projects, in six European cities.

The **Fairbrother Group** (c/o Urban Wildlife Group, 11 Albert Street, Birmingham B4 7UA or on 061 236 3626) co-ordinates and supports the network of urban wildlife groups.

The **Free Form Arts Trust** (38 Dalston Lane, London E8 3AZ or on 01 249 3394).

The **Groundwork Foundation** (Bennett's Court, 6 Bennett's Hill, Birmingham B2 5ST or on

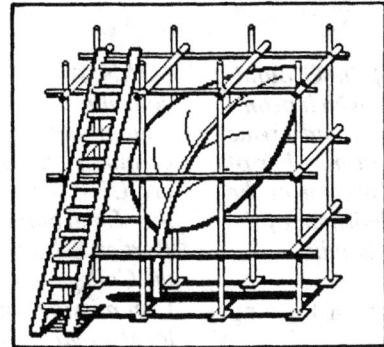

021 236 8565) is the national co-ordinating agency, with charitable status, which provides resources and support for the growing national network of Groundwork Trusts.

Landlife (Old Police Station, Lark Lane, Liverpool L17 9PF or on 051 728 7011).

The **National Council for Voluntary Organisations** (26 Bedford Square, London WC1B 3HU or on 01 636 4066) provides professional advisory services to voluntary organisations. It also protects their interests and promotes action, including a new initiative, Waste Watch, to support community-based recycling schemes. It published *How Green is Your City*, a book of environmental case studies early in 1988.

The **National Federation of City Farms** (Old Vicarage, 66 Fraser Street, Windmill Hill, Bedminster, Bristol BS3 4LY or on 0272 660663) is the national co-ordination and support agency for city farms.

Neighbourhood Energy Action (2-4 Bigg Market, Newcastle-upon-Tyne NE1 1UW or on 0632 615677) is the national co-ordinating agency promoting and supporting local energy projects, focusing on the insulation of the homes of the elderly and of low income families. It gives advice on grants and sponsorship, organises conferences and meetings, and publishes a bi-monthly journal.

The **Think Green Campaign** (Premier House, 43-48 New Street, Birmingham B2 4LJ or on 021 643 8899) is a nationwide campaign for greener towns and cities, and fosters the formation of 'think green' networks.

The **Town and Country Planning Association** (17 Carlton House Terrace, London SW1Y 5AS or on 01 930 8903) campaigns for effective planning and more local decision making.

The **Urban Centre for Appropriate Technology** (Philip Street, Bristol BS3 4DR or on 0272 669988).

JOHN DAVIDSON is Chief Executive of the Groundwork Foundation, a national organisation which promotes local action to improve environments and create jobs in and around British cities. A Board member of UK 2000, he was previously Assistant Director at the Countryside Commission and Deputy Chairman of the IUCN Commission on Environmental Planning.

JOAN DAVIDSON is an environmental writer and consultant, specialising in community-based environmental action in the UK and some Third World countries. Among the organisations she has worked for are UNESCO, OECD, IUCN and the Department of the Environment. She is a Research Fellow at the Bartlett School of Architecture and Planning, University College London, and a Member of the IUCN Commission on Environmental Planning. She studied local environmental action as a Leverhulme Fellow (1981–83) and with a research fellowship from the Economic and Social Research Council (1985–86).

transformation of a polluted quarry into a thriving commercial trout fishery.

The Bristol-based Urban Centre for Appropriate Technology is another good example. Its work has included the restoration of a terrace of derelict houses to show how homes can be cheaply adapted to save energy. From this base the Centre employs a team to insulate the homes of old and disabled people in the area. It also runs an energy workshop offering a range of training courses and is working with the local authority on an energy plan for the city.

Green businesses

The new vision is that citizens themselves have the skills and imagination to green the city. And their projects show that there is great scope for local environmental initiatives to be highly effective in tackling city problems. But they need help. They need better access to land and buildings: local authorities can often assist here by leasing properties at low or negligible rents. Funding for environmental improvements, especially to *maintain* them, is often limited and uncertain: local groups spend far too much time trying to raise small sums from many sources. Getting money from European agencies is often time-consuming. And where groups are trying to generate more of their own income, they often find it difficult to raise start-up grants and loans for new unconventional 'green' businesses.

An extension of technical aid and training is vital to ensure high quality work; 'enabling' organisations like the Groundwork Foundation, the National Federation of City Farms, and Neighbourhood Energy Action all have an important role to play in this. And if local groups are to thrive by becoming more financially independent, then they need good business advice – on marketing their products and services, communicating their achievements and managing their personnel. Companies already help here – in cash and kind – by sponsoring projects, events and materials, and by seconding staff.

Projects, too, must be enabled to share their knowledge, for although each one faces a different array of problems, there is much they could learn from each other. Some initiatives have already made contact with their counterparts in other European countries; many advantages could flow from a greater international exchange of experience and personnel – a worthwhile objective in the follow-up to European Year of the Environment.

URBAN RENEWAL

urban geographers, believes that many parts of Europe are moving back towards the settlement pattern which characterised the Middle Ages. In what the Germans have dubbed the 'flight to the green', growing numbers of people are moving out of the cities, via the suburbs, back to the countryside. 'The maps of population change in the 1980s are almost the precise inverse of those in the 1880s,' Professor Hall observed.

This trend is bound to be spurred by the release of considerable areas of land from agricultural production (page 150). In the remaining years of the 20th century we clearly have some hard decisions to make about whether the resulting spread city is something we are willing to live with – and in.

Export opportunities

Overall, however, the physical environment in the great cities of Europe has improved very considerably in recent years, at least when compared with the conditions prevailing when the Industrial Revolution was running at full throttle. The most pressing urban problems in the coming decades are likely to be found in the Third World.

While recent concern has tended to focus on problems of food supply, the main problem facing many Third World planners is massive urbanisation. By the year 2000, according to World Bank estimates, 40% of the world's population will be living in 450 cities, most of them in the developing world, each with a population of more than 11 million people.

Whereas the 1960s and 1970s saw a considerable investment in rural areas in general, and in agriculture in particular, to slow the pace of urban drift, the growth of mega-cities like Mexico City, Sao Paulo (which is expanding at the rate of one square kilometre every week), Cairo, Bombay, Manila or Lagos has hardly faltered. With the global population predicted to continue growing through the 21st century, the pressures will simply become more intense.

As a result, the focus is shifting towards urban projects designed to help the urban poor. The planner in the Third World today is more likely to be operating as an enabler than as a producer of static master plans. Increasingly, the emphasis is on helping urban communities to help themselves.

Although the greening of European cities may seem to have little to do with the problems facing Third World cities, planning consultants who have worked on such projects are often much better equipped for dealing with Third World problems. As Max Nicholson, a pioneer in urban ecology (page 162), points out, ecology not only has a great deal to offer in informing the management of small pockets of urban habitat, but must also now be integrated into all aspects of the design, construction, operation and management of our towns, cities and emerging mega-cities.

CUT THE COUPON. REAP THE REWARDS.

A better environment is rewarding for everyone. And in many ways, British Industry stands to gain more than most.

Groundwork works in partnership with local communities, private companies and local authorities to clear dereliction and regenerate Britain's environment in and around our towns and cities.

Find out today about how you – in partnership with Groundwork – could change tomorrow for the better.

Return the coupon for literature to: **Groundwork Foundation, Bennetts Court, 6 Bennetts Hill, Birmingham B2 5ST. Tel: 021-236 8565.**

We acknowledge the support of

Name
Company
Position
Address

PERSPECTIVES

The Cinderella Science

Max Nicholson has had an extraordinary career as an 'environmental revolutionary'. He has applied the principles of ecology, which he once described as the 'Cinderella science', to a series of top jobs. Indefatigable, he reviews the latest developments in his already 'rather-too-long career'.

MAX NICHOLSON, CB, CVO, *has 'tried to hold a balance between the importance of renewed learning and research, that of developing through lateral thinking a coherent outlook on – and strategy for – humanity's role on planet Earth, and that of actually bringing about change through innovative practical work.'*

In the first of these areas he has helped in building up the new ornithology as a founder of the British Trust for Ornithology, as Editor of British Birds *and, currently, as Editor of the definitive, seven volume* Birds of the Western Palearctic, *published by Oxford University Press. 'Taught mainly by birds,' he spent many years 'executing a national programme of applied ecology' as Director-General of the official Nature Conservancy, and then as Head of the Conservation section of the International Biological Programme.*

In public affairs he sought through decades, as a leader of Political and Economic Planning (PEP), to provide a factual and scientific base for national economic and social development, sector by sector. His books have included The System: The Mismanagement of Modern Britain *(1967),* The Environmental Revolution *(1970) and its sequel,* The New Environmental Age *(1987, see page 212).*

On the practical side, in addition to his World War II shipping role which took him to top-level meetings in Cairo, Quebec and Yalta, he served throughout the post-war reconstruction period as Head of the Lord President's Office, under Deputy Prime Minister Herbert Morrison. He was Chairman of the official launch committee for the Festival of Britain in 1951 and, later, Secretary of the Duke of Edinburgh's Conference on the Countryside 1970. More recently, as a founder Principal of Land Use Consultants (from 1966), he has advised on the environmental impact of such major projects as the National Coal Board's land restoration programme and the environmental repercussions of the Channel Tunnel Bill.

He regrets, but is not surprised, that – despite his best efforts – the full integration of human activities with their indispensable base in the biosphere has not yet been achieved. But, now well into his eighties, he intends to push on, 'holding senility at bay'.

' Ecologists try to understand how the complex systems of nature work, as they certainly do, with more robustness and efficiency than our own jerry-built and unbalanced economic systems.

During World War II, as Head of Allocation of Tonnage in London under the Anglo-American Shipping Adjustment Board, it was my task to apply the flow principles of ecology to extracting the utmost useful lift out of a chronically insufficient pool of cargo shipping, harassed by heavy sinkings, strategic setbacks and endless problems over matching points of supply to military and civil delivery theatres.

With the indispensable backing of many skilled and experienced shipping men, I found that the key patterns of strategic management arose naturally from ecological principles. However odd this may sound, I was fortified afterwards when Lord Alanbrooke told

URBAN RENEWAL

me that if we had got it wrong it could have lost us the war.

Facts of life

Looking at the state of the world today, and especially at what we now like to call 'wealth creation', I find a similar fundamental problem – our failure to adapt our basic attitudes and thinking to the obvious need to overhaul our use of our natural resource base.

The whole caboodle, to coin a phrase, is a misdirected shambles. And it is not a shambles for want of inventive ingenuity or any incapacity for immediate problem-solving. Instead, it is a shambles because those in business and elsewhere, who apply such talents so admirably, are content to do so within a framework of beliefs, attitudes, assumptions, politics and economics handed down to them by any number of prophets, moralists, philosophers, myth-makers, politicians and miscellaneous intellectuals who were never exposed to the facts of life on Earth as we now know them.

Unless and until wide-awake people insist that enough is enough, that our entire intellectual and social framework must be radically (hopefully peacefully) overhauled to cope with our changed circumstances and role on this planet, I see no hope for them or it.

My own experience suggests that this is an achievable goal. One only has to think back to the extraordinary growth of the world-wide environmental conservation movement during the space of a single generation, long before Chernobyl clouded the horizon, to see how resources can be mobilised for a pressing cause. Indeed, the firm, consistent, thoughtful way in which this movement functions has many lessons for business, where its principles could help companies not only to survive but to thrive.

Too little, too late

Detailed company audits published over the years by Environmental Data Services in the *ENDS Report* have shown a marked correlation between firms managed by environmentally enlightened directors and managers and business success, for the simple reason that both environmental thinking and successful strategic thinking demand similar capacities for looking ahead and for 'lateral thinking' (page 57).

The same potentially holds true for city planning and management. Indeed, one of the current failures which most troubles me in Britain is the almost total lack of recognition, both in business and government, of the real reasons why great American cities, which 20 years ago were heading for the same economic and social disasters as our own, have made such progress in recent years.

As the head of one of Britain's most successful firms recently told me, the only way to run a go-ahead, satisfied and loyal industrial team today is to ensure that employees and their families can enjoy an environment and amenities matching the best they know to be available. It is futile, indeed dangerous, for politicians and opinionated civil servants to insist on narrow, out-dated approaches based on throwing too little money too late at inner city problems.

The more I have worked in cities, the more convinced I have become that environmental rehabilitation is the key to their future. Britain's New Towns, decanting urban populations into greener surroundings, were an early attempt to move in this direction. But a far harder task – although in the end more important – is to green existing cities where they stand. Stoke-on-Trent has been one of the pioneers in this respect, regenerating many hundreds of acres as green spaces and greenways, advised by my firm, Land Use Consultants.

Through the early spadework of the Ecological Parks Trust (now the Trust for Urban Ecology, abbreviated to TRUE), I have laboured over the past decade to promote recognition of the important contribution that urban ecology, itself to date the Cinderella sister of ecology and conservation, to the greening of cities in its widest sense. If we are to create livable cities, and the alternatives are too awful to contemplate, then basic ecological principles will need to be integrated into all aspects of the design, construction, operation and management of the planet's villages, towns, cities and emerging megacities.

PERSPECTIVES
Wild about the City

London alone has 23 square miles of derelict and disused land.
David Goode looks at the prospect for coaxing more wildlife back into such areas.

'Concern for nature in towns and cities is a new phenomenon which has occurred spontaneously over the past ten years in many parts of Europe and North America. This novel aspect of nature conservation has rapidly grown in significance and has stimulated exciting new developments. A number of factors may have been responsible. Recent studies of city wildlife have demonstrated that a host of plants and animals are able to thrive in the city environment. Many have shown remarkable ability to take advantage of the variety of artificial habitats which we have created. Urban foxes are now commonplace in Britain and birds of prey such as kestrels are just as much at home in the city as in the countryside. Some introduced species have been so successful that they are reaching pest proportions – like Canada geese in Central London.

At the same time it has become appreciated that many city dwellers like to have contact with nature. This need has led to local communities arguing forcibly for the protection of local wildlife refuges, even though these places have for many years been regarded as nothing more than wasteland. Attitudes are changing, and it isn't only amongst local communities that new values are being established. Professional planners and landscape designers, as well as ecologists, have been responsible for new approaches to our use of urban greenspace.

Life in the cemetery

Urban nature conservation differs from other more traditional approaches to conservation in that it does not place priority on rare or endangered species or habitats, but gives considerable weight to the values and benefits of urban wildlife to local people. Places now valued vary from tracts of encapsulated countryside with traditional habitats such as woodland, heath or marsh, to the totally artificial habitats of abandoned railway yards, derelict industrial sites and even neglected cemeteries. Arguments for conservation of such places have established new precedents in the case-law of planning and the whole approach to conservation in urban areas has required new procedures and techniques for the creation and management of artificial habitats.

In West Berlin, meanwhile, the main stimulus has come from ecologists and planners working together to develop an overall ecological strategy for the city, which is now the most advanced of any city in Europe. In contrast the Dutch initiatives have been in landscape design. New urban woodlands were planted in Amsterdam in the 1930s and the past 40 years have seen a dramatic development of ecologically sensitive landscape design in many urban areas. British landscape designers have used this experience in places such as Warrington New Town, where tracts of birch woodland were planted in advance of new housing schemes, rather than adding trees as an extra.

The Dutch concept of local 'heem parks' composed of naturalistic vegetation has also been applied in Britain in developing inner city ecology parks which have proved remarkably successful. The very situations of some have captured people's imagination. The William Curtis Park by Tower Bridge was the first of these parks in Britain and provided a place for children to study nature right in the middle of London. That park was closed in 1986, to make way for new developments, but other permanent ecology parks have been constructed in London's docklands and at Camley Street, by King's Cross Station. Most of these new schemes have only occurred through partnership between local authorities and various voluntary organisations, such as the Trust for Urban Ecology (page 163).

But urban nature conservation is not just concerned with protection of nature reserves and ecology parks. It includes everything from city farms, community gardens and roof gardens right down to window boxes. It is concerned with environmental enhancement at all levels.

A grass-roots movement

In some cities planning authorities are now producing detailed ecological strategies to ensure that important places are protected. The Greater London Ecology Unit is developing such a strategy for London indicating all the significant sites throughout the capital. The Unit also identifies areas which are deficient in natural vegetation, so that efforts can be made to create new habitats or enhance the natural character of parks and other open spaces.

A fundamental feature of urban nature conservation in Britain is that it is a grass-roots movement. It is not imposed from above by statutory authorities, but has grown as a response to people's needs. People who feel themselves dispossessed of nature are taking action to save even the most unlikely spots, and they are winning. The proliferation of urban wildlife groups is a clear sign of the strength of this movement. During the past seven years over 80 urban wildlife groups have been set up in towns and cities throughout Britain and more are to come. New attitudes are

URBAN RENEWAL

becoming established, as well as a new ethos towards wildlife in the city.

One of the most powerful arguments in favour of this new movement is that ecological projects have a significant role in enhancing the quality of life in urban areas and may even help to reduce social tensions. There is evidence, too, that sensitively designed urban landscapes with natural qualities will in themselves attract investment and promote rehabilitation of inner city areas that have suffered in the past from dereliction and decay.

Urban nature conservation, in short, is a positive approach to the revitalisation of towns and cities which could have profound effects on our way of life if applied effectively through the planning and management of urban greenspace. **'**

Dr DAVID GOODE *worked for 15 years with the Nature Conservancy Council, where he was latterly Assistant Chief Scientist. He joined the Greater London Council in 1982 as its first ecologist, with a remit to develop an ecological dimension in all aspects of the Council's work. Since 1986 he has headed the Greater London Ecology Unit working to a new joint Committee of London Boroughs. He is Chairman for the Trust for Urban Ecology, a Trustee of the London Ecology Centre and a Director of the Think Green Campaign. His book* Wild in London *was sponsored by Shell UK and published by Michael Joseph (1986).*

SECTION 9

Boon or Bane?

Depending on how you tot up the balance sheet, tourism can be good, bad or ugly. Some see tourists as a godsend, others as a plague, but they – we – are now an inescapable fact of life. So how can tourism be harnessed to the cause of sustainable development?

Those clever people at Disneyworld may eventually come up with an answer to species extinction: robot animals whirring around robot ecosystems. They are already well down the track, particularly at the Epcot Center in Florida, where your cinema seat turns into a train and whisks you back into prehistory. On either side, dinosaurs browse trees which later became coal, while overhead pterodactyls stagger precariously back to their roosts and the reeking swamps wrap you in sulphurous Sensurround.

Having inherited something approaching an Eden, *Homo sapiens industrialis* has often seemed hell-bent on turning it back into a world fit only for such robust life-forms. Last year, for example, Britain's Royal College of Physicians warned that a holiday in the sun can kill. Ultraviolet radiation can promote malignant skin melanomas – a problem which is certain to get worse as the planet's ozone layer is eroded by aerosol propellants, refrigerants and other chemicals which drift inexorably up into the atmosphere long after they have fixed the latest hairstyle in place or cooled the car on the way home from the beach.

The average tourist may not spend much time thinking about the chemistry of the upper stratosphere, but some forms of pollution, like the radioactive fallout from the Chernobyl nuclear reactor accident in 1986, *have* significantly dented the tourism industry's receipts.

A few months after Chernobyl erupted into the headlines, for example, Intourist reported that bookings for tours in the Soviet Union had dropped by more than 30 per cent. Meanwhile, the Scandinavians, alarmed by Britain's contributions to their 'acid rain' problems, have threatened a tourist boycott unless real progress is made in cleaning up the emissions of power plants and other sources of sulphur and nitrogen oxides.

The commercial fallout

In today's world, such developments can spell economic ruin for countries that have hitched their fortunes to the international tourism industry. Tourists spent £10 billion in England in 1985, for example, of which some £5.5 billion was contributed by the 14.5 million overseas tourists visiting the country. Elsewhere, entire regions, like the Caribbean, have been turned into resort areas, with governments seeing tourism as their only means of filling the gaps in foreign earnings caused by depressed income from traditional commodity exports. Such revenues are taken seriously and the comings and goings of overseas visitors, particularly from the United States, are watched intently.

In some quarters, indeed, there has been a tendency to see tourism as an economic cure-all, a view smartly dismissed on behalf of the manufacturing sector by Sir John Harvey-Jones, while chairman of ICI. 'If we imagine the UK can get by with a bunch of people in smocks showing tourists around medieval castles,' he said, 'we are quite frankly out of our minds.'

The highly fragmented nature of the world tourism industry, coupled with the fact that most firms operate on precariously slim margins, makes it an unlikely recruit to sustainable development. Brian Jackman runs through the balance sheet on page 172, underscoring many worrying trends. But some parts of the industry may be ripe for greening.

Tourism, nonetheless, has grown at a very considerable rate worldwide. International arrivals alone increased more than 10-fold between 1945 and 1980, from 25 million to 280 million. The income from tourism in countries affiliated to the World Tourism Organisation (WTO) was $6.9 billion in 1960, but grew so rapidly that it breached the $100 billion mark by 1982. With world tourism growing at a rate of 5% a year, the chances are that demand will have doubled again by the year 2000.

As a result, very few areas remain sacrosanct from the tour operator's desire to open up new markets. In some instances, the results have been fairly positive (page 174), but elsewhere they have been tragic. The opening up of Australia's outback, for example, has led to a number of deaths following attacks by giant salt water crocodiles. As a result, Australian conservationists are having to fight hard to protect the crocodile population of the country's 'far north' from culling and hunting.

Paradoxically, the growing interest in wildlife is imposing increasing pressure on some of the world's

Aquaria are a US growth industry. Killer whales at Sea World, Florida.

most treasured ecosystems. 1986, for example, was a record year for tourist visits to the Galapagos Islands. Some years previously, a limit of 12,000 visitors had been set, but this was quickly breached and a new limit of 25,000 was imposed. In 1986, the numbers were in excess of 30,000. Unfortunately, while tour operators like Exodus Expeditions offer low-impact holidays, many arrivals come in large boats, all disgorged onto the islands at the same time. 'Apart from the environmental impact,' noted John Gillies, director of Exodus, 'such a sudden influx makes it impossible to appreciate wildlife and natural history. The proper way to enjoy the islands and preserve their ecology is in small boats carrying 10 to 12 people.'

The problem for a country like Ecuador, however, is that the big boats tend to bring the big profits, while the smaller, low-impact operators tend to bring lower returns. But such countries must increasingly realise that if they want to keep the goose that lays the golden egg, they are going to have to protect it against such pressures. The popularity of California's grey whales, for instance, has necessitated increasingly stringent controls to defend them from over-eager sightseers.

Another area which has been coming under growing pressure is Lapland, with travel agents selling nearly two million bed-nights a year north of the Arctic Circle and Lapland accounting for about one-tenth of all tourism in Norway, Sweden and Finland. But this region, billed as the Land of the Midnight Sun, Europe's Last Great Wilderness or even the Home of Santa Claus, is beginning to hit real

168 →

The Lindblad Explorer.

environmental carrying capacity problems. 'We are continually developing resort areas,' explained Ingrar Mattson, director of the Swedish Tourist Board, 'although there is always a conflict between the desire to build a new hotel, hunting lodge or ski-lift, and the need to preserve reindeer grazing land.'

Some of the Lapp herders are losing patience, complaining that visitors are trampling the vegetation and frightening the reindeer, often when the cows are giving birth or the animals are gaining weight for the winter.

Far better organised – and organisation and management are increasingly seen as the keys to sustainable tourism – have been the voyages of the *Lindblad Explorer* to Antarctica. These voyages have been chronicled by Jim Snyder, Keith Shackleton and Sir Peter Scott in the book *Ship in the Wilderness* (page 211). In 1985, every passenger who sailed on the ship *Salen Lindblad* gave £250 to the Falkland Islands Foundation, for use in its conservation programme. Such developments, however, remain the exception rather than the rule.

Tourist trends

In Europe, meanwhile, a number of emerging trends could influence tourism's economic and ecological impacts. Leisure is now big business, as research by the Henley Centre confirms. Consumers spend nearly £60 billion a year on leisure related goods and services in Britain alone. Indeed, leisure spending accounts for over a quarter of all consumer outgoings – and the sector is set to grow strongly. By 1992, it is estimated, the British leisure market could be worth £95 billion.

Second and third holidays are increasingly favoured, along with off-peak breaks. In some sectors there has been a decline in package tours, with visitors preferring to travel independently. There has also been considerable growth in the study, activity and countryside holiday sectors. Many of these holidays offer the prospect of learning while you relax, whether you are on a day-visit to the Centre for Alternative Technology in Wales or on a tour of the Galapagos Islands with David Bellamy.

Sometimes, of course, the desire to promote tourism can lead to worthwhile environmental improvements. To take just one recent example, the Italian Navy's training vessel, the *Amerigo Vespucci*, was recruited by the European Commission for EYE as a tour-ship, to put the media spotlight on the pollution of the Mediterranean and North Sea.

Back on terra firma, derelict land may be cleaned up to create theme parks (such as RMC's Thorpe Park, just outside London) or sites for garden festivals – as in Liverpool and Stoke-on-Trent. Companies such as Pleasurama are beginning to promote 'smokestack tourism', designed to explore the industrial and environmental heritage of cities which pioneered in the Industrial Revolution. The canal boat industry has also been working away quietly in this area for years.

COMMONWORK CENTRE AT BORE PLACE

Facilities available to

Schools • Colleges/Universities • Community Groups
Youth Organisations • Special Interest Groups • Individuals
Business Organisations

For

Personal Interest and Development • Curriculum Linked Study

Related to

Ecology/Conservation • Local History • Land Use/
Orienteering • Design/Process/Product • Visual Arts/
Music/Drama • Health & Personal Welfare

Our Resources are

18th Century Farm Buildings • Field Trail • Dairy Herd
Methane Digester • Organic Compost Unit • Brickworks
Exhibition Area • Study Space • Pottery/Ceramic
Workshop • Art Studio

RESIDENTIAL/NON-RESIDENTIAL
VISITS/COURSES AVAILABLE

PLEASE TELEPHONE FOR DETAILS
Sevenoaks (0732) 463255
– ask for Education Programme
and discuss with us your particular requirements

Commonwork Centre, Bore Place, Chiddingstone,
Edenbridge, Kent TN8 7AR.

TOURISM

Jams on the road, jams on the beach.

And no holiday resort relishes the idea of finding its polluted beaches in the headlines thanks to the efforts of the Coastal Anti-Pollution League. On the other hand, few indeed make it into the pages of the League's *Golden List* of safe, clean beaches (page 171). In short, actual or potential tourism revenues ensure that some environmental resources are more highly valued and more effectively protected than they otherwise would be.

Battery tourism

But tourism, too, can damage the very environmental resources which attracted the tourists in the first place. The publication of the *Broads Plan 1987* last year highlighted the damage caused to the ecology of the Norfolk Broads by the thousands of motor cruisers brought by the age of mass tourism. The more enlightened boat-hirers believe that the best way forward would be to return to sailing boats, which move more slowly, cause less wash and, in consequence, less damage.

What has been dubbed 'battery tourism', meanwhile, is often among the worst offenders, with once-beautiful stretches of coastline converted into a cacophony of soaring concrete and blazing neon.

One of the most controversial recent examples of the way in which modern tourism actively undermines environmental quality has been the development of Iztuzu, in Turkey. Despite a pledge by the Ministry of Agriculture in 1978 that the surrounding Dalyan region would be turned into a national park, permission was given for the construction of the 600-bed Kaunos Beach Hotel and a 1,200-bed holiday village on Iztuzu beach, in the heart of the nesting ground of a considerable colony of loggerhead turtles. Although the turtles were protected by a Council of Europe convention, which Turkey had signed, a spokesman for the builders noted: 'One thousand beds means $15 million in hard cash every year. Their [the Ministry of Tourism's] eyes don't see anything else.'

Such tourism developments can have enormously damaging effects – particularly where they exceed the carrying capacity of the local environment (page 170). The failure to prepare an environmental impact assessment for the project meant that the builders, by their own account, were unaware of the turtles until three days before the ground-breaking ceremony. With Turkey anxious to join the European Community, however, the criticisms of international conservation bodies forced the country's Prime Minister, Turgut Ozal, to take an interest. 'We will not allow the turtles to become the victims of the kind of crooked circumstances that tourism has brought to Greece,' he said, unable to resist a side-swipe at Turkey's long-standing rival.

At loggerheads

Greece, already a member of the European Community, has certainly faced similar problems. The uncontrolled growth of tourism around Laganas Bay, on the Greek Island of Zakynthos (Zante), is threatening the main Mediterranean nesting ground of the loggerhead turtle. These turtles need darkness and an undistrubed sandy beach if they are to lay their eggs, conditions which tourism is banishing.

'Speed-boats plough the bay all day and frighten the sea turtles which gather in the shallow water by the hundreds to prepare to come ashore,' explained Lily Venizelos of the Greek Sea Turtle Protection Society. When they finally emerge from the sea at night, they are faced with cars and motorcycles, beach parties and the blare of discos. If they succeed in running this gauntlet successfully and lay their eggs without incident, the resulting hatchlings, which find their way to the sea by the faint natural light at the horizon, can be misled by the dazzling hotel lights, falling easy prey to predators such as gulls and ravens.

Interestingly, however, Grecian Holidays, the Society and the World Wildlife Fund have worked together to produce a short set of guidelines for tourists visiting loggerhead nesting sites. Grecian Holidays, Horizon, Sun Med Holidays and Thomson Holidays have all helped to distribute the guidelines to visitors.

The turtles are part of the 'global commons', belonging to everyone, and have consequently been seen as of little direct economic value by the people of Zante, particularly when compared with tourism revenues. But the area may yet be declared a marine park, so that scientists can study the turtles and tourists can enjoy them too. 'The idea,' said project co-ordinator Dimitri Margaritoulis, 'is to get the local landowners and the villagers to become shareholders in this venture in order to give them a vested interest in the survival of the sea turtles. This is the only way to save them.'

Quarrying the environment

Part of the problem is the nature of the tourism business itself. Often highly fragmented, with intense pricing battles the rule in most sectors, the industry tends to 'quarry' environmental quality, with little interest in re-investing a proportion of its profits in the areas which it exploits. Tour operators struggle to build market share, cutting overheads and other costs to the bone. If one Shangri-La is wrecked, the industry's boom-town mentality suggests that another can always be found.

At the other end of the market, there are the specialised operators – many of whom now recognise that a growing number of tourists are becoming more discerning. Indeed, according to *Holiday Which?*, small holiday companies specialising either in a single country or a single type of holiday are now the most popular with their customers. Some of these companies operate in an emerging market sector with real potential for enhancing environmental quality, that targeted on the green tourist.

Interestingly, environmentalists increasingly use the tourism potential of living resources to argue the case for their conservation. As Friends of the Earth wrote in an open letter to the islanders of Islay during the long-running clash over peat-digging by whisky-makers Scottish Malt Distillers, 'there need be no clash and no losers. It is perfectly possible to combine work and wildlife, for the future of Islay depends not only on its farming, fishing and whisky, but also on its astonishing potential for tourism and recreation and its ability to attract new cottage industries. This means treating its wildlife and beauty as crucial resources, the foundations of sustainable prosperity.'

This argument is now being advanced in many parts of the European Community. In Greece, environmentalists have campaigned against plans to build a $500 million alumina processing plant five miles across the valley from the Temple of Apollo at Delphi, on the grounds that the emissions could destroy the delicate marble columns which have lasted more than 2,500 years. And the silver pelicans of Prespa, in Macedonia, have become a symbol of the struggle of Greek environmentalists against insensitive development. One report described the EEC-funded irrigation, agriculture and fish-farming works programme as 'a kamikaze exercise of disintegrated development.'

One strong critic of the Prespa developments has been Britain's Royal Society for the Protection of Birds (RSPB), attracted by the fact that the Prespa lakelands provide a haven for some 250 species of bird and a wealth of mammals, reptiles, amphibians and fish. The problem facing conservationists in such cases is that the revenues likely to be derived from 'kamikaze' developments is likely to be much higher in the short term than that to be derived from green tourism. But the RSPB, like some of the other organisations described below, is doing its utmost to promote sensitive exploitation of such areas, to ensure that they have a future.

Natural history tours are not yet as developed in Europe as they are in the United States – where operators like Betchart Expeditions, Biological Journeys, Earthwatch, Geo Expeditions, Kingbird Tours, Nature Expeditions International and Oceanic Society Expeditions are among the market leaders. But the potential for harnessing the spending power of the green tourist to the twin causes of conservation and sustainable development is increasingly recognised both in Britain and other parts of Europe. □

PEAK NATIONAL PARK STUDY CENTRE

LOSEHILL HALL

PROFESSIONAL TRAINING FOR COUNTRYSIDE STAFF

Courses for those involved in conservation and countryside management.

Losehill Hall can also be booked by groups who require special courses to be arranged.

For further details (sae please) from:
Peter Townsend, Principal,
Peak National Park Centre, Losehill Hall,
Castleton, Derbyshire S30 2WB.

Don't go Near the Water

Beaches that failed the test included the four at Blackpool, the four at Morecambe, the south bay at Tenby, all three at Barry, the south bay at Scarborough, Cleethorpes, two of the three at Great Yarmouth, Thorpe Bay at Southend, one of the two at Margate, Mawgan Porth, Bude and one of the three St. Ives beaches. The cleanest waters, the Department of Environment reported, are along the coasts of Yorkshire and East Anglia, while the dirtiest are in Wales and the North-west.

To try and rectify the situation, the Marine Conservation Society (MCS) and the Coastal Anti-Pollution League (CAPL) launched a public awareness campaign last year, focusing on the coast. The CAPL publishes a regularly updated listing of unpolluted beaches, *The Golden List,* priced at £2.50. It also publishes a bi-annual newsletter. Membership costs £5 a year, £7.50 for families, £10 for groups.

In the north of Italy, the problems are largely industrial, while in the south clean water alternates with sewage-polluted stretches. Even the sea off such tourist meccas as Amalfi and Positano was found to be chemically polluted. And when the Goletta Verde's crew went round the 'toe' of Italy, it again found a mixed picture: recommended tracts included Punta Safo and Belladonna.

In Britain, where the Blue Flag for Clean Beaches Scheme has been run by the Keep Britain Tidy Group, the Government has been very slow to act. While the Italians and the French designated thousands of their beaches to be monitored under the terms of a 1975 EEC Directive, Britain nominated a mere 27 – and left off such beaches as Blackpool, Brighton and Eastbourne. By the summer of 1987, 40% of Britain's beaches still failed to meet the EEC bathing cleanliness standards.

Anyone who cares to sample the waters around Europe's coastline is in for some unpleasant surprises. When the Italian news magazine *L'Espresso* took a yacht around the Italian coast, it found many areas of beautiful blue sea. If you want clean beaches in Italy, try Portofino, or search out an unspoiled length of the Ligurian coast. Elba, it seems, is swimmable, as is southern Tuscany. But the yacht also found a number of worrying pollution hot-spots.

Avoid swimming near Rome like the plague. The main pollutant in the Tiber is sewage, but *L'Espresso* found many other pollutants as it sailed around the country. Phosphate pollution in the Adriatic causes seaweed blooms and fish kills. You can find arsenic near Bari; mercury and solvents near Brindisi; lead and fuel near such ports as Reggio Calabria; mercury near Rosignano in Tuscany and just about every pollutant known to science in the Gulf of Naples – now considered an emergency zone by the Italian government.

PERSPECTIVES

The Millionaire Lions

In Kenya, every tourist wants to see a full-grown male lion. Someone once worked out that each male lion earns Kenya several hundreds of thousands of dollars a year. But tourism, as *Brian Jackman* explains, can be a double-edged sword.

'Ten years ago, the rare mountain gorillas of Rwanda seemed destined for extinction. Reduced in numbers to no more than 250, they clung on in the remote cloud forests of the Parc National des Volcans, on the border with Zaire. Yet even here, their last refuge was being cleared to make way for pyrethrum plantations; and the gorillas themselves were being shot and snared by poachers.

One of the first gorillas to be killed was the huge silverback male known as Digit, in whose company David Attenborough had been filmed for the TV series, *Life on Earth*. Digit's death touched the world's conscience. With the help of the Fauna and Flora Preservation Society, a fund was started. Thus began the Mountain Gorilla Project, which has not only saved the species but has made the national park financially viable for the first time.

It has done this by making the gorillas a major tourist attraction. Slowly, and with great care, some family groups of gorillas were habituated to the presence of tourists, enabling small parties of visitors to approach within a few feet of these gentle forest dwellers. The Mountain Gorilla Project is a textbook example of how tourism and wildlife conservation can work together for mutual benefit, and its implications are enormous.

A burden for the poor?

Nowadays there is nowhere so wild or so remote that it cannot be reached by package holidays. All too often the result is litter, noise, landscape destruction and a general devaluation of the wilderness experience.

Yet there are places where the very survival of the natural world could depend on the presence of tourists and the money they bring. Most countries, rich and poor, have set aside their outstanding wilderness areas as national parks and reserves. The honour of creating the world's first national park goes to a rich nation – the USA – which established Yellowstone in 1872. But increasingly these days it is the poor countries of the Third World who are expected to shoulder the burden of maintaining a disproportionate share of the world's wild heritage.

Africa is a classic case. A continent whose soaring birthrates and ever-present spectres of drought and famine may yet force governments to turn envious eyes towards their marginal lands: those remaining tracts of pristine bush and savannah where lions still roar their cadenzas at the dawn, and where elephant, buffalo, leopard, zebra, giraffe and wildebeest still roam as they did when the earth was young.

These are the world's hallowed places. Repositories of our most valued landscapes; sanctuaries like Zambia's Luangwa Valley, or Tanzania's vast Serengeti national park, where it is still possible to see one and a quarter million wildebeest, a million gazelles and half a million zebra – the greatest wildlife show on earth – blackening the plains as the bison must once have done on the American prairies.

Serengeti, Tsavo, Ngorongoro, Okavango; these magnificent wildlife refuges are the crown jewels of a continent, set aside in the hope – perhaps forlorn – that our children's children may also marvel at the bewildering diversity of life they contain.

Limited options

But sentiment is no longer enough. Such arguments carry little weight with hungry tribesmen. To ensure a future for wildlife today, the game must pay its way. The options are limited. Controlled trophy hunting – however distasteful it may be to some people – is one answer, successfully practiced in Zimbabwe. Tourism is another.

Everybody who goes on safari wants to see a lion. Ideally, it must be a male lion, powerful and full-grown, with a huge, shaggy mane. So someone did a simple sum. They counted the numbers of male lions in Kenya's parks, then totted up the numbers of tourists and the money they brought into the country. The result was astounding. It revealed that each male lion was earning Kenya several hundred thousand dollars in tourist revenue every year.

The lesson was not wasted. In Kenya the safari business is now highly organised. Every day, fleets of mini-buses set off from Nairobi to visit the game parks; north to Meru and Samburu, to the forest lodges of the Aberdares and Mount Kenya, and south to the arid thornscapes of Tsavo and Amboseli. In every park and reserve there are comfortable lodges, imaginatively designed, using local materials that blend in with the landscape, or permanent tented camps set under shady acacia trees.

So long as tourism continues to flourish, the parks are relatively safe from the powerful human predators who would like to plough up these last wild places or create immense new rangelands producing yet more

TOURISM

Burchell's zebra (inset: Brian Jackman).

beefburgers and butter mountains for the Western world.

A two-edged weapon

But tourism, too, can be a two-edged weapon. In general, the Kenyans have been astute and capable managers of their tourism and wildlife resources. They know that in the fragile ecosystems of a national park, tourism and wildlife can flourish only if they are in equilibrium. Too many vehicles, too many lodges, and the balance is upset, the joy of being in the wild devalued.

Such a situation has now been reached in Kenya's finest wildlife stronghold, the 540-square-mile Masai Mara national reserve. Here, the numbers of lodges and tented camps have doubled in a decade, and more are planned. The result is that nowadays, whenever a predator is sighted – leopard, cheetah, lions on a kill – the tourist vehicles swarm in like vultures, with little thought for the animals.

At the same time, the plains are being increasingly disfigured by a maze of unsightly tyre-tracks. The Mara is unusual in being one of the few reserves where off-track driving is allowed. This freedom to wander at will has always been one of the reserve's greatest delights; but for how much longer can it continue if the Mara's life-giving grasslands are wrecked beyond repair?

Every national park has a maximum carrying capacity in terms of the potentially destructive species, such as elephant, which it can support. Now it is becoming painfully clear that the same rules apply to tourists.

Deciding when enough is enough is the crucial question. The conservationists, concerned for the survival of species and the good health of the habitat, wisely err on the side of the animals. The tourist industry, eager for profit, will clearly press for continued expansion. Meanwhile, both sides can be thankful that the wealthy ranchers – Kenya's so-called 'wheat elite' – have been kept at bay.

BRIAN JACKMAN *is a journalist on the* Sunday Times Magazine *and script consultant for Anglia Television's* Survival. *In 1982, he was voted Travel Writer of the Year and won the award for best wildlife commentary script (for Osprey) at the Wildscreen International Wildlife Film and Television Festival. He has travelled widely in Africa and is the author of* The Marsh Lions *(with Jonathan Scott), published by Elm Tree Books in 1982. He is also the editor of Myles Turner's autobiography,* My Serengeti Years *(Elm Tree Books, 1987).*

The Green Tourist

A growing number of holiday firms and other organisations are offering packages put together with the green tourist in mind. Some involve conservation work, some take you on wildlife safaris and some introduce you to such green pursuits as organic gardening.

Although bird-watching holidays dominate the scene, a growing number of green holidays are now on offer. From a week spent cleaning out a pond to a bird-watching cruise aboard the *Canberra*, the range of options should cater to just about any taste.

Abercrombie & Kent Travel

'When you go on safari nowadays you are very fortunate indeed if you see a black rhino in the wild,' says Geoffrey Kent of Abercrombie & Kent. It is thought that fewer than 400 survive from a population of perhaps 20,000 in 1970. If you book the company's 'Luxury Tented Safari', however, it will make a donation to *Rhino Rescue* – and it encloses a copy of Rhino Rescue's brochure with every copy of its own promotional literature. Rhino Rescue, which is developing rhino sanctuaries in Kenya, can be reached at The Coach House, Yoxford, Suffolk IP17 3HX. Tel: 072877 305.

Among other specialist tours organised in 1987 was a game-spotting tour of Kenya and Tanzania in aid of the David Shepherd Charitable Foundation, which helps charities such as the World Wildlife Fund. The £2,135 price tag includes a 10% donation to conservation. Bird watching featured in a bird safari led by James Hancock, President of the British Trust for Ornithology. For £2,650, participants were promised over 300 species of birdlife, including the red-billed buffalo weaver and water dikkop. Specialised tours are organised to most regions of the world. *Contact:* Abercrombie & Kent Travel, Sloane Square House, Holbein Place, London SW1W 8NS. Tel: 01 730 9600 or on 01 235 9761. Telex: 8813352 ABKENT G.

Acorn Camps (National Trust)

Acorn Camps and Young National Trust Groups offer two ways in which volunteers can help the National Trust with conservation work. Work includes clearing waterways and replanting vegetation. Volunteers need not be members of the National Trust, but are encouraged to take an interest by being given a free admission card on completion of 40 hours' work. *Contact:* The National Trust, PO Box 12, Westbury, Wiltshire BA13 4NA. Tel: 0373 826302.

Aigas Field Centre Holidays

The wildlife of Scotland's Highlands and Islands features prominently in Aigas and Orkney Field Centre Holidays and Island Expeditions. A week's wildlife course in either Field Centre gives you six days out with qualified guides, with negotiated access to 500 square miles of uplands which the casual visitor could never hope to see.

Summer is the best time to see eagles, peregrines and divers. The newly established birders' course is not for the 'Twitcher' who likes to tick and move on, however. These courses focus on the way different species manage to survive and thrive in this tough wilderness area. Red deer are also often visible in the glens, particularly in the early morning or late evening. The cost is reasonable, at around £180 per week, plus accommodation, for holidays based at the Aigas Field Centre and £215, plus accommodation, for birdwatching holidays in the Orkneys. *Contact:* Aigas Field Centres, Beauly, Inverness-shire IV4 7AD, Scotland. Tel: 0463 782443.

Albannach Insight Holidays

'All organised holidays are in a sense a compromise,' notes Albannach, 'but we think ours is a happy one.' Insight Holidays are aimed at people who like wild country and lonely places. In a small group, travelling each day from the Strathpeffer centre, you can explore the natural history of the Highlands and Islands. *Contact:* Albannach Insight Holidays, Hamilton House, Strathpeffer, Ross & Cromarty, Scotland IV14 9AD. Tel: 0997 21577.

Alfred Gregory Photo Holidays

Designed for those who want to take photographs in remote parts of the world, such as the Khumbu and High Valleys around Mount Everest ('anyone joining this trek should have considerable experience of hill walking in Britain or similar and be very fit when leaving for Nepal'), the Cordillera Blanca Norte ('a paradise for botanists and bird watchers') and the Galapagos Islands ('where else can you swim with sea lions?'). *Contact:* Woodcock Travel Ltd, 25-31 Wicker, Sheffield S3 8HW, England. Tel: 0742 29428. Telex: 54520.

Ara Study Tours

An independent educational co-operative, with a general concern for the environment, particularly in developing countries. Workshops, study tours and vacation schools are organised in such areas as appropriate technology, organic husbandry and development issues. *Contact:* Study Tours, 10 Highfield Close, Wokingham, Berkshire RG11 1DG. Tel: 0734 783204.

Barn Owl Travel

Founded in 1973, Barn Owl Travel organises holidays, weekends and day trips for birdwatchers and naturalists. From boat trips on the River Medway to longer trips to Wales and Scotland, the idea is to get small groups of like-minded people close to the rich birdlife of the British Isles. Overseas tours take in France, Gibraltar, Iceland, Israel, Menorca and The Netherlands. *Contact:* Barn Owl Travel, 27 Seaview Road, Gillingham, Kent ME7 4NL. Tel: 0634 56759.

Birdquest

Whether you want to see the wildlife of the tropical forests of Thailand's Khao Yai National Park or the lemurs and other biological marvels of Madagascar, Birdquest should have something for you. 'What you do need, however,' say the company's directors, 'is a desire to watch birds for days on end, a certain sense of adventure and an ability to get on reasonably well with others in the group.'

In addition to better known countries, Birdquest also specialises in tours to Costa Rica ('an ornithological melting pot'), Turkey ('the most exciting birding in the Western Palearctic'), Siberia (see the 'far off breeding grounds of those rare autumn wanderers from Siberia and Central Asia'), Japan ('from the lovely Japanese Crane to the noisy but secretive Gray's Grasshopper Warbler'), Zimbabwe's Okavango Delta ('expensive, but worth every penny') and Australia, where more than 60 million years of separate evolution have resulted in a very rich avifauna – Australia has more endemic bird species than any other country. *Contact:* Birdquest Ltd, 8 Albert Road East, Hale, Altrincham, Cheshire WA15 9AL. Tel: 061 928 5945. Telex: 669108.

Brathay Exploration Group

Part of an educational trust, the Brathay Exploration Group (BEG) has been running expeditions for young people in many parts of the world since 1947. Many of these expeditions have involved fieldwork and project reports are published regularly. 'Over the years our fieldwork projects have regularly covered conservation matters,' notes expeditions co-ordinator June Tutin, 'from basic biological mapping (how do you know what to conserve if you don't know what's there?), through visitor surveys to direct conservation projects.'

TOURISM

The basic approach involves building up young people's skills and confidence, introducing them to the natural world – and, often, highlighting the pressures upon it. In BEG's Trans-Snowdonia Trek, for example, you can assess the environmental impact of hill farming, tourism, hydroelectric schemes and past mining and quarrying activities. *Contact:* Brathay Exploration Group, Brathay Hall, Ambleside, Cumbria LA22 0HP. Tel: 0966 33942.

British Trust for Conservation Volunteers (BTCV)

BTCV is a registered charity which aims to involve volunteers from widely varied backgrounds in practical conservation work throughout the British Isles. Over 400 Working Holidays are organised throughout the year for volunteers aged 16-70. The 'Natural Break' Conservation Working Holidays cost from as little as £20 per week, including food and accommodation. No experience is necessary. *Contact:* BTCV, 36 St. Mary's Street, Wallingford, Oxon OX10 0EU. Tel: 0491 39766. BTCV's sister organisation in Scotland is the Scottish Conservation Projects Trust, based at Balallan House, 24 Allan Park, Stirling FK8 2QG. Tel: 0786 79697.

Bushbuck Safaris

Bushbuck takes no more than 50 bookings a year, concentrating on safaris to game reserves in Botswana and Zimbabwe. At a cost of £3,000 – £5,000 per head, depending on the numbers going, the tour can be tailored to individual interests, be it birdwatching, game viewing, fishing or walking. Included are tours of the Okavango Delta, the largest inland waterway in the world. In both Botswana and Zimbabwe, say Bushbuck, 'you can visit game reserves reminiscent of those in Kenya 50 years ago, where man is still the rarest creature and the package tourist as yet an unknown species.' *Contact:* Bushbuck Safaris, 50 High Street, Hungerford, Berkshire RG17 0NE. Tel: 0488 84702. Telex: 846797 BUSH.

Caledonian Wildlife

'Most naturalists find birdwatching in the wilderness more refreshing than by a sewage farm,' says Sinclair Dunnett, the firm's founder. Although Caledonian Wildlife originally focused on the Scottish Highlands and Islands, it has increasingly diversified into wilderness areas of such countries as France, Iceland, Nepal, Poland, Tanzania and, in the United States, Alaska. *Contact:* Caledonian Wildlife, 30 Culduthel Road, Inverness IV2 4AP, Scotland. Tel: 0463 233130.

Cambrian Bird Holidays

If you like a friendly, informal style and want to see the birdlife of Wales, Cambrian Bird Holidays could be the answer. Included are visits to the bird-rich islands of Skokholm and Skomer. Previously a British Trust for Ornithology researcher and then a professional naturalist and conservationist for the Yorkshire Naturalists' Trust, director Graham Walker aims to communicate his deep interest in ornithology. Prices per week range from £190 in February to around £240 in August. *Contact:* Cambrian Bird Holidays, Henllan, Llandysul, Dyfed, Wales. Tel: 0559 370240.

Canberra Cruises

Operated by P&O Cruises, the *Canberra* offered an 'Oceans of Birds' cruise for the first time in 1987, as part of its World Cruise. Tony Soper, Britain's best-known birdwatcher and presenter of the live *Birdwatch* programmes and BBC2's *Nature* wildlife news magazine, led daily sessions of birdwatching from the ship's deck as it sailed west from Barbados. Ornithological tours were offered in Panama, California, Fiji, New Zealand and Australia. By the end of the cruise, participants should have been able to distinguish between petrels and boobies. P&O hoped to repeat the exercise. *Contact:* Canberra Cruises Ltd, 77 New Oxford Street, London WC1A 1PP. Tel: 01 831 1331.

Centre for Alternative Technology (CAT)

Opened in 1975, CAT has been visited by over half a million people. Set in an old slate quarry on the edge of Snowdonia, CAT is both a working demonstration of alternative technology and a living community. The Centre is open all year round, with energy and organic gardening displays, a blacksmith's forge, exhibition hall, bicycle-powered computer and maze. An affiliated manufacturing company, Dulas Engineering, makes electronic controls for renewable energy systems in a solar-powered workshop on site. *Contact:* Centre for Alternative Technology, Machynlleth, Powys SY20 9AZ. Tel: 0654 2400.

Cox & Kings Travel

'I regret we don't do much on the wildlife side,' replied Cox & Kings, 'but we are almost definitely the main operator for botanical tours.' The firm is certainly very strong in this area, with tours throughout Europe, but birds also feature, for example, in 14-day tours to the Spanish Pyrenees (£480), Northern Portugal (£749), Majorca (£395), Corsica (£650) and the Seychelles (£1,850). The guides include professionals working for such conservation organisations as the Nature Conservancy Council and the Royal Society for the Protection of Birds. *Contact:* Cox & Kings Travel, 10 Glentworth Street, London NW1 5PG. Tel: 01 723 5066. Telex: 28441 VJVTP.

Cygnus Wildlife

The Camargue region of southern France offers some of the most exciting birdwatching in Europe, and Cygnus can take you there on a 9-day tour for £580. For the more hardy, there are the Falkland Islands, with a 14-day tour likely to cost in the region of £2,500. Cygnus also offers tours to many other parts of the world, with new escorted birdwatching tours introduced last year in Florida (£1,290), Venezuela (20 days, check price) and Cyprus (£860). *Contact:* Cygnus Wildlife, 96 Fore Street, Kingsbridge, Devon TQ7 1PY. Tel: 0548 6178.

David Sayers Travel

A specialist in botanical and garden travel, David Sayers offers a range of tours with wildlife features, from the Elephant Safari which takes you through India's forests (£1,790), through wildlife tours of the Holy Land (£887) to tours of the Azores (£894), South Korea (£1,793), Kashmir (£1,690), Madagascar (£2,450) and Papua New Guinea (£2,900). *Contact:* David Sayers Travel, 10 Barley Mow Passage, London W4 4PH. Tel: 01 995 3642.

E & F Travels

For £1,300, E & F offer 'Kipling Camp – In Search of the Tiger', an Indian Safari in *Jungle Book* country. Kipling Camp is in the Kanha National Park and there is a good chance of seeing a tiger, since there are more than 80 in the reserve. *Contact:* E & F Travels Ltd, Creech Barrow, East Creech, Wareham, Dorset BH20 5AP. Tel: 0929 480548. Telex: 418253 LUMIC-G.

Encounter Overland

A number of tours with a wildlife focus are on offer from Encounter Overland, including the Mountain Gorilla Safari. This 5-week holiday costs around £1,200, plus an air fare of about £475. *Contact:* Encounter Overland, 267 Old Brompton Road, London SW5. Tel: 01 370 6951.

Erskine Expeditions

Arctic wildlife features in a number of the tours offered by Erskine Expeditions, including the muskox, caribou, polar bears and snowy owls of Bathurst Island in the Canadian archipelago (approximately £2,100) and the little auks, walrus, breeding geese and tundra flowers of Spitzbergen (approximately £2,000). Also check out their tours to St. Kilda and other Scottish Islands (£790) and to the Falkland Islands (£2,775). *Contact:* Erskine Expeditions, 1-8 Ferryfield, Edinburgh EH5 2PR, Scotland. Tel: 031 552 2673.

Exodus Expeditions

Check out their 'Naturetrek' expeditions, from 27 days travelling through a complete range of Himalayan habitats (£1,550) to 16 days in the High Atlas mountains of Morocco (£650). Naturetreks are designed to be gentle in pace, ideal for anyone who enjoys walking and wildlife. Ask for the Naturetrek dossier. *Contact:* Exodus Expeditions, All Saints Passage, 100 Wandsworth High Street, London SW18 4LE. Tel: 01 870 0151. Telex: 8951700.

ExplorAsia

A specialist company which aims to be the market leader in Nepal, India and the Himalayas. ExplorAsia is the exclusive UK agent for Nepal's Tiger Tops Jungle Lodge, in the heart of the Royal Chitwan National Park. Chitwan's forests, grasslands and rivers are home to the one-horned rhinoceros, sloth bear, the fish-eating garial crocodile, freshwater dolphin, a variety of deer and the Royal Bengal Tiger. There are also over 350 bird species. Prices are generally in the range £1,500-£2,000, with an 18-day tour of India's three finest game parks costing £2,125. *Contact:* ExplorAsia Ltd, 13 Chapter Street, London SW1P 4NY. Tel: 01 630 7102. Telex: 266774 EXPLOR G.

Fairways & Swinford

Botanical tours are a speciality with Fairways & Swinford, from the flowers of the Austrian Tyrol (5 days, £300) to the flowers of Uzbekhistan (£1,085). Each tour is led by a widely travelled botanist or horticulturalist. No specialist knowledge is needed to enjoy such holidays, however. *Contact:* Fairways & Swinford (Travel) Ltd, Sea Containers House, 20 Upper Ground, London SE1 9PF. Tel: 01 261 1744/928 5044. Telex: 8955803 SCN LDN for Swinfair.

HF Holidays

A non-profit organisation founded over 70 years ago, HF Holidays offer a range of wildlife and environmental special interest holidays – mainly set in Areas of Outstanding Natural Beauty or National Parks. HF Birdwatching Weeks take you to such destinations as Alnmouth (takes in Holy Island and the Farne Islands), Arran, Derwentwater, the Isle of Wight, Malvern, Conwy and Loch Awe. HF Wildlife Safaris take in Arran, Devon, Dorset, Pembrokeshire and Snowdonia. Prices for 1987 were in the range £180-£190 per week. *Contact:* HF Holidays Ltd, 142-144 Great North Way, London NW4 1EG. Tel: 01 203 0433.

Hosking Tours

Birdwatchers and other wildlife enthusiasts interested in exploring off the beaten track might like to try a two-week tour of North Yemen. A recent ornithological survey of North Yemen found 275 species, including 12 Bald Ibis (one of the rarest birds in the world) and 17 Arabian Bustards, whose future prospects in much of Arabia are tenuous at best. *Contact:* Hosking Tours, Hunworth, Melton Constable, Norfolk NR24 2AA. Tel: 0263 713969. Telex: 975458 HOSK G.

National Centre for Organic Gardening

Founded in 1958, the Henry Doubleday Research Association (HDRA) has been a pioneer in organic gardening. In 1986 it opened its 22-acre national showpiece for organic gardening methods, The National Centre for Organic Gardening. The Centre is open all year round and tens of thousands of visitors have seen such techniques as 'no-dig' gardening, composting and biological pest control in action. Alan Gear of HDRA has published an excellent book, *The New Organic Food Guide* (see page 215). *Contact:* The National Centre for Organic Gardening, Ryton-on-Dunsmore, Coventry CV8 3LG. Tel: 0203 303517.

National Federation of City Farms and Community Gardens

If you live in a city and want to see 'greening' in action, one interesting option is to visit some of the groups who have taken over derelict land and are managing it as organic farms or gardens. *Contact:* The National Federation of City Farms and Community Gardens, 66 Fraser Street, Bristol BS3 4LY. Tel: 0272 660663.

Ornitholidays

An impressive range of birdwatching and natural history holidays is on offer from

TOURISM

Ornitholidays. The firm's catalogue is packed with information on the birds likely to be seen – and on the best books and field guides for the areas visited. Ornitholidays was also the first corporate member of the Royal Society for the Protection of Birds. *Contact:* Ornitholidays, 1-3 Victoria Drive, Bognor Regis, West Sussex PO21 2PW. Tel: 0243 821230. Telex: 86736 SOTEX G for WESTRAV.

Papyrus Tours

Created in 1984, Papyrus aims to provide opportunities for wildlife enthusiasts to visit East Africa. Wildlife notes are provided for the areas visited and the pace of the tours is relatively leisurely, to allow participants to appreciate the environment. Costs are generally in the range £1,500-£2,000.

'As people committed to conservation in the UK,' says Roger Mitchell, 'we try to include this element in our own Kenyan tours, to the extent that we encourage (bully!) all participants to join the East Africa Wildlife Society for one year, in the hope that their membership will continue in the future.' *Contact:* Papyrus Tours, 4 Howden Close, Bessacarr, Doncaster DN4 7JW. Tel: 0302 530778.

Peregrine Holidays

Peregrine managing director Raymond Hodgkins not only offers wildlife tours, he also ensures that his firm contributes to wildlife conservation. Because of Peregrine's support for Monk Seal and Loggerhead Turtle conservation projects, Hodgkins was made an honorary life member of the Hellenic Society for the Protection of Nature. A newsletter circulated to some 3,000 clients keeps them abreast of developments – including new tours on offer. Among those leading tours are Anthony Huxley (bound for China) and Dr David Bellamy (who has led tours to the Galapagos and the Seychelles, and is due to take a group to New Zealand in November 1988). *Contact:* Peregrine Holidays, Town and Gown Travel, 40-41 South Parade, Summertown, Oxford OX2 7JP. Tel: 0865 511642.

RSPB Holidays

The Royal Society for the Protection of Birds (RSPB) co-operates with a number of tour organisers (including Ladbroke Centres, P&O's Canberra Cruises and Swan Hellenic Cruises) to offer tours to members. Destinations range from Norfolk to the Nile. *Contact:* Holiday and Conference Office, RSPB, The Lodge, Sandy, Bedfordshire SG19 2DL. Tel: 0767 80551. Telex: 82469.

Safari Consultants

If you want an old-style wildlife safari, try Safari Consultants, where almost all the safaris are tailor-made to individual requirements. As a guide, a two-week safari for two in Kenya would vary from £1,600 per person (including economy flights) to £5,500 per person (including economy flights) for a hosted private luxury tented safari. *Contact:* Safari Consultants Ltd, 83 Gloucester Place, London W1H 3PG. Tel: 01 486 4774. Telex: 264690 SAFARI G.

Sunbird

1988 is Sunbird's tenth year of operating birdwatching tours. Well-established tours to Majorca, Spain and Mexico have been supplemented by new tours to Cyprus, Kenya and Siberia. The Cyprus tour (cost about £800) run in co-operation with the magazine *British Birds,* was co-led by Bill Oddie. *Contact:* Sunbird, PO Box 76, Sandy, Bedfordshire SG19 1DF. Tel: 0767 82969.

Swan Hellenic

Among the natural history tours offered by Swan Hellenic are 8-day tours focusing on the alpine flowers of the Valais, Switzerland and the flora and fauna of Spain's Coto de Donana National Park; a 12-day natural history cruise around Greenland and a 15-day tour of Mauritius and Madagascar; a 17-day big game and bird safari in Kenya; a 22-day botanical tour of China; a 19-day tour of Ecuador and the Galapagos Islands; and a 19-day tour of Chile's Atacama Desert and Patagonia. *Contact:* Swan Hellenic, 77 New Oxford Street, London WC1A 1PP. Tel: 01 831 1616.

Tiger Tops Mountain Travel International

A range of wildlife-related holidays is on offer from Tiger Tops, via ExplorAsia (see above). *Details,* including copies of the Tiger Tops newsletter, *Tiger Mountain News,* from: Tiger Tops Mountain Travel International, PO Box 242, Kathmandu, Nepal.

Twickers World

1987 was Twickers World's 21st year of operation. 'Our original enthusiasm for the preservation of the world's wildlife and wild places, and our efforts to help the plight of some endangered species, have not diminished,' noted Hedda Lyons, the firm's managing director. 'In fact, whereas in our early days we were one of a small band of brothers, we are now delighted to be among an increasingly large group of those who care about our planet and its creatures.'

Many of the tours offered by Twickers World will be of interest to ornithologists and wildlife enthusiasts, but several are run under the auspices of the World Wildlife Fund. These include the Galapagos Cruise and Amazon Safari (£2,310 per person), the Peru Jungle-Desert Expedition (£1,850 per person) and a 20-day tour of Madagascar, Reunion and Mauritius (£2,295 per person). *Contact:* Twickers World, 22 Church Street, Twickenham TW1 3NW. Tel: 01 892 8164. Telex: 25780.

Wilderness Expedition & Survival Training (WEST)

Wilderness trekking, winter survival and mountaincraft are just some of the options available at WEST, where the aim is to 'live with nature, rather than against it.' Explore the coast of North-West Scotland by sea kayak, camp on deserted islands and 'play with the otters and seals beneath Ben Alligin and Liathach.' *Contact:* WEST, Arrina, Shieldaig, Strathcarron, Ross-Shire IV54 8XU, Scotland. Tel: 05205 213.

Wildfowl Trust

Formed over 40 years ago by Sir Peter Scott, the Wildfowl Trust promotes the conservation and study of wildfowl and their wetland habitats. From the outset, education has been the primary aim – and the seven centres scattered through Great Britain offer a host of educational activities and experiences – including 'birdwatching for the blind', with tactile exhibits and Braille signs. Of the 650,000 visitors to the Trust's sites each year, over 100,000 are children in organised groups. *Contact:* The Wildfowl Trust, Slimbridge, Gloucester GL2 7BT. Other sites are at Arundel, Sussex; Caerlaverock, Dumfriesshire; Martin Mere, Burscough, Ormskirk; Peakirk, Peterborough; Washington, Tyne and Wear; and Wenley, Wisbech.

Wildwatch

Birdwatching or botanical expeditions are offered on Walton Backwaters, including some 5,000 acres of tidal inlets, mud flats and saltings, with numerous islands. *Contact:* Wildwatch, Fah-Loong, Graces Walk, Frinton-on-Sea, Essex CO13 9PQ. Tel: 02556 78053.

Working Weekends on Organic Farms (WWOOF)

WWOOF is a non-profit exchange system whereby bed, board and experience are given in return for help on organic farms and smallholdings throughout the UK. *Contact:* WWOOF, 19 Bradford Road, Lewes, East Sussex BN7 1RB.

Youth Hostels Association

A registered charity founded in 1930, the YHA has the Queen as its Patron and David Bellamy as its President. Its aim is to help all, especially young people of limited means, to a greater knowledge, love and care of the countryside. Among the holidays on offer are special interest weekends focusing on natural history. *Contact:* YHA, Trevelyan House, 8 St. Stephen's Hill, St. Albans, Hertfordshire AL1 2DY. Tel: 0727 55215.

SECTION 10

A Picture Of Health

The growing consumer pressure for healthier products and healthier lifestyles is standing some existing industries on their heads – and opening up new market sectors. Some, like the organic foods sector, may eventually bring important environmental spin-offs.

If the links between environmental quality and personal health were still obscure for many people before the Chernobyl disaster, they became blindingly clear as the radioactive plume from the damaged reactor spread across Scandinavia and Europe.

Among the worst off were the Lapps, whose winter diet depends heavily on reindeer meat. Nine months after the disaster they were again warned to cut their consumption of reindeer – at a time when alternative foods are in extremely short supply – because the animals feed almost entirely on lichen in the winter months. And lichen, a rootless perennial, has shown a pronounced capacity to absorb radioactive contaminants. (The most radioactive reindeer meat was dyed blue and fed to mink, further food for thought among fur-fanciers.) Chernobyl hit Europe's supermarkets, too, whether it was East European vegetables which were in short supply or Welsh mutton.

Partly because of such disasters, Europeans have been showing a dramatically greater interest in their personal health. Opening Britain's 250th Little Chef restaurant, for example, Trusthouse Forte chief executive Rocco Forte noted that vegetarian dishes are increasingly demanded by health-conscious motorists and their families. In fact, a survey carried out by the *Egon Ronay Birds Eye Guide to Eating Out* (Automobile Association, £5.95) found that 83% of those questioned recognised the link between diet and health. And motorists are just the tip of the iceberg.

First to take advantage of – and promote – this trend towards healthier living were Europe's host of small health food stores. By the time Alan Gear's *New Organic Food Guide* appeared during 1987 (page 215), over 600 outlets were listed in Britain and Ireland. Many firms have been expanding. Cranks Health Foods, a leading health food store founded in 1961, now has half a dozen London outlets and has established footholds in the West Country and in Denmark.

Meatless eating

Vegetarians, according to a Gallup Poll carried out in 1986, account for 2.7% of all Britons, or around 1.5 million people. The work was carried out for the Realeat Company, from whom copies of the survey results can be obtained. In addition, another 3.1% of the population can be classified as 'non-meat eaters', avoiding red meat. The combined groups account for 3.25 million people, with women most likely to be moving in this direction. Overall, around 35% of the population claimed to be 'eating less meat.' To ensure that vegetarians abroad can find suitable restaurants, hotels, holidays and caterers, the Vegetarian Society has published the *International Vegetarian Handbook 1987*.

In West Germany, meanwhile, there were more than 1,500 health food stores by the time of Chernobyl and food grown without chemicals, nitrite-free ham

---

Many environmental problems, from acid rain to nuclear fall-out, affect human health. But the links between environmental quality and health are far from obvious to most Europeans. Now the rapidly growing organic food industry is helping them make that connection (page 179) and alternative medicine is taking off (page 182).

---

and eggs from 'happy hens' have become almost as popular as Wiener schnitzel and sauerkraut. Consumers, particularly at the top end of the market, seem more than happy to pay a premium to get products bearing the valued 'bio' label.

E for 'out'

Although it started out by resisting these trends, the food industry has increasingly been going with the tide. One reason for this shift has been the realisation that the tide is inescapable. 'Health foods,' noted US market analysts Frost & Sullivan in a European market research report, 'represent a buoyant market which is expanding at about twice the rate of the underlying general food market.' The report also predicted that the health food share of the EEC food market would grow by over 50% between 1984 and 1991.

Although the food industry has generally not gone nearly as far or as fast as 'organic' advocates believe it should, it has responded by deluging the market with new high-fibre, decaffeinated, low-salt, fat-free, better quality and more convenient foods.

The phenomenal success of books like *E for Additives* (Thorsons, 1987) has increased the pressure on industry to get the additives out. Indeed, the Soil Association has claimed that the average Briton eats eleven pounds of food additives each year – 'the equivalent of 23 soluble aspirin-sized tablets every day!'

Premium to pay

The Soil Association, in fact, has always explicitly linked the health and environmental implications of organic farming (page 143). Arguing that a small premium on food is a worthwhile price to pay for sustainable agriculture, it tells consumers that 'in choosing (organically grown food) you will be supporting increased rural employment, preserving the environment and protecting your own and your children's health.'

Worried by these trends, the Ministry of Agriculture, Fisheries and Food commissioned Questel to carry out a survey of women's attitudes to food additives. Although smoking and environmental pollution were seen to be greater hazards to health than food additives, 37% of those questioned claimed that they had already bought additive-free food, and over a third said they consulted packaging for details of food content.

Clearly, something needed to be done to pacify consumers. It has not proved an easy task. Indeed, food manufacturers who have tried to remove additives from their products have hit a number of problems. Kellogg, for example, found that the whole-grain cereals which sell so well in health food stores do not go down too well in supermarkets, because they tend to go rancid quickly without preservatives. Rather than give up, however the company identified special grains which stay fresh longer and then used computers to manage every step from field to factory, right down to the type of material used in the farmer's storage bins.

Big Mac goes green?

Now the trend has even reached fast food pioneer McDonald's. Long attacked by environmentalists, both because of the links between cattle ranching and the loss of tropical forests and because of the use of chlorofluorcarbons (CFCs) in the plastic packaging in which Big Macs and other fare are served, the company had not been notable for its responsiveness.

But in the United States it spent $10 million on a campaign designed to convince consumers of the nutritional value of its burgers and milkshakes. Magazines such as *Marketing* began to run stories with titles like 'Big Mac goes Green'. Not because the company was doing something to protect the rain forests or the ozone layer (although it subsequently did, see page 71), but because it was planning to offer salads for the first time.

Some market analysts, however, doubted that McDonalds could go very far down this route, arguing

that salads hardly fit into the fast food format. Indeed, they also suggested that the Wendy's chain, which ultimately shut down its UK operation, damaged its fast food reputation by installing serve-yourself salad bars.

Wherever Big Mac goes, however, European consumers are leaving food producers in no doubt that they want taste, freshness and 'natural' products. The demand for 'real' food – whether it be real bread, beer or fish – has been an increasingly important trend over the last decade.

Sales of organic vegetables could take 10% of the total UK vegetable market, according to Food from Britain, if only sufficient supplies were available. The result would be to push sales from a 1986 level of around £1 million to closer to £35 million. Both Sainsbury and Tesco said they would stock a wider range of organically grown produce if continuity of supply could be guaranteed. Overseas suppliers have already taken advantage of the market gap, flying in organic produce from as far afield as Israel.

The organic supermarket

Meanwhile, growing numbers of supermarket chains, like Germany's Tenglemann group, have been bringing out their own 'bio' product lines. In Britain, the Safeway group took the initiative in extending its own-brand products into the additive-free market. In addition, it was soon offering a wide range of organically grown produce, stressing that they were 'grown to Soil Association Symbol standards, on soil using natural manures and composts. All Safeway stores stock this ever-increasing range of quality products, all grown in the organic manner.'

Generally, the Soil Association and other organisations in this area have welcomed this trend. 'Safeway is to be applauded publicly for selling only organic foods of the highest quality,' said Soil Association chairman Lawrence Woodward, 'and Sainsbury, after discussion with the Association, are undertaking trials of organic produce in some of their stores.' But, he noted 'other companies, trying to meet a need, may not have such scruples.'

Irradiated Food

You can buy irradiated frozen prawns in the Netherlands and irradiated strawberries in Belgium, but countries like Britain and West Germany have been slower to permit the sale of foods pasteurised in this way. The public, particularly in the wake of the Chernobyl disaster, has been nervous about the whole idea. Peter Clarke of the *Guardian* is not the only cartoonist to have tackled the subject, but he nicely captured the public's response to this high-tech approach to food preservation.

When the magazine *Which?* asked consumers whether they would buy irradiated food, 50% said they would not – and 50% also said they would actually prefer to buy foods preserved with conventional additives. 30% felt that the technique should not be allowed in Britain, with only 10% thinking that it should.

Organic producers elsewhere in Europe have the same worries. 'There have been cases of things becoming "organic" in the hundred yards between the factory and the wholesaler,' was the way Ulrich Heinzel, an organic grocer in Cologne, put it.

Raising standards

Unfortunately, however, the word 'organic' on a food label can still mean different things to different people. This variability in standards, in fact, has been a major problem for genuinely organic producers. The Soil Association did come up with its own symbol of quality, awarded to farmers, growers and food processors who produce chemical-free foods – enforced by a small team of semi-voluntary inspectors.

But, as Lawrence Woodward put it, 'until there are government guidelines, there is nothing in the law to prevent producers from putting the word "organic" on their packaging, and their standards often vary. The trouble is that ignorance about wholefood and organic labelling abounds among retailers and consumers, and you also get the sharks who mislead the public with false claims.'

In the autumn of 1987, however, John MacGregor, Minister of Agriculture, Fisheries and Food, announced the imminent introduction of a new UK Register of Organic Food Standards, based on a voluntary code of practice. The idea was to replace several competing 'organic' labelling schemes with a single 'UK organic' scheme.

Enter the genetic engineer

One related development which did not win the Soil Association's automatic approval, however, was the growing use of genetic engineering methods to produce new strains of cereals and other crops which – if all goes well – will need fewer injections of agrochemicals (page 183). Organic farmers would be well advised to keep an eye on the activities of the new Sainsbury Laboratory.

In the longer term, in fact, genetic engineering and

other forms of biotechnology may offer ways out of the 'chemical trap' in agriculture. Critics of agricultural biotechnology point out that some of the first applications of plant genetic engineering have been designed to make crop plants more resistant to particular herbicides, so more herbicide can be used. But the launch of the Sainsbury Laboratory suggests that if the environmental pressure is sufficiently intense, real progress can be made towards the goal of sustainable, healthy food production.

A more speculative application of genetic engineering might be to convert grain crops into open-air 'chemical factories', producing compounds needed, for example, in alternative or 'complementary' medicine. The Ministry of Agriculture, Fisheries and Food, for example, has been looking at the potential for British farmers to switch to unorthodox crops, including crops which would produce the raw materials for alternative medicine. The main crop used in this way to date has been the evening primrose, a natural source of gammalinoleic acid (GLA). GLA is used for treating arthritis, eczema, pre-menstrual tension and multiple schlerosis.

The complementary medicine field is still some way behind the organic food business in terms of public acceptability, although it has won key supporters – including Prince Charles. In fact, there is growing government interest in complementary medicine, a term which includes homeopathy, osteopathy, acupuncture and herbalism. 1987, in fact, saw the opening of what was described as the first university research centre in the Western world for complementary medicine, at Exeter University. The focus of the centre's work will be on such techniques as acupuncture, herbalism, homeopathy and naturopathy, as well as yoga and meditation.

Although it may be many years before such remedies are readily available through the National Health Service, the British Medical Association and the Medical Research Council have been increasingly prepared to carry out comparative evaluations of such alternative therapies. A useful source of information is the Institute of Complementary Medicine, which publishes both a newsletter and a yearbook.

Standards needed

Once again, though, there is an urgent need for rigorous standards. There has been concern, for example, that some of the herbal preparations used by herbalists could cause unwelcome side-effects. Excessive doses of ginseng, it has been shown, can cause high blood pressure, swollen breasts and internal bleeding. The herb feverfew can cause mouth ulcers, while apricots, bitter almonds and the seeds of the plum, pear and cherry all contain significant quantities of cyanide. Comfrey may contain a substance known to cause cancer and several herbs, among them devil's claw, pennyroyal oil and broom, can cause miscarriages.

But those who use alternative medicine are generally in no doubt that they are benefitting. According to a survey carried out by the Consumers' Association, for example, four out of five people who have tried alternative remedies report either that they

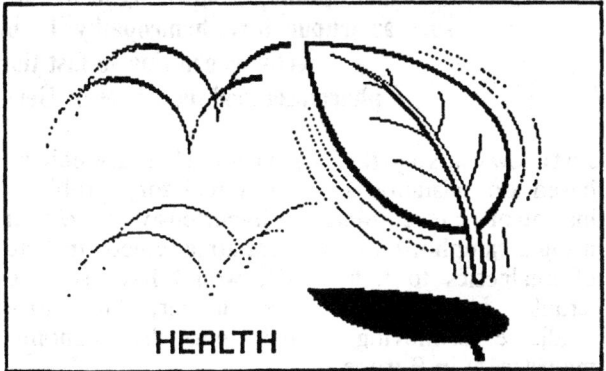

were cured or that their health improved. Only 1% of the respondents felt that alternative medicine had made their problem worse, while 14% said that it had proved ineffective.

Jogging in the smog

That still leaves a great many satisfied customers, however, although here again more attention will need to be paid to quality control and the introduction of appropriate standards. In the end, such products are as vulnerable to pressure from the environmental and health lobbies as those they have replaced.

Consider the West German mineral water industry. When the environmental magazine Natur tested 240 brands of bottled mineral water, it branded 121 as 'unhealthy' because of contamination by nitrates, acids and, in a few cases, arsenic. Sales of bottled water, normally in excess of nine billion litres a year, slumped as a result.

It will be interesting to see whether the 'designer water' industry, whose advertising has stressed the environmental protection legislation which keeps its water catchments pure, will try to exert pressure on farmers and other polluters to clean up their act.

In many people's minds, there is no automatic link between the health and environmental lobbies. But, as the public reaction to the lead-in-petrol debate and to the Chernobyl disaster showed, the links can be forged.

People who are diet-conscious may well be more interested in attempts to keep pesticide residues out of their food, for example. The loss of the world's rainforests may be seen as a more immediate threat if environmentalists talk in terms of the loss of potential cancer cures than if they point to the implications for the long-term climate. And joggers obliged to run through the fumes of city traffic may be less likely to resist calls for cleaner cars, even if they have to pay more for their own car. The challenge for the environmental movement (page 71) will be to help people make such connections. ☐

Healthy Growth In Alternative Medicine

Europeans are spending nearly $1.4 billion a year on alternative therapies such as acupuncture, homeopathy, herbal and natural medicines. Indeed, this market sector is growing so fast that it now poses a real threat to the pharmaceutical industries of Germany, France, the UK and Switzerland.

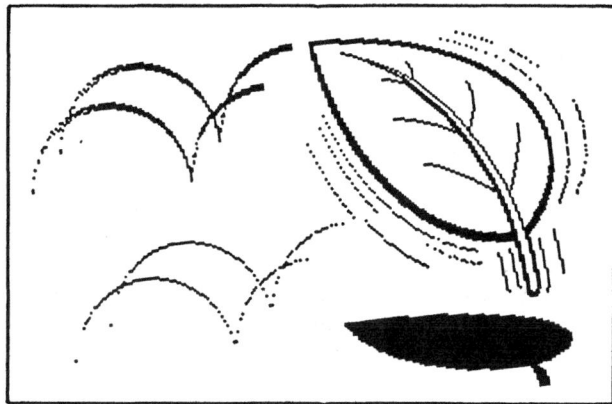

Just a few years ago the idea of using a herbal medicine based on mistletoe to treat circulatory problems instead of a conventional anti-hypertensive drug, or of using a camphor-based homeopathic remedy instead of analgesics to fight colds, would have seemed 'cranky' in the extreme. No longer. Alternative medicine is moving strongly into the economic mainstream in Europe.

West Germany is Europe's leading nation as far as sales of alternative medicines is concerned. Use of vitamins and other dietary supplements is 'generally at a much higher level' there than elsewhere in Europe, according to market analysts Frost & Sullivan. Homeopathy and other natural remedies are widely used, and acupuncture and manipulative practices (such as chiropracty) are well accepted by the medical establishment. Indeed, some 10,000 German doctors are reported to have used acupuncture on their patients.

The German market in alternative medicine accounted for a third of the European total in 1986, although Frost & Sullivan say it will grow more slowly than the overall market in the period to 1991 – averaging about 5% a year.

Homeopathy, herbal medicines and other natural remedies have a long tradition in France, too, which accounted for around a third of the 1986 European market – or $313 million (almost 2.4 billion francs). Despite the fact that all medical practices are heavily controlled by the French government, the French alternative medicine market is forecast to grow at 7% a year to 1991.

Across the Channel, in the United Kingdom, the National Health Service has been extremely conservative in adopting alternative therapies. Even so, homeopathic and other natural remedies are increasingly popular and are now widely available in health food stores. As a result, Frost & Sullivan predict that the UK market will grow at 9% a year to 1991 – reaching a value of £158 million ($182 million) that year.

Overall, consultations and physical therapies are the market leaders, accounting for 59% of the sales volume (see Figure 1). But natural dietary supplements, which account for a fifth of the volume, are expected to show the fastest growth rate.

If you want the latest facts on this rapidly developing market, Frost & Sullivan's 263-page report *Alternative Medical Practices in Europe* (No. E874) is an excellent – if, at $2,300 per copy, pricey – information source. If this area is one you want to move into, though, that may prove to be a relatively cheap entry fee.

What the company will tell you for free, meanwhile, is that increasing public concern about the long-term effects of drug usage and the favourable publicity that alternative treatments are receiving are combining to produce a market that will exceed $1.9 billion by 1991, in constant 1985 dollars. That means an average 7% growth rate across Europe – a market opportunity which is hardly to be sneezed at.

Frost & Sullivan Limited, *Sullivan House, 4 Grosvenor Gardens, London SW1W 0DH. Tel: 01 730 3438. Telex: 261671.*

Figure 1:

Expenditure on alternative practices and products in Europe in 1986 (source: Frost & Sullivan).

Consultations and physical therapies $796M

Natural dietary supplements $258M

Specific natural remedies $302M

HEALTH

Goodbye To Pesticides?

Growing concern about the use of pesticides in agriculture, coupled with intense interest in organic farming, is awakening the interest of many supermarket chains in organic food. But none has gone as far as David Sainsbury, who plans to invest £15m in plant science pathology in an attempt to design plants which shrug off pests with little or no help from agrochemicals.

Plant diseases cause severe crop losses all over the world, with the average crop failure in Europe sometimes exceeding 15% of the potential yield. In the UK, the annual loss to cereal crops due to fungal disease is estimated at around £150m, with a further £60m spent on fungicidal sprays. Molecular plant pathology promises to provide a far more effective solution to plant diseases by building in resistance through the use of genetic engineering.

In the largest private gift ever made to support plant science, David Sainsbury, through his Gatsby Charitable Foundation, is giving £15m over 10 years to create a new international laboratory for research into molecular plant pathology.

The Sainsbury Laboratory is directed by a steering committee chaired by Prof Harold Woolhouse, director of the Institute of Plant Science Research (IPSR). A Scientific Council includes such leading scientists as Prof Heinz Saedler of the Max Planck Institute, in Cologne, and Dr Brian Staskowitz from the University of California at Berkeley. Funded by the Agricultural and Food Research Council (AFRC), the IPSR is based at the John Innes Institute in Norwich, and will host the new laboratory. The idea, as Prof Woolhouse put it, is to: 'Create a brain drain in reverse.'

Third World benefits

David Sainsbury, who is finance director of J Sainsbury plc, personally endowed the Gatsby Charitable foundation in the 1960s. In the last decade, since the company went public, the combined Trusts set up by members of the Sainsbury family have grown to the point where their asssets are valued at over £350m. Buy why invest in this field? 'The fundamental study of the ways in which plants become diseased through infections with viruses, bacteria or fungi has emerged very strongly in the past three or so years as one of the most interesting areas in plant research,' Sainsbury replied. 'Unravelling how a bacterium gets into a plant and makes it ill or not is exciting science.' Developments in this area are also likely to produce important practical benefits, particularly in the Third World.

Equally important, Sainsbury noted, 'molecular plant pathology is an area of science in which the UK is strong. In viral work there is a long and deep history of UK research, not least at the John Innes Institute itself.' But, he stresses: 'This is not a "British-science-leads-the-world" story. There are people of comparable quality working in similar research programmes in places such as the USA, Germany and Holland. But the best UK scientists' publications are scrutinised every bit as closely in the US labs as the US publications are here.'

Plant pathology involves the study of the interactions between plants and pathogens, providing the scientific foundation on which crop protection strategies are based. At present, disease control depends on the use of fungicides and insecticides and on the breeding of disease-resistant crop varieties. Concerns about chemical crop protection methods are placing a premium on the development of disease resistance, but the problem here is that so little is known about the fundamentals of host-pathogen interactions that it is impossible to predict what kinds of genes will need to be transferred in order to confer useful disease resistance.

Private sector corrective

Despite an imaginative funding initiative undertaken by the Agricultural Research Council some nine years ago, however, the UK teams working in the molecular plant pathology field have been in trouble over the last three years. 'Existing teams are scarcely renewing themselves,' Sainsbury says, 'and our relative strength is beginning to erode. The new laboratory, developed in collaboration with the John Innes Foundation, the AFRC and the University of East Anglia, is seen as a private sector corrective to that trend.

Apart from the sheer excitement of this area of science, however, Sainsbury no doubt had his eye on a number of trends in agriculture and food markets. As Prof Woolhouse put it, 'we have to recognise that the use of crop protection chemicals is increasingly questioned from the standpoint of their effects on wildlife and as contaminants in human food and water supplies. I see the Sainsbury Laboratory as having a major part to play in acquiring the necessary basic knowledge needed to take us beyond this relatively crude era of chemical protection of crops, into a future where disease resistance can be properly understood and engineered. ☐

SECTION 11

Money Matters

Environmental fund-raising is now a highly professional business. Heinz captured the headlines when it became the first company to give £1 million to conservation, but hundreds of other businesses are now helping to finance the greening of Europe.

One of the most interesting questions for the 1990s is how Europe's environmentalists are going to move – as a growing number now recognise they must – from the charitable, non-profit periphery of the economy into the financial mainstream.

If sustainable development, as recommended by the Brundtland Commission (itself estimated to have cost $6 million), is to mean something in the real world, environmentalists cannot simply sit back and wait for development proposals to come forward – and then open fire with all guns. Instead, they should begin to operate as 'green investors'. They may even need to consider becoming developers in their own right, providing concrete examples of what more sustainable forms of development might look like.

Money, money, money

Meanwhile, the real world is changing rapidly, often in ways which run directly counter to the goal of sustainability. *'Money, Money, Money is the incantation of today,'* the leading US business magazine *Fortune* observed in the summer of 1987. *'Bewitched by an epidemic of money enchantment, Americans in the Eighties wriggle in a St. Vitus's dance of materialism unseen since the Gilded Age or the Roaring Twenties. Under the blazing sun of money, all other values shine palely.'* Things may not have been quite so bad in Europe, but the same trends have also been discernible on this side of the Atlantic.

The Big Bang in London's City, the privatisation of state industries and the emergence of the 'yuppie' were just some of the milestones along the road to a resurgence of materialism. Interestingly, however, environmentalism did not 'shine palely' as a result. Indeed Band Aid, which raised £56.5 million in Britain alone during 1984–85, demonstrated that a great many people still care what happens elsewhere on the planet.

Many of those who gave so generously to tackle starvation, however, are still unable to make the link between such problems and environmental mismanagement. If such funds could be mobilised and spent on preventative measures (page 50), they might be considerably more effective.

Fairy godparents

Meanwhile, there is no question that, potentially at least, the industrial nations have the resources needed for the transition to more sustainable forms of development. If Britain is valued at £1,630 billion in the official statistics, how much is Europe as a whole worth? And what proportion of that total value are we – and should we be – investing in environmental protection and sustainable development?

There are no ready answers to such questions, but the agenda laid out in the Brundtland Commission's report is as clear an indication as we are going to get that we are not currently spending enough on environmental protection, rehabilitation and management. Meanwhile, by force of necessity, green causes and organisations continue to tap into Europe's wealth in some highly innovative ways.

If we are serious about sustainable development, the bill is going to run into many billions of pounds. The money raised by shaking tins in the high street will help, but new ways must be found of greening mainstream financial institutions and money flows. The ethical investment funds discussed by Giles Chitty (page 186) are just the start.

Membership fees, of course, are an important source of income, even though they account for a relatively small proportion of the income of many major environmental organisations.

Another important, if little recognised, source of funding is the 'fairy godparent'. One such was Brigitte Bardot. 'I have dedicated my beauty and my youth to the human race,' said the French film actress when she auctioned almost all of her personal possessions to raise money for animal welfare. 'Now I am giving my wisdom and my experience, the best of myself, to the cause of animals.' That sale of Bardotbilia alone raised $500,000 for the new Bardot Foundation.

Few people are prepared to go quite that far, but wealthy individuals have played a considerable – and largely unsung – role in bankrolling the environmental movement. And the 'fairy godparent' approach to environmental fund-raising, with a wealthy individual appearing out of the blue to help a good green cause, can achieve dramatic results.

John Paul Getty, for example, gave nearly £90,000 to help the Dorset Trust for Nature Conservation and the Royal Society for Nature Conservation to raise the

MONEY

Godfrey Bradman funded CLEAR

£200,000 they needed to buy 328 acres of meadows and woodland at Lower Kingcombe, (page 143).

And remember the CLEAR campaign against lead in petrol? Des Wilson was funded by millionaire Godfrey Bradman. Among other services to the environmental cause, this radical philanthropist also saved Friends of the Earth from bankruptcy and helped fund their anti-nuclear campaign. In the wake of the Chernobyl disaster, too, he commissioned the Harwell Laboratory to develop a portable radiation monitor.

'I believe fervently that we have a duty to our children to leave the world at least as we inherited it,' Bradman explained later. But even such long-pocketed friends cannot sustain more than a small segment of the environmental movement for long.

A costly business

Environmental campaigning, it is worth stressing, can be an extremely costly business. At the activist end of the spectrum, for example, Greenpeace lost the *Rainbow Warrior* in New Zealand and, in 1987, was hit with a £296,000 damages claim by British Nuclear Fuels after trying to block the Sellafield effluent pipeline. Even the more conventional groups find that the cost of lobbying nationally and internationally imposes enormous financial strains.

Consider the cost of protecting the world's wetlands. 'Half of all wetlands have now been drained,' as HRH The Duke of Edinburgh pointed out a few months earlier in 1987. The Ramsar Convention on Wetlands of International Importance, the world's oldest global conservation treaty, protects over 350 wetlands totalling more than 20 million hectares. But to ensure that this protection could be maintained in existing areas and be extended to new areas, the annual bill for 1987 was just over $400,000. The amounts contributed by national governments ranged from Mauritania's $41 to the $109,000 given by the United States.

Few people would argue that this was too much money to spend on such a vital cause, but when you add in the funding requirements for the protection of other major natural resources, from coral reefs to rain forests, the total bill begins to look slightly daunting.

A $8 billion down-payment

When the US World Resources Institute published *Tropical Forests: A Call for Action* late in 1985, for example, it also announced that it would be looking for a total of some $8 *billion* over five years, to be spent by international and national government agencies, industry and other investors on initiatives designed to slow the pace of tropical deforestation. Some two-thirds of this total would be earmarked for the 56 most seriously affected countries.

'These sums are not small,' admitted the WRI Task Force, which pooled the expertise of WRI, the World Bank and the United Nations Development Programme, 'except in relation to the returns.' The proposed initiatives, it was suggested, 'will alleviate hunger and deprivation, arrest dangerous assaults on the planet's environmental support system, and provide the basis for sustainable economic growth. By any system of accounting that can encompass true costs and benefits, the investment that is required is nothing more than a small down payment on a far brighter future.'

These sums are not quite as forbidding as they might at first seem, given that they represent the greening of existing and planned spending by a large number of national and international government agencies, for example. But, even so, the challenge facing the international environmental movement is probably greater today than it has ever been.

Debt for trees

To meet their ever-growing requirements for finance and other resources, environmentalists have been steadily developing new strategies. One of the most extraordinary developments in recent years was the debt-for-nature swop arranged between Bolivia (which in 1987 had foreign debts to the tune of $4 billion) and the non-profit, Washington-based environmental group Conservation International.

By purchasing $650,000 of Bolivia's foreign debts for a knock-down price of just over $100,000, Conservation International won the right to protect

187 →

PERSPECTIVES

The Green Investor

Environmental considerations are as yet only a second-rank consideration in the booming ethical investment field. But, says *Giles Chitty*, the City should keep an eye on the emerging Green Investor.

'Two trends stand out in financial markets. The first, which has been extensively publicised, was initiated by the Government and the City with the Financial Services Act 1986 and the 'Big Bang'. It aims to make investment safer for the private individual. The second trend, 'ethical' (or socially responsible) investment, was not started by the City, but is now being actively investigated by the financial establishment.

The ethics on which the City's activities have traditionally been based are well-established and relatively narrow: investors should not be defrauded or misled, and inside information should not be used for financial gain. The ethics adopted by ethical investment funds, by contrast, are very much broader. They also vary widely according to the investor's interests and values. They may proscribe certain forms of investment (e.g. links with South Africa or nuclear arms) or actively seek out investments in particular types of project or venture (e.g. environmental protection, energy efficiency or inner city renewal).

Increasingly, there is common ground between different types of ethical investor, with a more 'holistic' approach tending to appeal to the 'inner directed' people identified by Taylor Nelson Applied Futures (page 52). Faced by growing numbers of investors who not only want a financial return from their investments but also want their portfolio to reflect their deeply-held personal convictions, the market has been scurrying to catch up.

How ethical?

Inevitably, some of the more recent ethical investment funds have been moving into this area with an eye on the profits to be made rather than on the need to carefully link financial yardsticks to broader social responsibility yardsticks. They are less interested, for example, in such questions as: How much tobacco- or alcohol-related revenue disqualifies an otherwise acceptable company? Experienced ethical investors also know that, however appealing a fund's publicity, a close eye may need to be kept on the performance of individual investment managers.

The investor will want to be assured that the fund's research is sufficiently rigorous. Some investors will also want to look at the nature and transparency of the fund's decision making process. Some, too, will want to develop a highly focused group of investments, a 'Green Portfolio', for example. But many others are simply looking for a reasonably safe, reasonably effective channel for their investments. So which are the funds which the ethical investor should turn to first?

The **Calvert Social Investment Fund** (contact: D. Wayne Silby, 1700 Pennsylvania Avenue, Washington, DC 20006, USA or on (301) 951 4260), founded in the United States in 1982 is a market leader. It has consistently outperformed stock market averages, has clear criteria and keeps investors informed about its decision-making process.

Small but growing

While it is claimed that $350 million is ethically invested in the USA (source: *Social Investment Forum Newsletter*), the UK has only a few acknowledged ethical investment vehicles, all small by any comparison. There are two established ethical investment funds of note here: **Friend's Provident's Stewardship Fund** (contact: Pixham End, Dorking, Surrey RH4 1QA or on 0306 885055), founded in 1984, now has more than £50 million invested. In the twelve months to June 1987 it outperformed the FT Ordinary Share Index.

The **Ethical Investment Fund** (contact: D. J. Bromige and Partners Ltd, 10 Queen Street, London SW1X 7PD or on 01 491 0558), unlike the Stewardship Fund, is independent of major financial groups

GILES CHITTY *is Managing Director of the Financial Initiative Ltd. Educated at Bryanston, University College London and Columbia University, he worked as a finance manager at Allied Chemical Corporation from 1966 to 1970, and at Warner Lambert from 1970 to 1973. He advised the Indonesian Minister of Finance on public enterprises from 1973 to 1975. He is Chairman of the Findhorn Foundation's Board of Trustees, having been a Trustee since 1978.*

operating outside the ethical investment sphere. Launched early in 1986, it had raised more than £1.75 million by mid-1987. It also outperformed the FT Ordinary Share Index in the twelve months to June 1987. Ethical investment outweighs market opportunism in its choice of investment opportunities.

A number of other funds advertise themselves as ethical, but you should ask them for details of their criteria and how compliance is researched. The Stewardship Fund does not release levels of materiality. The Ethical Investment Fund does. The others have not so far been publicly specific, seeking less risk and a fixed rate of interest.

Mercury Provident plc (contact: Christian Nunhofer, executive director, Orlingbury House, Lewes Road, Forest Row RH18 5AA or on 0342 823739) was founded in 1974 and is a licensed deposit taker, in effect a bank under the Bank of England's regulatory control. It promotes a conscious approach to money, aiming to channel funds to develop socially beneficial enterprises. Depositors make a conscious choice as to what projects their funds will support and choose the rate of interest, up to a maximum of 7%, in stark contrast to the 'pooled deposits' approach of most banks. Deposits approach £2 million, there are over 400 depositors and over 100 enterprises have been financed.

The Ecology Building Society (page 188) contributes to the regeneration of rural areas and inner cities, opposes wasteful use of land and resources, and lends to small-scale workshops, energy-saving homes, homes for people running businesses with an ecological bias, and properties which help promote the life of small communities. Terms of investment are typical for the building society sector.

For those looking for a full range of ethical investment services and products, **The Financial Initiative Ltd** (contact: Eversley House, 1 Elm Grove Road, Salisbury SP1 1JW or on 0722 338900) can help. Founded in 1983, it is the only ethical venture capital company in Britain and offers a full range of services, including venture capital brokerage, fund and portfolio management and financial consultancy. It handled £1 million of investment business in 1986. Investors have the opportunity for a more intimate knowledge of investee companies than is possible through funds or managed portfolios. Recent investments have included an organic packaged food company and an inner-city garden centre.

The Green Investor has a growing range of opportunities to choose from, as other sections of *Green Pages* demonstrate. Remember, though, that however successful companies like the Body Shop (page 70) may have been, if you are to avoid losing your money you will need to cast as careful an eye over the financial performance of a company as you do over its environmental performance.

3.7 million acres (an area larger than Northern Ireland) of forests and open savannah grassland in the north of the country.

Costa Rica was next in line. This time President Oscar Arias offered to recreate tropical forest in exchange for dollars to write off some of Costa Rica's foreign debt – which at the time stood at $3.7 billion. The project, undertaken with Dan Janzen, professor of biology at the University of Pennsylvania, will help protect a parcel of 15,000 hectares of forest in the north-west of Costa Rica, near the Nicaraguan border. An airstrip used by the US Central Intelligence Agency to supply the Contras in Nicaragua will be turned back into forest, with the proposed Guanacaste National Park as a whole effectively doubling the amount of protected dry tropical forest.

But how did the debt-for-forest swap work? 'It works like this,' reported Jeremy Cherfas in *New Scientist*. 'Foreign debt in Costa Rica sells for 38 cents on the dollar. That is, with your $38,000, the Costa Rican government can write off $100,000 of foreign debt. The government will then give Guanacaste National Park $75,000 worth of local currency in the form of a secure bond that earns a high rate of interest. On the strength of that bond, the park can borrow the same amount of money from a local bank, at a much lower rate of interest. The park uses the borrowed money to buy the land from owners while the bond sits earning interest. When the bond matures, part of the interest earned goes to paying off the local loan. The rest provides an endowment for running Guanacaste National Park.'

Environmentalists have long been worried that deeply indebted Third World countries are being encouraged to pillage their own natural resources in an attempt to break back into the black. 'The prospects for sustained economic growth are being undermined, not strengthened, by the growing pressures being placed on the resource bases of economically depressed nations,' explained Peter Seligmann, executive director of Conservation International.

For the long term future, Rafe Pomerance of WRI has been looking at the potential for a worldwide 'Carbon Tax', which would tax anyone burning fossil fuels or other sources of carbon dioxide, particularly in the developed world, generating funds which could be re-invested in tropical reafforestation programmes.

Business sponsorships

In the short term, however, a prime target of green fund-raising today is business, although the number of groups which can hope to develop workable partnerships with business is obviously limited.

Leading conservation organisations, most notably the World Wildlife Fund, have built up highly

PERSPECTIVES

Mortgaging the Future?

From small beginnings, the Ecology Building Society has built a growth business around the idea of green mortgages. Ecological lifestyles, says Bob Lowman, *are no longer a pipedream.*

'In 1981, a small group of people met to discuss ways to finance properties where ecologically sound projects could be got off the ground. Most major building societies were not helpful if a borrower was interested in buying derelict buildings or smallholdings. The result: a green light for the Ecology Building Society (EBS).

Ten founders each invested £500 to raise the minimum capital of £5,000. Since then, the EBS has grown to the point where it has 1,400 investors and £2 million in assets. Almost 100 borrowers have mortgages with the EBS on properties which embody the philosophy which underpins our activities. This is spelled out in Rule 5, as follows:

'Advances shall be made to persons or on properties which, in the opinion of the Board, are most likely to lead to the saving of non-renewable resources, the promotion of self-sufficiency in individuals or communities, or the most ecologically efficient use of land.'

The EBS's concern for the environment makes it opposed to the wasteful use of land and resources sometimes encouraged by orthodox lending policies. Instead, it aims to contribute to the regeneration of rural areas and inner cities, always promoting a more ecological and sustainable way of life.

Back-to-back and energy-efficient

Mortgage loans have been made on derelict – but sound – houses, which would otherwise have been abandoned; on houses incorporating special energy-efficient features; on back-to-backs, which by their very nature are energy-efficient; and on organic smallholdings and farms. The EBS also considers applications for mortgages from people purchasing homes from which they plan to run small businesses with an ecological bias, such as paper recycling or craft workshops.

There is a growing awareness of the vital necessity of saving our natural resources, but starting to take practical steps towards this goal can still be difficult. Many people have a dream of a different way of life. To have this they need to buy a property either to live in, to work in, to produce food or develop some ecological project. The EBS has been able to help some of them and looks forward to helping many more.

An example of where the EBS has helped in this way is provided by Pat Muir, who bought a derelict house with a smallholding in Nentsberry, Cumbria. Pat has suffered with allergies to many products which are an inescapable feature of modern life, and wanted to move away from her native Newcastle. She now has 22 acres in full use, with goats, hens, sheep and cows, seeking to be as self-sufficient as possible. The biggest change in her life is that she is now free from most of the reactions and allergies that previously had made her so ill. She now takes visitors who are suffering with the same problem, offering them advice and help.

A number of borrowers run small businesses, such as the growing of herbs, furniture making and paper recycling. The EBS has also helped with loans on wholefood shops.

Far from free-and-easy

Although it may sound as if the EBS is more free-and-easy than the High Street building societies, their lending criteria are in many ways more stringent – and therefore more prudential. At a time when many lenders are granting loans up to three times the borrower's annual income, the EBS will not advance more than twice the total income of the applicants. And, whereas 95% loans are the norm for most building socities, the EBS expects its borrowers to put

BOB LOWMAN *is General Manager of the Ecology Building Society. A Fellow of the Chartered Building Societies Institute, he spent the first thirteen years of his working life in banking, following up with 20 years working with building societies – including five years with the Halifax.*

The Ecology Building Society, *8 Main Street, Crosshills, Keighley, West Yorkshire BD20 8TB. Tel: 0535 35933.*

in at least 20% of the valuation of a property.

On the other hand, because of the Society's low percentage loans and its non-materialistic philosophy, it does not insist on extensive – and expensive – repair works being carried out to habitable properties.

Whilst the EBS is happy to lend where working or farm animals are raised under reasonably natural conditions, it is not prepared to lend where these animals are to be kept as pets, for show purposes or riding.

Bats and hardwoods

When talking to would-be borrowers, the EBS draws their attention to the fact that it is not an environmental organisation, but an ecological organisation. It is not, therefore, primarily concerned with natural beauty or with historic or architectural interest. It will lend on barns for conversion, but only if they form an essential part of an ecologically sound project and can no longer reasonably be used for their original purpose. The EBS does not lend on holiday cottages or second homes.

The Society has also become involved in other issues where it feels it can have a useful influence. For example, it insists that where timber needs to be treated to render a property structurally sound, permethrin-based products should be used. These are biodegradable and far less toxic to bats, house martins and other birds.

Another concern relates to the use of tropical hardwoods (page 64). The Society is advising borrowers to avoid tropical hardwoods wherever possible, although we may shift our policy if the Friends of the Earth 'sustainable hardwoods' scheme takes off.

The Ecology Building Society occupies a small but significant niche in the total financial market. By demonstrating that an ecological way of life is not a pipedream, we have helped a growing number of borrowers to find an alternative way of living. We aim to grow significantly as we move into the 1990s, but firmly intend to stick to our basic principles – in the belief that we cannot afford to mortgage the future of our world.

***

187 ←

professional corporate sponsorship units whose business it is to persuade corporate sponsors that conservation is at least as effective an investment as, say, sponsorship of the arts or sports. WWF produced a short booklet, *Conservation and Business Sponsorship,* showing how conservation sponsorship has proved beneficial for a wide range of business partners.

Fiat, for example, sponsored WWF's Madagascar Appeal. The company's UK managing director, Peter Quaglia, later commented that the Appeal had provided an excellent marketing vehicle. Geoffrey Dove, marketing director of Office Cleaning Services, reported that his company had landed new business through its sponsorship of a series of working lunches in aid of Britain's barn owls and other birds of prey. Ford, Kodak and the National Westminster Bank are among the companies which have sponsored major conservation award schemes.

Kellogg's have supported the British Wildlife Appeal. On a larger scale, BASF has given £40,000 towards a 12-month survey of birdlife in British gardens, co-ordinated by the British Trust for Ornithology. And the Prudential Corporation, which supported the British Trust for Conservation Volunteers' 'Natural Break' holiday programme (page 175), found its link with BTCV an effective way of reaching a specific target audience, the 18–25 age group. And the Central Electricity Generating Board, one of the sponsors of *Green Pages,* has built up a very considerable sponsorship programme, with £15,000 going to BTCV in 1987, £55,000 to the British Wildlife Appeal and £100,000 to BTO.

Now the spotlight is focusing on even the smallest industries. In a report commissioned by the Nature Conservancy Council, the Department of the Environment and the World Wildlife Fund, for example, Dr Mark Collins of the Cambridge-based Conservation Monitoring Centre argued that the small firms which make up Britain's £5 million-a-year butterfly house industry should put more resources back into conservation in the tropical countries which supply them with their most colourful exhibits.

Some companies, meanwhile, prefer to make their contribution in the form of non-cash donations. This may involve making donations in kind (unwanted or surplus materials or land), the loan of equipment (from typewriters to earthmoving machines), or help with specific problems, with some industrialists helping environmental organisations in their areas of professional expertise, on a voluntary basis. One of the most helpful ways in which business and industry can support such initiatives is to loan a member of staff for a period of time – often in the run-up to retirement.

Fairshares

Another form of help is to alert employees to the new tax provisions. BTCV is one of the groups which are now benefiting from the new tax regime in Britain, which encourages charitable giving by employees, whether in the private or public sectors.

Starting in April 1987, the 'Give As You Earn' scheme enables employees to give up to £120 a year to charity – at a cost of only £85.20. Assuming a tax rate of 29%, the taxman will make up the remaining £34.80. Or as Greenpeace put it, 'if you sign a tax recovery form, the Chancellor will give us £3.70 for

193→

PERSPECTIVES

Writing off the Environment

Conventional accountancy methods are highly misleading when it comes to
choosing between competing natural resource management strategies.
Norman Myers runs through some recent entries in our environmental accounts.

'The 'natural resource underpinnings' of our economies are becoming increasingly significant, especially when we consider they include not only soil, water, vegetation and wild creatures, but the atmosphere, indeed climate itself. Yet our economic accountancy procedures fail to reflect our use, or rather mis-use and over-use, of natural resources. National budgets and other annual audits rarely consider the depletion of natural resources, nor do they portray the decline in goods and services that these resources generate.

So while we hear much about rates of economic growth, we hear all too little, in equally systematized form at least, about rates of natural resource depletion. This gross discrepancy between the way we appraise our economic activities, and the way we evaluate the state of the natural resource base that ultimately sustains much economic activity, often leads us to a distorted view of our economic health (Leipert, 1986; Norgaard, 1985; Pearce and Markandya, 1986; Repetto, 1986).

When we make use of man-made assets such as equipment and buildings, we write off our use as depreciation. But we do not view our environment as productive capital, even though we utilize it as such. When we excessively exploit forests, overwork croplands until the soil erodes, and use our skies as a free garbage can and our rivers as cost-less sewers, our income as revealed via GNP actually registers an increase. And when we engage in efforts to reduce, neutralize or repair environmental damage, those economic activities are also registered as additions to GNP. Clearly we should modify our traditional accounting procedures to incorporate an environmental reckoning.

Corroding the future

An obvious illustration is the case of acid rain. According to the latest surveys, some 77,000 square miles of forests in Europe, or an area almost equivalent to Great Britain, are injured if not dying. In the worst-hit country, West Germany, the overall costs are now estimated at $2.8 billion per year (Leipert, 1987). In addition, the European Community believes that damage to crops amounts to at least $1 billion a year, and corrosion of buildings to more than $0.5 billion, possibly several times more. Yet the production functions that generate acid rain, notably power stations and automobiles, continue to be registered in national accounts as net contributions to GNP.

The acid-rain problem seems to be spreading. There are signs of it in the western Soviet Union and Japan, also in China, Malaysia and Brazil – even of an acid haze over the Arctic. These all demonstrate that the problem of pollution spillovers, or 'externalities' in the economist's jargon, is endemic to economic systems, West and East, North and South. Could there be more graphic evidence that we need to integrate the values of economics and environment?

Similar considerations apply to soil erosion. In the United States it is estimated to impose on-site costs to agriculture (in the form of reduced crop yields), plus off-site costs (in the form of siltation of reservoirs and other water bodies) worth more than $6 billion a year (Kneese, 1984). Worse, all forms of water pollution are estimated to detract from US GNP by more than $20 billion a year, or roughly 1% of GNP (Carson and Mitchell, 1984).

Conversely, measures to counter environmental problems can have a handsome payoff. In the United States, air-pollution control in 1978 was estimated at $4.3 billion for property damage avoided (counting both stationary and mobile sources of pollution), and at $17 billion for benefits to health (stationary sources alone) (Freeman, 1980). Avoiding damage to materials, known as 'soiling and cleaning costs', totalled a further $3 billion. Taken together, these items are worth over $100 to each American per year.

'Total picture' accounting

What we need, then, is a unified system of accounting that reflects the world outside the window – a seamless world that does not recognize man-made divisions of reckoning. Let us look forward to the day when we shall hear of a nation where a minister presents a regular 'total picture' accounting of his or her nation's economy *and* of its natural-resource base.

An integrative accounting of both 'economic flows' and 'environmental flows' is an even more urgent necessity in Third World nations. A greater share of their economies usually depends directly upon natural resources than is the case in developed nations; and these natural resources are often more susceptible to damage, due to the ecological sensitivity of many tropical environments. Consider Ethiopia, where tropical forests, which covered 25% of the country as recently as 1940, have declined to only 3%

MONEY

today. The result has been widespread soil erosion from the traditional farming areas in the country's highlands. It can be roughly calculated that this loss of soil with its plant nutrients cuts Ethiopia's agricultural output by at least one million tons of food per year – equivalent to two-thirds of all relief food shipped to the country in 1985 (Newcombe, 1984).

Moreover as trees disappear and sources of fuelwood go too, Ethiopian farmers turn to burning cattle dung and crop residues. So much of these materials are now being used as fuel instead of fertilizer that there is further agricultural output foregone, worth some $600 million a year. To restore tree cover and to safeguard topsoil, if undertaken in due time, would have cost some $50 million a year. Yet in 1985 the outside world spent almost $500 million on relief food alone.

We can trace a further linkage between deforestation and energy. One of the best prospects of plentiful and renewable energy in the Third World lies with hydropower. Of all electricity now consumed, 38% comes from hydropower; and the proportion could grow a good deal higher by the end of the century provided that water supplies remain adequate. But a recent World Bank survey of 200 major dams built in the last 45 years reveals that sedimentation, caused by washoff of soil in the wake of deforestation, leads to an average of 2% loss of storage capacity loss every year (Sfeir-Younis, 1986). Even a 1% loss per year would mean reduced output of electricity on such a scale that, were it to be generated by burning oil at a price of $15 a barrel, it would cost $3.5 billion per annum by the year 2000 – or a sum roughly equivalent to one-tenth of all OECD and OPEC aid per year right now.

Consuming our capital

In essence, then, we are consuming our environmental capital rather than the income from that capital.

Soil erodes from beneath eucalyptus trees planted in Ethiopia's Wollo region for building poles and firewood.

For instance, recent calculations in West Germany reveal that total pollution is levying costs on the economy worth no less than $51 billion a year, equivalent to 8.3% of GNP (Wicke, 1986). In developing countries, the spread of deserts imposes agriculture loss costs on 80 million desert-dwelling people to the extent of at least $26 billion a year – a figure which throws light on the proposed budget for the UN Anti-Desertification Campaign of less than $5 billion per year.

Fortunately a number of countries are moving to devise systems of environmental accounting (Collard et al., 1987; Pearce and Markandya, 1987; Peskin, 1987; United Nations, 1987). In Norway and France, depletion of natural resources is being incorporated into national economic analyses. In the United States and Japan, the main focus is on economic quantification of pollution and environmental quality. Somewhere in between these two categories lie the approaches of Canada and the Netherlands. The basic intent is to produce a well-defined measure of 'net national product', sometimes known as 'net national welfare indicator' – a measure that is free of compensatory activities such as defensive expenditures. The task is complex, partly because it lies so much outside of established perceptions of natural resource values. But while waiting for more realistic systems of national accounting, let us remember that the question to ask about environmental protection is not 'Can we afford to do it eventually?' It is 'Can we afford not to do it immediately?'

References

Carson, R.T. and R.C. Mitchell. 1984. *The Value of Clean Water*. Resources for the Future, Washington D.C.

Collard, D., D.W. Pearce and D. Ulph, eds, 1987. *Economics and Sustainable Environments*. Macmillan, London.

Freeman, A.M. 1980. *The Benefits of Air and Water Pollution Control: A Review and Synthesis*. Council on Environmental Quality, Washington D.C.

Kneese, A.V. 1984. *Measuring the Benefits of Clean Air and Water*. Resources for the Future, Washington D.C.

Leipert, C. 1986. *Social Costs of Economic Growth*. Journal of Economic Issues 20: 109–131.

Leipert, C. 1987. A Critical Appraisal of Gross National Product: The Measurement of Net National Welfare and Environmental Accounting. *Journal of Economic Issues* 21: 357–373.

Newcombe, K. 1984. *An Economic Justification for Rural Afforestation: The Case of Ethiopia*. The World Bank, Washington D.C.

Norgaard, R.B. 1985. *Linking Environmental and National Income Accounts*. Department of Agricultural Economics, University of California, Berkeley, California.

Pearce, D.W. and A. Markandya. 1986. *The Economic Benefits of Environmental Improvement*. Environmental Research Trust, Romford, Essex.

Pearce, D.W. and A. Markandya. 1987. *The Benefits of Environmental Policies*. Environment Directorate, OECD, Paris, France.

Peskin, H.M. 1987. *The Environmental Accounts Framework*. Resources for the Future, Washington D.C.

Repetto, R. 1986. *Natural Resource Accounting for Countries With Natural Resource-Based Economies*. World Resources Institute, Washington D.C.

Sfeir-Younis, A. 1986. *Soil Conservation in Developing Countries, a Background Report*. The World Bank, Washington D.C.

United Nations. 1987. *The System of National Accounts: Guidelines*. United Nations, New York.

Wicke, L. 1986. *Die Okologischen Milliarden*. Kosel-Verlag, Munich, West Germany.

Dr NORMAN MYERS *is a consultant in environment and development. He has worked in over 80 countries and is currently a Visiting Fellow at the World Resources Institute; a Senior Associate, International Union for the Conservation of Nature; Chairman and Visiting Professor, Department of International Environment, University of Utrecht; and Adjunct Professor, University of Florida. He has published more than 200 professional papers in scientific journals and several hundred popular articles. His books include:* The Long African Day *(MacMillan, 1972);* The Sinking Ark *(Pergamon Press, 1979);* A Wealth of Wild Species *(Westview Press, 1983);* The Primary Source: Tropical Forests and Our Future *(WW Norton, 1984); and* Gaia: An Atlas of Planet Management *(Doubleday, New York, and Pan, London, 1984).*

Dr Myers, Upper Meadow, Old Road, Headington, Oxford OX3 8SZ.

For the 'green consumer' with a sweet tooth. On-pack promotions are increasingly used to raise money for conservation.

189 ←

every £10.00 paid under covenant.' The benefit to such charities of donations from donors in higher tax brackets can be even higher.

An interesting approach pioneered by eight organisations in the Third World development field has involved joining forces to take full advantage of this changed tax regime for charitable giving.

The Fairshares consortium pulls together organisations such as AMREF (African Medical and Research Foundation), CARE Britain, the Commonwealth Society for the Deaf, the Leonard Cheshire Foundation Overseas, ITDG (the Intermediate Technology Development Group), IIED (the International Institute for Environment and Development), LEPRA and VSO (Voluntary Service Overseas).

Meanwhile, an American idea which has not yet spread to Europe to any great degree, is the 'credit card with a conscience'. As part of the trend towards socially responsible investments in the States (page 186), some credit card companies (notably Visa, in association with the San Francisco-based financial firm Working Assets) are making a donation every time the card is used to charitable groups – such as Amnesty International, Greenpeace or Oxfam. Again, an interesting way of enabling the ordinary individual to make his or her contribution to saving the world in a 'user-friendly', no-fuss way.

The possibilities for fund-raising are clearly almost endless, but the requirements for finance for environmental management and sustainable development are likely to grow nearly exponentially for the foreseeable future. In these circumstances, environmental organisations will have to become increasingly adept at tapping into the financial mainstream. The greening of the City, Wall Street and other financial centres is out of the most challenging targets left. □

Mercury Provident plc

We operate a creative financial channel between socially beneficial enterprises and our socially-aware depositor customers. To find out how to become part of all this, write for our information pack.

Simon Crosby, Mercury Provident plc,
8 Orlingbury House, Lewes Road, Forest Row,
E. Sussex RH18 5AA. Tel: 934282 3739.

Raising Money

Finding your way through the fund-raising maze can be the hardest part of getting a new project off the ground. But a number of directories and guides now available may help speed the process.

Whether you are involved in adventure playgrounds or woodland management, probably the most helpful starting point for a quick course in fund-raising is *Raising Money for Environmental Improvement: A Guide for Voluntary Groups.* The brainchild of the Macclesfield Groundwork Trust, the 44-page guide is available free from the **Shell Better Britain Campaign.**

Among the sources of funding covered are local authorities, business and industry and charitable trusts. Among the industrial sources of small grants, for example, are the **Trusthouse Forte Community Chest** and the **Ford Conservation Awards**, the **WWF Kodak Conservation Awards** and the **National Westminster Bank's Project Respond.**

The **Countryside Commission** publishes such booklets as *Countryside Grants for Voluntary Organisations* and *Conservation Grants for Local Authorities, Public Bodies and Voluntary Organisations.* If, on the other hand, you are setting up a nature conservation project, grant aid may be available from the **Nature Conservancy Council.** The NCC is most likely to support site management, although it may also help fund key posts in voluntary organisations, on the understanding that they are moving, wherever possible, towards financial self-sufficiency.

A growing number of directories can also help identify potential funding sources. The 1987 edition of the *Directory of Grant-Making Trusts*, for example, contained details on the location, objectives, policies and resources of over 2,450 grant-making bodies, with a

total income of over £638 million. The price, however, is high: £40 from the **Charities Aid Foundation.**

Cheaper, at £12.50, is *A Guide to Grant-Making Trusts*, available from **The Directory of Social Change.** Also available from the DoSC are: *A Guide to Company Giving* (£12.50), *Raising Money from Trusts* (£2.95), *Raising Money from Industry* (£2.95), *Industrial Sponsorship and Joint Promotions* (£2.95) and *Raising Money from Government* (£4.50).

The **National Council for Voluntary Organisations** also publishes a number of useful books, including *Government Grants*, priced at £3.95, and others covering grants from the EEC. The legal situation is different in Scotland, where the **Scottish Council for Community and Voluntary Organisations** provides advice and has published *Funds for Your Project: A Practical Guide for Community Groups and Voluntary Organisations*, priced at £2.00.

For the environmental entrepreneur thinking of setting up a small business, a number of publications may provide useful guidance. A good, independent first-stop information source is **Business in the Community,** which has reviewed the problems of raising loan capital and equity support for small businesses.

A helpful overview of the comparative benefits and costs of the different types of finance available is *Money for Business*, prepared by the **Bank of England** and the **City Communications Centre.** Copies are available, price £3.00, from the Bulletin Group at the Bank of England.

Bank financing remains the mainstay of small businesses, but there are other options, including local enterprise boards and the venture capital industry. A helpful guide here is *Sources of Venture and Development Capital in the United Kingdom*, published by **Stoy Hayward.** The **British Venture Capital Association** can provide information on the role of venture capital. Its European counterpart is the **European Venture Capital Association.**

And, by no means finally, anyone wanting to learn more about ethical investment should track down a copy of another Directory of Social Change publication, *Socially Responsible Investment*, priced at £5.95 and described as 'a guide for those concerned with the ethical and social implications of their investments' since a number of ethical investment funds are on the look-out for worthwhile projects in which to invest (page 186), however, they are worth tackling long before you start on the venture capital industry proper.

The EEC has declared 1987 as European Year of the Environment

THE EUROPEAN ENVIRONMENTAL YEARBOOK 1987

This "encyclopaedic volume" brings together for the first time in European history a subject by subject classification and survey of the legal and administrative environmental structures operating in EEC member states together with the very latest accounts of current policies and research in those fields.

Topics covered:
Agriculture & Rural Land
Cartography
Coasts
Cultural Heritage
Education
E.E.C.: Policy and Implementation
Energy
Environmental Impact Assessment
Fauna and Flora
Forestry
Information
Land Reclamation
Leisure Planning and Recreation
Mines and Quarries
Organizational Structure
Parks and Nature Reserves
Pollution: Air
Pollution: Noise
Pollution: Waste
Pollution: Water
Sea Protection
Town and Country Planning
Toxic and Hazardous Substances
Urban Renewal
Water Supply and River Management

Documentation:
Legislation on each Country's Topics
E.E.C. Legislation
International Agreements
International Charters and Declarations
Bibliographical References
International Organizations
Special Reports of Luxembourg and USA

Please send me ....copy/ies of the **European Environmental Yearbook 1987** to the following address. Price £45.

Name..

Job title/company..

Address...

....Postcode...........

☐ Please find enclosed my cheque/money order for ....
   payable to DocTer International UK.

☐ Please debit my credit account:

☐ Access   ☐ Visa   ☐ Diners   ☐ American Express

Account No........................Signature........................Expiring date...................

Send to: DocTer International UK, 27 Kensington Court, London W8, UK Phone 01-937 3660 Telex 895.3616 G

DocTer International UK Ltd
27 Kensington Court,
London W8, UK.
Tel: 01-937 3660
900 Pages   Price £45.00

SECTION 12

News and the World

The greening of the media and publishing industries has been one of the most extraordinary feats of modern environmentalism. But where do people get their information about the latest issues, problems and possible solutions?

'A picture,' it is often said, 'is worth a thousand words.' Whether still or moving, pictures can bring home the reality of complex issues in a way that the printed word cannot. Remember the first images of the Earth from space? Who now would dispute that they were worth millions of words? But, far from withering away, the Green Bookshelf (page 208) is expanding almost exponentially.

Indeed, as Harford Thomas points out on page 206, books have played a central role in igniting and sustaining the Environmental Revolution. According to Euromonitor's Book Report, Britons bought books to the value of £1.3 billion in 1986. Altogether there are something like 300,000 titles in print at any one time and 40,000 new titles each year. The Green Bookshelf is an attempt to help readers identify some of the key environmental titles from amongst these reams of print.

The overall conclusion must be that the printed word, whether in the form of books, newspapers, magazines or computer print-outs, remains a tremendously powerful medium for communicating environmental information. Before turning to look at the impact of TV and video, consider the role of the environmental correspondent in the newspaper industry.

Behind the headlines

Many people say they want to read more about environmental issues in their newspapers). Even today, however, a relatively small proportion of the literally hundreds of British newspapers have their own full-time environment correspondents, although many of the national dailies and several of the Sunday papers do. Geoffrey Lean of The Observer has probably had the most impact in recent years, but The Guardian has also devoted column-miles to environmental issues (including over 10 years of the pioneering 'Alternatives' column written by Harford Thomas and the weekly 'Futures' page) and most of the other dailies now regularly feature environmental stories.

Other *Green Pages* contributors who have made a career of environmental journalism include Brian Jackman of *The Sunday Times* (page 172) and Jon Tinker (page 204), for many years a highly effective environment correspondent at *New Scientist* and now president of the Panos Institute. And the field continues to attract new recruits, like Charles Clover of the *Daily Telegraph* (page 200). Some of these writers, like Brian Jackman, Richard North of *The Independent* and Catherine Caufield, another erstwhile *New Scientist* environment correspondent, have gone on to write important books. Catherine Caufield, for example, wrote the best-selling *In the Rainforest*.

Yet others, including Lloyd Timberlake (page 50), have increasingly straddled the great divide, writing highly original books but then turning up on radio or TV to get the message across to a wider audience. Among those who are happy in both camps are the two Davids, in this case Sir David Attenborough and Dr David Bellamy.

Both have been prolific authors, with David Bellamy's *Turning the Tide* appearing on the Green Bookshelf in 1987. But Sir David's books *Life on Earth* and *The Living Planet*, both of which were linked in with major 13-part TV series, are perhaps the most remarkable early examples of how TV can work in tandem with print. Both books have been extraordinary best-sellers in anyone's terms. *Life on Earth*, for example, had sold more than four million copies in all languages by mid-1987, two million of them in English.

A blip culture?

But, however well such books sell, they are unlikely to be the primary source of the general public's information on key environmental issues. We live in a world where the total amount of information potentially available to us is growing at an astounding rate. It is estimated, for example, that some 6,000 research articles are published around the world every day of the year, with the result that the amount of information available – on crude measures, at least – is doubling every five years.

So fast is the pace of development that it is said that a computer scientist's knowledge has a 'half life' of 2.7 years. Many areas of environmental science are moving quite as fast, with computers playing a key role in opening up new areas of research (page 94). As a result, anyone who needs to keep abreast of the latest environmental developments faces something of a problem.

We live, according to the Henley Centre, in a 'blip culture', the culture of the information age. As a result, the Centre believes, 'the old certainties and orders give way to an incoherent flood of new ideas and opinions. We are living in a post-literary society in which colours, symbols, pictures and images say as much (if not more) to the customer as numbers and words. All this reflects a long-term movement away from literary media towards a more visual form of information; we can absorb images very quickly.' Hence the power of the TV camera.

Environment on camera

So how fast are the non-print media taking up the environmental theme? The answer, as anyone who listens to the radio or watches television regularly will confirm, is that the greening of the radio, TV and video industries is also well under way.

Interestingly, the European Centre for Environmental Communication (ECEC) carried out a survey of European TV stations in 1986, in collaboration with the Commission of the European Communities. It confirmed that news on environmental issues is very strongly established in Northern Europe, but remains weak in Southern Europe (France, Spain, Portugal, Italy and Greece).

There are few specifically environmental programmes in Europe, with much of the coverage linked to events (such as Chernobyl) and handled within the scope of 'news and current affairs', even in those companies which do have a regular programme. Among the regular programmes identified by the ECEC survey were the following:

- The United Kingdom is particularly well-served, both in quantity and quality. Obvious examples include Central Television's 'Eco' series, produced by Vivica Parsons. Adopting a monthly format, running for 30 minutes and, transmitted on ITV or Channel 4, it has reached an estimated 2 million homes. 'Worldwise' Reports, from Acacia Productions, also went out on Channel 4. Programmes like 'Horizon' (BBC) and 'World in Action' (Granada TV) also regularly cover environmental issues.

There are also a number of quiz programmes, a range of special interest broadcasts such as live birdwatching and a plethora of high quality series. Among the more innovative programmes was 'The Longest Running Show on Earth', the culmination of the Worldwise Reports season of programmes, screened on Channel 4 in 1985. 'We aimed to entertain the Bank Holiday audience,' explained producer Paul Smith, of Celador Productions, 'and rescue a bit of Britain at the same time.' The show provided a live link between conservation projects around the country.

- Belgium also reported several regular programmes, including 'Autant Savoir', a prime time weekly magazine programme produced by Jacques Vierendeels and screened by RTBF, and 'Leven en Laten Leven', a weekly, 60-minute BRT programme reaching 1 million homes on Saturday afternoons.

- West Germany's main prime time programme was 'Globus', running for 45 minutes and reaching 1 million homes. Screened by Bayerischer Rundfunk (BRF) and Westdeutscher Rundfunk (RDF), the programme was produced by Dieter Kuhr of BRF and Alfred Thorwarth and Dieter Kaiser of WDR.
- Italy's main entrant was 'TG2 Ambiente', a weekly, 5-minute programme by RAI Channel 2.

Goodbye to disasters?

The Ecovision bi-annual events have shown what a vast array of TV material is now available (page 214). Ecovision will be back in 1989, with Wildscreen, the World Wildlife Film and Television Festival, scheduled to be held in Bristol in October 1988.

Despite the screening of films with such titles as 'Chernobyl Autumn' and 'Cubatao – The Valley of Death' at Ecovision 87, the ECEC survey had concluded that 'disaster' themes have gradually been abandoned in Northern Europe and replaced either by research and warning programmes put together by investigative journalists, or by televised debates. 'A chain reaction appears to have been established,' ECEC reported. 'Good programmes achieve high viewing figures and this in itself generates a high and varied output.'

In Southern Europe, meanwhile, environmental coverage is much thinner on the ground. The survey showed that the relevant programmes were generally relegated to off-peak viewing times, with the focus still primarily on disasters.

Although the TV companies contacted in the ECEC survey were not enthusiastic about being sent regular programme material by the Commission of the European Communities (64% said 'no thank you'), they were almost unanimous that the media response to cross-border pollution problems should be cross-border news programmes.

The acid test

One illustration of how a European market for environmental films is beginning to emerge was 'The Acid Test', produced by three European companies and broadcast by nine. This joint venture helped get the message about acid rain (thought to be affecting six million hectares of forest in 19 countries) across to at least 20 million people in Belgium, Denmark, Eire, the Netherlands, Italy, Norway, Sweden, Spain and the United Kingdom.

Another programme, 'Energie et Environnement', was co-produced by six European companies and transmitted by about a dozen. 95% of the TV stations in

the ECEC survey expressed a willingness to participate in environmental co-productions. Documentaries are the preferred option (94% of mentions), followed by magazine programmes (46%) and news and educational films (both scoring 23%).

Battle for the Planet

On an international scale, recent super-productions have included 'Only One Earth' (produced by BBC Television and North South Productions, in conjunction with the International Institute for Environment and Development) and 'Battle for the Planet' (screened on Channel 4).

'Only One Earth', which was launched simultaneously with a BBC book of the same name by Lloyd Timberlake (page 50), focused on individuals actively involved in successful projects in the sustainable development field. These ranged from population control to projects designed to slow soil erosion.

'Battle for the Planet', produced by the International Broadcasting Trust (IBT), was a particularly interesting venture. Each of seven programmes was followed by a debate and audience participation, with viewers responding YES or NO to particular propositions by phone or by letter. The results were passed on to the World Commission on Environment and Development, before the Commission reported its conclusions (page 46) direct to the UN General Assembly in November 1987.

Once again, however, the TV programmes were closely tied in with the printed word. A newspaper, *The Planet*, was produced and a book, *Battle for the Planet*, was written by series editor Andre

Where to find the Green Media

Looking for a listing of key British environmental journalists and other media contacts? Try CoEnCo's *Directory of Environmental Journals & Media Contacts*, compiled by Tom Cairns. *Details* from the Council for Environmental Conservation (CoEnCo), London Ecology Centre, 80 York Way, London N1 9AG. Tel: 01 278 4736.

Green Publishers

Two publishing groups which produce considerable numbers of 'green' titles are **Gaia Books** and **Green Books**. They are very different operations.

Gaia Books, started by Joss and David Pearson in 1982, has published such block busters as *The Gaia Atlas of Planet Management*, which pulled in over 100 contributors and publishers from a number of different countries. Because Gaia is a packaging operation, the books come out under other publishers' imprints. Other titles have included: *Green Inheritance* by Anthony Huxley (Collins/Harvill, 1984), Lee Durrell's *State of the Ark: An Atlas of Conservation in Action* (Bodley Head, 1986) and *Ship in the Wilderness* by Jim Snyder and Keith Shackleton (Dent, 1986).

Green Books, on the other hand, was founded by Satish Kumar of the Schumacher Society, and is supported by Friends of the Earth, the Council for the Protection of Rural England, the International Institute for Environment and Development and other environmental organisations. The first three books published by Green Books were: *New Renaissance*, by Maurice Ash; *People and Planet*, an anthology of speeches delivered by the winners of the Right Livelihood Award, popularly known as the 'Alternative Nobel Prizes'; and *Breaking Through* (page 215). Recent titles have included: *The Countryside We Want*, the manifesto of Lord Melchett's 1999 Committee, and *Economics of the Imagination*, by Hazel Henderson.

MEDIA & PUBLISHING

Singer and published by Pan Books and Channel 4, in association with IBT.

Keeping in touch

Clearly, keeping abreast of events in such a fast-paced field can prove extremely difficult. Apart from the newsletters and other publications published by IBT and the Television Trust for the Environment, whose activities are described on page 202, other sources of green films and videos include North South Productions and Concord Films and Videos.

As far as books are concerned, there is no foolproof way of keeping up with the evolution of the Green Bookshelf. Most of the publications listed on this page carry some reviews, as do many of the newsletters published by environmental organisations. *The Good Book Guide* is published bi-monthly and contains a 'Natural World' section, giving potted reviews of the latest titles. Another option is the *World of Nature* book club, run by W.H. Smith, which offers savings of at least 25% (and as much as 50%) on the publisher's listed price.

And what should you be buying? The *Green Pages* survey of environmental organisations came up with an interesting shortlist of 'key titles', headed by Marion Shoard's *This Land is Our Land* (Paladin, 1987). This and other titles in the Top 10 are given on page 217.

The Green Magazine

As far as newspapers, magazines and journals are concerned, the choice is almost endless. In addition to those mentioned in the main text, and the newsletters published by the various environmental lobbying organisations, periodicals which it might be worth getting a sample copy of are listed below in a (very partial) A-Z:

- *Ambio*, published by the Royal Swedish Academy of Sciences (Pergamon Press Ltd, Headington Hill Hall, Oxford OX3 0BW).
- *BBC Wildlife* (BBC Wildlife Subscription Department, PO Box 62, Tonbridge, Kent TN9 2TS).
- *Country Living* (National Magazine Company, 72 Broadwick Street, London W1V 2BP. Tel: 01 439 7144).
- *The Ecologist* (Worthyvale Manor Farm, Camelford, Cornwall PL32 9TT).
- The *ENDS Report* (Environmental Data Services Ltd, Unit 24, The Finsbury Business Centre, 40 Bowling Green Lane, London EC1R 0NE. Tel: 01 278 4745).
- *Environment Now*, launched late in 1987 by Holmes McDougall Ltd and the Conservation Foundation (Holmes McDougall Ltd, Ravenseft House, 302 St Vincent Street, Glasgow G2 5NL, Scotland. Tel: 041 221 7000).
- *The Environmentalist*, the journal of the Institution of Environmental Sciences (Science and Technology Letters, 12 Clarence Road, Kew, Surrey TW9 3NL). IES members get the journal free (Institution of Environmental Sciences, 14 Princes Gate, London, SW7 1PU).
- *The Environment Digest*, a monthly briefing on the latest developments in environmental affairs (Worthyvale Manor Farm, Camelford, Cornwall PL32 9TT).
- *European Environment Review* (Graham & Trotman Ltd, Sterling House, 66 Wilton Road, London SW1V 1DE. Tel: 01 821 1123).
- *Green Alliance Newsletter* (The Green Alliance, 60 Chandos Place, London WC2N 4HG. Tel: 01 836 0341).
- *Habitat* (CoEnCo, 80 York Way, London N1 9AG. Tel: 01 278 4736).
- *Industry and Environment*, published by the United Nations Environment Programme (UNEP Industry and Environment Office, Tour Mirabeau, 39-43 quai Andre Citroen, 75739 Paris Cedex, France. Tel: +33 (1) 45 78 33 33). The Office's activities are described on page 39.
- *Landscape*, launched in October 1987 by Marcus Binney (Domaine Publishing Ltd, Ransome's Dock, Parkgate Road, London SW11 4NP. Tel: 01 228 9099).
- *Mazingira* (Tycooly International Publishing Ltd, 6 Crofton Terrace, Dun Laoghaire, Co Dublin, Eire).
- *New Internationalist* (42 Hythe Bridge Street, Oxford OX1 2EP).
- *New Scientist* (New Science Publications, Holborn Publishing Group, 1-19 New Oxford Street, London WC1A 1NG. Tel: 01 829 7640).
- *Oryx*, published quarterly by the Fauna and Flora Preservation Society (c/o Zoological Society of London, Regent's Park, London NW1 4RY. Tel: 01 586 0872).
- *Panoscope*, published six times a year by the Panos Institute (page 204) and covering environment and development issues (8 Alfred Place, London WC1E 7EB. Tel: 01 631 1590).
- *Town & Country Planning* (Town & Country Planning Association, 17 Carlton House Terrace, London SW1Y 5AS. Tel: 01 930 8903).
- *World Magazine* (Hyde Park Publications Ltd, 27 Kensington Court, London W8. Tel: 01 937 3535).

PERSPECTIVES

Interesting, but is it News?

What makes a good environmental news story? *Charles Clover*, the *Daily Telegraph's* first environment correspondent spells out the difference between views and news.

'My first professional encounter with an environmentalist happened at a tender age and has marked me for life. It happened at the Reform club in 1982. As the youngest, and least used leader writer on the *Daily Telegraph* it had fallen to me to represent the editor at a dinner given by one Maurice Ash, former chairman of the Town and Country Planning Association, to introduce a small group of hacks from the broadsheet papers to his shadowy new organisation, the Green Alliance.

The Green Alliance is now rather better known. Many now know it to be a respectable charitable body dedicated to promoting discussion among opinion makers, opinion formers and the odd industrialist on the ragbag of issues infuriatingly lumped together as 'green'. Just then the Green Alliance was hardly known at all. Over pudding, a fellow scribe from the *Times* could bear the suspense no longer. The blunt commonsense questions, beloved of our trade, came tumbling out. What was the Green Alliance, who paid for it, what did it want, how could we help it, how could it help us? In short, was it going to provide the simple bread and butter of a journalist's job, a good story?

Answers came there plenty from Mr Ash, but few of us, with the exception of the sage Harford Thomas, could make head or tail of what he was saying. It had all to do with what he called 'changing the paradigm'. Only now, after some years of rubbing shoulders with environmentalists and six months of being a fully fledged environment correspondent (the *Telegraph's* first), have I a slightly better notion of what he was saying. He was talking about the concept of 'paradigm shift', a term coined by Thomas Kuhn. Some scientific discoveries are so important, like those of Copernicus or Einstein, that they change not only a small section of our view of the natural world but our whole intellectual 'paradigm'. That's what Maurice Ash thought had to happen, but the media were stuck in the same old paradigm. There was, he said, so little time. Was he ever pessimistic. Visions out of 'When the Wind Blows' seemed to trouble his mind. Conspiracy theories enmeshed him. Nuclear war threatened. Nuclear power stations leaked. Toxic wastes mounted up. Herb-rich meadows were cut down. It was all part of the same thing. We had to change our way of seeing altogether.

The eleventh hour?

I disagreed with Mr Ash then, and I disagree with him now. Not with his idealism, with which I side completely. But with the humble pressman's role of linguistic pioneer and front-line ideologue. That's not our job. 'Give us the facts', we implored, in Jack Moron-ish tones, 'the number of hedgerows ripped out, the location of the waste dumps which leak, the rivers which are polluted.' But Mr Ash was off again, on a tack about changing the whole language of debate, and about the philosophical difference between inductive and deductive reasoning. We were still asking the same old questions, he said, and, it was nearing the world's eleventh hour. We looked around confused. What *should* we be asking, we silently wondered.

I tell this story as an illustration of the almost deliberate incomprehension among diehard environmentalists of the media, and the media of them. There is, I believe, nothing whatsoever wrong with the same old questions. We environment correspondents (not 'environmental' correspondents, incidentally; we are reporters not environmentalists) cover *events* and on a daily paper that event must have happened that day. It must conform to Northcliffe's definition of news as being something that someone, somewhere, doesn't want to be known. To get on the front page it must be a story as important as a rise in unemployment, war in the Gulf, or a political scandal at home. That, I think, is as it should be.

To be fair to Mr Ash, there are times when one's colleagues fail to see the implications of a story and do not print it. But that appears to be changing. The British press has long had a poor record in giving space to some environmental matters. It looked on the safety aspects of nuclear power for many years with more equanimity than it does now. It has not questioned until the late 1970s the destructive power of subsidised agriculture. It took a long time to grasp acid rain. But in the past seven years Mr Ash's paradigm has been changing – through simple clear reporting of important events. International events like Chernobyl and Bhopal, and domestic political events like U-turns on building on the green belt and on the siting of low-level nuclear waste sites has given what the news media quite rightly thrives on, concrete examples.

Battle for space

Perhaps I flatter myself that I have become part of this change but as recently as the past year the environment has become an area of coverage on which the fatter newspapers feel obliged to compete. My counterparts at the *Guardian* and *Observer* now have Richard North on the *Independent* and myself on the *Telegraph* to put up with. We are beginning, even, to form a recognisable 'pack' at press conferences, like the industrial correspondents did in the industrially

MEDIA & PUBLISHING

stricken 1970s.

As far as coverage goes, the battle for space in the paper, post Chernobyl, has been won. Even, to a large extent, on the formerly cautious *Telegraph*. But we environment correspondents still have problems finding real 'events', and concrete examples to dramatise certain issues. We have not yet been able to find examples to show, or research to demonstrate, why huge impending, and continuing issues like industrial waste, the destruction of rain forests, and, bigger still, the greenhouse effect, matter, if indeed they do, to the housewife or house husband in Ongar. The true acid test of any story.

Very often we need those examples providing for us; like Friends of the Earth's brilliant use of the McDonalds carton to dramatise the dangers of chlorofluorocarbons to the ozone layer. (A little unfair, perhaps, since these make up a tiny proportion of the CFCs produced.) There is the challenge for responsible scientists and pressure groups. For us hacks the simple truth is that only a certain amount of research can be done with the daily pressure of three or so news stories a day and a feature hanging over your head. We depend on our sources.

And there lies the crux of the matter. We do depend on those who have an axe to grind to provide proper information and get it right. Friends of the Earth have grasped that it is not enough for them to say something, they have to find a respectable independent source to agree. Far too often some of the pressure groups rely on questionable science, rather than commissioning their own independent research or getting to know the appropriate independent scientist. Greenpeace, just now, are the worst offenders. I am not alone in being heartily sick of yet another press release from Greenpeace – e.g. a recent one on 'Acid rain and human health' – based on the findings of some unheard-of American scientist whose credentials are impossible to check out. Reporting scare stories unchecked just gets environmentalists, and environmental correspondents, a bad name.

So my contention is that old Maurice Ash's paradigm shift is coming about, slowly, for reasons not at all as esoteric as he would perhaps like. What used to be called Fleet Street now has its environment corps. We have our equivalents on radio and television. We are listening. We just wish, occasionally, we had a little better-grade information.

CHARLES CLOVER'S *father was a Suffolk farmer and his mother a foxhunting lifelong member of the Soil Association, which may explain how he became interested in countryside conflicts. He formerly had the important but meaningless title of assistant editor of the* Spectator. *Before coming to the Environment on the* Telegraph *he was a television critic and feature writer. He writes for* The Field, *the* Spectator *and* Country Life, *from time to time, whenever possible about fly fishing.*

THE DAILY TELEGRAPH, WEDNESDAY, OCTOBER 28,

Britain is 'still lagging behind' over acid rain

By Charles Clover, Environment Correspondent

BRITAIN is the largest producer of acid rain in Europe after the Soviet Union, and is doing less to tackle air pollution than its northern EEC neighbours, scientists were told yesterday.

Britain's air pollution exceeds that of East Germany, Poland and Czechoslovakia and is second only to the Soviet Union, according to Dr Graham Bennett of the Institute for European Environmental Policy.

...ain refused to pledge to do formally earlier this year.

Britain's case for not agreeing to the same standards of power station emissions is that made substantial reductions between 1970 and 1980, which are not taken into account the "30 per cent club"

PERSPECTIVES

Behind the News

Responding to new opportunities in visual technology – video, cable, video disc and satellites – the Television Trust for the Environment (TVE) acts as a bridge between environment and development organisations and the media. *Robert Lamb* reports.

ROBERT LAMB *is Director of the Television Trust for the Environment (TVE). With a background in television production (he has overseen the production of 25 television films) and environmental advocacy, he has been a science writer at Earthscan and an editorial and policy consultant to the United Nations Environment Programme. He has published three books on environmental subjects, numerous specialist articles and has had articles published in over 60 countries. From late 1987, TVE has had its own prime-time slot on Channel 4 and is on the look-out for new programme ideas from environmental groups and TV producers.*

The Television Trust for the Environment, 46 Charlotte Street, London W1P 1LX. Tel: 01 637 4602.

'The Television Trust for the Environment has been in existence since April 1984. A co-operative venture between UNEP and Central TV, the Trust is intended to bring programme-makers and environment and development groups together to make and distribute a new generation of programmes which deal in depth with issues concerned with major world environmental perils, of which deforestation and desertification are prime examples.

The concept has worked well. *Seeds of Despair*, the first film in TVE's desertification series, became the starting point for the famine relief appeal, later going on to win EMMY and Peabody awards. The follow-up series, *Seeds of Hope*, was the first film to show what it was like to be on the receiving end of aid.

Major productions involving the BBC, Worldview International Foundation (WIF), the International Broadcasting Trust (IBT) and a range of other companies are in the pipeline. TVE does not become involved in any production unless it is guaranteed transmission on a major network. Far too much money is wasted by organisations on films that never reach the general public.

On the job training

TVE is contributing funds towards the very high cost of making these documentaries. In return we secure the rights to distribute the programmes in developing countries and to make versions for different target audiences. And where feasible, we insist on the involvement of Third World institutions and film-makers with the aim of building up programme-making expertise. We believe that the best kind of training is on-the-job training.

The *Decade of Destruction* series on the development of Amazonia exemplifies this approach. The films are a co-production between Central TV and Brazil's Independent University of Goiaz. In the course of making the films, Director Adrian Cowell has helped the University establish what is now one of the most professional camera teams in Brazil. The University adapted the programmes for showing on all the major Brazilian TV networks where they have played a major role in arousing public concern about destruction of Amazonia's forest and other resources. Oxfam and a range of organisations are now providing support to the University.

Although TVE continues to be involved in catalysing new programmes, promoting the distribu-

Mark Edwards, Panos Pictures

tion of outstanding films is an equal priority. While carrying out research for our film catalogue we discovered just how many good quality films are available. TV companies are also switching on to the environment – a series of major productions are in the making. But media fashions come and go. When producers move on to new issues, TVE will still be there promoting the best of these programmes and starting new productions.

Clearinghouse

What tends to happen is that relatively few programmes are seen outside Western countries – profits are marginal and few companies can be bothered to sell to Third World countries. And productions made by Third World or Eastern European film-makers are rarely seen outside the country of origin. It became clear that a major priority for the next few years should be to concentrate on identifying and then promoting the best of these films. Our objective is to establish a Clearinghouse which will concentrate on getting films seen on TV in developing nations and in schools, colleges and training institutions.

The Clearinghouse is our most ambitious undertaking. From the outset we have recognised that if the idea is to work we will have to involve the major broadcast and distribution companies, international environment and development organisations and potential donors. Together with WIF, Earthscan, the Canadian Film Institute and the National Film Board of Canada, we are carrying out a feasibility study for presentation to interested groups.

Despite some encouraging developments, public awareness of the threat to the biological foundations of the global economy – the forests, grasslands, croplands and seas – is insufficient. The public outcry over the television pictures of the famine-victims is testament to the power of television to influence a global audience. The challenge now is to use that influence to alert the public to the threat to our global environment – to use television to go behind the news stories to explain why the environment is being impoverished and what can be done about it.

PERSPECTIVES

How Panos Makes the Headlines

From AIDS to the Arctic, Panos aims to boost the coverage of key
environmental and development issues in the Third World press and media.
Jon Tinker reports on some of the programmes currently in hand.

'The Panos Institute, founded in 1986 by former staff members of Earthscan, aims to provide a communications link between North and South, government agencies and non-governmental organisations (NGOs), and the development community and commercial media in the closely linked fields of development and environment.

In May 1987, for example, Panos helped provide background material for the Nordic Conference on Environment and Development in Stockholm. We commissioned Third World journalists to produce 14 case studies on projects funded by Nordic governments. The case studies focused on the environmental and social impact of projects, representing a major new departure in Third World evaluation of donor activities.

Several Panos units produce regular printed material for Third World users. Panos Features, for example, is funded by the Norwegian government and provides articles, news stories and short information briefs to over 400 leading newspapers and magazines in nearly 100 countries.

Panoscope, a bi-monthly magazine, is sent to a network of over 2,000 non-governmental groups and 700 decision-makers. The articles are designed to be reproduced freely by local groups and by the media in Third World countries.

And Panos Pictures, the source of a number of photographs used in *Green Pages*, is a photolibrary specialising in development and environment – with over 10,000 black and white photos and 5,000 colour slides from more than 50 countries.

The focal seven

Given the scale of the task in this area, Panos focuses its efforts both in terms of geography and issues. Our Focal Country Programme (FCP), started five years ago at Earthscan, concentrates on seven Third World countries: Kenya, Zambia, Tanzania, Bangladesh, India, Sri Lanka and Indonesia. Funded by the aid agencies of Sweden, Norway, Finland, Denmark and the Netherlands, the programme is directed by Donatus de Silva. Amongst the key FCP activities are:
- media workshops for journalists and NGOs;
- feature co-syndication schemes in local languages;
- fellowships to journalists and NGO writers;
- provision of briefing materials for decision-makers; and
- the development of a radio-tape/script service.

Panoscope carries regular contributions from FCP correspondents. A similar overall approach is now being developed for the Sahelian region, focusing on the Gambia, Senegal, Mali, Burkina Faso, Niger, Sudan and Ethiopia.

Getting the message across

Two ongoing Panos programmes illustrate our basic approach as far as specific issues are concerned: AIDS and children in cities. The first covers the global impact of AIDS, the second the plight of children struggling for survival in the world's cities.

JON TINKER *is President of the Panos Institute, which he founded in 1986 together with the former staff of Earthscan – where he had been Director since its foundation in 1975. With a degree in zoology and philosophy from Cambridge, he worked on an oceanographic research ship as secretary to Bertrand Russell. He then worked for a PR firm before becoming press officer to the Council for Nature in 1963. There he started the newsletter* Habitat. *For four years he edited a schools wildlife magazine owned by* Punch *and then went freelance, becoming Britain's first specialist environment journalist in 1969. Until 1979 he wrote regularly for* New Scientist *on environment and development. He has been a member of the Royal Commission on Environmental Pollution and a Churchill Fellow.*

MEDIA & PUBLISHING

Mark Edwards, Panos Pictures

The overwhelming majority of the 10 million people infected with AIDS worldwide live in the Third World. To help the Third World press and media come to grips with this modern scourge, Panos began its AIDS programme in September 1986. A couple of months later, we published the first accessible global overview of the AIDS pandemic and its impact in developing countries. This dossier of information led to major (often full page) articles in leading papers worldwide, including the *Bangkok Post, Zimbabwe Herald, Die Zeit,* Switzerland's *Berner Zeitung* and, in Britain, the *Independent*. Because of the pace of developments in this area, a second, revised edition was issued in February 1987 and an AIDS newsletter is in the pipeline.

But Panos does not simply rely on publications to get the message across. We organised a high-level consultative meeting on AIDS for bilateral and multilateral agency heads in Annecy, France, in March, 1987. We are also organising seminars on AIDS for decision-makers, the media and non-governmental organisations.

Meanwhile, millions of children – both in the Third World and in the North – sleep literally on the streets, rarely attend school and often work at illegal and dangerous jobs. With funding from Redd Barna (the Norwegian Save the Children), Panos is producing a popular book highlighting the lives of these children. Again, local case studies will be prepared by local journalists.

Electrification and the Arctic

Sometimes, too, Panos takes journalists from the North to the South, or vice versa, to alert them to the newsworthy trends which are not currently making the headlines. In July 1986 and April 1987, for example, we organised journalists' field trips to the Canadian Arctic to look at the impact of industrial development, hunting bans and other modern influences on the local people and their environment.

In the Third World, we are developing a programme which focuses on rural electrification. One of the largest single items in development assistance, rural electrification also figures very prominently in the rural investment programmes of many Third World governments. While its basic desirability is not in doubt, the paradox is that many projects achieve the reverse of what their promoters intended. They can easily deepen rural inequality, squander scarce capital resources, and bring their promised and highly subsidised benefits to only a tiny – and already privileged – minority.

Funded by the Netherlands Foreign Ministry and the European Commission, the Panos rural electrification programme began in January 1987 and will run to mid-1989. Among the outputs will be two policy studies, a popular paperback book, two dossiers, a series of working papers, feature articles and an electrification section in Panos Pictures. Panos will commission a series of studies on rural energy needs from NGOs in the South.

Our aim is to build bridges of many sorts between the North and South. And, as the communication capabilities of Third World countries continue to expand, Panos will increasingly be expanding its remit from the printed word to embrace radio, TV and video. Editorially independent of its donors, Panos is currently supported by the governments of Denmark, Finland, the Netherlands, Norway, Sweden and the UK; by the European Commission, the Norwegian Red Cross, Redd Barna, the American Foundation for AIDS Research (AMFAR), the Beldon Fund, the Noyes Foundation, the Carnegie Corporation and the Beijer Institute.

PERSPECTIVES

In the Beginning was the Word

Far from killing the book, TV has given the printed word new life.
Harford Thomas pulls out some key titles from the Green Bookshelf.

'There have been fanciful notions that the new communications technology would make the printed book obsolete. The evidence suggests the opposite. In plotting the pace of change and in determining its direction, books have been providing the landmarks and sometimes the turning points.

The mass media of broadcasting and the press may seem to dominate, at least in terms of quantity, but they very rarely originate. This is not to minimise their power to disseminate ideas which have first appeared in print, usually in the form of books, but also in the pages of so-called learned journals, these as often as not being inaccessible to the uninitiated generalist reader.

The process of dissemination of new information and the establishment of new attitudes towards the environment has been perhaps the most notable instance of communications shaping the pace of change and its direction. The MORI poll (page 22) undertaken in March 1987 for Friends of the Earth and the World Wildlife Fund found that four out of five people believe 'the Government should give a much higher priority to protecting the environment'; and 85% thought the Government should fix maximum levels of pesticides and residues in food and drinking water. It does not follow that they had come to this conclusion from reading books, but . . .

Twenty-five years ago the American biologist Rachel Carson wrote a book called *Silent Spring*. It reported the disappearance of birdlife from the farmlands of the Middle West where seed grain was being treated with new poisonous chemicals. This, in fact, had been going on for some years, and in the UK too. It was known to naturalists. It took Rachel Carson's book to set the alarm bells ringing worldwide. Twenty years later the Pelican reprint fairly claims, 'No single book on our environment has done more to awaken and alarm the world than *Silent Spring*.'

Doomsday and after

In the 1960s and the early 1970s there were more alarm-sounding books. One was *The Population Bomb* by Anne and Paul Ehrlich, in 1969, examining the implications of population growth rates. This was followed in 1972 by the first report from the Club of Rome, called *Limits to Growth*. At that time few people and no government had stopped to consider that there were limits to economic growth, that doubling and re-doubling economic output and consumption of resources every 18 years, which was the effect of four per cent annual growth rate (then a common target for governments) must at some point become unsustainable. Ten years later governments had taken to referring to *sustainable* economic growth.

The Club of Rome series of reports in the 1970s was a significant development because it was the work of a group of people – industrialists, academics, international civil servants, and other specialists – who operated collectively in identifying the key issues, many of them ignored or neglected at that time.

The collective approach has come to be widely adopted, partly because environmental issues do not fall neatly into the official categories of government and academic structures. The United Nations Conference on the Human Environment in 1972 commissioned a report from Barbara Ward and René Dubos which had the assistance of 152 corresponding consultants in 58 countries. But it carried the unmistakable imprint of Barbara Ward, not least in its title: *Only One Earth: the Care and Maintenance of a Small Planet*.

Barbara Ward went on to write *The Home of Man* for the UN Habitat conference of 1976 and *Progress for a Small Planet* for the UN Environment Programme in 1979. In this trilogy she developed the technique of working with a team of assistants and consultants. Only in this way can the horizon-spanning range of environmental issues, and their interlocking interdependence, be sifted out and presented comprehensibly to the interested but inexpert reader. For this the book is the indispensable means of communication.

Team efforts

A number of independent organisations and publishers have taken up this technique. The Worldwatch Institute, in Washington, headed by Lester Brown (page 240), has published books on specific issues, a regular series of substantial short reports called *Worldwatch Papers,* and an annual *State of the World* report, together providing up-to-the-minute monitoring of environmental issues by an expert staff and team of consultants.

An annual *World Resources* report was launched in 1986 jointly by the World Resources Institute of Washington and the International Institute for Environment and Development in London. This combines in-depth reports sector by sector with a substantial annexe of international resource and environmental statistics. Again, this is a collective team effort written with the general reader as well as the expert in mind.

MEDIA & PUBLISHING

The collaborative team approach was also the method adopted by a small publisher in getting together more than fifty consultants and contributors to produce in 1985 *The Gaia Atlas of Planet Management*, which has been widely praised.

The collective approach has also been developed on a global scale by the International Union for Conservation of Nature and Natural Resources in its *World Conservation Strategy* in 1980 and its affiliated national Conservation and Development Programmes.

The *UK Conservation and Development Programme*, running to nearly 500 pages and published in 1983, is the work of seven panels, each with an author briefed to write a section report (on industry, the city, the countryside, marine and coastal, overseas environmental policy, environmental ethics, and education). It was accompanied by a shorter 100-page overview, *Resourceful Britain*. Some 1,500 people were consulted in this process. Collaboration went about as far as it was practicable to go, perhaps farther. The resulting report deserves to be better known.

Sane alternatives

In emphasising the collective efforts to bring about an awakening to environmental and ecological awareness together into a single book, one must not overlook the inspirational individual and sometimes highly personal writers who have changed people's thinking.

The most notable was surely E. F. Schumacher, whose *Small is Beautiful* of 1973 has gone into more than twenty editions and many translations. This, and his other collected writings, retain an extraordinary relevance, because in a world where the fastest and biggest still claim to be best, his message of human scale and fitness for purpose sets the conditions for the building of a sustainable society and, as he put it, for economics as if people matter. The concept of appropriate technology is now acknowledged worldwide.

In this brief survey I must omit literally dozens of scene-setting books which take up particular issues from new and illuminating points of view and suggest alternative options. Some of these envisage quite new life-styles, in smaller, more self-reliant communities, as in James Robertson's *The Sane Alternative* and, more recently, *Future Work*.

Primary sources

Popularisation of specialist research and information is going to be increasingly important. If an educated awareness of ecological and environmental factors is to be brought into political debate, the specialist must reach the ordinary reader – and the ordinary politician, official and executive, indeed, all the ordinary and under-informed decision makers.

Some writers have turned themselves into specialists in order to take on this task. I will mention only two. Norman Myers (page 190) has made himself an authority on tropical forests, and by digesting a mass of highly specialised research material on loss of species has been able to write books (*The Sinking Ark* and *The Primary Source*) which have helped to create world-wide concern about forest and species conservation.

In the debate over intensive farming in the UK, meanwhile, Marion Shoard has established herself as an expert authority and a dedicated campaigner with her books *The Theft of the Countryside* in 1980 and *This Land is Our Land* in 1987. She has helped to set new parameters for decision-making on land use.

Words and pictures

This emphasis on the role of the printed word in the form of books (to which could be added some

HARFORD THOMAS *must qualify as the doyen of environmental journalists in Britain. His interest in environmental issues was sparked by the controversy over the relief roads around Oxford, where he was Editor of the* Oxford Mail *in the 1950s. He joined* The Guardian *as assistant Editor in 1961, subsequently becoming Deputy Editor, Managing Editor and Financial Editor. He covered the 1972 UN Conference on the Human Environment, in Stockholm, and was the first British journalist to review the* Limits to Growth *study. In 1975, he initiated a column on* The Guardian's *Financial pages which evolved into 'Alternatives', one of the most consistently innovative columns in the British press. 'The gaps and absurdities in conventional economics have been a recurring theme,' he says, 'a subject on which I have been writing for far too long.'*

The Guardian, *119 Farringdon Road, London EC1R 3ER. Tel: 01 278 2332.*

periodicals) is not to under-estimate the power of the broadcast picture nor of the broadcast word. Undoubtedly television and radio have vastly increased public awareness and understanding of environmental issues. But that leaves open the question, which came first, the book or the broadcast?

The answer is that they now increasingly go together. First comes the idea, probably soon put into printed words. But if the ideas yield a visual block-buster attracting a mass audience counted in millions, that then demands a book. This serves to make up for the fact that the instant impact of television is fleeting, you cannot turn back the pages or check a point through the index. So you find that the master-presenters, such as David Attenborough or David Bellamy, operate both as writers and broadcasters.

This inter-action of disciplines is symptomatic of an increasingly rapid transition to an ecological paradigm of inter-connection and inter-action in our thinking and in our professional practice.

The Green Bookshelf

The flood tide of environmental publishing continues unabated. We review some of the titles published while we were compiling *Green Pages*.

Before turning to green fact, consider green fiction. Publishers can churn out serious tomes on the environmental prospect until they are blue in the face, but until they start commissioning and publishing readable works of fiction revolving around some of these great issues of our times they will almost certainly fail to hit most people where it counts. Fiction, in short, can reach parts of the human brain that endless scholarly tracts leave unaffected.

The fiction end of the Green Bookshelf, however, remains fairly sparsely populated. Few genuinely popular authors have taken up environmental themes. Arthur Hailey is one exception, in that he did wrap them into *Overload*, which looked at what might happen if California's power supply systems failed.

One of the most interesting novels of 1987, however, was George Turner's *The Sea and Summer*, which projects the reader into a future long after what he dubs our 'Greenhouse Culture' has collapsed. The rapid build-up of carbon dioxide in the planet's atmosphere has led to the melting of the polar ice-caps, flooding many great cities and leading to profound climatic changes.

Turner, one of Australia's leading novelists, says that the book 'is not offered as a dire warning.' But, he adds in a postscript, although we do not yet know how serious the 'greenhouse effect' is likely to be, 'we can be sure that enormous changes will take place in the next two or three generations, all of them caused by ourselves, and that we will not be ready for them. How can we be? We *talk* of leaving a better world to our children but in fact do little more than rub along with day-to-day problems and hope that the longer-range catastrophies will never happen. Sooner or later,' he concludes, 'some of them will.'

Two books published in 1986 illustrate the ways in which today's novels are exploring and illuminating the environmental prospect. The first, *Always Coming Home,* is the work of a woman who can perhaps be described as the doyenne of green fiction, Ursula Le Guin. And it is a hugely ambitious work, running to over 500 pages, with technical appendices, plus an optional full-length tape of music composed by Todd Barton.

The music purports to come from the Valley, set in what we currently think of as North California, home of a people who call themselves the Kesh. They live in a future long after our civilisation has collapsed, thanks to wars, super-pollution, earthquakes and other natural disasters. The book, it has to be said, is a difficult read, but repays the effort. The lifestyles depicted are an extrapolation of elements of North American Indian and West Coast alternative lifestyles, but technology also looms large – from dishwashers to supercomputers.

More immediately readable is *Nature's End,* by Whitley Strieber and James Kunetka. This book only takes us as far as the middle years of the 21st century, but it is far enough. We see the way that today's world, with Denver yuppies coughing slightly because of air pollution as they listen to Madonna sing 'Material Girl' on the new Sony compact disc players in their cars, leads to eventual super-pollution incidents which leave thousands dead.

Carbon dioxide build-up in the atmosphere begins to affect the world's climatic systems, creating 'blocking highs'. These sit for weeks over cities, suffocating them in their own emissions. A key character, Tom Sinclair, dies in the opening pages while trying to save Colorado super-smog victims. But the key interest in the plot comes from the attempts by Sinclair's journalist father and a group of unlikely allies to stall the Depopulationist movement, headed by an apparently saintly, Gandhi-like demagogue, Dr Gupta Singh. He is calling for the voluntary suicide of a third of the world's population. But Tom Sinclair's computer proves to contain encrypted information which could help Singh's opponents to stop the Depopulationists before their Manifesto becomes law.

The interesting thing about *Nature's End* is that it takes today's events, like the 'Great Fire of Borneo', and weaves them into a highly credible plot whose pace is such that you get through 400-odd pages in a matter of hours. The book, in short, takes today's world and extrapolates it into a future when many of us could still be alive, but when the world will be a distinctly less livable place.

Someone else who is adept at turning his experience in the European Commission into eco-thrillers is Stanley Johnson, whose latest offering, *The Commissioner,* follows a junior minister who becomes a champion for the environment in Brussels.

Disasters provide much of the grist to the publishing mill. Some are almost instantly transformed into both fiction and faction. Within a few months of the Chernobyl disaster, for example, the science editor of *Pravda* (the first journalist on the scene) had written a play, *Sarcophagus,* subsequently translated into English. It took rather longer for the mainstream books, including *Mayday at Chernobyl: One Year On, The Facts Revealed* by Henry Hamman and Stuart Parrott, to begin to appear.

Even the best-known serious environmental writers have recognised the power of fiction. It is interesting to note that Rachel Carson's *Silent Spring,* first published in 1962, and ranked second in the SustainAbility listing of most recommended environmental books (page 217), started with a fictional portrait of a town where all the wildlife had died from pesticide poisoning.

The Green Bookshelf still contains many well-established titles, including E. F. Schumacher's *Small is Beautiful* (which was published in 1973 but still ranks fifth in our 'Top 10'), Jonathon Porritt's *Seeing Green* (the most recommended title) and *Gaia: An Atlas of Planet Management,* put together by Norman Myers and Gaia Books, which ranked joint second.

Schumacher's continuing influence is clear in *The Living Economy: A New Economics in the Making,* edited by Paul Ekins. The book is based on the first two years' work by The Other Economic Summit (TOES).

For an even more heavyweight review of the state of the world and of the global environmental agenda, the key title is *Our Common Future,* the World Commission on Environment and Development's report. The World Commission was set up as an independent body in 1983 by the United Nations and took very wide soundings both on problems and possible solutions. The project was headed by Gro Harlem Brundtland, Prime Minister of Norway, who concluded that 'the deepening and widening environmental crisis presents a threat to national security – and even survival – that may be greater than well-armed, ill-disposed neighbours and unfriendly alliances.'

The state of the global environment is monitored and reported on regularly by a range of organisations. The most useful publications include the *State of the World* series produced by the Worldwatch Institute (page 240) and the *World Resources* series produced by the World Resources Institute and the International Institute for Environment and Development. The latter is subtitled 'An Assessment of the Resource Base that Supports the Global Economy'.

The United Nations Environment Programme collaborated with Butterworths to produce *The State of the Environment,* by Essam El-Hinnawi and Manzur Hashmi, published to coincide with the fifteenth anniversary of the 1972 UN Stockholm Conference on the Human Environment.

Many of the issues and trends highlighted in *Our Common Future* have been written up for a wider audience. Lloyd Timberlake, for example, wrote *Only One Earth: Living for the Future,* which looks at these global problems from the perspective of individuals, including a Buddhist monk and a Kenyan nomad. Like a growing number of major environmental books, *Only One Earth* was linked into a (BBC) television series of the same name (page 198).

Other books which have been published alongside television series include several blockbusters by Sir David Attenborough (*Life on Earth,* 1979, *The Living Planet,* and *The First Eden,* 1987). As a book, *Life on Earth* has sold over 4 million copies and *The Living Planet* (which was also linked in to a 13-part series) looks set to repeat this extraordinary achievement. Another prolific TV environmentalist is David Bellamy, whose latest book, *Turning the Tide,* was co-authored with Brendan Quayle and published in 1987 to accompany an ITV series.

Most environmental series concentrate on wildlife, like *Kingdom of the Ice Bear* by Hugh Miles and Mike Salisbury, although there has been a growing interest in the impact of people on the environment. John Seymour and Herbert Girardet, for example, produced *Far from Paradise: The Story of Man's Impact on the Environment.* Population growth remains the mainspring of environmental destruction and was the focus of a TV series and accompanying book, *Earth,* by Paul and Anne Ehrlich. And the Television Trust for the Environment (page 202) reviewed a total of 1,000 films on environment and development when compiling its critical film guide, *Switching on to the Environment.*

But, as Harford Thomas points out (page 206), television generally follows in the wake of the printed word. Marion Shoard, to take one example, may have appeared on television, but her book *The Theft of the Countryside*

(which scored highest overall in the *Green Pages* survey) came first. She has since gone on to write another hard-hitting book, *This Land is Our Land: The Struggle for Britain's Countryside*. The book was the basis of a Channel 4 documentary, *Power in the Land*, made by London Weekend Television and presented by Marion Shoard. The basic thrust of her argument is that the general public should not only enjoy greater access to the countryside, but should also have more say in what happens there.

Among other campaigning titles, one which has captured the headlines very effectively is *Beyond the Bars: The Zoo Dilemma*. Edited by 'Born Free' actress Virginia McKenna, her son Will Travers and Jonathan Wray, the book is a forthright indictment of the mistreatment of animals. It fiercely criticises zoos, arguing that the best approach is to conserve animals in their natural environment. This is a subject of some controversy even within the environmental movement itself, but the book has done a great deal to raise the public profile of Zoo Check, the campaigning charity run by Virginia McKenna and her husband, Bill Travers.

Anyone wanting to learn the ins and outs of campaigning, meanwhile, should track down a copy of Des Wilson's *Citizen Action* and of his earlier book, *Pressure: The A to Z of Campaigning in Britain*. His political experience is very considerable, while his success with the CLEAR campaign for unleaded petrol demonstrates what can be achieved by a small number of determined people – if they choose the right subject, at the right time and pursue it in the right way.

There are many other titles which argue forcibly for conservation, including David Day's *Whale Wars* (1987) and, a spectacularly illustrated book, *Save the Birds*. For each of these popularly written books, there are more scientific titles covering the same subject. Whale conservation, for ex-

MEDIA & PUBLISHING

ample, is covered in *Conservation and Management of Whales,* by Radway Allen.

Put together by Anthony Diamond, Rudolf Schreiber, Sir David Attenborough and Ian Prestt, *Save the Birds* includes over 600 colour illustrations and helps explain why such a high proportion of 'green tourists' spend their leisure hours bird-watching. The same can be said of Sir Peter Scott's *Observations of Wildlife,* which is written around many of Sir Peter's glorious paintings and drawings of wildfowl, whales and other animals.

The extraordinary advances in colour printing have done wonders for environmental publishing, as the various books produced by Reader's Digest demonstrate. Among their richly illustrated offerings in this area are *The Reader's Digest Family Guide to Nature* and *The Reader's Digest Book of the Great Barrier Reef.* Books like these, and the *AA Book of the British Countryside,* help carry the conservation message to a readership it would not otherwise reach.

Marcel Proust said that the true journey would not be to pass through a thousand different landscapes with the same pair of eyes, but to see the same landscape through a thousand different pairs of eyes. Nowhere is this more true than in environmental publishing. One of the great fascinations is to see a landscape through a different pair of eyes. To see the Arctic landscape, for example, through the lens of Barry Lopez's extraordinary *Arctic Dreams: Imagination and Desire in a Northern Landscape.* Lopez views that world through the eyes of marine ecologists, eskimos, oil industry rough-necks and landscape painters.

Alternatively, journey through Antarctica with Jim Snyder and Keith Shackleton aboard the *Linblad Explorer* (page 167) in *Ship in the Wilderness.* Explore New Guinea with Benedict Allen in *Into the Crocodile Nest,* on his quest to find out how remote

peoples live in harmony with nature. In South America, it almost cost him his life. In New Guinea, he underwent the extremely painful initiation rites of the Sepik tribe. An intimate study of a culture at the crossroads.

Recall the roots of Brazil's current environmental problems with *Amazon Frontier: The Defeat of the Brazilian Indians*. Or see the

natural world through Japanese eyes, courtesy of *In the Shadow of Fujisan: Japan and its Wildlife*, another book linked to a BBC series. The Japanese draw much of their inspiration from natural landscapes, yet are doing at least as much to destroy their landscapes as any other nation. They are also having a much wider impact on the global environment. Japanese taste for whalemeat, for example, has been one of the main pressures behind continued whaling.

Other books which take the reader deep into the heart of threatened landscapes are *Wetland: Life in the Somerset Levels*, written by Adam Nicholson and powerfully illustrated with Patrick Sutherland's black-and-white photographs; Gareth Huw Davies' *England's Glory: A Photographic Journey through England's Threatened Landscapes*, with images by outstanding photographers from Terence Donovan to Koo Stark; and *Wild in London*, by David Goode (page 164). Goode's book is particularly interesting because it shows how wildlife can flourish even in the heart of cities.

A different sort of perspective is afforded by those with a long history of working in conservation. Try *The New Environmental Age* by Max Nicholson (page 162) or *The Bird of Time* by Norman Moore. Bill Adams, one-time editor of *Ecos*, may be a great deal younger, but he also has much to offer in *Nature's Place: Conservation Sites and Countryside Change*.

'One thing is certain,' Adams concludes, and that is 'that the prime need is for continued public pressure to back conservation and its statutory and voluntary agencies. The message of the past is clear: if the spirit is willing much can be achieved, even if for the moment the flesh and the legislation remain grievously weak.'

We are now well served with books on policy and legislation in the European Community. *EEC Environmental Policy and Britain*, written by Nigel Haigh (page

26), is essential reading for anyone wanting to know how environmental legislation is developed and implemented. David Hughes' *Environmental Law* is another useful – if somewhat dry – title in this field. And the *DocTer European Environmental Yearbook 1987* devotes over 800 pages to surveying policy and practice in the various EEC member states. At £45, however, it may be more directed at the institutional market than at individuals.

Anyone interested in London's smogs and the subsequent agitation for clean air legislation ought to track down a copy of *The Big Smoke,* by Peter Brimblecombe. Unfortunately, the technological solutions adopted in the wake of that legislation led directly to the acid rain problems which are now the subject of such controversy in Europe.

As far as environmental education is concerned, there have been major advances. An example of the best of the new breed of text books is *Chemistry in Action,* which is aimed at those studying A-level chemistry. Unlike most text books, this tackles head on such issues as the risk of environmental disasters, the health impact of food additives and the contributions of industrial chemistry to environmental pollution.

A useful survey of environmental inputs to the new GCSE exam system (page 236) can be found in the Council for Environmental Education's *GCSE and Environmental Education,* by Meryl Beek. For younger children, the World Wildlife Fund has produced a number of excellent multi-media educational packs, including *Earthwatch 2086,* developed by WWF as part of its Global Environmental Education Programme with Richmond Publishing. *Earthwatch 2086* helps schoolchildren come to grips with some of the issues highlighted by the *World Conservation Strategy* and, more recently, *Our Common Future.*

For older readers, the National Trust has teamed up with *The Reader's Digest* to produce a series of beautifully illustrated *Nature Notebooks,* all published in 1986 and priced at £4.95 each. Titles in the series cover Butterflies; Garden and Woodland Birds; Ornamental Trees; River, Wet-

Ecovisions

Julia Hailes watched the cream of European environmental films at Ecovision '87. She also talked to Ecovision organiser, Alain Sagne, to bring some of the trends into focus.

'The power of environmental films is that they can reduce complex problems to striking images which engage with the sympathies of the viewer,' said Alain Sagne. A total of 350 films from 28 countries were entered for Ecovision 1987. Held in Birmingham this was the fourth Environmental Film Festival organised by the European Centre for Environmental Communication (ECEC).

The Festival highlighted a number of trends in environmental film making which were succinctly summed up by Jane Cousins-Mills, chairman of the panel of judges. 'The films that impressed us most,' she said, 'were those which proposed positive solutions to the problems confronting our endangered planet. In almost all cases, the best films we saw showed that the problem is lack of political will on the part of governments, coupled with a refusal on the part of many scientists and industrialists to accept responsibility for the negative consequences of progress.'

The range of films also underscored a number of important trends in environmental filmmaking. Most notably, there is a shift away from wildlife and nature programmes to in-depth coverage of the key environmental problems of today.

Of the 88 films shown, there were 26 on pollution and health; 21 on conservation and management of natural resources; 17 on urban environments and land use; 10 on energy and environment; 8 on environment and development; and 6 on agriculture and environment.

A significant 20% of the entries came from Eastern bloc countries, including the winner of the top television prize, the Grand Prix, went to *Heritage*, a Polish film directed by Ireneusz Engler. This was the story of a north eastern Polish family forced to leave their ancestors' land to make room for a nuclear plant. The film's theme, the conflict between nature and progress, was a leitmotif which ran through many of the films shown.

Many of the issues addressed were international in character, including the radiological fallout from Chernobyl, acid rain and pollution of shared seas like the Baltic, the North Sea and the Mediterranean. Several of the films focused on the ways in which European countries are responding, or not, to some of these problems. These films are helping to mobilise the public support needed to push forward the recommendations of the World Commission on Environment and Development in *Our Common Future* (page 209), published in 1987.

Meanwhile there is an interesting divide in environmental film coverage. The 'north south divide' which splits a number of major

land and Lowland Birds; Seaside and Moorland Birds; and Wild Animals. Each is a field guide, gazeteer and notebook rolled into one.

The ways in which business and industry have responded to the environmental pressures of the last couple of decades are discussed in *The Green Capitalists: In Search of Environmental Excellence,* by *Green Pages* editors John Elkington and Tom Burke. Despite the negative images conjured up by the horrors of Bhopal and Chernobyl, and the ecological devastation of the Rhine disaster, a growing number of companies recognise that environmental excellence is now a key ingredient in longer term commercial success.

The book, which is based on visits to several hundred companies and other industrial organisations in Europe, North America and Japan, also looks at the environmental implications and applications of such emerging technologies as biotechnology.

Other useful books in this area include, in the United States, *Rating America's Corporate Conscience* and, on the investment front in Britain, *Socially Responsible Investment,* published by the Directory of Social Change.

Ultimately, the consumer must be persuaded to play a bigger role in the transition to more sustainable forms of development. Whether we are buying aerosols or holidays in the sun, our consumer decisions can have a considerable cumulative impact on the environment. *The Green Consumer Guide,* compiled by John Elkington and Julia Hailes of SustainAbility, represents a step in this direction.

Earlier books on consumption patterns and the environment have included *The Real Cost,* by Richard North; the Friends of the Earth Handbook; *Blueprint for a Green Planet,* by John Seymour and Herbert Girardet; *Environmental Impacts of Consumption Patterns,* by Liisa Uusitalo; and Charles Secrett's *Good Wood Guide* (page 64).

For those seeking practical advice on how to get involved in local greening projects, Chris

MEDIA & PUBLISHING

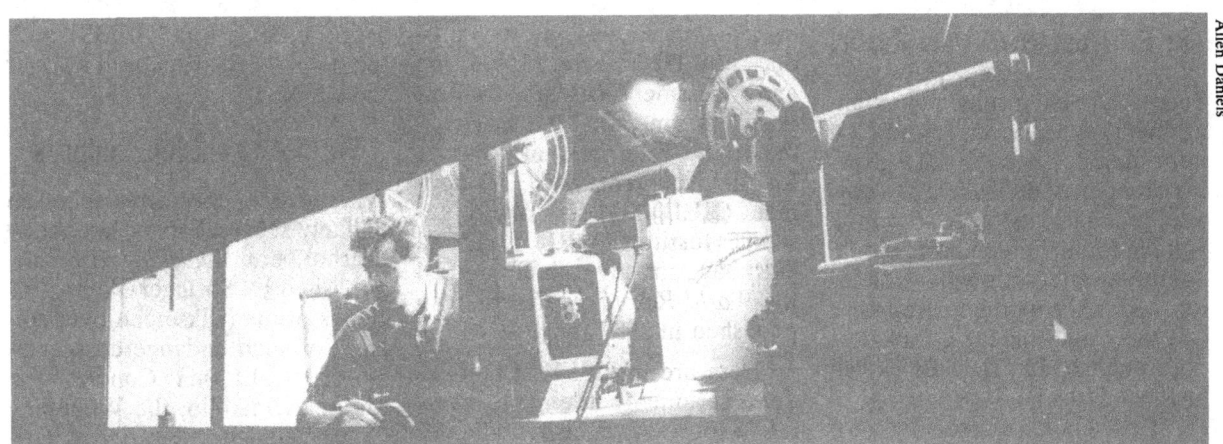

Reel power: Ecovision brings the issues into focus

European countries, and indeed the globe itself, also shows up in environmental film-making. The environmental media are most active north of a line drawn beneath the Benelux countries and, surprisingly, around the north of France.

Each country has a characteristic approach – Germany favours hard environmental problems like air, soil and water pollution, and the UK nature conservation and environment and development, whereas Spain, Portugal and Greece concentrate on wildlife and protection of marine species.

Although the UK apparently concentrates on the lighter and more entertaining side of environment, it has a long track record of high quality environmental film making and has won all the major awards in the past three festivals. This was one reason why the organising committee decided to stage the Festival in Birmingham during European Year of the Environment (EYE).

There is no automatic link between the productivity of a country's environmental film makers and the sensitivity of its government. The UK, for example, was the only EEC member state to refuse to join the '30% Club', set up to cut the emission of combustion gases which contribute to acid rain.

Strangely, France has had a fairly active political interest in environmental issues for some time which does not come across in their television scheduling. Alain Sagne found this mismatch difficult to explain. West Germany leads in that it is a hotbed of green politics and also produces many good environmental programmes. In Denmark, however, some people would argue that media coverage of such issues has reached saturation point.

Overall there is no question that there is growing demand for well made, topical and well researched environmental films with the next crop to be shown at Ecovision '89 to be held in Portugal. **'**

Baines is an excellent guide in *How to Make a Wildlife Garden* and *The Wild Side of Town*. And if all this leaves you desperate for addresses which you cannot find in the appropriate sections of *Green Pages,* try another Routledge & Kegan Paul title, Michael Barker's *Directory for the Environment*.

The growth of the green economy is providing new forms of employment, as James Robertson shows in *Future Work*. And new approaches are being developed, for example, to design (page 72). A book which shows how much we still have to learn from nature in this area is Robert Burton's *Egg: Nature's Miracle of Packaging*. From the tiny sculptured button of a butterfly egg to the perfect oval of a bird's egg, Burton explores the myriad ways in which new life is packaged and protected until the time comes to hatch.

One green growth sector which has been exploding in recent years is health food. Apart from Maurice Hanssen's *E for Additives*, whose first edition was published in 1984 and sold over half a million copies, useful titles include *Egon Ronay's Guide to Healthy Eating, Staying Vegetarian,* a guide to guesthouses and hotels for vegetarians, vegans and wholefooders, the *International Vegetarian Handbook* and Alan Gear's *New Organic Food Guide,* which lists over 600 suppliers of organically grown food in Britain and Ireland.

If you want to know what it is like to turn a farm organic, read *Rushall: The Story of an Organic Farm,* by Barry Wookey. More general guides to holistic living include *Breaking Through* and *The Green Alternative* by Peter Bunyard and Fern Morgan-Grenville. But, for something utterly different, try Russell Kyle's *A Feast in the Wild*. Kyle argues that one of the best ways to conserve rare animals is to eat them, encouraging rare breed farming and ranching ventures. The book ends with a number of recipes, ranging from wildebeest braised in beer to bisonburger with spiced sauce!

The Green Bookshelf conceals some unlikely delights.

The Environmental Data Report

Successful environmental management depends on up-to-date information, a need which a growing number of publishers are now attempting to satisfy. An essential volume for any green professional operating internationally – or interested in the world environment – is the Environmental Data Report, published by Basil Blackwell in 1987 (£19.95).

'This report summarises, in a single volume and in a way that has not been done before, the best environmental data that are currently available', says Dr Mostafa Tolba, executive director of the United Nations Environment Programme (UNEP), in the *Report's* introduction. The *Environmental Data Report* has been produced by UNEP, the Monitoring and Assessment Research Centre, the Department of the Environment, the International Institute for Environment and Development (IIED) and the World Resources Institute (WRI). IIED and WRI have already collaborated on the *World Resources Report*, also published in 1987 (page 209).

Data are included on population and human settlements, natural resources, energy, climate, pollution, natural disasters and accidents, health, transport, tourism and wastes. The data are presented in easy-to-read tables and two-colour figures. Currently in the pipeline: a series of environmental assessments prepared by UNEP's Global Environment Monitoring System (GEMS), with the help of scientists from all over the world.

Warhol's vanishing animals

Wildlife extinction may seem an unlikely subject for the late Andy Warhol, but *Vanishing Animals*, published by Springer-Verlag, includes prints (silkscreen over collage) of such endangered species as the California Condor, the Mouse Armadillo, the Whooping Crane and the Galapagos Tortoise.

The text is provided by Dr Kurt Benirschke, a leading pathologist and conservationist. Among other essential information, you learn how difficult it is to sex an endangered parrot – a vital activity in parrot breeding programmes. □

Books Reviewed

A Feast in the Wild, Russell Kyle, Kudu Publishing, 1987, £9.95

AA Book of the British Countryside, Hodder & Stoughton, 1984

Always Coming Home, Ursula Le Guin, Victor Gollancz, 1986, £10.95

Amazon Frontier: The Defeat of the Brazilian Indians, John Hemming, Macmillan, 1987, £19.95

Arctic Dreams: Imagination and Desire in a Northern Landscape, Barry Lopez, Macmillan, 1986, £14.95

Beyond the Bars: The Zoo Dilemma, Virginia McKenna, Will Travers and Jonathan Wray, Thorsons Publishing, 1987, £5.99

Bird of Time, The, Norman Moore, Cambridge University Press, 1987, £9.95

Blueprint for a Green Planet, John Seymour and Herbert Girardet, Dorling Kindersley, 1987

Breaking Through, Walter and Dorothy Schwarz, Green Books, 1987, £6.50

Chemistry in Action, Michael Freemantle, Macmillan

Citizen Action, Des Wilson, Longman, 1986, £3.95

Commissioner, The, Stanley Johnson, Century, £9.95

Common Ground, The: A Place for Nature in Britain's Future?, Richard Mabey, Hutchinson, 1980

Conservation and Management of Whales, K. Radway Allen, Butterworths, 1980

Directory for the Environment, Michael Barker, Routledge & Kegan Paul, £15.95

DocTer European Environmental Yearbook 1987, Achille Cutrera, Docter International UK, £45

E for Additives, Maurice Hanssen, Thorsons, 1987, £3.50

EEC Environmental Policy and Britain, Nigel Haigh, Longman, 1987

Earth, Anne and Paul Ehrlich, Methuen, £14.95

Earthwatch 2086, WWF-UK and Jordanhill College of Education in Glasgow, Richmond Publishing Group, 1986

Earthwatch Now, WWF-UK and The Centre for International Studies, Richmond Publishing Group, 1986

Egg: Nature's Miracle of Packaging, Robert Burton, Collins, 1987, £9.95

Egon Ronay's Guide to Healthy Eating, Alison Melvin, Automobile Association, 1987, £5.95

England's Glory: A Photographic Journey through England's Threatened Landscapes, Gareth Huw Davies, Weidenfeld & Nicholson, 1987, £14.95

Environmental Impacts of Consumption Patterns, Liisa Uusitalo, Gower, 1986

Environmental Law, David Hughes, Butterworths, 1986

Far from Paradise: The Story of Man's Impact on the Environment, John Seymour and Herbert Girardet, BBC, 1986, £9.50

First Eden, David Attenborough, Collins/BBC, 1987, £12.95

Friends of the Earth Handbook, Jonathon Porritt, Optima, 1987, £4.95

Future Work, James Robertson, Temple Smith/Gower, 1985

Gaia Atlas of Planet Management, The, Norman Myers, Pan Books, 1985, £7.95

GCSE and Environmental Education, Council for Environmental Education, 1985

Green Alternative, The, Peter Bunyard and Fern Morgan-Grenville, Methuen, 1987, £2.95

Green Capitalists, The: In Search of Environmental Excellence, John Elkington and Tom Burke, Victor Gollancz, 1987, £12.95

Green Consumer Guide, The, John Elkington and Julia Hailes, Victor Gollancz, 1988

Holding Your Ground: An Action Guide to Local Conservation, Angela King and Sue Clifford, Maurice Temple Smith, 1985, New Edition, Wildwood House, 1987

How to Make a Wildlife Garden, Chris Baines, Elm Tree, 1985, £6.95

In the Shadow of Fujisan: Japan and its Wildlife, Jo Stewart-Smith, Viking/Rainbird, 1987, £14.95

International Vegetarian Handbook, Vegetarian Society, 1987, £3.95

Into the Crocodile Nest, Benedict Allen, Macmillan, 1987, £12.95

MEDIA & PUBLISHING

The 'Top Ten' Environmental Books

Asked which environmental book they would recommend to a non-environmentalist, the respondents to the *Green Pages* survey came up with scores of different titles. But there was no dispute about the top three recommendations.

First came Jonathon Porritt's *Seeing Green*, followed by two titles in joint second place: *The Gaia Atlas of Planet Management*, edited by Norman Myers (page 190) and Marion Shoard's *The Theft of the Countryside*. When the 'most recommended' books were combined with 'other recommended' books, the following ranking emerged:

1. The *Theft of the Countryside*, Marion Shoard.
2. *Silent Spring*, Rachel Carson.
3. *Seeing Green*, Jonathon Porritt.
= *The Common Ground: A Place for Nature in Britain's Future?*, Richard Mabey.
5. *Small is Beautiful: Economics as if People Mattered*, E. F. Schumacher.
6. *Our Common Future*, World Commission on Environment and Development.
= *Only One Earth: The Care and Maintenance of a Small Planet*, Rene Dubos and Barbara Ward. (Note: *Only One Earth: Living for the Future*, an excellent book by Lloyd Timberlake was published in 1987.)
8. *The Gaia Atlas of Planet Management*, Norman Myers.
= *Holding Your Ground: An Action Guide to Local Conservation*, Angela King and Sue Clifford.
10. *The World Conservation Strategy*, International Union for the Conservation of Nature and Natural Resources (IUCN).

'Bubbling under', in eleventh position, was *Blueprint for a Green Planet*, by John Seymour and Herbert Girardet.

Life on Earth, David Attenborough, Collins/BBC, 1979. £14.95

Living Economy, The: A New Economics in the Making, Paul Ekins, Routledge & Kegan Paul, 1986, £8.95

Living Planet, The, David Attenborough, Collins/BBC, 1987, £8.95

Mayday at Chernobyl: One Year On, The Facts Revealed, Henry Hamman and Stuart Parrott, New English Library, 1987, £2.95

Nature Notebooks, Reader's Digest and National Trust, 1986 and 1987

Nature's End, Whitley Strieber and James Kunetka, Grafton Books, 1986, £10.95

Nature's Place: Conservation Sites and Countryside Change, Bill Adams, Allen & Unwin, 1986, £5.95

New Environmental Age, The, Max Nicholson, Cambridge University Press, 1987, £15.00

New Organic Food Guide, Alan Gear, J. M. Dent & Sons, 1987, £3.95

Observations of Wildlife, Sir Peter Scott, Phaidon Press, 1986, £7.95

Only One Earth: Living for the Future, Lloyd Timberlake, BBC/Earthscan, 1987, £6.95

Only One Earth: The Care and Maintenance of a Small Planet, Rene Dubos and Barbara Ward, Penguin Books, 1972

Our Common Future, World Commission on Environment and Development, Oxford University Press, 1987, £5.95

Overload, Arthur Hailey, Pan, 1980, £1.95

Pressure: the A to Z of Campaigning in Britain, Des Wilson, Heinemann, 1984, £4.95

Rating America's Corporate Conscience, Council on Economic Priorities (Washington DC, USA), Addison-Wesley, 1986, $14.95

Reader's Digest Book of the Great Barrier Reef, Hodder & Stoughton, 1984, reprinted in 1986

Reader's Digest Family Guide to Nature, Hodder & Stoughton, 1984, reprinted in 1986

Real Cost, The, Richard North, Chatto & Windus, 1986, £7.95

Rushall: the Story of an Organic Farm, Barry Wookey, Basil Blackwell, 1987

Sarcophagus, Penguin Books, 1987, £3.50

Save the Birds, Anthony Diamond, Rudolf Schreiber, Sir David Attenborough, Ian Prestt, Cambridge University Press, 1987, £17.50

Sea and Summer, The, George Turner, Faber, 1987, £10.95

Seeing Green, Jonathon Porritt, Blackwell, 1984, £3.95

Ship in the Wilderness, Jim Snyder and Keith Shackleton, J. M. Dent & Sons, 1986, £14.95

Silent Spring, Rachel Carson, Houghton Mifflin (USA) 1962; Pelican Books (UK) 1982

Small is Beautiful: Economics as if People Mattered, E. F. Schumacher, Blond & Briggs, 1973

Socially Responsible Investment, Sue Ward, Directory of Social Change, 1986, £5.95

State of the Environment, The, Essam El-Hinnawi and Manzur H. Hashmi, Butterworths, 1987

State of the World, Worldwatch Institute, 1987, $9.95

Staying Vegetarian, Lynne Alexander, Fontana/Collins, 1987, £3.95

Switching on to the Environment, Television Trust for the Environment, undated

The Big Smoke, Peter Brimblecombe, Methuen, £25

Theft of the Countryside, The, Marion Shoard, Maurice Temple Smith, 1980

This Land is Our Land: The Struggle for Britain's Countryside, Marion Shoard, Paladin Books, 1987, £5.95

Wetland: Life in the Somerset Levels, Adam Nicholson, Michael Joseph, 1986, £12.95

Whale Wars, David Day, Routledge & Kegan Paul, 1987, £10.95

Wild in London, David Goode, Michael Joseph, 1986, £8.95

Wild Side of Town, The, Chris Baines, Elm Tree, 1987, £6.95

World Conservation Strategy, International Union for the Conservation of Nature and Natural Resources (IUCN), 1980

World Resources, World Resources Institute and International Institute for Environment and Development, 1987, $16.95

SECTION 13

Acceptable Faces

There's nothing wrong with hiring Saatchi & Saatchi or Young & Rubicam to
clean up your image. But make sure you clean up your act first –
and don't expect miracles.

Most PR agencies would not rank environmental PR as a major business area, although there is increasing demand for top-flight services in this area as the 'environmental revolution' catches up with one sector of industry after another.

A company's image may not be an asset which shows up in its balance sheet, but sometimes it can be the most important asset the company has. Even though some environmentalists may see attempts by company X or Y to build a reputation for environmental excellence as little more than eyewash, once a company has such a reputation it is likely to want to protect it.

But can there really be such a thing as 'green' public relations? PR, you might say, is PR is PR. True, as far as it goes, but in the 'information age' the importance of communication skills can hardly be over-rated, and there is now a small – but increasingly effective – environmental sector of the communications industry which is helping a growing range of clients to understand and address the emerging green agenda.

First, though, a few words on the PR business proper. The PR profession is not universally popular. Outsiders often view public relations as little more than a corporate smokescreen, designed to cloak unacceptable practices and ensure business-as-usual. Company insiders, meanwhile, may see PR professionals as interlopers, or worse. In the United States, for example, there are those, including Marvin Olasky who used to work in Du Pont's public affairs department, who argue that the nature of the job means that public relations executives, caught between an ideology of openness and top-down commands to protect company secrets, generally end up 'speaking out of both sides of their mouths'.

Hard-liners such as Olasky have argued that PR has got out of hand. Companies should mind their own business and expect others to do the same, they say. Pressed by reporters or public interest groups, they argue, companies should be prepared to say: 'None of your business.' If companies once let their defences down, the argument runs, they have only themselves to blame for the inevitable result. 'The more corporations do,' Olasky stormed, 'the more they are asked to do. Indeed, once the corporate treasury comes to be seen as common grazing land, they can never do enough.'

End of argument? No, not if you look at the experience of those companies which have adopted a measured approach to PR. And the penalties of getting it wrong, of doing too little, too late, can be staggering.

The PR fallout

In 1976, for example, Switzerland's Hoffmann-La Roche was the world's largest pharmaceutical company. But that year an explosion at its subsidiary in Seveso, Italy, coated the surrounding area in 'snow-flakes' of dioxin. The controversy which ensued was intense and Hoffmann-La Roche was exposed to a great deal of highly unwelcome publicity. By 1987, following a series of subsequent mishaps, the company did not even rank among the top 15 drug firms.

Environment is no longer a 'no-win' issue for industry. Follow the '10 Steps to Environmental Excellence' on page 226 and green PR can pay real dividends. Although bridge-building between business and environmentalists can be expensive, frustrating and (occasionally) fruitless, it represents the vital next stage in the environmental debate.

No-one is saying that an effective PR strategy would have helped Hoffmann-La Roche to stay in that number one slot, nor that Union Carbide or Sandoz would have escaped censure if only they had handled their press conferences more professionally in the wake of the Bhopal or Rhine disasters. But even in the midst of the worst disaster, effective communications are essential, as part of a damage limitation strategy.

In the case of the Seveso disaster, the controversy reignited when 41 barrels of dioxin-contaminated waste, part of the fallout from the explosion at the Icmesa plant, disappeared without trace. Hoffmann-La Roche, it subsequently transpired, had consigned the barrels to Mannesmann, a West German company, for ultimate disposal. When it was realised that the barrels had not been incinerated, as was originally intended, the hunt was on in earnest. They eventually

PR & ADVERTISING

turned up in a disused abattoir in the village of Anguilcourt-le-Sart, in France. This second publicity disaster could so easily have been avoided, and no doubt Hoffmann-La Roche would now handle matters in a very different way.

Certainly, the climate in which industry operates in the major industrial nations has changed dramatically since 1976. 'Environmental groups, on balance, have dramatically more money and clout than they did in the early 1970s,' explained Harold J. Corbett, senior vice president at Monsanto. 'In fact, in many instances they can bring more resources to bear on specific issues than we can.'

Aiming to excel

PR professionals can play an important role both in helping industry to respond professionally to such growing pressures and by doing their best to ensure that avoidable disasters do not happen in the first place. To achieve these goals, traditional PR approaches will need to be revamped and success or failure will ultimately depend on the degree to which PR professionals and their clients follow the *10 Steps to Environmental Excellence* outlined on pages 226–227.

Even the most carefully considered PR strategy, however, will not solve industry's problems in this area on its own, a fact that many major companies now recognise. Take the case of Monsanto, an American multinational with a strong presence in

Sandoz drums up support for Europe's Greens.

Europe. It spends over $250 million a year on health protection and pollution control, and employs over 1,300 people full-time on safeguarding the environment, the company's workforce and the general public. In Europe alone, the equivalent time of some 90 people employed full-time is invested in developing and managing the company's environmental programmes.

Monsanto's Antwerp plant, in Belgium, has been spotlighted by a number of Greenpeace stunts, underscoring an inescapable trend in the European business environment. 'We have got to get used to managing our environment in the glare of some publicity and increasing freedom of information,' noted Carl Larsen, Monsanto's European director of environmental operations.

In today's world, in short, the pursuit of environmental excellence is no longer an option for industry. It is a pre-condition for staying in business. More and more, government agencies – and the public – want to know what industry is doing, what the implications are and what can be done to ensure that industry's operations are environmentally acceptable.

A key problem for industry, however, is that it often lacks credibility when responding to environmental challenges, whatever the facts of the matter. Too often, industry responds only when an issue has already surfaced, at which point conventional PR tactics are almost doomed to failure.

'It is vital that industry presents facts openly in a proactive and scientific manner,' commented Ken Baker, manager of science, technology and development at Monsanto Europe-Africa, 'rather than waiting until an issue reaches the media, when it becomes difficult to refute emotional statements. It's a difficult task to develop credibility, one you certainly can't achieve overnight, or even with a six month PR effort.'

Flannel soaked in gin?

So where does the PR professional fit into all this? To understand the potential contributions of PR to industry's pursuit of environmental excellence, it helps to know something about the way the PR industry itself has been changing in recent years.

PR professionals have been at some pains in recent years to counter the image that they are little more than purveyors of 'flannel soaked in gin,' as one industry executive put it. 'We are not paid high salaries to take people out to lunch,' said the head of PR at the National Farmers' Union. The real objective, he explained, involves 'managing the reputation of an organization, its products and services, and helping the organization to deserve its good reputation.'

For a start, and contrary to the general impression, British companies make considerable use of PR. Indeed, a report published last year by Shandwick, then the UK's leading quoted public relations consultancy, found that nearly 80% of the chief executives surveyed regularly used an external PR consultancy. Moreover, three out of every 10 companies also had an internal PR department. By contrast, only 15% of US companies surveyed had an internal PR department.

There has, in fact, been phenomenal growth in the European PR industry in recent years. By early 1987, the UK industry alone had a £100 million annual turnover and was growing at a rate of 20–30%. Industry was increasingly spending on PR programmes rather than on advertising – and growing numbers of PR agencies had been going public, with many of their share offerings on the stock market strikingly over-subscribed.

But there were those who saw dangers in this rush to market. 'Public-quoted consultancies tend to run their companies with one eye on the stock market and one on their client's business,' warned Mike Horton, chairman of the UK end of Burson-Marstseller, owned by a group headed by Young and Rubicam, the advertising agency hired to clean up the image of British Nuclear Fuels (page 134).

These pressures, Mike Horton noted, encourage many consultancies to 'react in a short-term and superficial way – and it is the superficiality of some PR activity that has given the industry a bad name in some quarters.' This is likely to be a particular impediment in the environmental field, where the issues are often unusually complex and the debate is constantly in flux as new evidence comes in.

Green masks?

Mainstream PR companies have not infrequently failed to protect their clients from environmental controversy. Ogilvy & Mather Public Relations, for example, landed what many considered the trickiest consultancy account in Britain in 1982.

Its client, NIREX, is the Government-appointed body responsible for finding sites for the disposal of nuclear waste. Around £250,000 was spent in 1985 alone and the fee income was considerable, but the investment of time, energy and money in persuading local communities, MPs and other interests that nuclear waste disposal was safe failed first in Billingham and, later, in four other rural sites around England – where the intention was to dump low-level nuclear waste. Then, in the run-up to the 1987 election, the Government abandoned the proposals.

NIREX had already spent £10 million on drilling and exploratory work, including £1.5 million on publicity, consultation and public relations, and estimated that a further £4 million would be needed for the winding up and reinstatement work.

In an effort to boost its public image and open out the debate, NIREX appointed three new directors to its board: Professor Sir Hans Kornberg of Christ's College, Cambridge; Ray Buckton, general secretary of the rail union ASLEF; and, most controversially,

PR & ADVERTISING

Angela Rippon, who had been Britain's first woman newsreader.

The reaction from the press was perhaps predictable. The *Sunday Times* wondered, tongue in cheek, whether the Government would follow up by appointing other celebrities to environmentally sensitive positions? 'Selina Scott,' it argued, 'must be a natural choice to investigate the sinking of the *Kowloon Bridge* off Ireland. True,' the correspondent continued, 'she has no great expertise in the design of super-tankers; but I am told she feels terribly strongly about pollution and on the whole would prefer ships not to sink.'

Angela Rippon presents a prize to Catherine Meaden for her project, 'Understanding Radioactivity'.

Such critics felt that Angela Rippon was being used to provide an acceptable face for unacceptable activities, just as film stars have long attached their names to advertisements for dubious products. It is difficult to imagine, however, that she would sell her soul for her director's fee of £4,500 a year. Indeed, she defined her natural constituency as the public and the environmental pressure groups, including Greenpeace and Friends of the Earth.

'I have no illusions,' she said at the time. 'It's going to be a very difficult job to do and I think that one of the biggest problems is going to be winning the confidence of the people I'm here to represent.' Such appointments can, in fact, work both ways. When NIREX chairman John Baker told his new directors that he thought they had been very brave to join up, Rippon replied: 'I think maybe it will turn out that NIREX has been very brave to have taken us on.' These are difficult, largely uncharted waters, but this trend does reflect the way in which environmentalism is now entering the political and economic mainstream.

Even more controversial, however, was the decision of two of Britain's leading environmental campaigners, Graham Searle and George Pritchard, to team up with companies which only a few months earlier they might have viewed as the enemy.

Searle, one of the founding fathers of Friends of the Earth in Britain, signed up as an environmental consultant with Rechem, one of the most sorely-troubled companies operating in the waste management field. Rechem's incineration plants had been the focus of a prolonged environmental battle, with pressure groups and local communities blaming the company's emissions for health problems in local cattle and for babies born with deformed eyes.

Having led major campaigns against such companies as Rio-Tinto Zinc and Schweppes, Searle now receives an annual fee for his part-time consultancy. More significantly, perhaps, he set a number of conditions. First, he insisted, information about the environmental performance of Rechem's plants should be made freely available to their critics and, second, he should be free to demand the closure of any plants that he felt were being operated in an unacceptable manner. But why did he join up? He explained that, having long campaigned against the dumping of toxic wastes in landfill sites, he had concluded that incineration was the best environmental option.

The news that George Pritchard, who had run rings around British Nuclear Fuels as Greenpeace's anti-nuclear campaigner, planned to help an entrepreneur to develop new ways of placing nuclear waste beneath the seabed, was an even greater surprise. While with Greenpeace, Pritchard had been utterly opposed to the disposal of nuclear waste either at sea or beneath the seabed. But, he said, he had changed his mind.

As long as such people take their principles with them, and there is no reason to believe that environmentalists with such extraordinary track records will turn their coats overnight, such appointments must be seen as a very positive development. If industry is to come to grips with the emerging environmental challenge, then it must not only talk to environmentalists, but increasingly needs to employ them too.

Nothing to hide

While no-one disputes the fact that industry can be both dangerous and environmentally problematic, public perceptions of the risks imposed by most major industries tend to be over-pessimistic. Part of the answer, many companies now believe, is to hold open days, when the public can visit industry and see with its own eyes what industry does – and how it does it.

This strategy has been employed by the nuclear industry with considerable success (page 134), and open day schemes were operated by many other industries around Europe as part of EYE. The British chemical industry had mounted a national open day in 1986, following discussions between the Chemical Industries Association (CIA) and its Dutch counterpart. Although there has been an extremely active environmental lobby in Holland for many years, open days held by Dutch chemical companies had not attracted hostile demonstrations. The aim, said Martin Trowbridge of the CIA, has been 'to put industry in perspective. The companies taking part in the open day programme are showing that we have nothing to hide.'

Although openness must be a guiding principle in effective corporate PR, however, companies should make sure that they immediately correct inaccurate or misleading stories in the media. 'We're aware that today's newspaper is tomorrow's fish wrapper,' explained Henry J. Kashka, director of public information at Eastman Kodak. 'But we don't turn the other cheek.' As an essential first step, such companies should call the reporter and straighten out the factual errors. If that fails to work, some take a stronger line.

Rechem, for example, sued the BBC over allegations made in the 'Newsnight' programme – and subsequently repeated four times on television and radio. The BBC claimed to have found a partially burned capacitor containing polychorinated biphenyls (PCBs) on a public waste tip in Wales. The context of the programme left viewers with the impression that it could only have come from the Rechem plant. The BBC apologised and paid estimated costs of £50,000.

If this seems a bit draconian, it is worth reflecting on the point that if industry wants to play an effective role in the environmental debate, it must do its utmost to ensure that the public believes that it always acts with integrity. An effective environmental communications package will be a key ingredient in the mix, but here again it is worth remembering that effective PR focusing on complex, highly charged issues has always involved a continuing process of confidence-building, not simply a one-off gala event designed to attract headline coverage.

Ultimately, money invested in building up a reputation for environmental excellence is likely to prove to have been well spent. 'Seven people in 10 among the general public says that "A company that has a good reputation would not sell poor products,"' noted Robert Worcester, chairman of MORI, the leading market and opinion research company (page 22). 'It is doubtful whether they are right,' he continued, 'but that is their perception, and it is perception with which you must deal.'

'Images', Worcester concluded, 'improve as slowly as glaciers move, but can be destroyed overnight'. As one observer put it, 'The building of a corporate image is like planting asparagus – you should have started three years ago.' □

British Nuclear Fuels Requests the Pleasure

They came, they saw – and many went away reassured
about BNF's efforts to clean up its Sellafield site.

'If I have one immediate objective,' said Christopher Harding introducing his first Annual Report as chairman of British Nuclear Fuels plc (page 134), 'it is for the Group to combine business success with public acceptability. Our primary concern over the next twelve months, and longer, must be to win back the confidence of the public in order that the issues of nuclear generated power can be debated openly, frankly and sensibly. The debate has to be in a language that everybody can understand.'

In 1986, an all-party committee of MPs had branded the company's Sellafield site, in Cumbria, as 'a byword for the dirty end of industry.' Employing over 16,000 people at five sites, the company had become a public limited company in 1984 and is perhaps best known for nuclear fuel reprocessing. New capital investment, particularly in effluent treatment and waste handling facilities, has made BNF's Sellafield site, in Cumbria, one of the largest construction sites in Europe.

The most immediate problem that BNF has faced is that Greenpeace has found a language that the public understands all too readily: direct action. Again and again, Greenpeace activists have returned to the company's effluent outfalls, identifying unusually radioactive slicks and attempting to block the effluent lines.

The interesting thing about the company's new chairman, meanwhile, has been the fact that he is something of a newcomer to the nuclear industry. Whatever one thinks of nuclear power or of nuclear fuel reprocessing, Christopher Harding's approach suggests lessons that many other companies could usefully study.

Recognising that 'the Chernobyl disaster has raised questions concerning the extent to which nuclear energy will be used for electricity generation in the future,' Harding stressed the need for much higher environmental standards. 'The public quite rightly expects us to meet the tightest safety and environmental standards,' he noted, 'even more stringent than in other industries. We accept that.'

On the technical side, BNF has pressed ahead with a programme of work designed to cut the Sellafield site's discharges of low level radioactive effluents into the Irish Sea. The commissioning of SIXEP – the Site Ion Exchange Effluent Plant – helped considerably, halving discharges. 'Nevertheless we will not stop there,' Harding stressed. 'Our aim must be to bring

PR & ADVERTISING

ARC: responsible communications

In America they have an Association for Responsible Communication (ARC). The idea is so simple and so important one wonders why it hasn't happened in Europe – or if it has, we haven't heard of it. ARC embraces people working in journalism, radio and television, film, video publishing, advertising, public relations and the entertainment business.

Tom Cooper, the man who founded ARC, is a Harvard professor and former assistant to Marshall McLuhan – who coined the term 'The Global Village'. In one project, 'The Entertainment Summit', Soviet and American film-makers got together to look at things like the negative stereotypes of each other's countries portrayed in popular films. What about something similar for environmental communications in Europe? Based in Denver, Colorado, ARC publishes a US newsletter and is developing European links.

them down to levels which are recognised as being as near zero as makes no difference. New plants which will achieve this have already been approved. They are due to come on stream in the early 1990s.'

That doesn't mean, of course, that Sellafield will no longer generate radioactive waste. It will. NIREX was set up to find a publicly acceptable final resting place for such wastes. But the key to BNF's new approach to PR has been a real willingness to talk to the public and other outsiders. 'We need to be completely open,' Harding told his staff. 'We have suffered from the charge that we are secretive. Of course we are not – but we must make greater efforts to show that we are not. We must actively demonstrate our commitment to this openness by getting people to come and visit us. When they do, we must ask them what they want to know. Then, within the constraints imposed by national security, we must explain thoughfully and patiently and certainly without condescension.'

BNF has supported the Nuclear Electricity Information Group, which has mounted a programme of national advertising, publications and other information material. Much more innovative, however, was the company's open invitation to Britain to come and see what it was doing. In 1986, for the first time, BNF advertised nationally on television, inviting the public to visit Sellafield and find out more about nuclear power in general and BNF in particular. The company, which aimed to spend £2.5 million on advertising and open days in 1987, laid on the Flying Scotsman, a brass band and even a birthday cake to encourage people to make 'a journey from the past into the future'.

'We want people to know they do not have to visit Sellafield in a radiation suit or with a geiger counter in their hands,' said Bob Philipps, BNF's senior press officer. 'If we reach 100,000 visitors, that would put Sellafield very high, say, on the list of stately home visits.' The idea came from research by Surrey University psychologists which showed that public attitudes to nuclear power were 'dramatically improved' by visits to nuclear industry sites.

In the month after the Chernobyl accident, the proportion of people who thought the nuclear programme should be shut down rose from 16% to 30%. But that same month the proportion who felt that BNF was good at protecting the public from radiation rose from 40% to 49% – and the proportion who thought that its performance was poor in this respect fell from 40% to 31%.

Unlike the average stately home, however, BNF has had to cope with environmentalists, including Greenpeace and CORE (Cumbrians Opposed to a Radioactive Environment), who have exploited the platform provided by the sightseeing visits to get their own message across. But that risk is one which BNF is prepared to take, given the considerable public response to its invitation. The new commitment to openness, it believes, has begun to pay off.

PERSPECTIVES

The Growth of Issues Advertising

Jackie Dickens describes how campaigners are learning to use the ultimate capitalist tool.

'The one thing that has changed the face of advertising most in the 1980s is the growth of issues advertising. Whilst the total spend on issues advertising is nowhere near that of the traditional brands and services areas, issues advertising is often highly visible, partly because it deals with matters of political or moral importance. Further, this visibility is often heightened by media comment, helping to make a little money go a long way.

So where is this growth coming from and why?

Government-sponsored advertising designed to shift public opinion in relation to issues such as smoking and drinking and driving is not new, but we have witnessed much growth in this area, with a reported total spend of 80 million plus in 1986, and further increases likely in 1987. The health education area received considerable funds, more recent campaign examples being those for drug abuse and AIDS, and one would anticipate further growth in this field.

More interestingly, we have seen the emergence of new faces in the issues advertising arena.

The TUC, which a few years ago might have eschewed advertising as an undesirable capitalist tool, produced a 'Guidelines on Advertising' booklet in 1986. The introduction said, 'we have to compete in the messages market with as much vigour and imagination as our competitors'. Pressure groups, charities, professional and industry bodies and local authorities have all increasingly been embracing professional marketing and advertising techniques.

100% annual growth

One might question why it has taken them all so long. Partly because we as a nation have been stubbornly slow to accord any respectability to selling, let alone advertising. The 'no hawkers or circulars' signs on the gates of middle class homes in my childhood are illustrative of earlier attitudes. In 1958 when the Conservative party admitted that it had employed the services of the advertising agency, Colman Prentis and Varley, the association of 'selling policies like soap suds' was made with scorn. How times have changed.

Companies' spend on corporate and issues advertising is estimated to have increased by an average 100% a year over the past five years, swelled by the highly visible take-over and merger campaigns. However most major companies now recognise that, with corporate take-overs proliferating in an aggressive fashion, the time to dig a well is before you need to draw the water. So we are seeing not just an increase in advertising to put over corporate policies and beliefs about specific issues, such as industrial disputes and prospective take-overs, but more consistent, long-term communication between companies and their shareholders, customers and the public.

Again, changing social attitudes are partly responsible. Society has grown less tolerant of secrecy and hypocrisy from those in authority. The increase in investigative journalism has meant that people in positions of power have had to become more accountable to those they represent. This has encouraged the belief amongst major corporations that being open about their activities will reduce their vulnerability in the longer term.

The fur flies

Is this increase in spending on issues advertising paying off? The key problem is that it is difficult to separate the advertising effects from those caused by broader media comment. So in many cases the answer has to be a don't know.

Yet one thing does seem fairly certain – that advertising can raise the saliency of an issue.

The 'Lynx' campaign, suggesting that women are 'dumb animals' if they wear furs, was initially laughed off by the trade, but the British Fur Trade Association retaliated with a campaign 'Be Fair about Fur' – a reaction to their belief that the issue has a high profile.

The growth of issues advertising is important, not just because there is more of it, but because such advertising has a potentially bigger role in shaping our attitudes. Whilst brand advertising is an invaluable marketing tool, which margarine ends up as brand leader in 1997 is less fundamentally important than what our nuclear energy policy will be.'

JACKIE DICKENS *began her career as a researcher in what was then the Social Survey Division of the Central Office of Information, later moving to the research department of Lintas Ltd., which became part of the newly formed Unilever research company, Research Bureau Ltd. In 1971 she re-joined RBL, firstly in the Technical Control and Development Division, later forming RBL's Qualitative Research Unit of which she was Operations Director. She joined Marplan as a Director in early 1978 and moved to Leo Burnett in October 1979, where she became an executive director heading up the planning function, and most recently Vice-Chairman.*

Leo Burnett Ltd., *48 St. Martin's Lane, London WC2N 4EJ. Tel: 01 836 2424.*

PR & ADVERTISING

PERSPECTIVES
Taking Green Into Account

Advertisers are increasingly interested in capturing green markets. Robin Sadler reviews some of the trends.

'Ten years ago the ethics of advertising agencies and environmental groups seemed diametrically opposed. Today they are sometimes synonymous, and sometimes co-existent in an uneasy truce. Understanding how green consumers are becoming, is now an inherent part of good marketing, and having a green pressure group as a client can have surprising advantages for an advertising agency's other clients, even it it can also raise a few problems.

The consumer trend that first made green concerns respectable (at least within the walls of this agency) was the growing interest in natural foods. Although some client and agency people for a while dismissed vegetarians and wholefood as 'cranky', the evidence of a developing trend was around for all to see in the 1970s – a growing interest in vegetarian diet among the young, and the success of wholefood stores and restaurants.

By using research techniques which identify future trends (e.g. 'Future Featuring') we showed that interest in additive free natural foods was likely to become widespread. *E for Additives* struck us immediately as a book destined to become a best seller. Slowly some of our food clients became concerned to offer more wholesome products. Further research showed us not only that vegetarian, additive free, and wholefood products would be popular, but also that pesticide-free frozen vegetables and hormone-free meat would have considerable appeal to some consumers, while the future might bring more concern about systems of land tenure or international trade. All these are factors which major food companies should be concerned about, if they are not to let smaller more flexible rivals nibble at their market share.

Inside information

Early in 1987 McCanns was appointed by Friends of the Earth as their advertising agency. The chance of working on this account brought many agency greens into the open, and there was a clamouring of creative people keen to work on the business. It not only gave the agency an opportunity to do great creative work – hadn't we all seen what Greenpeace had done for Yellowhammer? – it also gave the agency the chance to be more in touch with many vital environmental and consumer issues.

Friends of the Earth featured at once on our new client list at new business presentations, and as a 'Campaign of the Month'. Some of our other clients were puzzled, but none seemed put out. Better still, the inside knowledge we gained through our Friends of the Earth contacts suddenly became invaluable in helping us promote another client's product, Esso's Unleaded Petrol. Friends of the Earth were able to help with survey data which showed widespread public support for a reduction in pollution from cars, and also to provide us (and the ITCA who vet TV scripts) with the most comprehensive survey showing which car models could run on unleaded petrol, thereby helping us substantiate a claim that '40% of new cars since 1986' could run on it. The launch of Esso Unleaded was a success, bringing Esso a flood of congratulatory letters from a grateful public.

On the agenda

So green concerns are now on the agenda at McCanns, though not necessarily to everyone's universal approval. Nevertheless, whenever people meet to discuss a new project, product, or packaging, a green point of view is now an acceptable contribution to the debate. There will undoubtedly still be conflicts of interest in the future. No major agency with multi-national clients like Esso, Coca-Cola, Nestle, L'Oreal, and Unilever (as well as Friends of the Earth) is likely to get by without conflict. But perhaps McCanns is now better able to show a new green wisdom in resolving such future conflicts to the benefit of all concerned, and to the benefit of our fragile planet.'

ROBIN SADLER *is a partner in New Perspectives, a social and marketing research consultancy which also works on natural energy developments. He works part-time as an advertising planning consultant at McCann-Erickson Advertising Limited, a major international agency, where he plans and researches advertising for both Esso and Friends of the Earth. In the past he has worked for The British Market Research Bureau, Gillette, and General Foods in Canada.*

McCann-Erickson Advertising Ltd., *McCann-Erickson House, 36 Howland Street, London W1A 1AT. Tel: 01 580 6690.*

10 Steps to Environmental Excellence

Excellent companies are committed to people: their employees, their customers and those who are affected, in one way or another, by their operations. The difficulty they face in the environmental field, however, is in identifying everyone who is likely to be affected by their operations. Instead of concentrating on the area within the factory fence, or even on the communities living immediately around their manufacturing sites, such companies now recognise that their operations may have implications for people whom they may never meet, either because they are geographically remote or, in some cases, because they are not yet born.

But how should a given company set about achieving environmental excellence? There is no guaranteed route, but all of the ten steps outlined here have been followed by almost every one of the environmentally excellent companies mentioned elsewhere in *Green Pages*. As Sir Peter Parker has put it, 'there is an urgent need to simplify management ideas and action on this 360 degree challenge of the environment.' These ten steps are not the complete answer as far as environmental excellence is concerned, but they do represent a framework within which excellence can be pursued with real hope of success.

1

Develop and publish an environmental policy

The first step is to produce a company environmental policy. There is no standard format for such policies, with many of them being very short documents. But such a policy, adopted by the company's Board, effectively legitimises all the subsequent steps.

2

Prepare an action programme

A policy statement is a vital first step, but if it is to be implemented it needs to be spelled out in the form of a number of much more specific objectives for all company personnel, with guidelines on how these objectives should be met.

The purpose of an action programme is to determine where the immediate priorities for action lie and to ensure that the appropriate targets are clearly identified and the responsibilities for achieving them are given to people who have the power, initiative and resources to succeed in the task.

3

Organise and staff

Most excellent companies which operate in environmentally sensitive businesses ensure that the responsibility for the environmental agenda is vested in top management. For example, the responsibility for determining BP's policies on health, safety and environmental matters lies with the Board, advised by the Group Health, Safety and Environment Committee.

Any company aiming for environmental excellence will need to identify a 'champion' for health, safety and environment, typically a Main Board Director. He or she will need the advice and support of a sufficient number of appropriately trained people, with access to all of the company's operations. But the responsibility for ensuring that individual plants or processes are environmentally acceptable must be pushed down to individual line managers. Their suitability for higher positions in the company should be explicitly assessed, as is now the practice in a growing number of companies, on the basis of their success in meeting environmental targets.

4

Allocate adequate resources

If such environmental policies are to be translated into effective action, those responsible must be given adequate resources. As the 3M experience shows, such expenditure need not necessarily be a net drain on the company's resources. The key point, however, is that money spent in pursuit of environmental objectives should be subject to the same accounting procedures as the rest of a company's activities. Some of the benefits, particularly in the public relations and corporate image fields, may be hard to quantify, but the Board and shareholders must be assured that the environmental budget is professionally managed.

5

Invest in environmental science and technology

Sound environmental decision-making depends on the availability of sound scientific research. Industry must help ensure that the environmental debate is well-informed and that the necessary data-bases exist to ensure that pressing questions about potential environmental implications of particular decisions or activities can be assessed within a reasonable timescale.

New, environmentally acceptable technologies can be developed and deployed in an economically efficient manner if industry works closely with environmental interests and the regulatory agencies. The key objective must be to ensure that technology is designed from scratch to be cleaner, quieter or more energy-efficient, rather than having to be modified once in use.

6

Educate and train

People are much more likely to respond to company objectives and action plans if they know exactly what is expected of them and how they should respond. Company policy should be spelled out fully and effectively, while progress with the environmental action programme should be regularly reviewed and reported upon. The important thing is to get people launched on the path towards environmental excellence, even if the early steps are fairly small.

There is a considerable range of options in environmental education and training. Companies, for example, can decide to employ people with previous environmental education and training; they can ensure that managers, co-ordinators, scientists and technicians, operators and contractors are conversant with the company environmental policy, the related standards and the latest developments in this increasingly important area of corporate social responsibility; they can encourage staff to involve themselves in courses and programmes provided by others, including distance learning programmes; and they can encourage staff members to participate in local, regional or national environmental initiatives.

7

Monitor, audit and report

Once the appropriate management systems are in place, their performance should be assessed regularly. This will involve a number of separate activities. The state of the environment will need to be monitored, to check that the company's controls are effective. But there will also be a need to check on the extent to which impacts which were predicted in the initial environmental impact assessment work have been borne out in practice, to ensure that the base of environmental science on which the company's procedures have been erected is sound.

8

Monitor the evolution of the green agenda

The environmental agenda is constantly evolving. Any company which assumes that information it picked up two years ago, or even three months ago, is adequate may be in for an unpleasant surprise. As in any other area of business, the regular gathering and assessment of intelligence is the intelligent approach. Excellent companies also keep up to date on international developments which may influence the environmental agenda in other countries in which they operate.

9

Contribute to environmental programmes

There is a tremendous range of projects and programmes under way in the environmental field which need help from industry, whether it is in the form of money, help in kind or seconded staff. The return on voluntary, charitable contributions to conservation organisations can be very high indeed, provided the corporate sponsor selects a well-run charity or other organisation. Some companies, such as BP, are helping to train the staff of environmental charities and other non-governmental organisations in business management techniques. Internationally, too, industry should support programmes which make available environmental experts to countries which might not otherwise be able to afford them. Some of these experts should be drawn from industry itself.

10

Help build bridges between the various interests

One of the most critical needs in today's business environment is to build bridges between business, government and environmental interests. Any company which has worked its way through the previous nine steps will have found such bridges beginning to form naturally.

The key to environmental excellence is the recognition that such activities need not be a drain on the company's resources. Rather, they can help in training key personnel to operate effectively in today's world, in providing advance warning of impending pressures on core businesses, and in identifying the business opportunities of tomorrow.

Moreover, management must get across that it cares actively about the environment. This should be a positive process of listening and interpreting social and market trends, not merely of justifying what has been done. □

SECTION 14

A Job to Find

If you are an environmental scientist working in the government sector, your prospects may not be particularly bright – but other areas of the emerging green economy are booming as never before.

With unemployment still running at near-record levels in many parts of Europe, there has been intense interest in any area of the economy which seems to be creating jobs. Interestingly, the view today is that environmental protection is a job creator, not a job killer. Indeed, recent estimates suggest that between 1.5 and 2 million Europeans are now employed in the burgeoning environmental industry – supplying pollution control equipment, cleaner products and related services.

Demand for these products and services is growing rapidly, both in Europe and in international markets, with the result that the Commission of the European Communities expects to see a doubling in environmental jobs by the end of the century. But where will these new jobs be?

Green jobs

The answer will vary considerably by country. In Italy alone, a recent study estimated that over 18,000 additional trained personnel are needed to ensure that water pollution regulations are properly implemented there. And another 25,000 Italians are estimated to be needed in the toxic waste management sector. It is not at all certain that Italy will be prepared to pay for all these people, but the latent demand is certainly there – and the pressures for action are building (page 12).

In Britain, meanwhile, a study by the Labour Party, published just before the 1987 General Election, suggested that at least 200,000 new jobs could be created by vigorous investment in city greening projects, energy conservation, pollution control and environmental management programmes.

In another study, the Dartington Institute concluded that nature conservation, representing just one of many forms of environmental employment, provides some 15,000 full-time jobs in Britain. Even the voluntary sector is becoming a major employer: the Royal Society for the Protection of Birds, for example, employs some 300 people full-time, 50 part-time and 120 on a seasonal basis.

Is there a career path?

But such global figures mean very little to someone who is either looking for a first job or wanting to move from a different form of employment into the environment. Because this area has only become a major employer since the early 1970s, it is still difficult to point to a set of well-beaten career paths. Each of the many contributors to *Green Pages* – be they scientists, consultants, industrial advisors, lawyers, communicators, managers or investors – has followed a different route to his or her present position. Many, however, have been opening up totally new career paths (page 234), with their employers viewing them as something of an experiment.

Many also find it much easier to discern their 'career path' when looking back at the route they have travelled than when thinking about where that path might lead. But these people are living proof that if

---

With over 1.5 million Europeans employed in the green economy, and a doubling of that figure projected by the year 2000, the prospects for environmental employment have rarely been better. Building a 'green career', as Debbie Bruce points out (page 234), can be an extremely satisfying – and demanding – task.

---

you are sufficiently determined, and have suitable skills, a 'green' career path is not only now a real possibility but can be highly rewarding – particularly in terms of job satisfaction. Indeed, it is hard to think of many other areas of employment where people are so motivated.

The very fact that environmental organisations have been facing up to enormous challenges with relatively slim resources has made them a forcing ground for enterprising individuals. The Anita Roddicks of this world may capture the headlines (page 70), as they begin to develop mainstream businesses on green foundations, but they are simply the visible tip of a very substantial iceberg of environmental enterprise.

And perhaps that has been one of the key distinguishing features of those who have moved into this area to date. The very lack of an obvious career structure, at least outside such areas as the scientific civil service or the environmental health and planning professions, has exerted a form of natural selection: a very high proportion of those who have moved into environmental careers have done so because of a deep personal commitment to the environment.

Spoiled for choice

Since the green economy is not yet an obvious gold mine, it will continue to attract committed people. But, as other sections of *Green Pages* confirm, there is a profound social and economic transition under way in Europe. Hundreds of established organisations and thousands of new ones – including over 9,000 companies in the pollution control sector alone (page 108) – are helping to green Europe.

In fact, one problem facing anyone wanting to break into this area is the sheer range of options, from job creation programmes to mainstream career paths. There has been concern that some of the environmental job creation schemes launched by organisations such as the Manpower Services Commission are simply ways of getting young people 'filling in time, filling in holes'. But the MSC's regional offices have placed a very considerable number of young people (16 year old school-leavers, some 17 year olds and disabled schools leavers up to age 21) in various forms of environmental employment through the Youth Training Scheme. MSC teams, for example, have been a mainstay of many Groundwork projects (page 158). Details of the MSC schemes can be had from local jobcentres and careers offices.

The voluntary sector proper, meanwhile, is extraordinarily diverse and provides an important 'university of life' for growing numbers of young people. Indeed, it has been said that two years in the voluntary sector is worth three years of university. It should be noted that 'voluntary' in this case means non-government, rather than that volunteers are necessarily or exclusively used.

A fair number of people now working in mainstream environmental jobs started out in the voluntary sector. And for someone who wants to stay in the environmental field, volunteering can provide an opportunity to survey the career opportunities at closer quarters.

One interesting, and relatively recent, development which is enhancing the value of an environmental background has been the increasing use of training courses to build management expertise among those working in the voluntary conservation movement. Sponsored by BP and the Nature Conservancy Council, a series of training events have been offered covering 'The Business of Conservation'. The themes covered have included time and team management, negotiating skills and creating an effective organisation. Further details can be had from the Field Studies Council.

Volunteering

One of the most important things young people can do to enhance their employment prospects is to see more of the world and extend their horizons. Some may

CEDER
Consociation for Environmental, Development & Energy Research

In spring 1987, we began to create an international Green consultancy and research network of individuals and groups who share concern about economic and technological development.

Our services include project design, impact studies, resource evaluations, and a range of general advisory functions; CEDER study groups carry out their own research, and publish their findings.

If you would like to find out more about our work, and how you could be involved, please contact:

Tim Osborne
10/56 Griffin Close
Bristol Road South
Birmingham B31 2UZ
England

Dudley Stewart
148 Pearse Street
Dublin 2, Ireland

(Irish projects)

---

decide to take a green holiday (page 174), while others may opt for volunteer work. Young people wanting to travel overseas can do so through broad-based organisations like Voluntary Service Overseas or through more focused organisations like Green Deserts. A good guide to the opportunities for medium- and long-term international volunteering is *Volunteer Work,* published by the Central Bureau for Educational Visits & Exchanges.

For those interested in voluntary work in the UK, there is an even larger range of opportunities. A key organisation in practical conservation is the British Trust for Conservation Volunteers.

BTCV, in fact, is one of the organisations associated with UK 2000, whose initial objectives included helping to green Britain's cities, to restore the country's industrial heritage and to develop imaginative forms of litter control. Other organisations involved are: the Civic Trust; Community Service Volunteers; the Groundwork Foundation; the Keep Britain Tidy Group; and the Royal Society for Nature Conservation.

Individual employers, like the Nature Conservancy Council and Countryside Commission, may also provide their own short guides to employment prospects. The latter, for example, publishes a

Directory of Training Opportunities in Countryside Conservation and Recreation.

Professional paths

As the greening of the economy proceeds, so a growing number of mainstream professions have also been emphasising the environmental facets of their work. Environmental lawyers (page 28) are a case in point. A number of professions, however, deal fairly directly with the environment and may offer an entry route for those who find the volunteering path too uncertain. Among other options are careers as: biologist (contact: Institute of Biology); landscape

CAREERS & EDUCATION

Testing careers in the environment: BMW's exhaust emissions are analysed while Thames Water Authority biologist takes samples (inset).

architect (The Landscape Institute); teacher (National Association for Environmental Education); town planner (Royal Town Planning Institute); or environmental health officer (Institute of Environmental Health Officers).

Onto the payroll

Voluntary work with such organisations can be an excellent way of telling whether or not one is cut out for a career in the environment. Remember, too, that such organisations also need secretarial, administrative, managerial and promotional help. A checklist for would-be environmental employees can be found on page 233. Many have publishing operations, creating a demand for editorial and graphic skills, while most have computing, campaigning, fund-raising and transport needs. Some job vacancies are advertised in CoEnCo's *Habitat* magazine.

If the trial period works out well, some volunteers are taken onto the payroll, while others find it much easier to get subsequent employment because of the experience they have gained – whether that was in using a chain-saw or programming a computer.

232→

World Wildlife Fund UK
Along came man

231 ←

For anyone whose appetite has been whetted by such work, there are a number of publications which can help plot out a game-plan for the next steps. Among the publications offered by the Manpower Services Commission's Careers & Occupational Information Centre, for example, is *Working in Nature Conservation*. This looks at the employment prospects in the voluntary sector, in statutory bodies like the Department of the Environment, the Nature Conservancy Council, the Countryside Commission, the Natural Environment Research Council, the National Parks, in national and local government, and in the private sector. Other COIC 'job outlines' cover such areas as arboriculture and forestry, and water supply and sewerage.

Another helpful book is John McCormick's *Careers in Conservation*, the second edition of which was published in 1986 by Kogan Page. A more dated, but possibly still useful pamphlet is *Careers in the Environment: A First Guide*, available from the Council for Environmental Conservation. More general in orientation is *Which Subject? Which Career?*, available from the Consumers' Association.

Such professions are not for those who simply want to work with animals or in the open air, however. They involve dealing with ordinary people's everyday problems. So, for example, an environmental health officer does not just deal with air pollution or noise problems, but with a wide range of housing, food contamination and infectious disease problems.

But many such environmental professionals are also attracted to such work by, as Hampshire county planning officer Roger Brown put it, 'concern for the human race, if that doesn't sound too pompous.' Some local authorities, Hampshire included, have professional in-house ecologists, to advise planners and other staff on the environmental implications of their work.

Another possibility is forestry or woodland management. Dutch elm disease and the ravages of acid rain have made the sustainable management of Europe's timber resources and treescapes an increasingly pressing priority. Apart from the COIC brochure already mentioned, advice on possible career paths in this field is available from the Arboricultural Association and from the Forestry Commission.

By no means finally, there are also various career paths opening up in 'alternative technology'. The key source of information here is the Intermediate Technology Development Group. A useful background paper on the opportunities in this area is *Careers in Alternative Technology*, produced by the Network for Alternative Technology and Technology Assessment.

And if you want to see such technologies in action, interesting places to visit include the National Centre for Alternative Technology, the Urban Centre for Alternative Technology and Commonwork.

Government paths

Anyone wanting to combine environmental science with the security of a civil service career could start off by tracking down a copy of *Scientists: Civil Service Careers*, a brochure published by Her Majesty's Stationery Office (Demand 8841769 20M 6/86), and by getting in touch with the Civil Service Commission. The main Civil Service employer in this respect is obviously the Department of the Environment, although other ministries also have a need for environmental expertise.

Then there are the plethora of statutory agencies, including the Countryside Commission, Forestry Commission, Nature Conservancy Council and the Water Authorities, and the local government sector – which is the main employer of professionals such as planners and environmental health officers.

For those who want to carry out environmental research, there are again many options, depending on whether the goal is a career in a university, a public sector agency or institute, or in industry. The Natural Environment Research Council (NERC) is a useful source of information on environmental research careers in the public sector, as are the Countryside Commission and the Nature Conservancy Council.

237 →

CAREERS & EDUCATION

Getting Started

Young people of all ages are now exposed to more information on environmental issues than ever before. Among organisations with major programmes in this area are the World Wildlife Fund and the Watch Trust for Environmental Education.

In addition to impact of the media and of the Green Bookshelf (page 208), growing numbers of lecturers are out converting people of all ages to the conservation cause. A classified Directory of Lecturers in Natural History and Environmental Conservation is available from the Council for Environmental Conservation.

As a result, there is growing interest in green careers. But anyone who asks 'How do I get a job in the environment' is posing a difficult question, as the Council for Environmental Education (CEE) notes. 'There is no single "environmental profession" and therefore no set path to qualifying and obtaining a career in this field.' The choice of direction will largely depend on individual's interests and objectives.

The very fact that the environmental field is not easy to define, however, means that it is possible to break into some areas, particularly in the voluntary sector, with diverse experience and qualifications. 'Nevertheless,' says CEE, 'there is competition for these jobs, too, despite the fact that they are often characterised by long hours, comparatively low wages and job insecurity.'

If you are looking for university or college courses covering some aspect of the environment, check through the latest handbook from the Universities Central Council on Admissions. For first degree, diploma and postgraduate environmental courses offered by the polytechnics and other college, track down copies of the director-

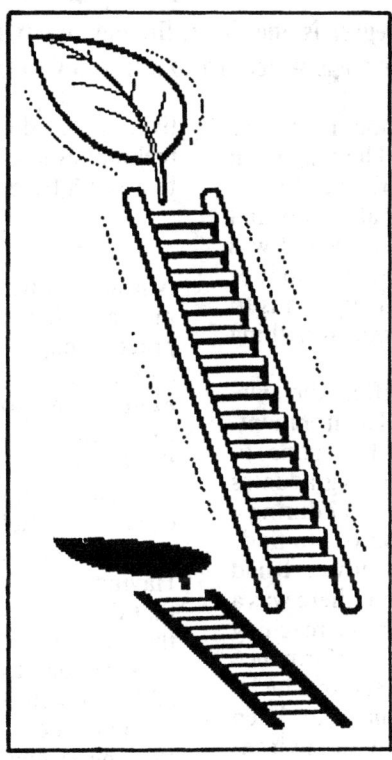

ies published by the Council for National Academic Awards.

Other useful advice offered by CEE includes the following general pointers:
- decide which areas are of most interest and most suited to your experience and qualifications;
- try to think beyond the more obvious 'conservation careers', because (a) they are in short supply and (b) you could make a worthwhile contribution by bringing your concern and skills to bear in an environmentally relevant occupation where the concepts of conservation and environmental excellence have yet to engage;
- become informed by reading the relevant magazines, newsletters, annual reports (page 40) and so on. Get to know what is going on and what sort of job vacancies are likely to come up. A now out-of-date, but extremely helpful document on the opportunities for environmental scientists is available from Sunderland Polytechnic;
- do voluntary work, particularly if you would like eventual employment in the voluntary sector. But, wherever you end up, experience as a volunteer with organisations like the British Trust for Conservation Volunteers, the National Trust or the Royal Society for the Protection of Birds should stand you in good stead;
- be persistent – and discerning. Vacancies are often advertised, so keep an eye out. Talk to people in the field and follow up leads and contacts. But don't spend a great deal of time and effort writing to all the organisations which might potentially employ you. Make sure that the organisations you do contact are in the market for new recruits;
- consider other routes, perhaps by joining or helping to set up a co-operative or other venture operating in such fields as recycling, insulation or environment-based leisure activity.

Europe-wide, there are a number of sources of information of the latest developments in employment, training and related policies, programmes and projects. The Commission of the European Communities, for example, runs:
- the Transition programme to help young people prepare for adult and working life;
- Eurydice, an education information network in the European Community, for the mutual exchange of relevant information between Member States; and
- Informisep, a publication on developments in employment, training and related policies in Member States.

PERSPECTIVES

An Electrifying Start

Achieving an environmental degree is one thing, finding an environmental job quite another, *Debbie Bruce* on the steps which led to a 'green career' with the CEGB.

'I received two pieces of advice about my future career when I graduated in 1977. The first, from an academic, was that my duty to society was now to join a prominent environmental group and protest in order to save the world. The second was from the university careers adviser. 'There are no jobs in the environment,' he said. 'Your only option is to take a graduate secretarial course and hope something turns up.'

At the time, some five years after the UN Stockholm Conference on the Human Environment, this was not unreasonable advice. I had gone to university in 1974 when environmental graduates were a rare commodity, but emerged in 1977 during a recession when jobs of any kind were harder to find.

Determined not to take any of the advice I had been given, I turned to industry. I thought there was a real need to work with companies with far-reaching environmental impacts to improve their performance in this area. My first post came as the result of a lucky break – a civil engineer I knew who had been employed by Wimpey told me they had an environmental section. When I turned up on their doorstep with a degree on environmental sciences, then unheard of, I was in.

An experiment

It is fair to say that both Wimpey and the Central Electricity Generating Board (CEGB), where I went next, took me on as something of an experiment. They wanted to find out if a degree in environmental sciences was worth the paper it was printed on. Both, I am glad to say, have subsequently employed other generalist environmental science graduates. However, while generalists are in increasing demand, most industries still have an urgent need for specialists.

The work at Wimpey was a mixture of field work (monitoring construction and transport noise and undertaking noise surveys for proposed residential developments), analysis of the results and production of reports. Unfortunately, very little of my time was spent dealing with people outside the company and there seemed little hope of the work developing in this direction. It was time to move on.

However, this early experience proved to be the key to the CEGB. They, too, were experimenting, but this time the work was very different. Initially, it involved a study for a proposed power station, the sort of work later dubbed 'environmental impact assessment' or EIA. I was sent to Brussels to develop industry's comments on the EEC's draft EIA Directive. And then we set about introducing EIA techniques into the CEGB. The Board adopted them two years before the Directive came into force.

Pan-European impact

Normally, one would expect to move into environmental policy development only after many years of practical experience. It is a 'top-of-the-pile' job. From an environmental point of view, it is also extremely exciting: the potential rewards of achieving a significant shift in the policies of an industry on the scale of the CEGB are pan-European in impact.

Being a small cog in a very large wheel, however, can be extremely daunting. One must be prepared for policy developments to take a very long time indeed. Having been with the CEGB for nine years, it is clear that the organisation *has* changed its attitude towards the environment.

On a day-to-day basis, though, any movement is all but undetectable. Indeed it often feels as though the machine is going backwards. It is all a bit like steering a supertanker. You have to be thinking many, many miles (or years) ahead.

Overall, however, it is clear that once a big organisation begins to turn, the changes can come relatively quickly. The environmentalist working in industry has to have the stamina to create an institutional will to change, and to do that, help is needed from environmental groups outside.

Expect mistrust

As an environmental scientist in industry one has few friends. The public and pressure groups tend to distrust you because you are employed by the 'enemy'. Many of your colleagues inside the company or organisation view you as little more than grit in the works. Your job, at least in the short term, is often going to make their work more difficult. Like-minded friends, both inside and outside, are therefore critically important to sustain your morale.

Luckily, the CEGB encourages its staff to accept positions on external specialist committees and study groups. It has been possible for me to develop strong contacts with environmental campaigners and professionals. I was asked to join the industry sector working group which developed the industrial component of the UK response to the *World Conservation Strategy,* for example, and the University of Aberdeen faculty for a series of World Health Organisation seminars on environmental impact assessment. I was also able to accept an invitation to sit on the Council of the

CAREERS & EDUCATION

Institution of Environmental Sciences and to join the Green Alliance.

Because conflict often leads to stalemate, I began to develop a new role in the CEGB, concerned with creating low-conflict situations in which pressure groups of all kinds can discuss their ideas with CEGB staff. After a year, this role was formalised and a second person was appointed to help develop it. While this extra effort increases costs in the short-term, in the long run, with the Board seen to be taking environmental concerns into account, industry's costs (particularly those generated by planning delays) will be reduced.

Increasingly, too, the CEGB has been helping environmental organisations to undertake their work, so it can put something back into communities which face the unavoidable disbenefits of electricity generation. The 'culture of conflict' between the industry and environmentalists is difficult to overcome, but it is essential to work towards this end to ensure that industrial decisions are both economically and environmentally acceptable and efficient.

Over-worked

Paradoxically, and much against the grain for those with a 'green' education, to build a career in environmental policy development you may need to join a large organisation or government department and work in London, tied to a desk. It is ironic that almost all those who are involved in environmental policy making, and this includes the pressure groups, are based in big cities. Contact with the natural world, which may have seemed a main attraction of the job in the first place, is often severely limited both by the place and pace of work. Almost all the environmental specialists I know are overwhelmed with work.

The alternative is to be a larger cog in a smaller wheel. This is an area of environmental employment which has grown substantially since 1980. The British Trust for Conservation Volunteers, the County Naturalist Trusts, the Farming and Wildlife Advisory Groups and Groundwork: these are just some of the smaller units now working to achieve day-to-day progress in the real world, content to win small prizes very much more often, rather than to go after the big prizes available on a very occasional basis at the policy level in an organisation like the CEGB.

DEBBIE BRUCE *worked in the Environmental Studies Section at the CEGB until late 1987. With a BSc in Environmental Sciences from the University of East Anglia, she was employed in a self-created post, responsible for building bridges with environmental organisations and using their contributions to the debate to develop environmental policy recommendations for the CEGB. Early work on air pollution by nitrogen oxides led on to work on the CEGB's environmental assessment policy. She then worked on the environmental assessments for a proposed pumped-storage power station and for the Sizewell 'B' nuclear power station. She is now an independent consultant.*

PERSPECTIVES

Seeds of Understanding

An innovative twinning scheme links UK schools with Third World schools and puts the spotlight on genetic resources, including seeds and under-utilised plants. *Roger Hammond* and *Niall Marriott* report.

'Environmental education has evolved very considerably in recent years. Early on, the main emphasis was on informal nature studies, but the 1970s saw the beginning of a dramatic increase in the number of schools offering more formalised teaching of environmental science subjects. More recently, in a third stage of evolution, environmental studies have been developed as a context for learning across the curriculum, rather than as a free-standing subject.

The recent introduction of the General Certificate of Secondary Education (GCSE) examination system in Britain has encouraged a more issue-based approach to learning than the traditional subject areas of the old Certificate of Secondary Education (CSE) and General Certificate of Education (GCE) examination systems. As a result, there is now a large emerging market for cross-curricular, project-oriented educational materials.

Rainforests resource pack

But with education authorities under enormous financial pressures, it is essential that any new environmental education package be designed to help teachers meet a number of objectives – or teach a number of different age groups – simultaneously. This approach also lends itself particularly well to helping students and teachers explore the complex, inter-related issues surrounding the impact of environmental problems on the performance of local and global economies.

One of the projects we have worked on recently was the Earthlife Rainforests Resource Pack, developed with the assistance of The Partners, a leading London-based design consultancy. Backed with £30,000 in commercial sponsorship, the pack has been built around the rainforest supplement compiled by Earthlife and published by *The Observer* in 1986.

Working with a group of practising primary and secondary teachers, we produced a range of subject-oriented briefings to accompany the supplement. These can be used separately or as part of cross-curricular projects, and show ways in which rainforest issues can enhance teachers' existing work programmes. Among the subject areas highlighted are: English, Drama, Physics, Chemistry, Biology, Geology, Craft Design Technology, Religious Education, Geography, History and Home Economics. Also included is a set of four posters, with notes and outline schemes of work, enabling teachers to adapt the resources to particular age groups.

Twinning for sustainability

Another project, undertaken for the Royal Botanic Gardens at Kew, has explored the potential of 'twinning' schools in Britain and the developing

ROGER HAMMOND *is Director of Education for the Earthlife Foundation and* **NIALL MARRIOTT** *is Assistant Director of Education. They are both Directors of Marriott Hammond Resource Consultants. Previously they worked with the Urban Wildlife Group in Birmingham, Hammond as Founder-Chairman in 1980 and then Vice-Chairman of the Group and Chairman of the Education Sub-Committee, and Marriott as the Education Unit Supervisor. Both have produced a number of publications and have been involved in Central TV series such as 'ARK' and 'Nature Watch'.*

Marriott Hammond Resource Consultants, 37 Bedford Square, London WC1.

countries, to encourage research on the planet's plant resources. There are thousands of known food plants, yet the world depends for its staple food on a mere handful. The danger of relying on such a narrow genetic pool is obvious, especially in the less developed countries, where people are struggling to survive in marginal environments.

The idea is that the twinned schools would carry out research, under the guidance of Kew, aimed at identifying local plant food resources which are better adapted than the main commercial crop species. There is relatively little information on the biology of these under-used plants, so the project offers young people the chance to become involved in a real-world project with the possibility of real benefits for Third World communities.

Due to the largely experimental nature of traditional twinning projects in schools, a lack of resources has often led to a lack of continuity, despite the educational benefits. Part of our work within the project is to explore and establish mechanisms which will facilitate and enhance twinning as a viable and effective component of the learning environment in schools.

---

232 ←

Government cut-backs have forced NERC to reduce staff numbers in recent years, but its span of interests are unique in the UK. Alphabetically, its numerous component organisations extend from the British Antarctic Survey (BAS) through to the Unit of Comparative Plant Ecology. Scientifically, they extend from work on the deep ocean floor to satellite monitoring of the physics and chemistry of the upper atmosphere. And the recent BAS discovery of the Antarctic 'ozone hole' (page 88) provides an excellent example of the ways in which the frontiers of environmental science are constantly being rolled back.

Industrial environmentalists

An increasing proportion of the environmental research undertaken around the NERC system is now carried out under contract to outside clients, including industry. Indeed, it is worth noting that at the same time as industry is employing more external environmental consultants it is also employing increasing numbers of environmental professionals in-house. Roughly, between 40% and 50% of students successfully completing MSc courses supported by NERC – and between a quarter and a third of PhD students – are subsequently employed by industry and commerce.

Among the contributors to *Green Pages* there are a number of industrial environmentalists. Generally such people are appointed from other roles in the company, rather than from the outside, although increasing numbers of new graduates have also been taken on to carry out environmental research.

At the pollution control end of the employment spectrum, meanwhile, there is a strong preference among employers for people with a sound grounding in a traditional subject such as chemistry or engineering, possibly followed by further environmental training, rather than for those with a broad training in environmental sciences.

Interestingly, a number of senior industrialists have recognised one important spin-off benefit from the employment of industrial environmentalists, of whichever type. A given company's chances of recruiting well-qualified people are very much influenced by its public image. If it can clean up its reputation, its general recruitment task can be considerably eased.

Distance learning

One of the most comprehensive surveys of the level of environmental awareness in industry was carried out for the Department of the Environment by the Centre for Environmental Education. And one of its conclusions was that there are major gaps in the environmental training market.

This gap was to some extent filled in 1987 when a new distance learning package was launched by William Waldegrave. Funded to the tune of £600,000 by the Manpower Services Commission's Open-Tech scheme, the package was put together by Leicester Polytechnic, Imperial College and Loughborough Polytechnic.

The distance learning material is aimed at the sort of industrial personnel – including technical, supervisory and managerial staff – who might not otherwise receive adequate environmental training. The 85 work units in the package cover six main areas, including the control of air, water and noise pollution, hazardous waste management, and the law relating to pollution control. The sixth unit, on environmental management, deals with more general topics, such as sources of environmental information, costing pollution control, and trends in environmental policy.

10 steps to employment

By no means all these industrial environmentalists are involved in pollution control, however. Some are involved in policy advice or public relations, while others mainly focus on training or other environment-related activities. In fact, the *10 Steps to Environmental Excellence* outlined on pages 226–227 provide an agenda for business and industry which will take many years to achieve.

Viewed in the right light, each of the sections of *Green Pages* – be it Design, Energy, Marketing, Money or Tourism – can serve as an initial guide to some of the new employment opportunities in Europe's emerging green economy. □

Into the 1990s

Compiling *Green Pages* has been like painting the Firth of Forth Bridge. Even before we
finished, new events, facts and trends were jockeying for a place on pages which
had already been typeset and laid out. But the underlying trends remain the same.
Whether you are an optimist or a pessimist, the challenge is clear:
the real question is whether we have the political will to respond in time.

A pessimist, they say, is simply a well-informed optimist. Certainly, the problems outlined in earlier sections of *Green Pages* are enough to take the wind out of the sails of even the most rampant optimist. And, as if to drive the message home, the world seemed to rock on its very foundations as the last few sections of *Green Pages* were manoeuvred into place and readied for the cameras.

A hurricane swept across the south east of England in the early hours of October 16, uprooting or damaging over 15 million trees. We emerged to find scenes reminiscent of the Blitz, with giant trees splintered and toppled like so many matchsticks. A mile or two down the road, Kew Gardens sustained massive damage. Some scientists questioned whether the build-up of carbon dioxide in the atmosphere was to blame, with shifting weather patterns presaging much broader climatic changes.

Ten days later, we emerged into the street to find all the cars covered in a mottled coat of red Saharan dust. Accelerating soil erosion in African countries like Algeria, Morocco and Mauritania is leading to more episodes of so-called "blood rain" – and their tempo is increasing. The dust had been stripped by fierce winds from the denuded earth of Africa and carried well over 1,000 miles before being washed out of the sky in London rain.

Between 1900 and the time we put the finishing touches to *Green Pages,* there had been 17 major Saharan dustfalls over Britain. Ten had occurred in the 1980s alone. Norman Myers explains some of the contributory trends on pages 190–192, but there is nothing like having to wash the Sahara off your car in London to concentrate the mind on what is happening to the global environment.

Meanwhile, the media brimmed over with environmental features and surveys. *Time* ran a cover story on the 'greenhouse effect,' while *International Business Week* did one on the state of the world's seas and oceans. At the other end of the Earth, the US National Science Foundation was becoming increasingly concerned about the safety of scientists working in Antarctica, where the 'ozone hole' continued to grow. First identified by British scientists (pages 88–89), this alarming phenomenon could be seen as the 20th century equivalent of the writing on the palace wall which so troubled King Belshazzar in Biblical Babylon. It provides further evidence, were it needed, that many of our industrial technologies are being weighed in the balance and found wanting.

But, whereas the ill-fated Belshazzar, desperate to have the writing on his plaster decoded, promised to clothe the interpreter in scarlet, to hang a chain of gold about his neck and to make him the third ruler in the kingdom, today's environmental scientists have tended to receive much shorter shrift in recent years. The Natural Environment Research Council, which funds the British Antarctic Survey's work, has suffered major cuts in both funding and manpower.

Yet, everywhere you look, human populations are pressing harder on their environment. The prospects for slowing – let alone reversing – such critical processes as desertification or tropical deforestation seem bleak. With the world's population expected to 'stabilise' at around the 10 billion mark, double today's 5 billion figure (pages 244–245), these pressures can only increase – and, with them, the value of environmental research.

Clearly, governments cannot be expected to tackle the environmental agenda on their own. Indeed, broad new coalitions of interest are already forming to experiment with new ways of solving environmental problems. Some, like those active in the inner cities (pages 152–165), operate mainly at the local or project level. Others operate primarily at the policy level. Whichever level they work at, the process of developing such partnerships is rarely easy, as Janet Barber of the World Wildlife Fund points out on pages 242–243. But there *is* a new willingness, both in the government and business sectors, to experiment with alternatives to confrontation.

The message is certainly beginning to get through to many leading European industrialists. "It will no longer be sufficient to have good products, an efficient organisation and a strong balance sheet," as Ciba-Geigy chairman Alex Krauer summed up the challenge one year after the Rhine disaster led to a storm of protest in Basle, where both Ciba-Geigy and Sandoz have their headquarters. "To be successful in the 1990s," he warned his fellow industrialists, "you will have to win the acceptance of the people who live near your plants. People will have to believe in your professional competence and your ability to manage technology."

Speaking on behalf of the chemical industry at the European Conference on Industry and Environmental Management (ECIEM), held in Interlaken, Switzerland, during October 1987, CEFIC President Mr A. A. Loudon admitted that "our attempts to communicate to the public our achievements have

BRITISH COAL

A Mine of the Times

A modern coal mine is one of the more complex forms of industrial development to introduce into the environment – and the task is becoming steadily more challenging as the coal industry begins to move into areas with no tradition of coal-mining. Although most of a deep mine development goes underground, enough happens on the surface to ensure that the level of environmental work required is constantly rising. Consider the environmental impact assessment (EIA) prepared by British Coal, a *Green Pages* sponsor, for the South Warwickshire Prospect at Hawkhurst Manor, near Coventry.

"British Coal had been carrying out exploration work on the South Warwickshire coalfield since the early 1970's," says Ted Allett, who co-ordinates the Corporation's activities in relation to the surface environment. "The local authorities were informed in 1979, when we began to assess the feasibility of exploiting the reserves. The outline development proposals, published as a consultation paper during 1985, encouraged comment and suggestions on the nature and extent of the environmental studies likely to be required."

Since British Coal began carrying out environmental assessments in the early 1970s, the trend has been towards increasingly comprehensive environmental studies, more consultation at an earlier stage of planning and the use of more sophisticated techniques. The South Warwickshire EIA is the most comprehensive British Coal has prepared to date.

Local authorities were invited to help identify sites for the mine and its associated infrastructure. This phase of the consultation process proved enormously helpful, but the local authorities concluded that the choice of site was best left to the developer. By late 1985, two possible mine sites had been identified and Environmental Resources Ltd were engaged to pick the environmentally preferable option and produce an EIA.

80 groups were consulted. Hawkhurst Moor emerged as the favoured site. The ensuing EIA considered the mine, the road and rail links and traffic, and soil disposal, focusing on land use, ecological, noise, dust, water and visual impacts, as well as subsidence, planning and socio-economic effects. The EIA was carried out alongside the design process, so that the design could be modified as potential constraints – and opportunities – were identified. The spoil, for example, will help restore local sand and gravel workings, while the road link to the A45 has been designed to ensure that coal or spoil lorries cannot use local minor roads.

British Coal's planning application was submitted in July 1987 and called in by the Secretary of State for the Environment in November. The Hawkhurst Moor EIA will be among the first to be considered at a public inquiry in the wake of the EEC's new EIA Directive. Copies of the main EIA report from: The South Warwickshire Project Team, British Coal Corporation, Central Area, Coleorton Hall, Coleorton, Leicestershire LE6 4FA, price £10.00.

---

failed to boost our credibility." Instead, he accepted, industry would increasingly need "to establish alliances with those who are now among our most vocal critics."

The following month, Alan Rae, President of the UK Chemical Industries Association, told 1,300 senior executives that "ecology and safety must be the first charge on profitability. The improvements we can make in the fields of ecology and safety will probably never come to an end". European Year of the Environment (EYE), however, helped to build new bridges – and reinforce existing links – between industry and environmental interests, although many of the evolving partnerships will take many years to bear fruit.

Looking beyond EYE, Environment Commissioner Stanley Clinton Davis has stressed the real contribution which the environmental industry is already making to Europe's economy (page 3). No doubt many ears in the industry pricked up when Herr Krauer also announced that Ciba-Geigy would spend SFr1 billion (some £400 million) over the next three years on anti-pollution measures, double its previous rate of spending.

Whatever happens in the global markets in the wake of the Wall Street crash, which began a few days after the European Industry Conference on Environmental Management closed its doors, the longer term market outlook for green technologies, products and services continues to look very promising indeed. In an attempt to attract the new breed of socially and environmentally aware investor, new ethical investment funds have been launched. Several have been announced in Britain in the short period of time since Giles Chitty sent us his review (page 186–187), including N.M. Schroder's Conscience Fund, advertised as "a partnership of profit with principles".

As the greening of the European economy proceeds, and hopefully accelerates, we expect that the need for a second edition of *Green Pages* will grow. Currently, our thinking is that this would appear in 1990. Meanwhile, having completed this first edition of *Green Pages,* the SustainAbility team has moved on to a new generation of projects, among them *The Green Consumer Guide* (pages 19 and 71).

Consumer power can be deployed in many ways. In Japan, for example, one of Tokyo's top department stores has been selling cans of compressed oxygen as an antidote to the exhaust fumes which pervade the city. The real challenge is not to develop new markets for expensive gimmicks like this, but to encourage consumers to consciously seek out and buy green products and services. Don't buy oxygen, in short, buy a cleaner car or switch to public transport.

We emerge from *Green Pages* as optimists. But some optimists are pessimists who have seen the way the world is headed and have decided that the best way to market difficult changes is to show people what is in it for them, whether they are operating as investors, consumers, managers, employees or – perhaps most important of all – voters. But it is important to recognise the real limits to the powers that governments have at their disposal. Whoever we are, wherever we may live, whatever we may do, we all have an important stake in the success or failure of the green markets whose early progress has been charted in these pages.

PERSPECTIVES

The State of the World

The Worldwatch Institute's annual series of State of the World *reports are now published in most of the world's major languages.* Lester Brown *looks at the political and educational impact of a publishing phenomenon.*

'When we decided, with the encouragement of the Rockefeller Brothers Fund, to launch the *State of the World* reports, beginning with 1984, we expected there would be a strong demand. We did not anticipate the rate at which the demand would grow. Using virtually any indicator – sales, translations, orders from policymakers, or course adoptions on college campuses – interest in *State of the World* expands each year.

The first printing of the US English edition of *State of the World 1984* totalled 16,000 copies. By year's end, it had gone through five printings for a total of 27,000 copies. For *State of the World 1987*, the first printing of 50,000 copies was quickly joined by a second printing of 20,000 copies.

State of the World now appears in most of the world's major languages. In addition to English, it is published in Spanish, Arabic, Chinese, Japanese, Javanese, German, Polish and Italian. It also appears in several less widely spoken languages, including Romanian and Thai. We estimate that the worldwide market in all languages is now in excess of 200,000 copies.

State of the World 1986 is used as a textbook in nearly 200 US colleges and universities. As in 1985, the University of Wisconsin campus at Madison still leads the way, with five separate courses having adopted the book. The University of California at Berkeley uses the text in four courses and several other institutions, including Harvard, use *State of the World* in three different courses.

Media coverage

Worldwide media interest in *State of the World* has also risen with each annual volume. Without this extensive print and electronic media coverage, it would be virtually impossible to reach a worldwide audience. Whether through an article in *The People's Daily* (China) or an appearance on *The Today Show* (United States) all media coverage of *State of the World* raises public awareness of both the long-standing and the newly emergent environmental issues that now confront the entire world.

Last year, we reported that we had been approached by the producers of NOVA to collaborate on a 10-part television series based on *State of the World*. Most of the $6 million for this project has been raised. We are excited by this major initiative not only because it adds a new dimension to our global public educational effort in its own right, but also because the film and print versions of *State of the World* will reinforce each other throughout the world. For educators, a telecourse and instructional guide are being developed with the support of the Carnegie Corporation and the Hitachi Foundation. Another promising complement to the television series is the preparation of a *Citizen's Guide to a Sustainable Society* by the Global Tomorrow Coalition, a Washington, DC based organisation of some 70 public interest groups, from the Audubon Society to Zero Population Growth.

The phone never stopped

Occasionally a news reporter, an editorial writer, or a columnist will write a piece on *State of the World* that strikes a responsive chord, measurably raising public awareness. When Hugh Sidey devoted his *Time* magazine column, 'The Presidency,' to a comparison of President Reagan's State of the Union address and *State of the World 1986*, such a chord was struck. Sidey concluded that *State of the World* was 'arguably a more accurate and provocative picture of the globe than the one sketched by the President.' For the following week, our phones rang on average once every six minutes as *Time* readers called to order the report.

Sometimes the information in *State of the World* contributes directly to shaping policy. In other cases, the contribution is more indirect. An annual two-day retreat of the senior staff at the World Bank held in November of 1985 was devoted to sustainable development and addressed by the project director of *State of the World*. And in April 1986, the African Development Bank invited the authors of last year's chapter on 'Reversing Africa's Decline' to lead a seminar for directors and senior staff in Abidjan on the links between the environment and the economy. No policy decisions were made at either the November retreat or the April seminar. But key decision makers in the field of international development discussed what was sustainable and what was not, considering sustainability along with the financial concerns that have traditionally dominated development policymaking.

Crossing the threshold

For the world to respond to global challenges such as soil erosion, species extinction, or human-induced climate change, we must cross what Harvard University professor Harvey Brooks terms a 'perceptual threshold.' Enough people must perceive the threat for a cogent response to emerge. Information is the key to crossing such thresholds. Once public concern

INTO THE 90'S

is aroused, it becomes possible and indeed necessary for politicians to act.

One such threshold was crossed when Congress passed the Food Security Act in December 1985. After two comprehensive USDA soil surveys and several studies by environmental groups indicated erosion severe enough to undermine US agriculture, farm groups joined national environmental organisations to demand action. Congress voted overwhelmingly to establish a conservation reserve designed to convert 45 million acres of the most highly erodible cropland into grassland or woodland.

The information that underpins change may come in more dramatic form. For societies weighing the pros and cons of nuclear power, the accident at Chernobyl in April 1986 confirmed the consequences of a core-damaging power plant accident. European countries exposed to the radiation from Chernobyl were soon re-examining the future of their nuclear power programmes. Although statistical models of the risks and consequences of a nuclear accident had long been available, the magnitude of the Chernobyl accident prompted actions that even widely publicised studies had never inspired.

State of the World is intended to help societies cross perceptual thresholds *before*, rather than after, such disruptive events occur. The task of the series, in part, is to highlight the risks that confront societies, and to indicate the most promising avenues for pre-emptive policies and actions. Soil conservation, energy efficiency, materials recycling, and population stabilisation – a few of the themes emphasised here – can broaden the options open to societies and enhance the prospects of the next generation.

LESTER R. BROWN is *President of the Worldwatch Institute, which he helped found in 1974. In 1986, he was awarded a MacArthur Foundation Fellowship for 'voicing the key environmental concerns of his own and future generations.' He has been described by* The Washington Post *'as one of the world's most influential thinkers' and the Library of Congress has requested his personal papers, while he is still in mid-career, because of the leadership role he and the Worldwatch Institute have played on global environment, population and resource issues. In 1984, he launched the Institute's* State of the World *reports, now translated into most of the world's major languages, including Spanish, Arabic, Chinese, Japanese, Indonesian and German.*

The Worldwatch Institute, *1776 Massachusetts Avenue, NW, Washington, DC 20036, USA. Tel: +1 (202) 452 1999.*

PERSPECTIVES

How Long a Spoon?

Mounting pressures on developers and aid agencies create a growing demand for information and assistance. Conservation organisations, says *Janet Barber*, must be in a position to respond.

'Radical environmentalists say it is too dangerous to sup with the Devil, no matter how long your spoon, but many are now cautiously taking a seat at his dinner table. The environmental movement is entering a challenging and interesting experimental phase with the most powerful agencies involved in international development, for example the World Bank, and the Asian and African Development Banks. Further opportunities for co-operation are emerging with national government development agencies, such as the Overseas Development Administration (ODA) in the UK.

Two kinds of non-governmental organisation (NGO) are involved in the emerging relationships, those with financial and philosophical stakes overseas in the form of field projects and personnel, for example WWF and OXFAM, and those with first and foremost a strong moral and intellectual interest about the emphasis of development aid, for example Friends of the Earth, the International Institute for Environment and Development (IIED) and Survival International. These groups work very successfully in the UK together combining to present a varied range of concerns to appropriate civil servants and ministers. WWF finds it helpful to have a portfolio of projects, and therefore practical issues, to discuss with ODA, who appreciate the need to co-operate with NGOs in the field in Sri Lanka or Zambia.

WWF, with other groups, began taking the occasional cup of coffee with ODA about 18 months ago on the basis of the potentially strong role the UK was well placed to play at the World Bank on environmental issues. At that time the main issues were (and still are to a great extent), Bank funding of the Narmada Valley power and reclamation project in India; human transmigration into tropical forests in Indonesia, development in the Amazon and cattle ranching in Botswana.

Pandora's Box

The Botswana case is particularly interesting, because the World Bank's role in the project has by and large been misunderstood by NGOs, and it demonstrated the complexity of the development issue. Large wilderness areas unsuited to intensive cattle raising were being brought under production. Mainly as a result of a WWF project it became clear that many animals like the rare spotted hyena and lions were being shot and poisoned to protect stock, and thousands of migratory antelopes, giraffe and zebra were dying on veterinary cordon fences and those of newly established ranches. Severe degradation of the dry habitat was taking place. The lifestyles of people in the Kalahari were being disturbed by the great influx of cattle. The main stimulus to the cattle industry was the already overloaded European Community beef market. The World Bank's role was mainly to provide generous credit facilities for farmers wishing to take advantage of the EC market, and this certainly fuelled beef production.

It took the combined resources of interested people in the European Commission, the European Parliament, the World Bank, WWF, the International Union for Conservation of Nature and Natural Resources (IUCN), the Kalahari Conservation Society and other groups and individuals in Botswana, and UNEP to explore the situation and act. As a result, the EC is trying to introduce a natural resources conservation programme to the country, the World Bank is more appreciative of the cost of environmental degradation, the Kalahari Conservation Society role has been strengthened and the Botswana government is now preparing a National Conservation Strategy. However, apart from lots of people and organisations learning some salutary lessons, the situation was not really saved. For instance, it has had to be recognised that the days of animal migration are over and henceforth wildlife will be contained by more formal management within reserves.

Another part of the experiment with relationships concerns the British Government's recent grants to WWF for three of its field projects which meet 50% of the budget for these projects. The money, so far totalling over £300,000, will go to an education project in Ecuador, which will enable every child in the country to receive environmental education, and research and field experiments in Zimbabwe leading to multi-species management in marginal areas. It was only two years ago when some officials at ODA were referring to the Zimbabwe project, as 'opening a Pandora's box' of uncertainty about the direction of aid. ODA has also supported the conservation of wetlands in the Kafue and Bangweulu areas of Zambia.

Natural resource profiles

The last project is perhaps particularly significant as it demonstrates the importance of not looking at development aid in isolation from other policy issues. Funding of the Zambia project sits well within the priorities for wetland conservation encompassed by the Ramsar Wetlands Convention, the Parties to which held their triennial meeting in Canada in 1987. This occasion was used to announce the ODA grant to this project which will help demonstrate how the natural resources of wetlands can be used sustainably. Other international treaties, including the Convention on International Trade in Endangered Species (CITES), and the Convention on the Conservation of Marine Living Resources (CCAMLR), are important instruments for sensitive natural resource use and adherence to their principles (by nearly 100 countries in the case of CITES) demonstrates the growing interest by governments in many aspects of sustainable natural resource management.

National Conservation Strategies, stimulated in particular by IUCN, provide a framework for governments in 50 countries to consider the long term use of their natural resources. The preparation of these strategies is funded in part by development agencies, who themselves are now undertaking natural resource profiles of countries to guide investment and grants.

Burden of debt

The role of NGOs in the development process is being explored and increasingly encouraged by the World Bank and other agencies. Opportunities are likely to increase for many NGOs to participate in their thinking and programme planning. The importance of national NGOs in developing countries cannot be over-estimated, and their views on the kind of development most appropriate in a particular country have rapidly increasing relevance for development agency thinking. NGOs now have ideas about relieving the debt burden suffered by the Third World, realise the impact of trading policies conceived in the North on the future of the people and the natural resources of countries in the South, and are disturbed about the future of indigenous people in countries like Malaysia and Indonesia, where massive destruction of tropical forest annihilates tribal cultures.

The development agencies are feeling as expectant and experimental as are the NGOs. What is going to count most in the very near future is the urgent pooling of ideas, views, experience and resources by all those anxious to resolve many key development issues. In order to do this, NGOs should be prepared to at least take hors d'oeuvres with the devil and should bear in mind that he may have made the invitation with more diffidence than rapacity.

JANET BARBER *is Head of Conservation at the World Wildlife Fund UK. She has worked for WWF since 1970, the Council of Europe's European Conservation Year. In 1972 she was awarded a Winston Churchill Travelling Fellowship to look at the impact of human population growth on the natural resources of Central America. That year, in fact, marked a watershed in the public's interest in the environment and wildlife, and the range and scale of WWF's activities have since grown accordingly. In addition to her work on wildlife conservation generally, she takes a particular interest in international conservation agreements and international aid issues.*
World Wildlife Fund UK, *Panda House, 11-13 Ockford Road, Godalming, Surrey GU7 1QU. Tel: 04868 20551.*

Michael Freeman, WWF

PERSPECTIVES

My Five Billionth Baby

As the world awaited its five billionth inhabitant, *Geoffrey Lean's* own child was born. Only by limiting the population growth, he says, can she and her generation have a decent future.

'Last summer I was invited to a solemn celebration – a special United Nations conference to mark the imminent birth of the five billionth inhabitant of the planet.

I could not go. I was in the delivery suite at our local hospital attending the arrival of our second child.

So it is just possible that our daughter Eorann is rather special – not just to her parents, but to the world as a whole. No one, of course, knows the time of arrival of the baby who took the world's population to five billion (lacking evidence, the UN designated Saturday 11th July as a special day), but experts agree that it is some time this summer.

The first 'billion baby' did not arrive until around the beginning of the last century – three million years or so after humans appeared on earth, and about the time that Thomas Malthus published his *Essay on the Principle of Population*.

The second 'billion baby' arrived sometime in the 1920s, the third about 1958, the fourth in 1975. The acceleration is staggering. Four of the five 'billion babies' are probably still alive.

The pace continues. By the time Eorann is 12, there will be another 'billion baby'; by the time she is 23, another. It is even possible that, if she waits for children as long as her parents, her own first baby could be the eighth billion – born in the early 2020s. Demographers hope that the pace of increase will slow after that, but they do not expect world population to stabilise until it has reached 10 billion – double what it is today.

A world of people on top of the present one! What on earth would it be like? Bottom-heavy for a start, for the greatest increases will be in the Third World, and the greatest strains, as ever, upon the world's poorest people.

Already three-quarters of humanity live in the Third World, and 95% of future growth will occur there. And the most rapid growth of all is in the poorest developing countries, particularly in Africa, which will become the second most populous continent.

In 1950 Africa's population was half the size of Europe's; before 2050 it will be three times as great. Kenya's population is doubling every 17 years; Nigeria is expected to become the world's most populous nation after China and India.

So the burden piles up intolerably on the weakest shoulders. If the five billionth baby was born in Africa last summer, its prospects will be very different from Eorann's. A newborn baby is nearly 20 times more likely to die before its first birthday in Sierra Leone, for example, than in Britain. It can expect to live to the grand old age of 34.

Even now only half the children in the world's poorest countries (mostly in sub-Saharan Africa) complete primary school; fewer than a quarter of the boys – fewer than a tenth of girls – even start secondary education. Only a quarter can get safe drinking water; less have any form of sanitation.

Trying to improve these woeful statistics would be hard enough, given the chronic poverty of the continent, even if the problem remained the same size. But the problem is doubling every 25 years along with the population.

As it is, enormous achievements have already been destroyed. Since independence, Africa has increased food production faster than Europe and the United States. But population has grown so fast that each African has a fifth less food to eat.

The effects are universal. 'Can we imagine,' asked Robert McNamara, while president of the World Bank, 'any human order surviving so gross a mass of human misery piling up at the base?'

By the time Eorann has reached my age, virtually all of the world's tropical rainforests will have disappeared, with incalculable consequences for the climate – a catastrophe rated by a meeting of world leaders last year as second only to nuclear war. And the burning of fossil fuels and use of aerosol sprays by those of us in the rich world will be causing further alarming climatic changes.

It is, of course, easier to outline the problem than to suggest answers. Easier for most of us, that is, for few subjects so attract the fundamentalists.

On the one side, there are those – strengthened by the rise of Reagan's Right and Khomeini's disciples – who say that population growth is neutral, or even beneficial, in its effects and that nothing should be done. The United States and other countries are already reducing their support for population control.

On the other hand, there are those who attribute virtually all the world's problems to population growth, and preach control to the exclusion of everything else. At worst this degenerates into something close to racism – 'Sterilise them before they destroy our world.'

To the rest of us, population growth is highly destructive, but it is neither the root of the world's problems, nor could it be simply controlled. It is a

INTO THE 90'S

A Balanda mother in Southern Sudan (above) and Geoffrey Lean and Eorann (below) ponder the future.

highly complicated social and economic issue.

When Eorann's namesake – Sweeney's queen, in the ancient Irish ballad – lived in seventh century Ireland, both birth rates and death rates were high – as for most of human history. Then health and sanitation improved in Europe in the nineteenth century, death rates fell, and population soared. Our great-grandparents did not start breeding like rabbits, but they did stop dying like flies. As they got richer people had fewer children, and population stabilised.

The same 'demographic transition' has begun, much more savagely, in the Third World. Death rates dropped from the 1950s, as life expectancy grew, and diseases like cholera, smallpox and typhus were beaten back. But birth rates are only beginning to turn down.

Medical technology provided death-control, so it was natural to look to it for birth control. But many early contraceptive programmes in the Third World proved disappointing – because people *wanted* lots of children.

They want them for good reasons. From the age of 10, children often produce more for the family by work in the fields than they consume. They provide security in old age. And infant mortality is still so high than an Indian couple needs to have more than six children to be statistically sure of having one surviving son.

As people become a little less poor and more secure, their desire for large families generally falls. And as women receive more education, better opportunities, and more rights the birth rate falls even faster.

At the same time, surveys have shown that many women would have fewer children if they could get effective contraception. So the best hope lies both in providing the technology and in fighting poverty. Where the two have gone hand in hand there have been astonishing successes. But attempts to short-circuit the process by compulsory sterilisation, as in Mrs Gandhi's India, have ended in disaster.

Providing the contraceptives is relatively easy. Fighting poverty is extraordinarily difficult, for it involves changing entrenched economic and political relationships both between and within countries.

Yet – quite apart from the moral imperative – it must be done, not just to defuse the population bomb, but to address the appalling conditions of the billion poorest people already on earth, and to relieve the threats to farmland and forest, which are caused as much by poverty as by population growth.

Nothing else has a chance of producing a world fit for the five billionth baby – whoever it is – to live in.

GEOFFREY LEAN *is environment correspondent at* The Observer, *where this article first appeared.*
The Observer, *8 St. Andrew's Hill, London EC4 75JA. Tel: 01-236 0202.*

FOLLOW UP

Abbey National Building Society, Abbey House, Baker Street, London NW1 6XL. Tel: 01 935 2121.

Acacia Productions, 80 Weston Park, London N8 9TB. Tel: 01 340 2619.

Agricultural and Food Research Council (AFRC), 160 Great Portland Street, London W1N 6DT. Tel: 01 580 6655.

Agricultural Training Board, Bourne House, 32-34 Beckenham Road, Beckenham, Kent BR3 4PB. Tel: 01 650 4890.

Arboricultural Association, Ampfield House, Romsey, Hampshire SO51 9PA. Tel: 0794 68717.

Association for Responsible Communication (ARC), Mickleton House, Mickleton, Gloucestershire GL55 6RY. Tel: 0386 438727.

Atlas Copco, PO Box 79, Swallowdale Lane, Hemel Hempstead HP2 7HA. Tel: 0442 61201.

Babcock International plc, Cleveland House, St. James's Square, London SW1Y 4LN. Tel: 01 930 9766.

Band Aid, PO Box 4TX, London W1A 4TX. Tel: 01 408 1999.

Bank of England, London EC2R 8AH. Tel: 01 601 4444.

BASF, BASF Aktiengesellschaft, D-6700 Ludwigshafen, Federal Republic of Germany.

BAT Industries plc, Windsor House, 50 Victoria Street, London SW1H 0NL. Tel: 01 222 7979.

Bayer UK Ltd, Bayer House, Richmond, Surrey TW9 1SJ. Tel: 01 940 6077.

Better Environment Awards – see Royal Society of Arts.

Bio-Dynamic Agricultural Association, Woodman Lane, Clent, Stourbridge, West Midlands DY9 9PX. Tel: 0562 88493.

Biosphere II, PO Box 689, Oracle, Arizona 85623, USA. Tel: +1 (602) 622 0641.

BioTechnica Ltd (BTL), 5 Chiltern Close, Cardiff CF4 5DL. Tel: 0222 766716.

BioTreatment, 5 Chiltern Close, Cardiff CF4 5DL, Wales. Tel: 0222 766716.

Blue Circle Industries plc, Portland House, Aldermaston, Berkshire RG7 4HP. Tel: 07356 78541.

Body Shop International plc, Dominion Way, Rustington, West Sussex BN16 3LR. Tel: 0903 717107.

Boots Company plc, Nottingham NG2 3AA. Tel: 0602 56111.

Bosch, Postfach, D-7000 Stuttgart 1, Federal Republic of Germany. Tel: +49 711 8110.

British Aerospace plc, Aircraft Group HQ, Richmond Road, Kingston-upon-Thames, Surrey KT2 5QS. Tel: 01 546 7741.

British Gas plc, Rivermill House, 152 Grosvenor Road, London SW1V 3JL. Tel: 01 821 1444.

British Nuclear Fuels plc, Risley, Warrington WA3 6AS. Tel: 0925 832000.

British Organic Farmers (BOF), 86 Colston Street, Bristol, Avon BS1 5BB. Tel: 0272 299666.

British Organic Standards Board (BOSB), Elm Farm Research Centre, Hamstead Marshall, Newbury, Berkshire RG15 0HR. Tel: 0488 58298.

British Petroleum Company plc (BP), Britannic House, Moor Lane, London EC2Y 9BU. Tel: 01 920 2703.

British Renewable Energy Forum, 19 Albemarle Street, London W1X 3HA. Tel: 01 439 6601.

British Telecommunications plc, 81 Newgate Street, London EC1A 7AJ. Tel: 01 356 5000.

British Tourist Authority, Thames Tower, Blacks Road, London W6 9EL. Tel: 01 846 9000.

British Trust for Conservation Volunteers (BTCV), 36 St. Mary's Street, Wallingford, Oxon OX10 0EU. Tel: 0491 39766.

British Trust for Ornithology, Beech Grove, Tring, Herts. HP23 5NR. Tel: 044 282 3461.

British Venture Capital Association, 1 Surrey Street, London WC2R 2PS. Tel: 01 836 5702.

British Wildlife Appeal, 164 Vauxhall Bridge Road, London SW1V 2RB. Tel: 01 828 1657.

British Wind Energy Association, 4 Hamilton Place, London W1V 0BQ. Tel: 01 499 3515.

Broads Authority, The, 18 Colegate, Norwich, Norfolk NR3 1BQ. Tel: 0603 610734.

Bulletin Group – see Bank of England.

H P Bulmer Ltd., The Cider Mills, Plough Lane, Hereford HR4 0LE. Tel: 0432 6411.

Burson-Marsteller Ltd, 24-28 Bloomsbury Way, London WC1A 2PX. Tel: 01 831 6262.

Business in the Community, 227A City Road, London EC1V 1LX. Tel: 01 253 3716.

Business Network, 18 Well Walk, London NW3 1LD. Tel: 01 435 5000.

Cambridge University, Department of Botany, Downing Site, Downing Street, Cambridge CB2 3EA. Tel: 0223 333900.

Campaign for Lead Free Air (CLEAR), 3 Endsleigh Street, London WC1H 0DD. Tel: 01 278 9686.

Campaign for the Countryside, 11 Cowley Street, London SW1P 3NA. Tel: 01 222 9134.

Castrol Ltd, Castrol Research Laboratories, Whitchurch Hill, Pangbourne, Reading, Berkshire RG8 7QR. Tel: 07357 4321.

Celador Productions, 39 Long Acre, London WC2. Tel: 01 240 8101.

Central Bureau for Educational Visits & Exchanges, Seymour Mews, London W1H 9PE. Tel: 01 486 5101.

Central Electricity Generating Board (CEGB), Sudbury House, 15 Newgate Street, London EC1A 7AU. Tel: 01 634 5111.

Central Television, Central House, Broad Street, Birmingham B1 2JP. Tel: 021 643 9898.

Centre for Agricultural Strategy, University of Reading, 1 Earley Gate, Reading RG6 2AT. Tel: 0734 875123.

Centre for Economic and Environmental Development (CEED), 12 Upper Belgrave Street, London SW1X 8BA. Tel: 01 245 6440.

Centre for Environmental Education (CEE), School of Education, University of Reading, Reading RG1 5AQ. Tel: 0734 85234.

Centre for Environmental Interpretation (CET), Manchester Polytechnic, John Dalton Building, Chester Street, Manchester M1 5GD. Tel: 061 228 6171.

Charities Aid Foundation, 48 Pembury Road, Tonbridge, Kent TN9 2JD. Tel: 0732 356323.

Chemical Industries Association (CIA), Kings Buildings, Smith Square, London SW1P 3JJ. Tel: 01 834 3399.

Ciba-Geigy (UK) Ltd, 30 Buckingham Gate, London SW1E 6LH. Tel: 01 828 5676.

FOLLOW UP

City Communications Centre, 14 Austin Friars, London EC2. Tel: 01 628 8522.

Civic Trust, 17 Carlton House Terrace, London SW1Y 5AW. Tel: 01 930 0914.

Civil Service Commission (CSC), Alencon Link, Basingstoke, Hampshire RG21 1JB. Tel: 0256 29222.

Clean Britain's Beaches Campaign – see Marine Conservation Society.

Cleanaway Ltd, The Drive, Warley, Brentwood, Essex CM13 3BE. Tel: 0277 234 567.

Coastal Anti-Pollution League, Alverstoke, 94 Greenway Lane, Bath BA2 4LN. Tel: 0225 317094.

Commission of the European Communities (Belgium), Rue de la Loi 200, B1049 Brussels, Belgium. Tel: +32 2 235 11 11.

Commision of the European Communities (UK), 8 Storey's Gate, London SW1P 3AT. Tel: 01 222 8122.

Common Ground, 45 Shelton Street, London WC2H 9HJ. Tel: 01 379 3109.

Commonwork, Commonwork Land Trust, Bore Place, Chiddingstone, Edenbridge, Kent TN8 7AR. Tel: 0732 463255.

Community Service Volunteers, 71 West Street, St. Phillips, Bristol BS2 0BX. Tel: 0272 541952.

Concord Films and Videos, 210 Felixstowe Road, Ipswich, Suffolk IP3 9BJ. Tel: 0473 715754.

Confederation of British Industry (CBI), Centre Point, New Oxford Street, London WC1. Tel: 01 379 7400.

Conservation Foundation, 11a West Halkin Street, London SW1X 8JL. Tel: 01 235 1743.

Conservation International, 10-15 18th Street, Northwest, Suite 1002, Washington DC 20036, USA. Tel: +1 (202) 429 5660.

Conservation Monitoring Centre (CMC), 219c Huntingdon Road, Cambridge CB3 0DL. Tel: 0223 277314.

Consumers' Association, 2 Marylebone Road, London NW1 4DX. Tel: 01 486 5544.

Convention in Trade of Endangered Species (CITES) – see Conservation Monitoring Unit.

Cotswold Farm Park, Guiting Power, Cheltenham, Gloucestershire. Tel: 04515 307.

Council for Environmental Conservation (CoEnCo), London Ecology Centre, 80 York Way, London N1. Tel: 01 278 4736.

Council for National Academic Awards (CNAA), 344-354 Gray's Inn Road, London WC1X 8BP. Tel: 01 278 4411.

Council for the Protection of Rural England (CPRE), 4 Hobart Place, London SW1 0HY. Tel: 01 235 9481.

Council of Europe, BP 431R6–, F67006 Strasbourg, Cedex, France. Tel: +1 (88) 614961.

Countryside Commission, John Dower House, Crescent Place, Cheltenham, Glos. GL50 3RA. Tel: 0242 521381.

Countryside Commission for Scotland, Battleby, Redgorton, Perth PH1 3EW. Tel: 0738 27921.

Countryside Commission for Wales, 8 Broad Street, Newtown, Powys SY16 2LU. Tel: 0686 26799.

Cranfield Institute of Technology, Cranfield, Bedford, Bedfordshire MK43 0AL. Tel: 0234 750111.

Cranks Health Foods, 8 Marshall Street, London W1V 1LP. Tel: 01 437 9431.

Cumbrians Opposed to a Radioactive Environment (CORE), 98 Church Street, Barrow-in-Furness, Cumbria LA14 2HJ. Tel: 0229 33851.

Daily Telegraph, The, Peterborough Court, South T Plaza, 181 Marsh Wall, London E14 9SR. Tel: 01 538 5000.

Dartington Institute, Central Office, Shinner's Bridge, Dartington, Totnes, Devon TQ9 6JE. Tel: 0803 862271.

Department of the Environment, 2 Marsham Street, London SW1P 3EB. Tel: 01 212 3434.

Design Council, 28 Haymarket, London SW1Y 4SU. Tel: 01 839 8000.

Directory of Social Change, Radius Works, Back Lane, London NW3 1EL. Tel: 01 435 8171.

Domestic Fowl Trust, Honeybourne Pastures, Honeybourne, Evesham, Worcestershire. Tel: 0386 833083.

Dorset Trust for Nature Conservation, 39 Christchurch Road, Bournemouth, Dorset BH1 3NS. Tel: 0202 24241.

Earth Resources Research, 258 Pentonville Road, London N1 9JY. Tel: 01 278 3833.

Ecology Building Society, 8 Main Street, Crosshills, Keighley, West Yorkshire BD20 8TB. Tel: 0535 35933.

Economic and Social Research Council (ESRC), 1 Temple Avenue, London EC4Y 0BD. Tel: 01 353 5252.

Ecosphere Associates, 2521 East 6th Street, Tucson, Arizona 85716, USA. Tel: +1 (602) 327 5558.

Ecotec Research & Consulting, Priory House, 18 Steelhouse Lane, Birmingham B4 6BJ. Tel: 021-236 9991.

Ecovision – see Central Television.

Energy Efficiency Office, Department of Energy, Thames House, South, Millbank, London SW1P 4QJ.

Energy Equipment Testing Service, Department of Mechanical Engineering and Energy Studies, University College, Newport Road, Cardiff CF2 1TA. Tel: 0222 44211, ext 7116.

Environment Foundation, c/o Bain Clarkson Ltd, Ibex House, Minories, London EC3N 1HJ. Tel: 01 709 0744.

Environmental Data Services (ENDS), Unit 24, The Finsbury Business Centre, 40 Bowling Green Lane, London EC1R 0NE. Tel: 01 278 4745.

Esso UK plc, Esso House, Victoria Street, London SW1E 5JW. Tel: 01 834 6677.

Essochem Europe, Arundel Towers, Portland Terrace, Southampton SO9 2GW. Tel: 0703 634191.

European Centre for Environmental Communication (ECEC), 55 rue de Varenne, F-75341 Paris, Cedex 07, France. Tel: +33 1 42 22 12 34.

European Centre for Work and Society, PO Box 3073, NL 6202 NB Maastricht, Netherlands.

European Conference on Plastics in Packaging, Association of Plastics Manufacturers in Europe, Avenue Louise 250 Box 73, 1050 Brussels, Belgium. Tel: +32 2 640 2850.

European Council of Chemical Manufacturers' Federations (CEFIC), 250 Avenue Louise, Box 71, B-1050 Brussels, Belgium. Tel: +32 2 640 2095.

European Environmental Bureau, 29 rue Vautier, 1040 Brussels, Belgium. Tel: +32 2 647 0199.

European Network for Environmental Technology Transfer (NETT) – see Commission of the European Communities.

European Unit of Eurydice, 17 rue de Archimede, Bte 17, B-1040 Brussels, Belgium.

European Venture Capital Association, Clos du Parnasse, B1040 Bruxelles, Belgium. Tel: +32 3 513 7439.

Fairshares, 3 Endsleigh Street, London WC1H 0DD. Tel: 01 388 2117.

Farming and Wildlife Advisory Group (FWAG), The Lodge, Sandy, Bedfordshire SG19 2DL. Tel: 0767 80551.

Feruzzi Group, Calata Paita, 19100 La Spezia, Milano, Italy.

Field Studies Council (FSC), Preston Montford Field Centre, Montford Bridge, Shrewsbury SY4 1DX. Tel: 0743 850880.

Fisons plc, Fisons House, Princes Street, Ipswich, Suffolk IP1 1QH. Tel: 0473 56721.

Food from Britain, Market Towers, New Covent Garden, Market 1, Nine Elms Lane, London SW8. Tel: 01 720 2144.

Ford Conservation Awards – see The Conservation Foundation.

Forestry Commission (Scotland), 231 Corstorphine Road, Edinburgh EH12 7AT. Tel: 031 334 0303.

Forestry Commission, Forestry Commission Research Station, Alice Holt Lodge, Wrecclesham, Farham, Surrey GU10 4LH. Tel: 0420 22255.

Friends of the Earth (FoE), 26-28 Underwood Street, London N1 7JQ. Tel: 01 490 1555.

Frost & Sullivan, Sullivan House, 4 Grosvenor Gardens, London SW1W 0DH. Tel: 01 730 3438.

Gaia Books, Umbrella Studios, 12 Trundle Street, London SE1 1QT. Tel: 01 403 5124.

Gist-Brocades, PO Box 1, Wateringsweg 1, 2600 MA Delft, Netherlands. Tel: +31 15 799111.

Glasgow Garden Festival 1988 Ltd, Princes Dock, Glasgow G51 1JA. Tel: 041 429 8855.

Golden List, The – see Coastal Anti-Pollution League.

Greek Sea Turtle Protection Society, PO Box 51154, G.R. 14510 Kifissia, Greece.

Green Alliance, 60 Chandos Place, London WC2. Tel: 01 836 0341.

Green Books, Ford House, Hartland, Bideford, Devon EX39 6EE. Tel: 02374 293/621.

Green Deserts, Rougham, Bury St Edmunds, Suffolk IP30 9LY. Tel: 0359 70265.

Green Leaf Housing Awards, New Marketing Board, 82 New Cavendish Street, London W1M 8AD. Tel: 01 580 5588.

Greenpeace UK, 30-31 Islington, London N1 8XE. Tel: 01 354 5100.

Greentown Group, 19 Cawardon, Stantonbury, Milton Keynes, Buckinghamshire. Tel: 0908 310066.

Groundwork Foundation, Bennetts Court, 6 Bennetts Hill, Birmingham B2 5ST. Tel: 021 236 8565.

Guardian, The, 119 Farringdon Road, London EC1. Tel: 01 278 2332.

Habitat Magazine – see Council for Environmental Conservation (CoEnCo).

Halifax Building Society, Trinity Road, Halifax. Tel: 0422 65777.

Hawker Siddeley Group plc, 32 Duke Street, St James's, London SW1Y 6DG. Tel: 01 627 7718.

Hellenic Marine Environmental Protection Association (HELMEPA), 1-3 Mavrokordatou Street, Athens 142, Greece.

Henry Doubleday Research Association (HDRA), National Centre for Organic Gardening, Ryton-on-Dunsmore, Coventry CV8 3LG. Tel: 0203 303517.

Hoechst UK Ltd, Hoechst House, Salisbury Road, Hounslow, Middlesex TW4 6JH. Tel: 01 236 5336.

Hoggett Bowers Search and Selection, Abbott House, 1/2 Hanover Street, London W1R 9WB. Tel: 01 734 6852.

IBM UK Ltd, IBM South Bank, 76 Upper Ground, London SE1 9PZ. Tel: 01 928 1777.

ICC Information Group, 28-42 Banner Street, London EC1Y 8QE. Tel: 01 253 9736.

ICI – see Imperial Chemical Industries.

IFAPLAN, 32 Square Ambiorix, 1040 Brussels, Belgium.

Imperial Chemical Industries plc (ICI), Imperial Chemical House, Millbank, London SW1P 3JF. Tel: 01 834 4444.
– Biological Products Division, PO Box 1, Billingham, Cleveland TS23 1LB. Tel: 0642 522323.
Brixham Laboratory, Freshwater Quarry, Brixham, Devon TQ5 8BA. Tel: 08045 6411.
Paints Division, 1 Wrexham Road, Slough, Berkshire SL1 5DS. Tel: 0753 78218.
Plant Protection Division, Fernhurst, Haslemere, Surrey GO27 3JE. Tel: 0428 4061.

Independent, The, 40 City Road, London EC1. Tel: 01 253 1222.

Institute of Biology, 20 Queensberry Place, London SW7 2DZ. Tel: 01 581 8333.

Institute of Complementary Medicine, 21 Portland Place, London W1N 3AF. Tel: 01 636 9543.

Institute of Environmental Health Officers, Chadwick House, 48 Rushworth Street, London SE1 0QT. Tel: 01 928 6006.

Institute of Plant Science Research (IPSR) – see John Innes Institute.

Institute of Terrestrial Ecology (ITE), Merlewood Research Station, Grange-over-Sands, Cumbria LA11 6JU. Tel: 04484 226416.

Institute of Terrestrial Ecology (ITE), Monks Wood Experimental Station, Abbots Ripton, Huntingdon, Cambridgeshire PE17 2LS. Tel: 04873 381/8.

Institute of Virology, Mansfield Road, Oxford OX1 3SR. Tel: 0865 512361.

Intermediate Technology Development Group (ITDG), 9 King Street, London WC2E 6HN. Tel: 01 836 9434.

Intermediate Technology Development Group (ITDG), Myson House, Railway Terrace, Rugby, Warwickshire CV21 3HT. Tel: 0788 60631.

International Broadcasting Trust (IBT), 2 Ferdinand Place, London NW1 1LX. Tel: 01 482 2847.

International Chamber of Commerce (ICC), 38 Cours Albert, 75008 Paris, France. Tel: +33 14 562 3456.

International Coalition for Development Action, 22 rue des Bollandistes, 1040 Brussels, Belgium, or Apartado 23398, 08080 Barcelona, Spain.

International Environment Bureau, 61 Route de Chene, Ch-1208 Geneva, Switzerland. Tel: +41 22 865111.

International Institute for Applied Systems Analysis (IIASA), A-2361 Laxenburg, Austria.

International Institute for Environment and Development (IIED), 3 Endsleigh Street, London WC1H 0DD. Tel: 01 388 2117.

International Institute of Biological Husbandry, Abacus House, Station Approach, Needham Market, Ipswich, Suffolk IP6 8AT. Tel: 0449 720 838.

International Union for the Conservation of Nature (IUCN), IUCN Secretariat, 1196 Gland, Switzerland. Tel: +41 22 647 181.

John Innes Institute, Colney Lane, Norwich NR4 7UH. Tel: 0603 525711.

John Paul Getty Junior Charitable Trust, 149 Harley Street, London W1N 2DH. Tel: 01 486 1859.

Johnson Matthey plc, New Garden House, 78 Hatton Garden, London EC1N 8JP. Tel: 01 430 0011.

Johnson Matthey Chemicals, Orchard Road, Royston, Herts SG8 5HE. Tel: 0763 44161.

Joint Committee for Conservation of British Insects, c/o Institute of Terrestrial Ecology, Furzebrook Research Station, Wareham, Dorset BH20 5AS. Tel: 09295 51518.

Keep Britain Tidy Group, Bostel House, 37 West Street, Brighton, East Sussex BN1 2RE. Tel: 0273 23585.

La Metalli Industrialle Spa, Borgo Pinti 99, I-50121 Firenze, Italy.

Landscape Institute, Nash House, Carlton House Terrace, London SW1. Tel: 01 839 4044.

Lead Development Association, 34 Berkeley Square, London W1. Tel: 01 499 8422.

Leicester Polytechnic Centre for Educational Technology and Development, PO Box 143, Leicester LE1 9BH. Tel: 0533 554228.

Leigh Environmental, Leigh Interests plc, Lindon Road, Brownhills, Walsall, West Midlands WS8 7BB. Tel: 0543 375151.

Lloyds Bank plc, PO Box 95, Hay's Lane House, 1 Hay's Lane, London SE1 2HN. Tel: 01 407 1000.

London Docklands Development Corporation (LDDC), West India House, Millwall Dock, London E14. Tel: 01 515 3000.

London Energy and Employment Network (LEEN), 99 Midland Road, London NW1 2AH. Tel: 01 387 4393.

Lonhro, Cheapside House, 138 Cheapside, London EC2V 6BL. Tel: 01 606 9898.

Manpower Services Commission's Careers & Occupational Information Centre, COIC Sales Department, Freepost, Sheffield S1 4BR. Tel: 0742 753275.

Marine Conservation Society, 4 Gloucester Road, Ross-on-Wye, Herefordshire HR9 5BU. Tel: 0989 66017.

McCann Erickson International, McCann Erickson House, 36 Howland Street, London W1P 6BD. Tel: 01 580 6690.

McDonald's Corporation, McDonald's Plaza. Oak Brook, Illinois 60521, USA.

FOLLOW UP

Medical Research Council (MRC), St Bartholomew's Hospital, Medical College, Charterhouse Square, London EC1M 6BQ. Tel: 01 253 1537.

Midland Bank plc, Poultry, London EC2P 2BX. Tel: 01 260 8000.

Milton Keynes Development Corporation, Saxon Court, 502 Avebury Boulevard, Central Milton Keynes MK9 3HS. Tel: 0908 74000.

Ministry of Agriculture Fisheries and Food (MAFF), Whitehall Place, London SW1. Tel: 01-233 3000.

Ministry of Agriculture Fisheries and Food (MAFF), MAFF Publications, Lion House, Willowburn Trading Estate, Alnwick, Northumberland NR66 2PF. Tel: 0665 602881.

Naisbitt Group, The, PO Box 25536, Washington DC 20007, USA.

National Association for Environmental Education, c/o West Midlands College of Higher Education, Gorway, Walsall, West Midlands WS1 3BD.

National Centre for Alternative Technology, Llwyngwerm Quarry, Machynlleth, Powys SY20 9AZ. Tel: 0654 2400.

National Centre for Organic Gardening, Ryton-on-Dunsmore, Coventry CV8 3LG. Tel: 0203 303517.

National Council for Voluntary Organisations, 28 Bedford Square, London WC1B 3HU. Tel: 01 636 4066.

National Seed Development Organisation, Newton Hall, Newton, Cambridge. Tel: 0223 871167.

National Society for Clean Air (NSCA), 136 North Street, Brighton BN1 1RG. Tel: 0273 26313.

National Trust, 36 Queen Anne's Gate, London SW1H 9AS. Tel: 01 222 9251.

National Westminster Bank plc, 41 Lothbury, London EC2P 2BP. Tel: 01 726 1000.

Natural Environment Research Council (NERC), Polaris House, North Star Avenue, Swindon, Wiltshire SN2 1EU. Tel: 0793 40101.

Nature Conservancy Council (NCC), Northminster House, Peterborough PE1 1UA. Tel: 0733 40345.

Nature Conservancy Council (NCC Scotland), 12 Hope Terrace, Edinburgh EH9 2AS. Tel: 031 447 4784.

NETT (European Network for Environmental Technology Transfer) – Directorate-General XI – see Commission of The European Communities.

Network for Alternative Technology and Technology Assessment (NATTA), c/o Alternative Technology Group, Faculty of Technology, The Open University, Walton Hall, Milton Keynes, Buckinghamshire. Tel: 0908 74066.

New Economics Foundation – see The Other Economic Summit.

New Scientist, New Science Publications, Holborn Publishing Group, Commonwealth House, 1-19 New Oxford Street, London WC1A 1NG. Tel: 01 829 7777.

North South Productions, Woburn Buildings, 1 Woburn Walk, London WC1H 0JJ. Tel: 01 388 0351.

Novo Industri A/S, Novo Alle, 2880 Bagsvaerd, Denmark. Tel: +45 2 982333.

Nuclear Electricity Information Group, 22 Buckingham Gate, London SW1. Tel: 01 828 8248.

Observer, The, 8 St Andrew's Hill, London EC4V 5JA. Tel: 01 236 0202.

Ocean Environmental Management Ltd, Bloomsbury House, 74-77 Great Russell Street, London WC1B 3DA. Tel: 01 255 3363.

Open Tech Distance Learning Pack – see Leicester Polytechnic.

Organic Farmers and Growers Ltd, Abacus House, Station Approach, Needham Market, Ipswich, Suffolk IP6 8AT. Tel: 0449 720838.

Organic Food Manufacturers' Federation, The Tithe House, Peaseland Green, Elsing, East Deerham, Norfolk NR20 3DY.

Organic Growers' Association, 86 Colston Street, Bristol BS1 5BB. Tel: 0272 299800.

Organisation for Economic Co-operation and Development (OECD), Chateau de la Muette, 2 rue Andre Pascal, 75775 Paris, Cedex 16, France.

PA Design Ltd, 49 Princes Place, Holland Park, London W11 4QA. Tel: 01 221 2828.

PATAS (Pollution Abatement Technology Awards) – see Royal Society of Arts.

Pergamon Press Ltd, Headington Hill Hall, Oxford OX3 0BW.

Pilkington Brothers plc, Prescot Road, St Helens WA10 3TT. Tel: 0744 692554.

Plant Breeding Institute, Maris Lane, Trumpington, Cambridge CB2 2LQ. Tel: 0223 840411.

Plant Genetic Systems, Jozef Plateaustraat 22, 9000 Gent, Belgium. Tel: +32 91 242525.

Pollution Abatement Technology Awards (PATAS) – see Royal Society of Arts.

Pollution Control Distance Learning Project, Leicester Polytechnic, PO Box 143, Leicester LE1 9BH. Tel: 0533 554228.

Polmark – Directorate-General XIII – see Commission of the European Communities.

Project Respond – see National Westminster Bank, Schools Liaison Officer, Personnel Division, Recruitment Department.

Prudential Corporation plc, 142 Holborn Bars, London EC1N 2NH. Tel: 01 405 9222.

RealEat Company, 2 Trevelyan Gardens, London NW10 3JY. Tel: 01 459 7354.

Rechem International, 80 Shirley Road, Southampton SO1 3EY. Tel: 0703 898915.

Recycling Advisory Unit, Warren Spring Laboratory, Gunnels Wood Road, Stevenage, Hertfordshire SG1 2BX. Tel: 0438 313388.

Right Livelihood Foundation, School of Peace Studies, University of Bradford, Bradford BD7 1DP. Tel: 0274 737143.

Rockware Reclamation, Riverside House, Riverside Way, Northampton NN1 5DW. Tel: 0604 21255.

Rolls-Royce Ltd, 65 Buckingham Gate, London SW1E 6AE. Tel: 01 222 9020.

Royal Bank of Scotland plc, 42 St Andrew Square, Edinburgh EH2 2YE. Tel: 031 556 8555.

Royal Commission on Environmental Pollution, Church House, Great Smith Street, London SW1P 3BL. Tel: 01 212 3434.

Royal Environmental Health Institute of Scotland, 62 Virginia Street, Glasgow G1 1TX. Tel: 041 552 1533.

Royal Society for Nature Conservation (RSNC), The Green, Nettleham, Lincoln LN2 2NR. Tel: 0522 752326.

Royal Society for the Prevention of Cruelty to Animals (RSPCA), Causeway, Horsham, West Sussex RH12 1HG. Tel: 01 794 6224.

Royal Society for the Protection of Birds (RSPB), The Lodge, Sandy, Beds SG19 2DL. Tel: 0767 80551.

Royal Society of Arts, John Adam Street, Adelphi, London WC2N 6EZ. Tel: 01 930 5115.

Royal Town Planning Institute, 26 Portland Place, London W1N 4BE. Tel: 01 636 9107.

Saatchi & Saatchi plc, 15 Lower Regent Street, London SW1. Tel: 01 930 2161.

Safeway Food Stores Ltd, Beddow Way, Aylsford, Nr Maidstone, Kent ME20 7AT. Tel: 0622 77822.

Sainsbury plc, Stamford House, Stamford Street, London SE1 9LL. Tel: 01 921 6000.

Sainsbury Laboratory – see John Innes Institute.

Saint-Gobain Les Miroirs, Cedex 27, 92096 Paris-La-Defense, France.

Sandoz Ltd, CH-4002 Basle, Switzerland.

Science and Engineering Research Council (SERC), Polaris House, North Star Avenue, Swindon, Wiltshire SN2 1ET. Tel: 0793 26222.

Scientific Committee on Problems of the Environment (SCOPE), SCOPE Secretariat, 51 Boulevard de Montmorency, 75016 Paris, France. Tel: +33 1 4 525 0498.

Scottish Council for Community and Voluntary Organisations, 18-19 Claremont Crescent, Edinburgh EH7 4QD. Tel: 031 556 3882.

Sea Mammal Research Unit, c/o British Antarctic Survey, High Cross, Madingley Road, Cambridge CB3 0ET. Tel: 0223 311354.

Sea Turtle Protection Society, PO Box 51154, GR 14510 Kifissia, Greece.

Shell, Shell Centre, London SE1. Tel: 01 934 1234.

Shell Better Britain Campaign see – Nature Conservancy Council.

Shell International Petroleum Company Ltd, Shell Briefing Service, PAC/221, Shell Centre, London SE1. Tel: 01 934 1234.

SIA Ltd, 23 Lower Belgrave Street, London SW1. Tel: 01 730 4544.

Societé Nationale Elf-Aquitaine, 7 rue Nelaton, F-75015 Paris, France.

Soil Association, 86-88 Colston Street, Bristol BS1 5BB. Tel: 0272 290661.

Solvay & Cie, Ixelles (Bruxelles), rue du Prince Albert 33, Brussels.

Species Conservation Monitoring Unit – see Conservation Monitoring Centre.

Stoy Hayward, 8 Baker Street, London W1M 1DA. Tel: 01 486 5888.

Sunday Times, The, 1 Pennington Street, Wapping, London E1 9XW. Tel: 01 481 4100.

Sunderland Polytechnic, Careers Advisory Service, Edinburgh Building, Chester Road, Sunderland SR1 3SD. Tel: 0783 761 91.

SustainAbility Ltd, 1 Cambridge Road, London SW13 0PE. Tel: 01 876 1125.

Taylor Nelson Applied Futures, 44-46 Upper High Street, Epsom, Surrey KT17 4ZS. Tel: 03727 29688.

Technica, Lynton House, 7-12 Tavistock Square, London WC1H 9LT. Tel: 01 388 2684.

Television Trust for the Environment (TVE), 46 Charlotte Street, London W1P 1LX. Tel: 01 637 4602.

The Other Economic Summit (TOES), 4 Streche Road, Swanage, Dorset BH19 1NF. Tel: 0929 425 627.

Thermalite, Station Road, Coleshill, Birmingham B46 1HP. Tel: 0675 62081.

Think Green, Midland Business Centre, Temple House, 43-48 New Street, Birmingham B2 4LJ. Tel: 021 643 8899.

Thorn EMI Lighting Ltd, Tricity House, 284 Southbury Road, Enfield, Middlesex EN1 1TJ. Tel: 01 363 5353.

Thorn EMI Security Systems, Thorn EMI House, Upper St Martin's Lane, London WC2. Tel: 01 836 2444.

Total, 5 rue Michel-Ange, 75781 Paris, Cedex 16, France. Tel: +33 (1) 47 43 80 00.

Town & Country Planning Association, 17 Carlton House Terrace, London SW1. Tel: 01 930 8903.

TRAFFIC – see Conservation Monitoring Centre.

Transport 2000, Walkden House, 10 Melton Street, Euston, London NW1 2EJ. Tel: 01 388 8386.

Trusthouse Forte Community Chest, 11a West Halkin Street, London W1 – see Conservation Foundation.

Turning Point, The Old Bakehouse, Cholsey, Nr Wallingford, Oxon OX10 9NU.

UK 2000 Secretariat, 95-99 Ladbroke Grove, London W11 1PG. Tel: 01 229 1282.

Unilever plc, Unilever House, Blackfriars, London EC4P 4BQ. Tel: 01 822 5252.

United Nations Development Programme, New York, USA. Tel: +1 (212) 906 5000.

Universite de Perpignan, Faculté des Sciences Exactes et Naturelles, Laboratoire de Thermodynamique et Energetique, Avenue de Villeneuve, F-66025 Perpignan Cedex, France.

Universities Central Council on Admissions (UCCA), PO Box 28, Cheltenham, Glos GL50 1HY.

University of East Anglia, School of Environmental Sciences, Norwich NR4 7TJ. Tel: 0603 561161.

Urban Centre for Appropriate Technology, 82 Colston Street, Bristol BS1 5BB. Tel: 0272 272530.

Vegetarian Society, Parkdale, Dunham Road, Altrincham, Cheshire WA14 4QG. Tel: 061 928 0793.

Vitrifix, 39 Scotland Street, Sheffield S3 7BT.

Volkswagen AG, Postfach, D-3180 Wolfsburg 1, West Germany.

Voluntary Service Overseas (VSO), 9 Belgrave Square, London SW1X 8PW. Tel: 01 235 5191.

Volvo AB, S-405 08 Goteborg, Sweden. Tel: +46 31 590000.

Watch Trust for Environmental Education, 22 The Green, Nettleham, Lincoln LN2 2NR. Tel: 0522 752326.

Wholefood Trust, 24 Paddington Road, London W1N 4DR. Tel: 01 935 3924.

Wildfowl Trust, Gatehouse, Slimbridge, Glos GL2 7BT. Tel: 045389 333.

Wildlife Trade Monitoring Unit (WTMU) – see Conservation Monitoring Centre.

Wildscreen, Bristol & West Building Society, PO Box 27, Broad Quay, Bristol BS99 7AX. Tel: 0272 292656.

Wimpole Hall Park Home Farm, Arrington, Nr Royston, Hertfordshire. Tel: 0223 207257.

Wind Energy Group, 345 Ruislip Road, Southall, Middlesex UB1 2QX. Tel: 02 578 2366.

Woodland Trust, Autumn Park, Dysart Road, Grantham, Lincs NG31 6LL. Tel: 0476 74297.

Working Weekends on Organic Farms (WWOOF), 19 Bradford Road, Lewes, East Sussex BN7 1RB.

World Bank, 1818H Street, N.W. Washington DC 20433, USA. Tel: +1 (202) 4771234.

World of Nature Book Club, Swindon X, SN99 9XX.

World Resources Institute (WRI), 1735 New York Avenue, NW Washington, DC 20006, USA. Tel: +1 (202) 638 6300.

World Tourism Organisation (WTO), Capitan Hiya 42, Madrid-20, Spain. Tel: Madrid 279 2804 or 279 5107.

World Wildlife Fund, Panda House, 11-13 Ockford Road, Godalming, Surrey GU7 1QU. Tel: 04868 20551.

WWF Kodak Conservation Awards, c/o Hesketh House, 43-45 Portman Street, London W1H 9FG. Tel: 01 935 2655.

Young & Rubicam Ltd, Greater London House, Hampstead, London NW1. Tel: 01 387 9366.

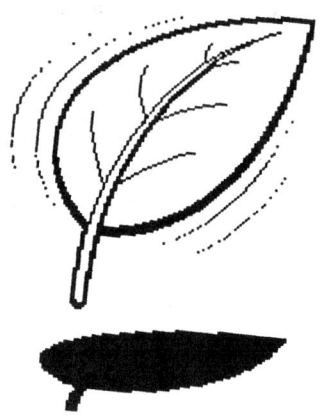

Index

3M 18, 48, 124, 125, 226
A T & T 95
Abbey National 44, 246
Abbott Laboratories 142
Abercrombie & Kent Travel 174
Acacia Productions 197, 246
acid rain 16, 19, 22, 23, 24, 26, 33, 35, 42, 77, 83, 85, 87, 109, 128, 166, 178, 190, 201, 214, 215, 232
Acorn Camps 174
acupuncture 181, 182
Adams, Bill 212
Adams, Richard 62
Addis 115
additives 19, 179, 213, 225
- food 90
- additive free foods 33
Adriatic 171
Advanced Micro Devices 95
advertising 57, 218-227
aerosols 19, 72, 78, 214, 244
- propellants 71, 86, 166
- aerosol sales 75
Africa 51, 68, 69, 74, 94, 96, 220, 238, 240, 244
Africa in Crisis 51
Africa Wildlife Society 177
African Development Bank 240
African Medical and Research Foundation (AMREF) 193
Agricultural and Food Research Council (AFRC) 85, 140, 183, 246
Agricultural Research Council 183
Agricultural Training Board 141, 246
agriculture 16, 26, 43, 85, 90, 110, 138-151, 190, 214
- policy 149
- pollution 29
- Third World 92
- wastes 131
agrochemicals 16, 103, 142, 148, 180, 183
Agrochemicals Association 138
agroforestry 147
aid agencies 204
aid issues 243
AIDS (Acquired Immune Deficiency Syndrome) 204-205, 224
Aigas Field Centre Holidays 174
air pollution 16, 23, 26, 29, 32, 79, 87, 103, 108, 113, 116, 124, 134, 190, 232
Air Resources Board 118
air travel 94
aircraft, noise 31
Albannach Insight Holidays 174
Alcan's Cash-a-Can scheme 115
Alfred Gregory Photo Holidays 174
Algeria 238
Allen, Benedict 211, 216
Alliance, Liberal-SDP 24
Aloisi de Larderel, Jacqueline 39
alternative medicine 182
alternative technology 175-176
Alternative Trading Organisations (ATOs) 62
Amazon 177, 202, 242
Ambio 199
America - see United States
American Foundation for AIDS Research (AMFAR) 205
Amnesty International 193
anaerobic digestion 108, 110-111, 139
animal welfare 19, 184
annual reports 40-44, 49
Antarctica 89, 168
appropriate technologies 68-69
Aquabase paints 61
Ara Study Tours 174
Arabia 176
Arboricultural Association 232, 246
ARC 18
Arctic 70, 190
ARKS (Animal Records Keeping) 103

Ash, Maurice 198, 200-201
Asia 174, 176
Asian and African Development Banks 242
ASLEF 220
Aslib (Association for Information Management) 105
Asociacion Ecologista de Defensa de la Naturleza - AEDENAT 16
Associated Portland Cement Manufacturers (now Blue Circle)
Association for Responsible Communication (ARC) 223, 246
Association for the Conservation of Energy 137-138
Association for the Protection of Rural Scotland 15
Association of Community Technical Air Centres 159
Atlas Copco 246
Attenborough, Sir David 172, 196, 208, 209, 211, 217
Austin Rover 11
Australia 37, 116, 174, 175, 208
Austria 20, 36, 43, 57, 70, 84
Baader-Meinhoff group 21
Babcock Hitachi 111
Babcock International plc 43, 246
Babcock Power 111
Baines, Professor Chris 155, 214-215, 216, 217
Baker, John 221
Baldock, David 138, 148-149
Baltic 86, 214
Band Aid 21, 50, 184, 246
Bangladesh 68, 204
Bank of England 187, 194, 246
Barbados 175
Barber, Janet 238, 242-242
Bardot, Brigitte 184
Bardot Foundation 184
Barker, Michael 215, 216
Barn Owl Travel 174
BASF 41, 86, 189, 246
BAT Industries - see British American Tobacco Industries
batteries,
- cadmium 19
- Duracell 19
- recycling 26
Baugh, Dr Ian 101
Bayer UK Ltd 86, 246
BBC 51, 197, 198, 202
- Enterprises 106
BBC Wildlife 44, 199
Beek, Meryl 213
Beggs, Mike 61
Beijer Institute 205
Belgium 20, 23, 36, 41, 70, 129, 138, 147, 180, 197, 220
Bellamy, Professor David 168, 177, 196, 208, 209
Berridge Incinerators 117
Betchart Expeditions 170
Better Environment Awards 9, 246
Bhopal 47, 87, 95, 126, 200, 214, 218
BICC 155
'Big Bang' 184, 186
Bio-Dynamic Agricultural Association 246
biocides 40
biofuel technologies 122
biogas 869, 3, 139
Biological Journeys 170
Biological Records Centre 101, 105
biomass 128
- energy 131
biopesticides 142
Biosphere II 72, 76-77, 246
BioTechnica - see BTL
biotechnology 16, 29, 43, 44, 87, 92-93, 109, 118-119, 138, 142, 181, 214
Biotechnology Bulletin 9
BioTreatment - see BTL
bird holidays 174-177
Birdquest 174
Blue Circle Industries plc 43, 121, 246
Blue Flag for Clean Beaches 171
Body Shop International plc 15, 18, 19, 49, 53, 56, 63, 70-71, 80, 83, 86, 246

Bolivia 185
Bookchin, Murray 37
Booker 142
Boots Biocides 60
Boots Company plc 40, 49, 60, 246
Bosch 117, 246
Botswana 175, 242
bovine somatotropin (BST) 144
Bowman, Dr John 84, 88-89
boycotts 19, 37, 61, 64, 71, 166
Boyle, Godfrey 152
Bradman, Godfrey 185
Brathay Exploration Group 174
Brazil 190, 202, 212
British Aerospace plc 113, 246
British Aluminium 18
British American Tobacco Industries 44, 246
British Antarctic Survey (BAS) 89, 237
British Coal 18
British Coal Corporation 8, 239
British Deer Society 100
British Fur Trade Association 224
British Gas plc 18, 41, 120, 246
British Hedgehog Society 19
British Lichen Society 100
British Medical Association (BMA) 181
British Nuclear Fuels (BNF) 8, 18, 43, 129, 134-135, 185, 220, 221, 222, 246
British Organic Farmers (BOF) 143, 246
British Organic Standard Board (BOSB) 143, 246
British Petroleum Company plc (BP) 9, 18, 31, 41, 98, 101, 131, 226, 227, 229, 246
British Rail 18
British Renewable Energy Forum 246
British Telecommunications plc 44, 246
British Tourist Authority 246
British Trust for Conservation Volunteers (BTCV) 9, 14, 15, 35, 41, 98, 99, 100, 158, 159, 175, 189, 230, 233, 235, 246
British Trust for Ornithology 98, 100, 162, 174, 189, 246
British Venture Capital Association 194, 246
British Wildlife Appeal 189, 246
British Wind Energy Association 132, 246
Broads Authority, The 246
Broads Plan 1987 169
Brown, Lester 141, 240-241
Brown, Roger 232
Bruce, Debbie 8, 234-235
Brundtland Commission (World Commission on Environment & Development) 46, 47, 50, 51, 126, 184
Brundtland, Gro Harlem 32, 33, 46, 50, 209
Brundtland Report - see Our Common Future
Brunt, Keith 49, 60-61
BTL (previously Biotechnica) 43, 116, 246
- Biotreatment 44, 92, 246
Buckton, Ray 220
building societies 188-189
Bulletin Group 246
Bulmer, H P Ltd 83, 246
Bundestag 8, 20, 21, 24, 37
Bunyard, Peter 215, 216
Burke, Tom 8, 9, 20, 214, 216
Burson Marsteller Ltd 220, 246
Bushbuck Safaris 175
Business in the Community 42, 194, 246
Business Network 246
butterfly house industry 189
Button, John 10
cadmium, batteries 19
Caledonian Wildlife 175
California 167, 175
California Institute of Technology 76
Calvert Social Investment Fund 186
Cambridge University 246

Cambrian Bird Holidays 175
Campaign for Lead Free Air (CLEAR) 185, 210, 246
Campaign for Nuclear Disarmament (CND) 24
Campaign for the Countryside 246
Canada 192, 243
Canadian Film Institute 203
Canberra Cruises 175
carbon dioxide 30, 31, 33, 77, 85, 86, 87, 110, 128, 187, 208, 238
carbon monoxide 116, 118
carcers 228-237
Carnegie Corporation 205, 240
Carson, Rachel 138, 206, 209, 217
Castrol Ltd 48, 61, 63, 246
catalogues 62
catalytic converters 31, 43, 77, 83, 108, 109, 116, 117, 118
Caufield, Catherine 196
CEDER 230
Celador Productions 197, 246
Central America 243
Central Bureau for Educational Visits & Exchanges 230, 246
Central Electricity Generating Board (CEGB) 8, 9, 18, 42, 86, 109, 111, 127, 129, 132, 156, 189, 234-235, 246
Central Television 197, 202, 246
Centre for Agricultural Strategy 144, 246
Centre for Alternative Technology 168, 175-176
Centre for Economic and Environmental Development (CEED) 15, 44, 246
Centre for Environmental Education (CEE) 213, 216, 233, 237, 246
Centre for Environmental Interpretation (CET) 246
Centre for Organic Gardening 176
Centre for World Development Education (CWDE) 96
CFCs - see chlorofluorocarbons
Channel 4 197, 198, 199, 202
Channel Tunnel 162
charities 227
Charities Aid Foundation (CAF) 194, 246
Chataway, Christopher 155, 156
chemical fertilizer 143
Chemical Industries Association (CIA) 30, 221-222, 246
chemical industry 16, 18, 29, 44, 87, 95, 103, 111, 114, 139, 140, 142
- fertilizer 143
- hazardous chemicals 59, 206
- pollution 77
(see also under e.g. pesticides and individual chemical names)
Cherfas, Dr Jeremy 94, 106, 187
Chernobyl disaster 22, 23, 29, 42, 47, 83, 85, 90, 129, 163, 166, 180, 181, 185, 197, 200, 201, 209, 214, 222, 223, 241
Chester, Dr Peter 8
Chile 177
China 177, 190, 240, 244
Chitty, Giles 184, 186-187, 238
chlorofluorocarbons (CFCs) 59, 71, 75, 85, 89, 179
Christian Ecology Group 15
Ciba-Geigy 41, 238, 246
CITES - see Convention on International Trade in Endangered Species
City Communications Centre 194, 247
Civic Trust 25, 230, 247
Civil Service Commission (CSC) 247
Clarke, Tim 110-111
Clean Britain's Beaches Campaign 247
clean technologies 63
Clean Up: It's Good Business 30
Cleanaway Ltd 117, 247
Cleaver, Tony 44
Clifford, Sue 216, 217
Clinton Davis, Stanley 3, 87, 239
Clover, Charles 196, 200-201

Club of Rome 31, 206
Coastal Anti-Pollution League 169, 171, 247
Coca-Cola 225
Coffee, Dr Ron 74
Commission of the European Communities (CEC) 3, 14, 84, 86-87, 91, 113, 114, 115, 147, 149, 168, 197, 205, 228, 233, 247
Common Agricultural Policy (CAP) 14, 138, 139, 148-149
Common Ground 247
Commonwealth Society for the Deaf 193
Commonwork 232, 247
Community Landscapes 155
Community Service Volunteers 230, 247
complementary medicine 181
computers 91, 94-107, 196
Concord Films and Videos 199, 247
Confederation of British Industry (CBI) 11, 30, 35, 48-49, 80, 111, 114, 135, 247
Conscience Fund 239
Conservation and Business Sponsorship 189
Conservation and Development Programme for the UK 15
Conservation Books 11
Conservation Foundation 199, 247
Conservation International 185, 187, 247
Conservation Monitoring Centre (CMC) 104, 105, 189, 247
Conservative Party 224
consultants, environmental 90
Consumers' Association 19, 63, 181, 132, 247
consumers 52, 55, 64, 67, 70, 78, 168, 178, 214, 225
– green consumer 19, 46, 56-59, 62, 63, 75, 77, 83, 193, 238
– markets 33
– products 77
contraception 68, 245
Contras 187
Control of Pollution Act, 1974 29
Convention on International Trade in Endangered Species (CITES) 66, 104, 243, 247
Convention on the Conservation of Marine Living Resources (CCAMLR) 243
Cooley, Dr Mike 37
Corado, Michelle 22
CORE (Cumbrians Opposed to A Radioactive Environment) 223
Corsica 176
cosmetics 33
Costa Rica 174, 187
Cotswold Farm Park 247
Council for Environmental Conservation (CoEnCo) 198, 231, 233, 246, 247
Council for National Academic Awards (CNAA) 233, 247
Council for the Protection of Rural England (CPRE) 25, 148, 150-151, 198, 247
Council of Europe 105, 169, 247
Council of Industrial Design 73
Council on Economic Priorities 217
Council of Europe's Campaign for the Countryside 147
Country Landowners' Association 140
Country Living 199
Countryside Commissions 15, 49, 98, 100, 145, 147, 155, 160, 194, 230, 232, 247
County Nature Conservation Trusts 19, 150
Cousins-Mills, Jane 214
Cox & Kings Travel 176
Cranfield Institute of Technology 139, 247
Cranks Health Foods 247
Cubatao 197
Cumbrians Opposed to a Radioactive Waste (CORE) 247
Cygnus Wildlife 176
Cyprus 176, 177
Czechoslovakia 20

Daily Mail 23
Daily Mirror 63
Daily Telegraph 196, 200-201, 247
Dale, Philip 8
Dartington Institute 228, 247
databases 79, 101-104
David Sayers Travel 176
Davidson, Joan 158-160
Davidson, John 155, 158-160
Davy 33
Davy McKee 111
Day, David 210
De Beers 9
De Bono, Edward 56, 75
debt, foreign 16
deforestation 16, 51, 64, 71, 74, 77, 85, 131, 191, 202
– tropical 64, 85
demographic transition 245
Denmark 23, 116, 118-119, 138, 139, 142, 178, 197, 204, 215
Department of Energy 42, 83, 132
Department of the Environment 8, 114, 115, 171, 189, 216, 232, 237, 247
desertification 96, 192, 202
design 47, 72-83, 237
– Design Centre 42, 83, 114
– Design Council 10, 72-73, 80-81, 83, 247
– green designer 10, 42, 72, 76, 80-81, 83, 114
Deutsche Babcock 111
development (see sustainable development)
development agencies 68
Dialog Information Retrieval Service 105
Dickens, Jackie 224
Die Grunen 37
Directory of Social Change, The 194, 247
disarmament 51
DOCTER European Environmental Yearbook 213
Domestic Fowl Trust 247
Donovan, Terence 212
Dornier-System 114
Dorset Trust for Nature Conservation 143, 184, 247
Double Dividends? The US Biotechnology Industry and Third World Development 92
Du Pont 218
Dubos, Rene 217
Duke of Edinburgh 185
Dulas Engineering 176
Durrell, Lee 198
Dutch Elm disease 92, 232
E & F Travels 176
E for Additives 179, 215, 225
Earth Resources Research 9, 98, 149, 247
Earthlife Foundation 8, 9, 100
earthquakes 208
Earthscan 51, 202, 203
Earthwatch 170, 213
East Africa 177
Eastern Europe 20, 37
Eastman Kodak 222
Eco series 197
Ecodisc 106-107
Ecodisc 94, 96, 106-107
Ecological Parks Trust 163
Ecologist, The 24, 199
Ecology Building Society 157, 187, 188-189, 247
Ecology Party 24
Economic and Social Research Council (ESRC) 85, 102, 105, 247
economic growth 16, 32, 46, 126, 187, 206
Economist, The 144
Ecosphere 72, 76-77
Ecosphere Associates 247
Ecotec Research & Consulting Ltd 79, 114, 247
Ecovision 197, 214-215, 247
Ecuador 167, 177, 242
education 52, 227, 228-237, 245
Ehrlich, Anne and Paul 206, 209, 216
Ekins, Paul 51, 209, 217

electricity 191
– privatisation 29
(see energy)
Electrodyne sprayer 75
Elkington, Elaine 8
Elkington, John 8, 9, 18, 19, 71, 94, 214, 216
emissions
– nitrogen 109
– vehicle 24, 30, 31, 43, 83, 84, 116, 117, 118
employment 228-237
Empressa Nacional de Residuos Radioactivos 129
Encounter Overland 176
endangered species 13, 16, 19, 147, 148, 177
ENDS Report 9, 58, 163, 199
energy 26, 47, 74, 90, 128-137, 153, 214, 237
– conservation 19, 32, 130, 228
– consumption 76, 124, 128, 132
– efficiency 16, 42, 52, 56, 80, 83, 113, 118, 128, 130, 136-137, 186, 241
– hydropower 191
– nuclear 16
– renewable 16, 110, 129, 130, 131, 132, 135
Energy Development International (EDI) 68
Energy Efficiency Office 247
Energy Efficiency Year 136, 137
Energy Equipment Testing Service 247
Energy Technology Support Unit (ETSU) 132
Environment Digest, The 199
Environment Foundation 114, 247
Environment Now 199
Environmental Data Report 216
Environmental Data Services (ENDS) 8, 9, 86, 163, 199, 247
environmental impact assessment (EIA) 47, 77, 169, 234
Environmental Law Association (UK) 28
environmental monitoring 94
Environmental Resources Ltd (ERL) 84, 90-91
Environmentalist, The 199
Environmentally Sensitive Areas 146
Esso UK plc 18, 41, 156, 225, 247
Esscohem Europe 31, 247
ethical investment 18, 19, 33, 56, 184, 186-187
Ethical Investment Fund 186, 187
Ethiopia 94, 190-191
Euromonitor's Book Report 196
European Centre for Environmental Communication (ECEC) 197, 198, 214, 247
European Centre for Work and Society 247
European Commission Host Organisation (ECHO) 105
European Community (EC) 3, 26, 116, 132, 136, 144, 146, 148, 169, 170, 212
European Confederation of Trade Unions 37
European Conference on Industry and Environmental Management (ECIEM) 238
European Conference on Plastics in Packaging 59, 247
European Council of Chemical Manufacturers' Federations (CEFIC) 30, 247
European Economic Community (EEC) 14, 24, 28, 31, 65, 121, 124, 131, 148-149, 171, 178, 212, 215, 234
– environment policy 26-27
European Environment Review 199
European Environmental Bureau (EEB) 9, 247
European Foundation for Living and Working Conditions 159
European Investment Bank 146
European Parliament 20
European Venture Capital Association 194, 247

European Year of the Environment (EYE) 3, 9, 14, 19, 41, 43, 109, 114, 160, 168, 215, 221, 238
– EYE Task Force 8
Eurydice 233, 247
Exodus Expeditions 167, 176
ExplorAsia 176, 177
Exxon Chemical International 31
EYE – see European Year of the Environment
Fairbrother Group 159
Fairchild Camera and Instrument 95
Fairshares 247
Fairways & Swinford 176
Falkland Islands 176
– Foundation 168
Farm and Food Society 143
Farm Gas Ltd 110-111
Farming and Wildlife Advisory Group (FWAG) 140-141, 235, 247
farming industry 16, 138-151, 245
– organic 56, 142-145, 183
fast food 71
Fauna and Flora Preservation Society (FFPS) 99, 172, 199
Ferranti 156
fertilizers 69, 110, 118, 139
Feruzzi Group 72, 247
Fiat 116
fibre optics 33, 76
Field Studies Council 229, 247
Fiji 175
Financial Initiative Ltd, The 157, 186-187
Financial Services Act 1986 186
Financial Times, The 23, 49, 111, 146
Finland 57, 167, 204
Fisher, Florence 84, 90-91
Fisons plc 40, 247
Flakt 111
Flood, Dr Mike 120-122, 132, 151
flue gas desulphurisation (FGD) 111, 127
Flux, Mike 126-127
Food and Agriculture Organisation (FAO) 69, 104
Food from Britain 144, 247
Ford 189
Ford Conservation Awards 194, 247
forestry 16, 86, 92, 138-151, 187, 203, 245
Forestry Commission 98, 99, 146, 232, 247
fossil fuels – see energy
Foster Wheeler Energy 111
Fountain Forestry 18, 146
Fourth Environmental Action Programme 14, 26-27, 29, 84, 86-87, 113
France 22, 39, 41, 57, 72, 116, 124, 129, 132, 137, 140, 143, 171, 174, 175, 182, 192, 197, 199, 215, 219
Free Form Arts Trust 158, 159
French Ministry of Environment 39
Friend's Provident Stewardship Fund 186
Friends of the Earth (FoE) 9, 12, 14, 15, 16, 19, 20, 22, 25, 63, 64-66, 70, 71, 79, 92, 117, 170, 185, 198, 201, 214, 221, 225, 242, 247
Frost and Sullivan 57, 178, 182, 248
fuel-efficient stoves 68-69, 83
fundraising 184-194
fur trade 19
Gaia Books 198, 209, 248
Gaia: An Atlas of Planet Management 207, 209
Galapagos Islands 167, 168, 174, 177
Game Conservancy 98, 138
Game Dr Meg 100
Gatsby Charitable Foundation 183
Gear, Alan 178, 215, 217
General Certificate of Secondary Education (GCS) 236
General Electric 111

genetic engineering 85, 86, 144, 180
Geo Expeditions 170
Getty, John Paul 184, 248
Gibraltar 174
Girardet, Herbert 209, 214, 216, 217
Gist-Brocades 92, 114, 248
Give As You Earn scheme 189
Glasgow Garden Festival 1988 Ltd 248
Glaxo 9
Global Environment Monitoring System (GEMS) 104, 216
Global Environmental Education Programme 213
Global Tomorrow Coalition 240
Global Village 94, 223
Globus 197
Gold, Professor Thomas 131
Golden List, The 169, 171, 248
Gollancz, Victor 19, 71
Good Wood Guide, The 63, 64–66, 71
Goode, Dr David 164–165, 212, 217
gorilla safari 176
Granada TV 197
Grant, Keith 80–81
Greater London Ecology Unit 100, 102, 105, 164–165
Grecian Holidays 31, 169, 170
Greece 22, 23, 31, 149, 169, 170, 197, 215
Greek Sea Turtle Protection Society 169, 248
Green Alliance 8, 9, 235
– newsletter 199
Green Bans 37
Green Books 248
green capitalists 49, 53
Green Capitalists, The 33, 214, 216
green consumer (see consumers)
Green Consumer Guide, The 9, 19, 71, 214, 216
Green Cuisine 56
Green Deserts 230, 248
green designer – see design
green growth 16, 33, 37, 46
green investor – see ethical investment
Green Leaf Housing Awards 155, 248
Green Parties 24, 36
Green Party, The (West Germany) 149
green politics 20–21, 24–25, 36–37, 215
green tourist 46, 211
greenhouse effect 16, 31, 86, 128, 134, 238
GreenNet 104, 105
Greenpeace 12, 14, 17, 23, 25, 53, 63, 70, 92, 104, 185, 189, 193, 201, 220, 221, 222, 223, 225, 248
Greens, The 20, 21, 36–37
Greentown Group 152, 248
Groundwork Foundation 9, 14, 35, 41, 42, 44, 98, 100, 152, 155, 156, 158–160, 230, 235, 248
Grove-White, Robin 138, 150–151
Guardian, The 23, 63, 99, 180, 200, 207, 248
guidelines, environmental 30
– International Chamber of Commerce (ICC) 30
– Nature Conservancy Council (NCC) 31
Habitat 231, 248
Haigh, Nigel 26–27, 212
Hailes, Julia 8, 9, 19, 71, 214–215, 216
Hailey, Arthur 208, 217
Haines, Dr Richard 79
Halifax Building Society 44, 248
Hall, Professor Peter 157
hamburgers 71
Hammond, Roger 236–237
Handley, Dr John 155
Hanssen, Maurice 215, 216
Harding, Christopher 8, 128, 134–135, 222
Harrison, Paul 49, 68–69
Harvey-Jones, Sir John 40, 75, 166

Harwell Laboratory 185
Hawker Siddeley Group plc 42, 248
health 37, 52, 55, 90, 119, 126, 178–183, 201, 214, 220
– foods 19, 144
Heathrow 153
Heineken beer 19
Heinz 184
Hellenic Marine Environmental Protection Association (HELMEPA) 31, 248
Hellenic Society for the Protection of Nature 177
Henderson, Hazel 198
Henley Centre 168, 196
Henry Doubleday Research Association 143, 176, 248
herbalism 181, 182
Hertfordshire & Middlesex Trust for Nature Conservation 14
HF Holidays 176
Himalayas 176
Hobelink, Henk 92
Hoechst UK Ltd 41, 248
Hoffmann-La Roche 218
Hoggett Bowers Search and Selection 57, 248
holidays (see tourism)
Holland 14, 19, 92, 139, 157, 183, 221
Holmes, Peter 42
homeopathy 181, 182
Horizon (BBC) 170, 197
Horizon Holidays 31
Hosking Tours 176
Hughes, David 213
Hungary 20
Huw Davies, Gareth 212, 216
Huxley, Anthony 198
hydropower 191
IBM – see International Business Machines
ICC Information Group 109, 248
Iceland 174, 175
ICI – see Imperial Chemical Industries
IFAPLAN 248
Illich, Ivan 36
Imperial Chemical Industries (ICI) 9, 40, 63, 74, 75, 83, 92, 114, 127, 135, 142, 156, 166, 248
– Brixham Laboratory 86
– ICI Paints 61
– ICI Pharmaceuticals 156
Imperial College 113, 237
– Centre for Environmental Technology 151
Independent, The 196, 200, 248
India 69, 95, 176, 204, 242, 245
Indonesia 74, 204, 243
Industry and Environment 199
Industry Year 1986 9, 10, 42, 72, 114
information technology 94, 97
Informisep 233
inner city renewal – see urban renewal
INSEAD (European Institute of Business Administration) 39
Institute for European Environmental Policy (IEEP) 15, 27, 124, 148–149
Institute for Terrestrial Ecology 101
Institute of Biology 230, 248
Institute of Complementary Medicine 181, 248
Institute of Ecotechnics 77
Institute of Environmental Health Officers, 231, 248
Institute of Plant Science Research (IPSR) 248
Institute of Terrestrial Ecology (ITE) 85, 100, 105, 147, 248
Institute of Virology 248
Integrated Mediterranean Programme 26
Intel 95
Intermediate Technology Development Group (ITDG) 73–74, 83, 193, 232, 248
International American Development Bank 51

International Association for Environmental Affairs 91
International Biological Programme 162
International Broadcasting Trust (IBT) 198, 199, 202, 248
International Business Machines (IBM) 11, 18, 44, 97, 98, 101, 102, 103, 248
International Centre for Conservation Education 18
International Chamber of Commerce (ICC) 30, 248
International Coalition for Development Action (ICDA) 92, 248
International Council for Bird Preservation (ICBP) 104
International Energy Agency (IEA) 128
International Environment Bureau (IEB) 39, 248
International Institute for Applied Systems Analysis (IIASA) 84, 248
International Institute for Environment and Development (IIED) 9, 31, 32, 51, 193, 198, 209, 216, 242, 248
International Institute for Tropical Agriculture 69
International Institute of Biological Husbandry 143, 248
International Labour Organization (ILO) 39
International Oceans Institute 31
International Planned Parenthood Federation (IPPF) 69
International Research Institute for Social Change (RISC) 55
International Tropical Timber Organisation (ITTO) 65–66
International Union for the Conservation of Nature and Natural Resources (IUCN) 31, 32, 104, 160, 207, 217, 242, 243, 248
International Wildfowl Research Bureau (IWRB) 104
investment 20, 41, 53, 69, 90, 136, 146, 184–194, 222, 226
(see also ethical investment)
Ireland 22, 23, 197
irradiated food 180–181
Israel 174
Italy 22, 23, 57, 72, 95, 116, 171, 174, 197, 218
Jackman, Brian 166, 172–173, 196
JANET (Joint Academic Network) 104, 105
Japan 54, 73, 108, 111, 116, 190, 192, 212, 214
Jersey Wildlife Preservation Trust 14
Jet Propulsion Laboratory (JPL) 76
John Brown Engineering 111
John Elkington Associates 31, 41
John Innes Foundation 183, 248
Johnson Matthey plc 33, 43, 48, 56, 109, 116, 117, 118, 248
– Chemicals 83, 116, 248
– Metals 63
Johnson, Stanley 209, 216
Joint Committee for Conservation of British Insects 101, 248
Joint European Torus (JET) 131
Joseph, Michael 217
Judd, Adrian 78–79
Jungk, Professor Robert 36
Kalahari Conservation Society 242
Keep Britain Tidy Group 171, 230, 248
Kelloggs 179, 189
Kelly, Petra 8, 14, 36–37
Kenya 13, 69, 172–173, 177, 204, 236, 244
Kew, Royal Botanic Gardens 42, 101, 236, 238
Khomeini, Ayatollah 244
Kidder, Peabody 108
King, Angela 216, 217
Kingbird Tours 170
Kodak 18, 189
Kodak Conservation Awards 194

Kohl, Helmut 24
Kornberg, Professor Sir Hans 220
Krauer, Alex 238
Kyle, Russell 215
L'Oreal 225
Labour Party 24, 228
Lamb, Robert 202–203
land contamination 79
Land Rover 11
Land Use Consultants 163
Landlife 159
Landscape 199
Landscape Institute 140, 231, 248
Lapland 167
lateral thinking 56
Latin America 9, 37
law, environmental 28, 49
Lawyers Ecology Group 24
Layfield enquiry 129
Le Guin, Ursula 208, 216
Lead Development Association 63, 248
lean burn technology 31, 117, 118
Lean, Geoffrey 16, 196, 244–245
Leicester Polytechnic 237, 248
Leigh Environmental 117, 248
leisure 144, 150, 153, 168, 211
Leo Burnett 9, 224
Leonard Cheshire Foundation Overseas 193
LEPRA 193
Les Amis de la Terre 92
Letchford, Dr Brian 61
Liberals 25
Life on Earth 172, 196
Limits to Growth, The 44, 206
Lindblad Explorer, The 167–168
Linnaean Society 101
Live Aid 94
Living Earth Rainforest Resource Pack 236
Living Economy: a New Economics in the Making, The 51
Living Planet, The 196
Lloyds Bank plc 44, 248
Lodge Cottrell 111
London Docklands 152, 157
London Docklands Development Corporation (LDDC) 152, 248
London Ecology Centre 165
London Energy and Employment Network (LEEN) 115, 248
London Research Centre 105
London Weekend Television (LWT) 210
Longman Cartermill Ltd 105
Lonhro 44, 248
Loudon, A.A. 238
Loughborough Polytechnic 237
Love Canal 44
Lovins, Amory 36
Lower Kingcombe 143, 185
Lowman, Bob 188–189
Lucas Aerospace 37
Luxembourg 22, 23
Lyon, Nicola 63
Mabey, Richard 216, 217
Macclesfield Groundwork Trust 194
Macrory, Richard 28
Madagascar 174, 177, 189
Majorca 176, 177
Malaysia 190, 243
Mali 96
Mammal Society 101
Management Information Services (MIS) 108
Manpower Services Commission (MSC) 113, 229, 232, 237, 248
Marine Conservation Society 14, 101, 171, 247, 248
Market and Opinion Research International (MORI) 22, 206, 222
Marketing 70
markets 48–49, 56–71
– market research 57
– marketing 68–69, 237
Marriott Hammond Resource Consultants 236
Marriott, Niall 236–237
Marshall, Lord 42, 129

Mauritania 238
Mauritius 177
Max Planck Institute 183
McAughtry, Georgina 8
McCann Erickson Advertising Ltd 67, 225, 248
McCormick, John 232
McDonalds 44, 71, 179, 201, 248
McKenna, Virginia 210, 216
McLuhan, Marshall 94, 223
McNamara, Robert 244
McNulty, Kirk 19
media 196–217
Medical Research Council (MRC) 85, 181, 249
Mediterranean 70, 86, 101, 146, 168, 169, 214
Megatrends 67
Melchett, Lord 198
Menorca 174
Mercedes 116
Mercury Provident plc 187
Metal Box 18
Mexico 161, 177
Microbial Resources Ltd (MRL) 142
Microinfo 105
Microsystems Centre 105
Middle East 43
Midland Bank plc 44, 249
Miles, Hugh 209
Milton Keynes Development Corporation (MKDC) 83, 152, 249
Milton Keynes Energy World 42
Ministry of Agriculture, Turkey 169
Ministry of Agriculture, Fisheries and Food (MAFF) 138, 146, 148, 179, 180, 181, 249
Mitsubishi 111
Monergy 42, 137
money 184–195, 237
Monitoring and Assessment Research Centre (MARC) 216
Monsanto 9, 113, 116, 219, 220
Moorcroft, Sheila 52–55
Moore, Dr Norman 212, 216
Moore, Tim 8, 9
Morgan-Grenville, Fern 215, 216
Morocco 176, 238
motor industry (cars) 18, 63, 67, 77, 117
Mountain Gorilla Project 172
Myers, Dr Norman 190–192, 207, 209, 216, 217, 238
Myxoma virus 92
Naisbitt, John 67, 249
National Aeronautics and Space Administration (NASA) 76, 96
National Association for Environmental Education 231, 249
National Association of Retail Furnishers 65
National Audit Office 146
National Centre for Alternative Technology 232, 249
National Centre for Organic Gardening 143, 176
National Computing Centre 105
national conservation strategies, 242, 243
National Council for Voluntary Organisations (NCVO) 9, 159, 194, 249
– Waste Watch 35
National Environment Agency 118
National Farmers Union (NFU) 148, 220
National Federation for Biological Recording 101, 105
National Federation of City Farms and Community Gardens 158, 159, 160, 176
National Federation of Zoos 105
National Film Board 203
National Health Service 181, 182
National Parks 232
National Seed Development Organisation 142, 249
National Semiconductor and Texas Instruments 95

National Society for Clean Air (NSCA) 140, 249
National Trust 25, 101, 150, 174, 213, 233, 249
– for Scotland 14
National Westminster Bank plc 44, 122, 189, 194, 249
– Project Respond 249
Natural Environment Research Council (NERC) 9, 84, 85, 88, 102, 232, 237, 238, 249
Nature Conservancy Council (NCC) 9, 14, 15, 31, 41, 44, 63, 67, 98, 99, 101, 105, 130, 138, 147, 162, 176, 189, 194, 229, 230, 232, 249
Nature Conservation Bureau (NCB) 16
Nature Conservation Guidelines for the Onshore Oil and Gas Development 31
Nature Conservation Trusts 98, 100
Nature Expeditions International 170
NEI International Combustion 111
Neighbourhood Energy Action 159, 160
Nepal 74, 174, 175, 176
Nestle 225
Netherlands, The 23, 36, 70, 114, 158, 174, 180, 192, 197, 204, 205
NETT (The European Network for Environmental Technology Transfer) 113, 247, 249
Network for Alternative Technology and Technology Assessment (NATTA) 232, 249
Network Foundation 8
networking 53
New Age 36–37
New Economics Foundation 157, 249
New Guinea 211–212
New Homes Marketing Board 155
New Hope or False Promise: Biotechnology and Third World Agriculture 92
New Internationalist 199
New Opportunities for the Countryside 145
New Organic Food Guide 178
New Organic Food Guide, The 176
New Scientist 10, 99, 187, 196, 199, 249
New Zealand 175, 177, 185
News of the World 23
Nicaragua 187
Nicholson, Adam 212, 217
Nicholson, Max 9, 161, 162–163, 212, 217
Nickson, Sir David 11, 46, 48–49, 80, 111
Niger 69
Nigeria 141, 244
NIREX 18, 23, 220–221, 223
Nissan 116
nitrogen tax 145
NOAH (National Online Animal History) 103
noise 79, 87, 103, 232
– aircraft 31
Nordic Conference on Environment and Development 204
Norfolk Broads 169
North America 52, 67, 120, 164, 169, 214
North, Richard 196, 200, 214, 217
North Sea 86, 168, 214
North South Productions 198, 199, 249
North Yemen 176
Norway 32, 46, 50, 57, 86, 145, 167, 192, 197, 204, 205, 209
Novo Industri 93, 113, 118–119, 138, 139, 142, 249
Noyes Foundation 205
nuclear 90, 124, 129, 185, 221
– energy 16, 23, 24, 36, 42, 87, 128, 131, 200, 222, 214, 235
– fall-out 178
– industry 129, 134–135
– war 21, 200, 244

– waste 16, 128, 129, 200, 221
Observer, The 23, 196, 200, 236, 249
Occidental Chemical Corporation 44
Ocean Environmental Technology 117
Oceanic Society Expeditions 170
Office Cleaning Services 189
Ogilvy & Mather Public Relations 220
Only One Earth – TV 51, 198, 209
Operation Groundwork 155–156
organic 143
– agriculture 16, 56, 142, 143–145, 148–149, 151, 183
– gardening 174
– produce 19, 37, 178–179, 180, 183
Organic Farmers and Growers 143, 144, 249
Organic Food Manufacturers' Federation 143, 249
Organic Foods Production Association of North America 143
Organic Growers' Association 143, 249
Organisation for Economic Cooperation and Development (OECD) 29, 31, 32, 58, 92, 113, 160, 191, 249
Organization of Petroleum Exporting Companies (OPEC) 116, 128, 191
Orion Royal Bank 155
Ornitholidays 176
Oryx 199
osteopathy 181
Our Common Future 10, 33, 46, 47, 50, 51, 126, 209, 213, 214
Overseas Development Administration (ODA) 242
Oxfam 51, 193, 242
ozone layer, 16, 31, 59, 71, 77, 78, 85, 86, 88–89, 166, 201, 238
package tour holidays (see tourism)
packaging 55, 79, 78–79, 94
Packaging Council 9
paints industry 61
– anti-fouling 86
Panama 51, 175
Panos Institute 199, 204–205
Panoscope 199, 204
paper 26, 114, 120
– recycled 11, 19, 55
Paperback Ltd 11
Papua New Guinea 176
Papyrus Tours 177
Parker, Sir Peter 226
Parsons, Vivica 197
Partners, The 236
Peabody Process Systems 111
Pearson, Joss 198
Peregrine Holidays 177
Pergamon Press Ltd 249
Peru 177
pesticides 13, 23, 80, 90, 92, 93, 142, 183, 206
– biological 139
– pollution 138, 148
petrol, unleaded 19, 117, 225
Philippines 62
phosphate fertilizers 69
Pilkington Brothers plc 42, 155-156, 249
– Energy World House 42
Pilkington, David 155
Plansee Metals 63
Plant Breeding Institute 142, 249
Plant Genetic Systems 93, 138, 249
plant pathology 183
plastic 59, 120
Poland 20, 175, 214
policy, environmental 226
politics – see green politics
pollution 11, 30, 61, 63, 77, 83, 95, 108–127, 139, 151, 192, 208, 213, 214, 221, 232
– agricultural 16, 29, 138, 145, 148, ¼G

– air 3, 16, 23, 26, 29, 32, 79, 87, 103, 108, 113, 116, 134, 190, 225, 232
– carbon dioxide (see under this heading)
– chemical 77
– nitrates 26
– radioactive (see nuclear)
– water 32, 87, 103, 110, 113, 138, 148, 190, 215
(see also emissions)
pollution control 3, 27, 46, 48, 56, 60, 75, 77, 79, 138, 190
– technology markets 33, 79, 109, 113, 118, 228, 229, 237
Pollution Abatement Technology Awards (PATAS) (now The Better Environment Awards) 9, 40, 60, 74, 91, 111, 114, 249
Pollution Prevention Directorate 39
Pollution Prevention Pays 45, 124
Polmark 79, 249
polychlorinated biphenyls (PCBs) 44, 58–59, 222
population 16, 33, 47, 48, 57, 74, 131, 150, 209, 241, 243, 244–245
Porritt, Jonathon 15, 16, 209, 216, 217
Portman Building Society 18
Portugal 23, 129, 197, 215
Prince Charles 9, 55, 140, 181
Princess of Wales Conservatory 42
Pritchard, George 221
privatisation 29
Protected Areas Data Unit 104
Prudential Assurance 18
Prudential Corporation plc 44, 189, 249
public relations 57, 58
publishing 56, 196–217
PVC 59, 61, 69
radiation 85, 88, 103, 143, 166, 221
Rae, Alan 239
radioactive waste 33, 223
– management 42, 87
Rainbow Warrior, The 185
rainforests – see tropical, forests and deforestation
Ramsar Convention on Wetlands of International Importance 185
Ramsar Wetlands Convention 243
Reader's Digest, The 23
Reagan, President Ronald 240, 244
Realeat Company 178, 249
Rechem 18, 117, 221, 222, 249
Recycling Advisory Unit 249
recreation – see leisure
Recycler's Guide to Greater London, The 115
recycling 11, 78–79, 81, 87, 110, 241
– batteries 26
– cans 114
– paper 19, 55
– wastes 115
Red Cross 205
Redd Barna 205
refuse derived fuel (RDF) 120–122
renewable energy – see energy
renewable resource technology 125
research 47, 53, 69, 84–93
Research Cottrell 111
Reuters 51
Rhine 10, 11, 29, 40, 83, 87, 214, 218
rhinoceros
– conservation 13
– rescue appeal 174
Rifkin, Jeremy 9
Right Livelihood Award 198, 249
Rio-Tinto Zinc (RTZ) 221
Rippon, Angela 221
Robertson, James 207, 215, 216
Rockware Reclamation, Vend-a-Can 83, 249
Roddick, Anita 53, 56, 63, 70–71, 228
Rolls-Royce 42, 73, 117, 249
Rowcliffe, Nick 8, 9
Royal Bank of Scotland 44, 249
Royal Botanical Gardens, Kew 101, 104, 105, 236

Royal Commission on Environmental Pollution 75, 92, 249
Royal Forestry Society 100
Royal Society for Nature Conservation (RSNC) 15, 42, 98, 99, 100, 101, 184, 230, 249
Royal Society for the Prevention of Cruelty to Animals (RSPCA) 14, 15, 249
Royal Society for the Protection of Birds (RSPB) 14, 25, 63, 100, 101, 141, 147, 150, 170, 176, 177, 228, 233, 249
– holidays 177
Royal Society of Arts (RSA) 9, 73, 91, 111, 114, 246, 249
Royal Town Planning Institute (RTPI) 231, 249
Rural Areas Database (RAD) 102
rural land use 16, 150–151
Saarberg-Holter 111
Saatchi & Saatchi 218, 249
Sadler, Robin 225
Safari Consultants 177
safari holidays 174–177
Safeway 144, 179, 249
Sagne, Alain 214–215
Sainsbury, David 183
Sainsbury Laboratory 138, 180–181, 183
Sainsbury plc 18, 44, 179, 249
Saint-Gobain 43, 249
Salisbury, Mike 209
Sandoz 11, 29, 40, 41, 218, 219, 249
Sankey Canal Restoration Society (SCARS) 156
satellites 202–203
Scandinavia 21, 85, 128, 166
(see also under individual countries)
Schumacher, Dr E F 37, 73–74, 207, 209, 217
Schweppes 221
Science and Engineering Research Council (SERC) 85, 97, 249
Scientific Committee on Problems of the Environment (SCOPE) 85, 249
Scott, Selina 221
Scott, Sir Peter 168, 211, 217
Scottish Council for Community and Voluntary Organisations 194
Sea Mammal Research Unit 85, 249
Sea Turtle Protection Society 31, 250
Sea World 97
Searle, Graham 221
Secrett, Charles 64–66, 214
Seligmann, Peter 187
Sellafield 42, 129, 222, 223
Seveso disaster 87, 95
Seychelles 177
Seymour, John 209, 214, 216, 217
Shackleton, Keith 168, 198, 211, 217
Shell Group 9, 18, 19, 41, 42, 98, 133, 165
– motor mileage marathon 133
– Shell Better Britain Campaign 18, 42, 194, 250
Shoard, Marion 138, 148, 199, 207, 209–210, 217
Shopley, Jonathan 8, 9, 94
SIA Ltd 95, 250
Siberia 174, 177
Sierra Leone 244
SimChem 111
Singer, Andre 198–199
Single European Act 28
Sizewell 'B' 129, 132, 235
Slapton Ley 106–107
Snyder, Jim 168, 198, 211, 217
Social Democrats 21
Social Investment Forum Newsletter 186
Soil Association 19, 179, 180, 143, 179, 180, 250
soil conservation 241
soil erosion 87, 131, 141, 147, 148, 190, 191

Soil Survey 140, 141
solar energy 130, 131, 132
Solvay 41, 250
Somerset Nature Conservation Trust 96, 98
South Africa 37, 186
Soviet Union 20, 77, 166, 190
Space Biosphere Ventures (SBV) 77
Space Shuttle 96
Spain 129, 148, 176, 177, 197, 215
species conservation 207
Species Conservation Monitoring Unit 104, 250
Sports Council 157
Sri Lanka 68, 74, 204, 242
State of the World, The 32, 209, 240–241
Stewardship Fund 187
Stichting Natuur en Milieu 14, 19
Stockholm Conference 32, 39
Stoy Hayward 194, 250
straw burning 140
Strieber, Whitley 208, 217
Sun Med Holidays 31, 170
Sunbird 177
Sunday Times, The 23, 173, 196, 221, 250
superconductivity 86
Survival International 242
Sussex Trust for Nature Conservation 14
SustainAbility Ltd 8, 14, 19, 40, 50–51, 71, 98, 209, 214, 250
sustainable agriculture 141, 179
sustainable development 8, 10, 16, 20, 32–33, 35, 36, 44, 46–47, 49, 50–51, 63, 64, 75, 84, 86, 88, 94, 97, 113, 126, 127, 166, 168, 184, 214
SustainAble Development of the Biosphere 84
Swan Hellenic 177
Sweden 43, 48, 57, 83, 86, 111, 116, 129, 131, 167, 197, 204, 205
Swedish Tourist Board 168
Switzerland 11, 43, 48, 57, 59, 129, 182, 218
Synchronicity 105
Tachmintzis, Joanna 8
Tanzania 62, 174, 175, 204
Taylor Nelson Applied Futures 19, 52–55, 57, 63, 186, 250
Technica 95, 250
technology
– appropriate 68–69
– clean 63
– low waste 74, 113, 126
– resource efficient 60–61
Telecom Gold 105
television 202–203
Television Trust for the Environment (TVE) 199, 202–203, 209, 217, 250
Tesco 144, 179
textile industry 114
Thatcher, Prime Minister Margaret 129
The Other Economic Summit (TOES) 19, 209, 250
Thermalite 75, 250
Think Green 155, 159, 165, 250
Third Environmental Action Programme 29
Third World 16, 37, 47, 62, 68, 69, 74, 80, 83, 92, 115, 131, 141, 161, 172, 183, 187, 190–192, 193, 202–203, 204–205, 236, 237, 243, 244–245
– debt 44
Thomson Holidays 31, 170, 196, 200, 206–208, 209
Thorn EMI 83, 137, 250
Threatened Plants Unit 104
tidal power 129
Tiger Tops Mountain Travel International 177
Timber Trade Federation 65
Timberlake, Lloyd 8, 50–51, 196, 198, 209, 217
Time 240
Times, The 153, 200
Tinker, Jon 196, 204–205

Tioxide 40
TNT 113
Tolba, Dr Mostafa 216
Torrey Canyon, The 85
Total 41, 250
tourism 31, 56, 155, 166–177, 237
– holidays 19, 31, 53
– package tours
tourist – see green tourist
Town & Country Planning Association (TCPA) 152, 199, 200, 250
toxic chemicals 116
toxic waste 44, 221
– management 228
Trade Union Congress (TUC) 18, 224
TRAFFIC (Trade Records Analysis of Flora and Fauna in Commerce) 104, 250
Traidcraft 18, 62
training 227
Transport 2000 25, 157, 250
transport 26, 153
Travers, Bill 210
Travers, Will 210, 216
Treaty of Rome 28, 29
Tree, Michael 73
tropical
– forests 16, 22, 50, 71, 77, 187, 190, 202, 207, 236, 244
– hardwoods 19, 64–65
(see deforestation, tropical)
Tropical Forests: A Call for Action 185
Trowbridge, Martin 222
Trust for Urban Ecology (TRUE) 163, 164–165
Trusthouse Forte Community Chest 194, 250
Turkey 169
Turner, George 208, 217
Turning Point 19, 250
turtles 31
– loggerheads 169
– sea 170
Twickers World 177
UK 2000 35, 41, 160, 230, 250
UK Conservation and Development Programme 207
UK Reclamation Council 115
UK Register of Organic Food Standards 180
unemployment 228
UNESCO 22, 104, 160
UNICEF 68
unilateral disarmament 24
Unilever 44, 225, 250
Union Carbide 18, 218
Unit of Comparative Plant Ecology (UCPE) 237
United Engineers 111
United Nations (UN) 33, 50, 91, 198, 209, 244
United Nations Development Programme (UNDP) 185, 250
United Nations Environment Programme (UNEP) 31, 103, 104, 105, 199, 202, 209, 216
– Industry and Environment Office 39
United Nations General Assembly 198
United Nations Stockholm Conference on the Human Environment 209, 234
United States 37, 43, 54, 65, 73, 76, 80, 86, 108, 111, 116, 143, 144, 163, 166, 175, 183, 185, 186, 190, 192, 193
– Agency for International Development 68
– Central Intelligence Agency 187
Universities Central Council on Admissions 233
University of California 183
University of East Anglia 183
University of Florida 192
University of Pennsylvania 187
University of Southampton 105
University of Stirling 44
unleaded petrol (see petrol, unleaded)

Urban Centre for Appropriate Technology 159, 160, 232, 250
urban nature conservation 165
urban renewal 16, 152–165, 186, 214
Urban Spaces Scheme 15
Urban Wildlife Group 236
Uusitalo, Liisa 214
vegetarianism 215, 225
Vegetarian Society 178, 216, 250
Venables, Dorothy 57, 63
Venezuela 176
video industry 197, 202–203
Vitrifix 83, 250
Volkswagen 43, 250
Voluntary Service Overseas (VSO) 193, 230, 250
Volvo 43, 116, 117–118, 250
von Weizsacker, Professor Ernst 124
W H Smith 199
Waitrose 144
Waldegrave, The Rt Hon William 111, 237
Ward, Barbara 217
Ward, Sue 217
Warhol, Andy 216
Warmer Campaign 104, 105
Warren, Andrew 136–137
Warren Spring Laboratories (WSL) 83, 115
waste 108–127
– agricultural 131
– disposal 16, 18, 78, 117
– hazardous 16, 30, 35, 79, 221
– management 42, 46, 87, 228
– materials 120–122, 148
– radioactive 16, 33, 42, 87, 221, 223
– technologies 74, 120–122
– treatment 3, 57, 58, 79, 110
(see also recycling)
Waste Management Advisory Council 9
Waste Watch 35, 159
Watch Trust for Environmental Education 233, 250
water 47, 48
– industry 35,
– pollution 32, 87, 103, 110, 113, 148, 190, 215
– privatisation 29
– treatment 3, 58
Water Authorities Association 138
Water Research Centre 102
West German, 8, 13, 21, 22, 24–25, 36, 41, 43, 57, 83, 70, 92, 111, 114, 115, 116, 117, 124–125, 140, 143, 149, 155, 178, 179, 180, 181, 182, 183, 190, 192, 197, 215, 218
whale conservation 210, 212
What to Buy for Business 99
Which? 19, 63, 155, 180
– Holiday 170
Wholefood Trust 143, 250
Wild Side of Town, The 155
Wilderness Expedition & Survival Training (WEST) 177
wildflowers 147
Wildfowl Trust 98, 100, 177, 250
wildlife 147, 151, 155, 166, 170, 174–177, 215
– African 242
– city 164
– conservation 144, 172–173
– habitat 148
– lions 172
– safaris 174–177
Wildlife and Countryside Act 147
Wildlife Appeal 42
Wildlife Link 99
Wildlife Trade Monitoring Unit (WTMU) 104, 250
Wildscreen International Wildlife Film and Television Festival 173, 197, 250
Wildwatch 177
Wilson, Des 185, 210, 216, 217
Wimpey 18, 234
Wimpy Restaurants 71
Wind Energy Group 137
wind power 129
Windmill Hill City Farm 159

Wolf, Edward 141
Woodland Trust 150, 250
Woodward, Frank 86
Wookey, Barry 139, 143, 215, 217
Woolhouse, Professor Harold 183
Worcester, Robert 22, 222
Working Weekends on Organic Farms (WWOOF) 143, 177, 250
World Bank 48, 65, 69, 91, 161, 185, 191, 240, 242, 244, 250
World Commission on Environment & Development (WCED) 8, 10, 32, 33, 46, 50, 198, 209, 214
World Conservation Strategy, The 9, 15, 46, 158, 207, 234
World Health Organisation (WHO) 234
World in Action 197
World Industry Conference on Environmental Management (WICEM) 39, 126
World Magazine 199
World Ocean Circulation Experiment (WOCE) 86
World Resources Institute (WRI) 9, 32, 86, 92, 94, 141, 185, 187, 192, 209, 216, 217, 250
– WRI Report 32, 216
World Tourism Organisation (WTO) 166, 250
World Wildlife Film and Television Festival 197
World Wildlife Fund (WWF) 12, 14, 15, 19, 22, 23, 31, 35, 42, 44, 51, 64, 66, 98, 100, 101, 169, 177, 187, 189, 194, 206, 213, 232, 242–243, 250
Worldview International Foundation (WIF) 202–203
Worldwatch Institute 32, 141, 209, 217, 240–241
Worldwise Reports 197
Wray, Jonathan 210, 216
WWF Kodak Conservation Awards 194, 250
Wytch Farm Oil Field 131
Yellowhammer 225
Young & Rubicam 218, 250
Youth Hostels Association (YHA) 177
Zaire 172
Zambia 204, 242
Zimbabwe 13, 174, 175, 242
Zoo Check 210
Zoological Society of London 98, 100, 103, 105, 199
zoos 210, 216

9781138503250